I JUST KEEP TALKING

ALSO BY NELL IRVIN PAINTER

Old in Art School: A Memoir of Starting Over

The History of White People

*Creating Black Americans: African-American History
and Its Meanings, 1619 to the Present*

Southern History across the Color Line

Sojourner Truth: A Life, A Symbol

Standing at Armageddon: The United States, 1877–1919

*The Narrative of Hosea Hudson: His Life as a Negro Communist
in the South*

Exodusters: Black Migration to Kansas after Reconstruction

Self-Portrait Normal, Self-Portrait Triptych, 2011, ink, collage on paper, 12" × 12". This is a detail of *Self-Portrait Triptych,* 2011, which also includes *Self-Portrait Black* and *Self-Portrait White,* inspired by Stephen Colbert's question on *The Colbert Report* in 2010 whether I was White, on account of having written a scholarly history of White people.

I JUST KEEP TALKING

A LIFE IN ESSAYS

Nell Irvin Painter

DOUBLEDAY · NEW YORK

www.doubleday.com

DOUBLEDAY and the portrayal of an anchor with a dolphin
are registered trademarks of Penguin Random House LLC.

Pages 417–18 constitute an extension of the copyright page.

Jacket art: *Self-Portrait 11* (2010) by Nell Irvin Painter
Jacket design by John Fontana

Library of Congress Cataloging-in-Publication Data
Names: Painter, Nell Irvin, author.
Title: I just keep talking : a life in essays / Nell Irvin Painter.
Description: First edition. | New York : Doubleday, 2024.
Identifiers: LCCN 2023001197 (print) | LCCN 2023001198 (ebook) |
ISBN 9780385548908 (hardcover) | ISBN 9780385548915 (ebook)
Subjects: LCGFT: Essays.
Classification: LCC AC8.5 P35 2024 (print) | LCC AC8.5 (ebook) | DDC 080—dc23/eng/20230417
LC record available at https://lccn.loc.gov/2023001197
LC ebook record available at https://lccn.loc.gov/2023001198

MANUFACTURED IN CHINA

1 3 5 7 9 10 8 6 4 2

First Edition

To my steadfast correspondents

Jackie Bryant Smith

Jill Sheppard

Nellie McKay in memoriam

Thadious M. Davis

Glenn Shafer

Art and history are the indelibles.

ELIZABETH ALEXANDER
in *The Trayvon Generation,* in the last chapter,
"There Are Black People in the Future"

Contents

Contents

HISTORY—SOUTHERN HISTORY

WHITENESS

Contents

VISUAL CULTURE

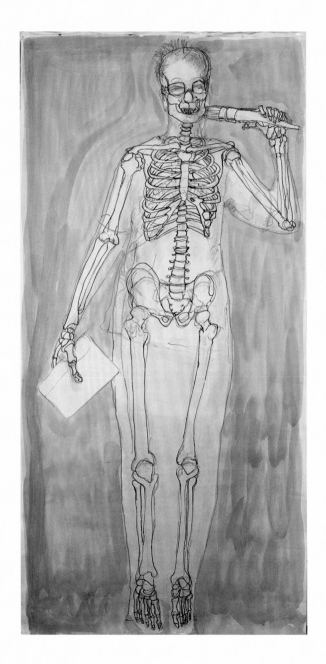

Self-Portrait Skeleton, 2009, ink and graphite on paper, 73″ × 36″. This drawing, a kind of memento mori warning against excessive self-regard (odd for someone who draws scores of self-portraits) is related to *Self-Portrait Quilt,* but not in dimensions or mediums.

Introduction

It's a good thing I didn't die young. Meaning it's a good thing for my reputation that I didn't die during the full-blown era of White-male-default segregation, discrimination, and disappearance that wound down only yesterday. I would have disappeared from memory, just another forgotten Black woman scholar, invisible to history and to histography. So much in me—a dark-skinned Black woman, always very smart, born in Houston in the Houston Hospital for Negroes in 1942—was suited for disregard. No family drama. My parents were married; they stayed married in as good a heterosexual marriage as Americans born in 1917 and 1919 could have and that lasted seventy-two years—until my mother's death. We were never poor, though never rich, and physical violence and addiction played no part in my family. My parents supported me emotionally and materially for more than forty years. There's not much there in my life to match what my country likes to recognize as a Black narrative of hurt. I remember speaking about *Old in Art School* in Seattle to a wonderful, warm audience largely of women. A questioner asked me what I do for healing. "Nothing," I said. "I'm not broken." Not broken, but on occasion

    frustrated,
    indignant—self-righteously—
    pissed off with cause,
    often exhausted,

but mostly and permanently grateful for the people who have protected me, mentored me, supported me over so many decades. Without you, there would be no me.

My Blackness isn't broken. It faces a different way. Mine is a Blackness of solidarity, a community, a connectedness to other people who aren't known personally, of seeing myself as part of other people, other Black people. My Blackness also brings with it an understanding of how other people see oneself, a seeing that can be hurtful, but not one's own fault. What W. E. B. Du Bois called "twoness" is not merely an exhausting from-the-inside/from-the-outside identity, but also an ability to understand more than one way of seeing oneself in the world, an awareness that some non-Black Americans lack. The history of that seeingness brings with it strategies, its armor—usually communal—for fending off hurt. Those strategies of protection aren't always as robust as society's strategies of meanness, which are legal, financial, and personal. But ours are better than nothing, better than going into a cruel world naked and unarmored. I wish other Americans weren't so wedded to an individualist identity, that they could understand themselves more as connected to other people, locally and nationally, and less with having to do with guns and not caring how one's behavior endangers other people. I wish we had more solidarity, even if that makes me sound like a socialist.

My Blackness celebrates itself through art—music, dance, painting, talking, writing—what I term Black studies. Since the opening of the cultural realm in the twenty-first century, people of all sorts have been able to savor the art of Black artists, and I'm proud to say that early on in this century that is no longer new, I brought Black visual art to the fore in my narrative history *Creating Black Americans: African-American History and Its Meanings, 1619 to the Present* (2006). Black history is full of pain, but it's full of something more: creativity. Since my years in art school, I've been adding to that legacy through my own visual art, including what you see in this book.

At the same time, I think it's right to tally up the injuries of slavery, to the enslaved and to their descendants in psychic and material terms—to the nation in its politics and social norms. What lives in me, specializing in post–Civil War history as a historian, are the wrongs that came after slavery and that live with me as experiences in my historical research, the terrorism, the lasting imprint of the politics of White supremacy enforced through violence, experienced for me intellectually, but harrowing nonetheless.

I live with the insults of the era of segregation; the grudging, thrown-togetherness of my parents' college, even though its little library inspired me before I was born; the economic scrimping of my family in the early 1950s to purchase our first home at Sixty-First Street and Telegraph Avenue in Oakland, because the Federal Housing Administration did not extend its favorable mortgages to African Americans. The automatic discounting of one's worth.

As a historian and as a visual artist, I have prospered, thanks to hard work and essential allies all along the way. But I know, I have seen, how the habits of sexism and racism discouraged others, and how the injuries of class held other women back, even held them down. In my final analysis, my own personal sorrow for my country's ways with race traces back less to slavery than to what came after in the decades of cruelty, extending into my own life.

I want to tell you some crucial things about me that have influenced my life's choices and, thereby, my work—what I have written as I have just kept talking over the course of more than fifty years and the fact that nowadays my talk is visual as well as verbal. How and why I stress specificity—individual specificity, geographical and chronological specificity—rather than generalization; as I read the past, one person cannot simply be substituted for another merely on account of sex or race. Just because I cannot know one person doesn't allow me to put another in her place. Knowing what, say, Harriet Tubman said or did doesn't let me assume the same for, say, Sojourner Truth. That said, I want to tell you when and where it was and with whom I was when my shaping, my molding, took place.

My family's roots reach back into Ascension, Baton Rouge, and St. Landry Parishes, Louisiana; low country South Carolina around Charleston; and Harris County, Texas. A century ago, their names— McGruder, Donato, Lee, Irvin, Ashley—might have meant something, might have conveyed relative standing (McGruder, Donato, Lee) or not (Irvin, Ashley I don't know about). So far as I know, all but two of my ancestors were of African descent. My father's parents were Edward Irvin, an exquisitely skilled locomotive machinist, and Sarah Lee, a housekeeper. She, a very dark-skinned Geechee originally from a low country of South Carolina farming family who sought opportunity in Harris County, Texas. My grandfather, a half-White bastard, a Texan born and bred. I met my Irvin grandparents only once, on a trip back to Spring with my father when I was a girl. I returned to Spring twice later, after their deaths, once during my dissertation research trip in 1971 and again during my book tour in 2018. In 1971 Spring was still very rural, still famed for the excellence of its white lightnin' whisky, whose excellence I can attest to.

In 2018 Spring still had fields and cattle whose days were numbered as Houston's suburbs encroached. The little house where my father grew up was still there in 2018, still with a horse in the yard, right beside the railroad tracks, but on the wrong side, the side away from the little (White) town center that now strives to market itself as a railroad tourist destination. My grandfather was a skilled machinist but was always classified as a machinist's helper, even as he had to train the White man who became his boss. My grandfather's half Whiteness wasn't enough to get him paid as a machinist, and my grandfather is the main reason I could never share the distinguished historian David Montgomery's fondness for American machinists.

My mother's father, Charles Hosewell McGruder, originally from Ascension Parish, was a professor at Straight University in New Orleans (now within Dillard University) who married Nellie Eugenie Donato, a pretty, light-skinned-enough-to-pass student from St. Landry Parish, in 1902. She was a descendant of Donato Bello from Naples, Italy. By the 1930s Charles McGruder was one of Houston's leading Colored men; he died before my parents' marriage of "aggravated indigestion," caused, I reckon, by tiptoeing between Black and White Houstons in the 1920s and 1930s. In the late 1940s Nellie McGruder—"Maman"—came to live with us for a while. I remember her as a mean, paper-colored old woman who thought me ugly and trouble-bound because I was dark-skinned. My mother wrote about her difficult relationship with her mother in a memoir, *I Hope I Look That Good When I'm That Old* (2002). Maman spent her days with us crocheting funny-looking multicolored doilies, which we threw away as soon as she left. Did I, a knitter, inherit her needlework vocation?

My parents, Frank and Dona, fell in love at first sight in the library of the then Houston College for Negroes (now Texas Southern University), so I come by my bookishness from my very beginnings. They married and moved to Oakland, California, in 1942. For their migration, I remain eternally grateful. I never was meant to be a Southerner.

Frank and Dona didn't escape right away; I was born in the Houston Hospital for Negroes, an institution that Texas had named specifically to let everyone know it was meant to be lesser, as in separate not intended to be equal, one of many Southern institutions created after the Second World War against Nazi Germany had given outright, unmitigated racism unsavory connotations. My parents knew these hastily created institutions, having met in one of them, as the NAACP Legal Defense Fund was harrying the South over the lying, mean-spirited state of its public education. Texas jerry-built my parents' college, the Houston College for Negroes, under another discounting name. Frank and Dona escaped to the San Francisco Bay Area. They stayed married. I stayed bookish.

I was their only surviving child. Tragedy made that so, for my older brother, Frank Jr., died during a routine tonsillectomy, a procedure then that was the right thing to do for one's children.

My brother didn't survive his surgery, but how do your parents survive the loss of their son, picking up his body in death, not in life? How could they get to the next day? How could they carry on from this "unbearable grief," as my colleague at Princeton Elaine Pagels termed it after just such a loss?

Frank and Dona gave me the same reply every time I asked: "We had you," they said to me. They poured all the love they had for one lost child into me, Nell, endowing me with love for two children, two children's bounty of love, two children's expectations. From my earliest childhood, I flourished in the love for two children, not just one. In the mid-twentieth-century America I grew up in, I needed it all.

How did all this play out for me as a young woman around 1960?

Frank, Dona, and Frank Jr. Irvin in Houston, Christmas 1941, Dona pregnant with Nell. This is the only image I have of my brother, whose death when I was an infant profoundly marked my youth.

First of all, I have to say it wasn't all sorrow. I belonged to Black communities at our Downs Memorial United Methodist Church of civic-minded peers, with the Berkeley teens around my parents' friends and art-minded friends in high school. During my time there, Oakland Technical High School was turning from all-White to all-Black, with my cohort right in the middle of the transition. Tech was then still largely White but strictly tracked, segregated internally. Its physical plant was well tended, and its teachers were excellent and experienced. Half a decade later, with the intentional segregation created by a new high school, Tech was all-Black. The expert teachers who had taught me in AP classes that gave me a head start at the University of California had moved on to the new high school, the White high school in the hills.

I got a first-rate high school education, but after my little lifetime of only-Black isolation and loneliness in my severely tracked gifted classes, I wanted a change. I wanted to go east to Howard University,

Blue Nell on Kaiser with Jacob Lawrence's Migrants, 2010, digital collage on paper. Like many Black Californians with roots in the segregated South, where Black people could not enjoy the outdoors freely, we Irvins drove around California in our enormous Kaiser automobile, where my dog, Christopher Robin, and I could stretch out in the back seat, even though I was a tall kid.

where my mother's brother had studied to be a doctor. I applied to Howard and was admitted. A dinner at home took Howard away from me, and a good thing it was, too, given the times.

The Irvins had a scholarly guest at dinner, the distinguished Howard University sociologist E. Franklin Frazier, who was teaching summer school at Cal. My father, the longtime chief technician of chemistry, though not on the faculty, was a sort of magnet for Black faculty and graduate students in the sciences. We often hosted Black American, African, and other international graduate students. E. Franklin Frazier was an especially honored guest. A few years earlier Professor

Frazier had published *Black Bourgeoisie* (1957), a scathing critique of his subjects' grasping materialism and shallow political awareness, a book that accorded with the Irvins' suspicions about their peers.

After dinner I proudly announced to him that I was going to Howard. Professor Frazier sat me down and decreed, "Nell Irvin, you are too smart and too dark to go to Howard." And that was that. (Many decades later, in a conversation at a meeting of the Southern Historical Association, my esteemed history colleague and friend John Hope Franklin responded to my anecdote by chuckling, noting it sounded exactly like his erstwhile Howard colleague "Frank Frazier," that he—John Hope—could just hear him—Frazier—saying that.) Back in the day, when women were expected to gain only their MRS degrees in college, and every Black man with class standing sought as light-skinned a mate as possible, Frazier, of course, was right. Just look around. I hadn't paid strict attention to this pattern, even though it held in the marriages of my parents' friends. My own dark-skinned mother had snagged a light-skinned man by dint of extraordinary beauty and, perhaps, the gloss of a respectable, cultured family (though reduced in means after Dona's father's death, bringing her from Prairie View A&M to Houston College for Negroes).

E. Franklin Frazier saved me from the maw of Howard University's voracious, vicious colorism, for light-skin preference wasn't so pernicious at the University of California–Berkeley, where I went because I was smart and proud of it. At Cal I was active in student government and in art circles and drew two covers for the campus humor magazine. I also hung around the edges of a proto-Afrocentric movement, the Afro-American Association, which was mostly the speaking on campus of the lawyer Donald Warden, who wasn't a student but whose lectures filled a gigantic void around Blackness on campus. (I should also note that Warden and the Afro-American Association inspired Huey Newton and Bobby Seale at Merritt College in Oakland. Huey Newton and I were in the same Oakland Technical High class of 1959, though on very separate tracks.) A standout of the Afro-American Association circle was a fellow undergraduate, the late Cedric Robinson, who became a prominent scholar of Black Marxism. Like so much Blackness back in those days, the racial default was male. That assumption, with its merging of race and gender, permeated Black organizations (informal as well as formal) in the early 1960s. I wonder if sexism saved me from a twentieth-century affliction of Black manhood: too deep a fascination with Whiteness as male and too much seeing oneself through the eyes of White men. That was my thought decades ago hearing and reading Eldridge Cleaver. Returning to Frantz Fanon, the same thought crosses my mind.

My undergraduate education culminated in an honors degree in anthropology within the tradition of Franz Boas's crucial distinction between culture and biology, a particularly useful distinction in the context of thoroughly racialized US society.

The Bay Area Irvins were a left family of proud progressives, an identity whose sources I find in Oakland's traditional progressivism and my parents' awareness of the meanness of Texas politics, which they escaped. One of my earliest memories is sitting on the floor with a gathering of my parents and their friends to listen to the presidential election results in 1948. They were sweet people who wanted the best for their country, seemingly at a turning point from segregation to openness. They were all so naively disappointed by Henry Wallace's dismal showing, after he had so straightforwardly run an anti-racist, progressive campaign, even in the South. Lorraine Hansberry, Pauli Murray, and the young Coretta Scott (five years before her marriage to Martin Luther King Jr.) also supported the Wallace campaign in 1948.

When I try to situate the Irvins at midcentury, I think of our reading. We read *Freedomways* and *The Nation*, admired W. E. B. Du Bois and Paul Robeson, followed the Highlander Folk School, and were among the first to join the Berkeley Food Co-op. My father's very best friend, Josh Theriot, seemingly more representative of our class, didn't share our politics or our anti-consumerism. As a student at Xavier University in New Orleans, Josh, like so many of his collegiate peers, was an enthusiastic Greek, an Omega Psi Phi fraternity brother.

We Irvins disdained Black Greeks' conspicuous consumption in those mid-twentieth-century days, when Black sororities and fraternities were—or so it seemed to us—insufficiently attuned to the social and economic needs of Black people as a whole. It wasn't like now, when Black social organizations are proudly philanthropic. Looking back, I recognize that the Irvins were mostly as stiff-necked about the Black bourgeoisie as Professor Frazier. My father trivialized his friend Josh's dedication to social events and fashionable possessions. But Irvin stiff-neckedness didn't mar their friendship, which lasted more than half a century, until death.

My childhood's safety I look back on as an absence, which is why I could hardly see it, a safety that endowed me with resources that I recognize now as resilience. I've been able to remain relatively optimistic in my character, as opposed to fundamentally anxious or fearful of injuries familiar from hurtful experience. I've been blessed with the gift of an inner sense of a basic all-rightness that is a class privilege, even when both the class and the privileges in question are limited and contingent.

I always knew beneath the surface of my consciousness that disregard was not a correct appraisal of my worth, of my intelligence, of the soundness of my thinking and my being. Like my mother, I knew in truth I was more than what other people saw—assumed, as they quickly turned away—in me. I started, like my mother and father started, from blessings not to be taken for granted in a society that shoves so many Black people into poverty and exclusion. I gratefully count myself fortunate.

My family's education made my transit into scholarship seamless. They always understood what I was pursuing and supported it, materially as well as emotionally. I never had to explain why I was following a path that would never lead to wealth. Or fame. They underwrote my trip—my trips. When I say "my family," I mean it beyond my own parents. In 1974, when I got my PhD in history from Harvard, my cousin Charles McGruder received his PhD in astrophysics from Heidelberg University.

If I had wanted to continue in art, my parents would have said yes to that too. My father, after all, had taught me to draw early on and continued his woodworking hobby throughout his life, until glaucoma dimmed his eyesight and made work with sharp tools frustrating and dangerous. But we didn't know professional artists well enough for me to see them as role models, while the university was familiar terrain. Drawing classes at California College of Arts and Crafts and UC Berkeley were as far as I got in art until very much later, when Sojourner Truth led me away from text and into images in the 1990s.

I said at the beginning of this essay that it was good that I didn't die young, because I would have died in obscurity. Stopping right there makes me sound careerist, which I'm not, and I wasn't. But I wanted recognition for my work when recognition was due. I wanted my work to be known for its value, even though for decades I just kept talking even when it seemed only a saving remnant was listening. If recognition had been crucially important for me years ago, it's a good thing I wasn't a visual artist. For recognition for one's work has come much later and more haltingly to Black women artists who began working in the twentieth century. The shining example being Faith Ringgold. Over the course of a long life, she has gone from being dismissed by Romare Bearden in the 1960s to being included in the Museum of Modern Art in the 2020s. Margo Humphrey, a fine original printmaker who took drawing classes with me at CCAC and continued as a professional artist, is more representative. Even now, she has only partially received her work's due in Adrienne L. Childs's 2009 monograph, *Margo Humphrey,* in a series edited by David Driskell, who did so much to bring Black artists to the attention of the White art world, which, until recently, was *the* art world. Driskell's own artwork was only prominently exhibited late in his life.

This isn't to say all has gone along smoothly and painlessly. Some insults I never have forgotten or forgiven, for instance, the refusal of the Institute for Advanced Study at Princeton to let me use an office there to complete *Sojourner Truth: A Life, A Symbol,* even though I requested no money (I had a National Endowment for the Humanities fellowship), a courtesy appointment that was routine for Princeton University professors on leave. I'm still pissed. It still annoys me that *The History of White People,* a bestseller, was totally overlooked for book prizes—didn't get a single one. And a prominent historian reviewed it negatively, claiming I had ignored Franz Boas. Franz Boas! I didn't fucking ignore Franz Boas! Boas is in several chapters, and chapter 16 is entitled "Franz Boas: Dissenter." No, all has not run smoothly in this career of mine. Some festering remains, as you see.

However . . . not having an office in the institute for one year a long time ago and a stupid review, also a long time ago, don't begin to compare with real insults and real losses, like not getting a job or not getting tenured or promoted, not getting published, contracting a chronic disease, making a bad marriage, being orphaned early in life, or losing one's child. I have lived a charmed life.

During my Cal-Berkeley years, I hung around Stiles Hall, the YMCA near campus that hosted speakers, including Malcolm X—a brave act at the time. I wrote about my sense of his speaking at Berkeley in "Malcolm X across the Genres" (page 287). There was more for me at Stiles Hall, for I learned there about Operation Crossroads Africa, a program that took US college students to Africa to work together with African counterparts on worthy projects. In the summer of 1962 I went with Crossroads to northern Nigeria, where, together with northern Nigerian students, we built a lopsided elementary school in the countryside outside Kano. This was well before the ethnic bloodshed in the northern region that led to the creation of Biafra in 1967. I wondered if any of the students we had worked with knew of—or even took part in—attacks on people from southern Nigeria.

In 1962 the Kano region seemed to be peaceful to me. One of our counterparts, Serajo Muhammad Wudil (I'm spelling this by memory, so forgive mistakes), invited me to his home and to meet his wife, younger than me but a mother, whom he had married when she was thirteen. Operation Crossroads Africa introduced me to African people in a Muslim part of the continent that I hadn't known about before. My Oakland family had graduate student friends from Ghana and southern Nigeria, but no one Muslim, no one from a place that seemed so exotic to me. More reason not to be able to generalize about some all-encompassing Blackness.

After Operation Crossroads Africa I went directly to France to spend my junior year abroad in Bordeaux. At the University of Bordeaux I discovered a history that wasn't the lying, partial American stories of my 1950s public schooling. In Bordeaux I learned to love medieval French history. Even so, I learned only in 2019 that in the early 1960s, I missed one of the biggest unfolding stories in French history, what French people call a *non-dit,* something we don't want to talk about.

Bordeaux's *non-dit* was the settlement of hundreds—thousands?—of *Harkis,* Algerians who had served with the French forces during the bloody war for Algerian independence in the 1950s and early 1960s, a very dirty war of torturous atrocity. *Harkis* were resettled in France for their own safety after Algerian independence made them into symbols of treason. Thanks to reading *The Nation,* I already knew about French atrocities in that war. But nothing prepared me to see this complicated dimension of the post–Algerian War situation in Bordeaux, the city where I was getting to know France's storied medieval history. I learned all about the Guerre de Cent Ans and Bertrand du Guesclin, Beau Marechal de France, whose body was dismembered (*dilaceratio corporis*) after his death, so his heart, guts, muscles, and bones could be buried separately in four different tombs in Paris. I learned nothing about the *Harkis* in Bordeaux.

After my last year at Berkeley, I traveled once again, this time to join my parents in Ghana, in 1964–66. Ghana changed my life, as I describe in my Hers column "A Sense of Place" (page 7). Ghana let me see around and beyond the American ideology of race and encouraged me to look around and beyond categories into specifics. If any one concern permeates my thinking still, it's the importance of specificity, to see where generalities serve generalities' purposes, but not to stop at generalities. I still credit my years in Ghana for whatever sanity I retain as a Black American.

I had started graduate study in African history at the University of Ghana and even published one of my research papers. (Don't ask me for that long-ago citation.) Though we socialist-Nkrumaist-Afro-Americans had to leave Ghana after a coup d'état deposed Kwame Nkrumah, I stuck with the history of Africa and earned a master's degree in the field at UCLA in 1967. I had planned to continue in African history at Harvard, but arriving before the distinguished professor K. O. Dike, I slipped into the roiling field of US history at Harvard. As a historian of the United States, I nonetheless could never generalize or spin satisfyingly dramatic narratives about the peoples and their histories in the vast continent of Africa.

Looking back, I see (to speak like a historian) a periodization in my long life. Around 1968–1969 I emerged from my mid-twentieth-century youth in the era of segregation into a new time of promised intellectual openness. I started to feel that I could contribute to this new historiography in work that would be read and began graduate school at Harvard in 1969. Inspiration for my dissertation came from my own peripatetic 1960s: the usefulness of leaving. Why, I wondered, did formerly enslaved people remain in the South after Reconstruction's end unleashed so much disaster?

My research revealed disaster and impediments to leaving, but there was also something I hadn't known about, a major leaving of thousands of people from Louisiana, Texas, Tennessee, and Kentucky. People *had* tried to leave, and thousands had succeeded in leaving. Their escape succeeded. The meager existing historiography said absolutely nothing of their success.

Much in that research broke my heart. More than forty years after the publication of my book *Exodusters,* a woman's description of torture, of murder, in East Feliciana Parish, Louisiana, still brings me to the brink of tears. Let me quote it at length from pages 85–86, because it stands as a warning of what atrocities Americans are capable of. My book's protagonist, the political activist Henry Adams, took down the words of the widow of one of his colleagues, Joe Johnson:

> She said to me that she had lost her husband; that he was burned to death in his own house; that him and I [his wife] had worked together, but he was gone now to return no more forever; but, thank God, he is going to rest. He [Johnson] asked me not to grieve for him. They made me and my children wrap our heads up in bed-quilts and come out of the house, and they then set

it on fire, burning it up, and my husband in it, and all we had. They then took all my husband's papers from me. There were about fifty or sixty of them terrorists. They killed him because he refused to resign his office as constable, to which he was elected on the Republican ticket. They sent him several notices, warning him to leave his place and resign his office, but he said he would not until his time was out. So they warned him the last time, but he did not leave, so they burnt him near to death; at least they thought he was dead, but he was not quite dead; he got out and fell into a hole of water and lay there; but all the skin was burnt off of him. So the white men saw him and shot him, and he lived four days and died, and leaves me, a poor widow with a housefull of children, and no one to help me.

Reading this account in Harvard's Widener Library a century later hurt on account of sheer physical anguish and familial loss and deep injustice. But looking back now, I can recognize something I could not sense as I did my research: my assumption of the past-ness of that post-Reconstruction past. In the 1970s I subconsciously assumed that what I was reading of Tensas Parish, Louisiana, in 1876 belonged to another century, a century gone by, an era long ended. I was unwittingly assuming a gulf separated me in Widener Library from Joe Johnson's searing assassination, setting this bloody history behind me, behind us as a nation. The New Deal, the Second World War against Nazism, the Cold War against Stalinism, the civil rights movement of the 1950s and 1960s, the Civil Rights Act of 1964, and the Voting Rights Act of 1965, even the Vietnam War, which was causing such upheaval as I researched the nineteenth-century South—all of that felt separate from the time of Joe Johnson, his widow, and Henry Adams.

I no longer feel that. Now my dissertation and first book seem not yet present but, after January 6, 2021, a warning of what can come again, closing up the space between the Exodusters in post-Reconstruction 1879 and now. Frighteningly present.

On third thought, though, maybe beside my unconscious assumptions of pastness, the immediate twentieth-century past was also playing its part in my research: the savagery of young Emmett Till's fatal torture, the cold calculation of Medgar Evers's assassination in the driveway of his own home, and the brutal cunning of the Sixteenth Street Baptist Church bombing in Birmingham, timed to succeed in slaughter. Those atrocities occurred within my lifetime and lived in my consciousness while I was at Harvard.

Graduate school at Harvard brought me a sympathetic dissertation adviser, Frank Freidel; many fine friends, beginning with Preston and Connie Williams and Jean and David Layzer; and, most intensely, the literary scholar Nellie Y. McKay, who died in Madison, Wisconsin, in 2006. Nellie and I exchanged real letters, personal and professional, candid about it all, on paper and in email to each other for nearly thirty years, a friendship that sustained me until her death. Overlapping with Nellie and outliving her, Thadious Davis has offered me more than forty years of friendship's essential gifts, also grounded in writing. I dedicated *Creating Black Americans* to Thadious, for she shepherded my writing of history into visual art. As long as my attachments to Nellie and Thadious have lasted, they aren't my oldest friends. Jackie Bryant Smith, an Oakland friend from my high school art club and Downs Memorial United Methodist Church, has been with me over sixty years, with art as our tie. After Jackie, there's Jill Sheppard in London, whom I've been talking with and visiting nearly as long as with Jackie. Among my friends of more than thirty years is my husband, Glenn Shafer, whom I met at the Center for Advanced Study in the Behavioral Sciences at Stanford in 1988 and married in 1989. We've spent most days together since then. This book is dedicated to Glenn and my lifelong friends.

Thadious was present at the beginning of *Creating Black Americans*, but Nellie was there at the inaugural of the project that became my second book, *The Narrative of Hosea Hudson: His Life as a Negro Communist in the South*. Nellie accompanied me on my first trip to Atlantic City in 1976 to meet Hudson, whom one of Nellie's colleagues in

Boston had described as a fascinating character. Fascinating Hosea Hudson certainly was. Later on, my Knopf editor turned down my Hudson biography on the grounds that Hudson didn't "tug at one's heart strings." Hudson—feisty, mouthy, unrepentant Communist—certainly did not. And, as a reviewer noted, neither do I.

I say here I just keep talking, and that's long been true. I just keep talking and writing and publishing books that made their way haltingly, bringing me just enough of a following for a very nice, no, a distinguished scholarly career, but not sufficient for major book prizes or high visibility. My third book, *Standing at Armageddon,* is an engaging book; it tells readers what happened in a coherent manner. But radical historians, its natural constituency, ignored it, which they really should never have done, and it has not entered the historiographical canon. *Standing at Armageddon* has managed to stay in print as a useful text in AP history courses, and every few years, a graduate student or young professor writes me after having just discovered it on their own.

My fourth book, *Sojourner Truth: A Life, A Symbol,* published in 1996, has become a classic in its quarter-century existence, as over the decades American readers have come to accept a more nuanced depiction of Truth than the slogan—*which she did not say*—"Ar'n't [or Ain't] I a woman?" An audience I respect deeply, the Black Caucus of the American Library Association, gave *Sojourner Truth: A Life, A Symbol* its annual book award, a prize to cherish, the only prize this book received, amidst a strange critical reception. The *Women's Review of Books* did not review it, and when Nellie McKay investigated the slight, she reported back that a couple of reviewers "had trouble with the book." That "trouble," I expect, was my insistence, my exceedingly painstaking documentation, that Sojourner Truth did not say, "Ar'n't/Ain't I a woman?" Frances Dana Gage, a White journalist talking back to Harriet Beecher Stowe, twelve years after the fact, made up the phrase. The essay "Difference, Slavery, and Memory" (page 15) explains where the slogan came from.

As you see in my 2022 letter to the editor of *The New Yorker* (page 34), I'm still struggling against the way Gage's popular slogan has not only flattened a fascinating New Yorker into a unit of vaguely

Southern sex-race but also obliterated the history of other nineteenth-century Black women feminist abolitionists, Frances Ellen Watkins Harper most notably. Here I'm speaking as a historian comfortable with the complexities, the challenges, even the contradictions within historical biography. Years later I would come to interpret my struggle with Frances Dana Gage's slogan as part of a larger, contentious coexistence of history and biography, i.e., me, on the one hand, and art, i.e., Gage, on the other. But only years later.

Back in the 1980s, radical historians' disregard of *Standing at Armageddon* dismayed me a lot, just as the refusal of the *Women's Review of Books* to review my *Sojourner Truth* hurt in the 1990s. Both experiences distanced me from communities I had thought I belonged to. This was disappointing but, ultimately, not devastating, because even my belonging had been contingent. Too many prior discussions had alerted me to our differences. Now enough readers agree with me that the naysayers are in retreat. I received a Guggenheim Fellowship in the 1980s, was inducted into the American Academy of Arts and Sciences in 2007, and two historical organizations have voted me president: the Southern Historical Association and the Organization of American Historians.

During the late 1980s and into the 1990s, I published several essays with racially mixed casts of characters. Scattered in journals and in books under other people's names, these pieces eluded those trying to track them down. I collected several biographical pieces, which the University of North Carolina Press published as *Southern History across the Color Line* in 2002, with a second edition in 2021. After *Sojourner Truth: A Life, A Symbol,* I have written more visually. In 2006 I published *Creating Black Americans: African-American History and Its Meanings, 1619 to the Present,* a narrative history whose illustrations are Black fine art. In that book, I wanted to balance the horrific history of racial trauma with the enormous Black achievement of survival and creativity. Visual art offered a means of capturing the beauty of Blackness. By using the work of fine artists, I sought to harness art's power to entice viewers and readers and said so in that book.

My most recent scholarly history book, *The History of White People* (2010), appeared during my first year of art graduate school (a coincidence I emphatically do not recommend). This book, so clearly attuned to the importance of physical appearance, makes "the Father of Art History," Johann Joachim Winckelmann, a leading character and dedicates an entire chapter to "The White Beauty Ideal as Science." Yes, indeed, a very visual book. Its research and writing took a decade, and its voluminous notes, intended prophylactically, make plain the depth and breadth of its research foundation in English, French, and German. *The History of White People,* a *New York Times* bestseller, still circulates widely, with editions in Japanese and French. What it is—the work of a Black historian that concentrates on White people—has made it hard for Americans to situate me culturally and, I suspect, cost it any book prize whatever. It's as though Black scholars are supposed to write only about Black people. But I know I'm not the first or the last to depart from tradition. The distinguished John Hope Franklin widened the trail of W. E. B. Du Bois's *Black Reconstruction,* as did Charles Wesley (educated at Fisk University and Yale and the third Black Harvard PhD, author of *The Collapse of the Confederacy* [1937, 1968]). John Hope Franklin, whom I had the honor of knowing personally, inspired me deeply. I dedicated *Southern History across the Color Line* to him and link his uniqueness with that of my mother in "Humanity, Scholarship, and Proud Race Citizenship: The Gifts of John Hope Franklin" (page 36). I framed his letter of thanks for the dedication and mounted it on my writing room wall.

Readers often ask me why I wrote *The History of White People,* sometimes with an extra edge of curiosity, as though a damned good explanation were compulsory. As with my Sojourner Truth biography, my impetus for *The History of White People* came from a question in my mind. With Sojourner Truth, I wondered about the apparent conflict between the fiery figure portrayed in the words attributed to her, which, I quickly learned, were words Frances Dana Gage had invented, and the settled bourgeoise in the photographic portraits she had taken of herself. In the case of *The History of White People,* I wondered why White Americans were called "Caucasians," when few Americans knew who and where actual Caucasians were. They were in

Georgia and Chechnya, in the borderlands between Europe and Asia. When the Russians were bombing Grozny in Chechnya into a Berlin 1945, I wondered why White people were, in effect, called Chechens. Usually the answer came back that White Americans thought they should know and were too embarrassed to ask. Or they skipped over my question and accused me of wanting to get back at White people after all the terrible things White people had done to other people. Was I writing my book "as a Black person"?

I would say—self-righteously—that I was writing as a historian. Then, when that got tiresome, I'd ask what my options were. I was about to show the ridiculousness of the question by answering that I was writing as a White man, when defensive questions died down. Maybe the quieting down was due to the presence of President Obama. My hundreds of pages explain how conceptions of White race have changed since the notion of scientific human races was invented in the eighteenth-century Enlightenment. Even so, my American readers, thinking that race is somehow a permanent and biological fact rather than an ideology, have had tremendous difficulty grasping the fact that definitions of White race have changed with time and place. Apart from the actual material manifestations of racism, so many Americans are convinced that race is real—White race, Black race, Other race—and somehow unchanging. The hardest part to convey is that a century ago, educated Americans believed in the actual existence of more than one White race.

The 2010 publication of *The History of White People* marked the second watershed in my personal periodization after my emergence from mid-twentieth-century segregation into scholarly history in the 1970s. After that book, I had, for the first time in my life, a plan: first a BFA from Mason Gross, then an MFA from the most demanding art school I could get into, which turned out to be the Rhode Island School of Design; then I would make art worth serious recognition. My father always encouraged my art. My mother, who taught me to read and write, also showed me how to start over after retirement and to use the word "old" in a book title, hers: *I Hope I Look That Good*

When I'm That Old. Sojourner Truth taught me to heed and to love visual images.

When word of my plan spread among my friends and colleagues, they were envious. Leaving the gray halls of scholarship for the excitement of art! I would say outrageous things and wear outrageous clothes, Technicolor scarves that would billow in the wind. Would I please report back? Report back I did, in *Old in Art School: A Memoir of Starting Over*, not my first non-scholarly writing—I had been writing opinion pieces, journalism, op-eds in *The New York Times* for years—but my memoir was my first extended piece of creative nonfiction.

I Just Keep Talking ends with "I Knit Socks for Adrienne" (page 356), a work combining visual art and text, image with discourse, how I work now in my own personal twenty-first-century, third era since art school. Text, rooted in history, supplies one sort of meaning, while art, a work of the imagination, conveys meanings that exceed the historical archive. They are not the same thing. It's too simple to say that text speaks historical truth, while art ranges further, reaches beyond the limits of the archive. But the contrast between what history says

Photograph of Eastman Studio wall, MacDowell, 2021. One of a series of process photos of organizing these essays.

Organization Drawings, Eastman Studio wall, MacDowell, 2021, ink and graphite on paper. Visual art's depiction of the process of organization. The circular shapes represent balls of yarn and the occupation of my time out.

IJKT Drawings, wall of Pigeon East studio, Yaddo, 2022, ink, graphite, and collage on paper. Only some of the images on the wall made it into this book.

and what art suggests is well worth recognizing. History and art draw on two different kinds of power, and I want to tap both in this book.

Text + art is not the only hybridity in my work, for as an artist, I work manually + digitally, toggling back and forth between the hand and the computer, and embracing unexpected results springing from combination. Here the texts, many created before I went to art school, inspire the art; increasingly the way I see inspires thoughts and questions I take into words, in a both-ways exchange. Organizing this book became a visual as well as a discursive undertaking in late 2021 during a residency at MacDowell, where I documented my process of organization.

Once the organizing was done, I moved on from organization to visualization in a series of drawings I mounted on my studio wall.

Once the texts had found their places, and I had made a few drawings in 2021, I needed more images than already existed in my portfolio. In a 2022 residency at Yaddo, I made new drawings and pinned them to my wall in Pigeon East studio.

This text + art is the way I work, the way I think, now, with each aspect living its own life, though originally inspired by my text. Accordingly, the images in this book are informally captioned, so that they remain both related to and independent from the texts and free to inspire various meanings, visual and discursive, in readers as readers and as viewers.

August 2022

AUTOBIOGRAPHY

Hers: Whites Say I Must Be on Easy Street

I'VE ALWAYS THOUGHT affirmative action made a lot of sense because discrimination against Black people and women was prolonged and thorough. But I've been hearing talk in the last several years that lets me know that not everyone shares my views. The first time I noticed it was shortly after I had moved to Philadelphia, where I used to live. One evening I attended a lecture—I no longer remember the topic—but I recall that I arrived early and was doing what I did often that fall. I worked at polishing my dissertation. In those days I regularly carried chapters and a nicely sharpened pencil around with me. I sat with pencil and typescript, scratching out awkward phrases and trying out new ones.

Next to me sat a White man of about thirty-five, whose absorption in my work increased steadily. He watched me intently—kindly—for several moments. "Is that your dissertation?" I said yes, it was. "Good luck in getting it accepted," he said. I said that it had already been accepted, thank you.

Still friendly, he wished me luck in finding a job. I appreciated his concern, but I already had a job. Where? At Penn, for I was then a beginning assistant professor at the University of Pennsylvania. "Aren't you lucky," said the man, a little less generously; "you got a job at a good university." I agreed. Jobs in history were, still are, hard to find.

While cognizant of the job squeeze, I never questioned the justice of my position. I should have a job, and a good one. I had worked hard as a graduate student and had written a decent dissertation. I knew foreign languages, had traveled widely, and had taught and published. I thought I had been hired because I was a promising young historian. Unlike the man beside me, I didn't think my teaching at a first-rate university required an extraordinary explanation.

"I have a doctorate in history," he resumed, "but I couldn't get an academic job." With regret he added that he worked in school administration. I said I was sorry he hadn't been able to find the job he wanted. He said: "It must be great to be Black and female; because of affirmative action, you count twice." I couldn't think of an appropriate response to that line of reasoning, for this was the first time I'd met it face-to-face. I wished the lecture would start. I was embarrassed. Did this man really mean to imply that I had my job at his expense? The edge of competition in his voice made me squirm.

He said that he had received his doctorate from Temple, and yet he had no teaching job, and where was my degree from? "Harvard," I said. It was his time not to reply. I waited a moment for his answer, then returned to my chapter.

Now I live in North Carolina, but I still hear contradictory talk about affirmative action. Last spring I was having lunch with some Black Carolina undergraduates. One young woman surprised me by deploring affirmative action. I wondered why. "White students and professors think we only got into the University of North Carolina because we're Black," she complained, "and they don't believe we're truly qualified." She said that she knew that she was qualified and fully deserved to be at Carolina. She fulfilled all the regular admissions requirements. It was the stigma of affirmative action that bothered her; without it, other students wouldn't assume she was unqualified.

Another student said that the stigma of affirmative action extended to Black faculty as well. She had heard White students doubting the abilities of Black professors. Indeed, she herself tended to wait for Black professors to disprove her assumption that they did not know their fields. She was convinced that without affirmative action, students would assume Black faculty to be as good as White.

That's what I've been hearing from Whites and Blacks. White people tell me I must be on easy street because I'm Black and female. (I do not believe I've ever heard that from a Black person, although some Black people believe that Black women have an easier time in the White world than Black men. I don't think so.) White people tell me, "You're a twofer." On the other side of the color line, every Black student knows that he or she is fully qualified—I once thought that way myself. It is just the other Black people who need affirmative action to get in. No one, not Blacks, not Whites, benefits from affirmative action, or so it would seem.

Well, I have, but not in the early 1960s, when I was an undergraduate in a large state university. Back then, there was no affirmative action. We applied for admission to the university like everyone else; we were accepted or rejected like everyone else. Graduate and undergraduate students together, we numbered about 200 in a student body of nearly 30,000. No preferential treatment there.

Yet we all knew what the rest of the university thought of us, professors especially. They thought we were stupid because we were Black. Further, White women were considered frivolous students; they were only supposed to be in school to get husbands. (I doubt that we few Black women even rated a stereotype. We were the ultimate outsiders.) Black students, the whole atmosphere said, would not attend graduate or professional school because their grades must be poor. Women had no business in postgraduate education because they would waste their training by dropping out of careers when they married or became pregnant. No one said out loud that women and minorities were simply and naturally inferior to White men, but the assumptions were as clear as day: Whites are better than Blacks; men are better than women.

I am one of the few people I know who will admit to having been helped by affirmative action. To do so is usually tantamount to admitting deficiency. To hear people talk, affirmative action exists only to employ and promote the otherwise unqualified, but I don't see it that way at all. I'm Black and female, yet I was hired by two history departments that had no Black members before the late '60s, never mind women. Affirmative action cleared the way.

Thirty-five years ago, John Hope Franklin, then a star student, now a giant in the field of American history, received a doctorate in history from Harvard. He went to teach in a Black college. In those days,

Black men taught in Black colleges. White women taught in White women's colleges. Black women taught in Black women's colleges. None taught at the University of Pennsylvania or the University of North Carolina. It was the way things were.

Since then, the civil rights movement and the feminist movement have created a new climate that permitted affirmative action, which, in turn, opened areas previously reserved for White men. Skirts and dark skins appeared in new settings in the 1970s, but in significant numbers only after affirmative action mandated the changes and made them thinkable. Without affirmative action, it never would have occurred to any large, White research university to consider me for professional employment, despite my degree, languages, publications, charm, grace, despite my qualifications.

My Philadelphia White man and my Carolina Black women would be surprised to discover the convergence of their views. I doubt that they know that their convictions are older than affirmative action. I wish I could take them back to the early '60s and let them see that they're reciting the same old White-male-superiority line, fixed up to fit conditions that include a policy called affirmative action. Actually, I will not have to take those people back in time at all, for the Reagan administration's proposed dismantling of affirmative action fuses the future and the past. If they achieve their stated goals, we will have the same old discrimination, unneedful of new clothes.

December 1981

Hers: A Sense of Place

GHANA IS ONE OF THE BEST THINGS that ever happened to me, even though it was a very long time ago, when my family and I lived there for two years in the mid-1960s. Ghanaians impressed me from the moment I stepped off the plane. For aside from a few travelers, everyone was Black, an even, opaque, velvety Black that I had never seen in the United States. The customs officials, families greeting passengers, taxi drivers, policemen, they were all intensely and beautifully Black.

The people in the airport not only looked different from American Black people; they also carried themselves differently. They stood with self-assurance and spoke without implied apology. Their dress seemed to announce they were sure of themselves. They wore the bright colors and large prints that respectable African Americans eschewed for fear of being conspicuous or seeming to reinforce unfortunate stereotypes. Ghanaian women wore long, two-piece dresses of a batik-like print that I learned to call wax print. The dresses were designed to flatter African figures and to take advantage of the prints, whether flowers or portraits of public figures.

Most of the men wore Western dress, white shirts with plain, dark ties and trousers. The contrast between dark skins and white shirts dramatically reinforced the blackness of skin and the whiteness of cloth. A few men wore traditional dress, a toga-wrapped cloth of either printed cotton or kente cloth, made of several narrow hand-woven strips of blue, yellow, red, and white silk sewn together. Kente cloth, both beautiful and expensive, announced the wearer's national pride and his importance. Men wearing traditional dress showed off their calves and their sumptuously decorated sandals. In comparison, American men travelers in their boxy suits seemed dowdy.

The city of Accra and the university at Legon presented me with a new spectrum of color. I squinted into an enormous, brilliant sky. All the buildings and walls presented complex patterns of textures and colors, for something grew on every surface—bushes, flowers, or mold. The California Bay Area that I had left was a gray-blue place with mostly light-colored people. But now I moved in a world of bright contrasts. The dirt was red, the trees and grass blue green, the buildings white with red tiled roofs. Cerise bougainvillea climbed whitewashed walls and cascaded over fences. This colorful landscape and the very black people in white or brilliant clothes together altered my visual sense of everyday life.

Many Ghanaians invited us into their homes, chemistry professors, a carpenter, an herb doctor, and our landlord, among others. We ate in mansions more luxurious than anything we could ever afford and in bungalows so crowded that we winced. At every point on the scale of wealth, the people were Ghanaian, every one dark-skinned.

As Black Americans unaffiliated with the United States Embassy, we enjoyed several advantages. Nearly everyone regarded us as kindred, and they called us Afro-Americans, not American Negroes. Ghanaians disassociated us from their main grievances against the United States: imperialism and racial discrimination. Those who had studied in the United States or visited for any length of time included us in their nostalgia, if their memories were fond.

With our unstraightened hair and in wax print dresses, my mother and I looked enough like locals to pass, provided we kept our mouths shut. This silent assimilation made me something new. I felt inconspicuous and free. This is not to say that I felt Ghanaian. The better I came to know the various sorts of Ghanaian lives and customs, the more I realized how thoroughly American I was. Yet I never felt terribly foreign in Ghana. Knowing full well that I could never take part in Ghanaian national life, I yet felt far less an outsider than I had sometimes felt in California. As a Black person in a Black country, I felt very much at home.

At first I found being a member of the racial majority disorienting. I had grown up in Northern California as a member of one of several racial minorities. In the 1940s and 1950s my family had encountered outright discrimination in housing and occasional difficulties in getting decent service in restaurants. But by and large, racism didn't present us with serious problems on a day-to-day basis. My parents taught me about racial discrimination, however, and for as long as I could remember, I felt connected to people of African descent in the South, the West Indies, and Africa. Any failure of mine, I was convinced, reflected badly on four hundred million Black people throughout the world. My successes, of course, made them all proud. I bore my responsibilities without complaint, certain that my actions counted in the world.

Growing up as I did with a strong Pan-African orientation, I took my social and political bearings by race. How to decide which sports team to root for? Favor the one with the Black players, then later, the one with the most Black players. (This system doesn't work so well anymore.) Which side of a political issue to support? See how it will affect Black people as a whole. Which movie to see? The one with a Black character. Without my realizing it, my response to racism was a keen sense of race.

In Ghana, however, racial solidarity in the American way made little sense. I realized this first in politics, mostly at the Star Hotel. Ghanaian and African American students and my friends and I spent many tropical nights at the tables around the Star's outdoor dance floor, drinking Ghanaian beer, smoking Ghanaian cigarettes, and talking politics. That is, my friends talked politics. At first, all I could sort out was colonialism, which was related to racism.

In the independent republic of Ghana, however, the issues were not racial, but economic. Should the inefficient collective state farms expand, although they were losing money hand over fist? Should the prosperous, private cocoa farms, which brought in most of the nation's hard currency, be nationalized? Should the government emphasize the development of agriculture or industry? When those who profited and those who suffered were all equally Black, I couldn't figure the racial angle. But as economic questions superseded racial ones in my mind, I slowly discovered the politics of class and issues of economic development.

Similar processes occurred in other areas of my life, as the racial thinking I had brought from the United States gave way. At the university, where geniuses, dumbbells, and average students were Black, I discovered the quality of ordinariness, which American race relations denied to Blacks. In my studies of African history, I began to separate the politics of power from color. The outlines of human nature emerged.

Ordinary humanness affected me deeply as a woman. In the United States I was a woman, but always—outside the tight circle of family and close friends—a Black woman. A Black woman in the United States was not the same thing as just a woman, without a racial qualifier.

In Ghana, I became just a woman. I let down my burden of responsibility to the four hundred million people of African descent, for I was surrounded by friends who were thinking seriously about the future and also having a good time. I had love affairs. I had my heart broken and broke hearts in my turn. I was free to enjoy myself and be something I have often missed intensely in the years since I came home—ordinary.

December 1981

Regrets

THIS LITTLE ESSAY bothers me greatly, because I want to write it and I want to write it right: to think about what has changed, what research remains to be done, what advice I'd give to younger scholars. But try as I may, I'm not sure I can even show up. Every time I sit down to write, especially when I think about the academy in the next five years, exasperation overflows my computer.

For twenty-five years I've been hearing too much of the same frustrations from my colleagues of color. Too little has changed for me to cherish the "progress" I know to lie at the core of a mandatory narrative from scholars of color. We can complain, but only after praising how far we have come and how much things have changed for the better, thank you. But I can't write the "progress" narrative. Managing mainstream feminists just saps too much energy for me to perform it at the end of the academic year.

How can I reflect on how far we have come when American historians still divide not only the American past but also American historiography into "real" history, which counts, and African American history, which does not count and need not be read or cited, unless produced by Whites?

How can I speak of progress when I know that young African American historians fear that they will not be judged fairly by their peers?

How can I assure my younger colleagues that things have changed when it's White historians who receive prestigious prizes for writing African American history?

Same Frustrations, 2022, ink on paper, 5″ × 7¼″. I wish this no longer felt true.

When Black women professors are vulnerable to harassment from male students of all races?

When White colleagues routinely forget they have Black colleagues?

When we in the minority are still expected to smile gently when we're the only one, time after time after time?

When isolation, exhaustion, and frustration sit at the end of every working day, little energy remains for the contemplation of issues beyond how to make it to the next day and the end of each semester.

After such a long time and still so many of the same old frustrations, I'm just plain worn out.

Summer 2000

BIOGRAPHY

Difference, Slavery, and Memory

SOJOURNER TRUTH IN FEMINIST ABOLITIONISM

T HE ISSUE OF RACE is always present in American culture, especially in large areas such as women's rights. Understandably, Americans often try to avoid the issue, for race can still sabotage analysis of terms as essential as the nineteenth-century formulation of "woman." Whenever race is acknowledged in discussions of American culture, the significance of the whole and the parts alters, subtly or drastically. Words and phrases acquire additional connotations, and lines of reasoning may twist imperceptibly. Large parts of social equations may disappear, as other parts are enhanced. Often the undeniable importance of race makes it too facile an explanation; it seems to provide answers to hard questions that are too easy.

In American antislavery feminism, few of the principals who have been remembered were of African descent, but the movement was tethered both to the racially charged institution of slavery and to notions of gender that are deeply but subtly influenced by race. If the need for a Black presence was felt in the early histories of American feminism, merely quoting the speeches of Sojourner Truth—an unforgettable Black woman who frequented the halls where women organized for the abolition of slavery and the achievements of their own rights—apparently filled that need. With the flowering of Black women's studies, however, merely quoting Sojourner Truth no longer substitutes for carefully analyzing Truth's persona and her place in the history of American reform.

Formerly enslaved in the Hudson River valley near the Shawan-gunk and Catskill Mountains of Ulster County, New York, Sojourner Truth (ca. 1797–1883) appeared often on the antislavery and women's rights lecture circuits in the 1850s, 1860s, and 1870s. She is still one of the two most famous nineteenth-century Black women; the other, Harriet Tubman, was also a mature, dark-skinned, unlettered former slave. Since Truth's heyday as an abolitionist and women's rights advocate, she has symbolized the connection of sex and race in liberal reform. The line most closely identified with her persona, *which she did not say,* is "and ar'n't I a woman?" It demands that the category of "woman" include those who are poor or not White.

This message bears repeating on a regular basis, particularly as feminists seek to make their movement more broadly representative. The very fact that Truth's message has remained pertinent for so long inspires investigation into her place in feminist abolitionism and the function of her public persona in the history of American reform. The women's rights conference in Akron, Ohio, in 1851, at which Truth made her most famous appearance and at which she first gained prominence as a feminist, will serve here as the touchstone of my analysis.

As attractive as the scene in Akron has become to modern readers, its meaning is no longer as straightforward as it had seemed. Reexamining the meeting at Akron and Truth's own personal history in light of scholarship on feminist abolitionists raises new questions about the use of a naive persona among Americans who are educated, particularly when the naif is Black and the educated are White. Was Sojourner Truth unique in 1851? What made her remarkable and how intentionally created was her persona? Why is Truth remembered while other Black women reformers have mostly been forgotten? Could nineteenth-century Black women feminist abolitionists be "woman"?

Comparing Truth with antislavery female leadership and the rank and file, I reconsider the prophetic persona of Sojourner Truth—a persona that Truth herself invented and that educated White women further invented and helped to preserve in American memory. I employ two different strategies. First I present a narrative history of

Sojourner Truth; because Truth's life is less well known than her persona, this section runs long. In the second part of my essay, I analyze the discursive approaches that preserved Truth's place in cultural history.

Even though Black women had already been active in women's reform for decades, the Ohio women's rights convention held in Akron in May 1851 is primarily remembered today, as in the nineteenth century, as the occasion when Sojourner Truth inserted Black women into women's reform and reclaimed physical and emotional strength for all women. As was often the case, Truth was the only Black person present. This was an event of enormous rhetorical and symbolic, as well as historical, importance. Not surprisingly, therefore, the only report that has been widely reprinted features Truth prominently. Its author was Frances Dana Gage (1808–1884), a White antislavery writer and lecturer from McConnelsville, Ohio, who chaired the meeting.[1]

In Gage's account, Truth stands out immediately: "A tall, gaunt, black woman in a gray dress and white turban, surmounted with an uncouth sunbonnet," Truth makes an unusual entrance and takes an unorthodox seat. She "march[ed] deliberately into the church, walk[ed] with the air of a queen up the aisle, and [sat] upon the pulpit steps." During the first day, Gage writes, Truth said nothing. On the second day, still according to Gage, several ministers in the audience vehemently denied women's claim to equal rights, arguing that women lacked intelligence, that Jesus Christ was a man, and that Eve, who had tempted man into original sin, was a woman. Throughout this onslaught, Gage reports, none of the White women in the convention was brave enough to counter the charges. As respectable White women cowered, silenced by the Pauline prohibition against women's public speech, scoffers and small boys in the gallery enjoyed the women's chagrin.

Then, says Gage, Sojourner Truth acted: "This almost Amazon form, which stood nearly six feet high, head erect, and eye piercing the upper air" instantly riveted everyone's attention. Whereas the White women organizers of the meeting failed to respond to the ministers' denunciation of women's rights, Truth, an uninvited participant, spoke for all the women in phrases that effectively silenced the male opposition. Gage quotes what she says are Truth's words:

Wall, chilern, whar dar is so much racket dar must be somethin' out o' kilter. I tink dat 'twixt de niggers of the Souf and de womin at de Norf, all talkin' 'bout rights, de White men will be in a fix pretty soon. But what's all dis here talkin' 'bout?

Dat man ober dar say dat womin needs to be helped into carriages, and lifted ober ditches, and to hab de best place everywhar. Nobody eber helps me into carriages, or ober mud-puddles, or gibs me any best place! And ar'n't I a woman? Look at me! Look at my arm! (and she bared her right arm to the shoulder, showing her tremendous muscular power). I have ploughed, and planted, and gathered into barns, and no man could head me! And ar'n't I a woman? I could work as much and eat as much as a man—when I could get it—and bear de lash as well! And ar'n't I a woman? I have borne thirteen chilern, and seen 'em mos' all sold off to slavery, and when I cried out with my mother's grief, none but Jesus heard me! And ar'n't I a woman?

Four times, Gage has Truth exclaim, "And ar'n't I a woman?" Subduing what Gage terms the "mobbish spirit of the day," Truth reverses this tide of denigration. Her speech brings "roars of applause" and turned a rout into triumph.[2]

Modern readers generally focus on one aspect of this report, Sojourner Truth's demand that poor Black women like herself be included with people classed as women. Some women are workers, Truth says, making the ability to work a womanly characteristic. Truth reminds her audience that although women belong to different classes and races, they nonetheless remain women, no matter what their material condition. Such conclusions are faithful to the spirit, if not the actual words, of Truth's utterance.

But Gage has still more to say about Sojourner Truth in this setting. Inventing the rhetorical formula that made Truth's theme so memorable, Gage also delivers an important message about Truth's relative efficacy. Gage underscores Truth's authority by contrasting the timidity of the White women who had organized the meeting with the fearlessness of Sojourner Truth. Summing up the symbolic significance of the scene, the critic Jean Fagan Yellin says that Gage paints the Black woman as the "powerful rescuer" of powerless White women.[3]

The seat that Gage has Truth assume—on the steps of the pulpit rather than in the pews—manifests the rhetorical degree to which she stood (or rather sat) apart from the rest of the gathering. This physical placement hints at a distinction separating Truth from her feminist abolitionist peers that exceeds racial difference. Truth not only looks different from the White women; she appears stronger as well. In the midst of the long quotation in dialect, Gage interrupts Truth's exotic phrasing to insert her own stage business in standard English, again contrasting two modes of expression and being. Gage does not explain how Truth came to exercise such power, leaving the curious reader to search out her own explanations. Truth's prior experience would seem a likely place to start, for compared with other women in the church that day she apparently traveled a singular life's road to Akron.

In the late 1840s Truth joined the antislavery lecture circuit, speaking and selling *Narrative of Sojourner Truth*, which she had dictated to Olive Gilbert, a Connecticut abolitionist also in residence in the Northampton Association of Education and Industry, and published herself in 1850. Her sale of the book to antislavery and women's rights audiences allowed her to support herself and to pay off the mortgage on her home in Northampton, Massachusetts, where she had lived from 1843. In 1851 she went to the women's rights convention in Akron primarily to sell her book, and Frances Dana Gage reports that indeed she did a brisk business on the first day.

When Truth and White feminists met in Akron in 1851, the outspokenness of the one and the silence of the others might have seemed natural, given the very different routes they apparently had traveled. Feminist abolitionists had begun to seek their own rights within the antislavery community, but Truth had come out of religious cults and an itinerant ministry.[4] Like the prophet Matthias, whose Kingdom she lived in during the mid-1830s, she had changed her name when God told her to preach her truth. Like her brother and sister evangeli-

Sojourner Truth Pink Green Tusche, 2022, tusche, ink, and digital collage on paper. One of several Sojourner Truth drawings I made at Yaddo in 2022, the only one with text. The text comes from the back of Truth's cartes de visite, which notably does not quote Frances Dana Gage's 1863 version of Truth in 1851.

cals of the Second Great Awakening, she gloried in massive outdoor camp meetings. And like other Black women preachers, she heeded her inner spiritual voice and spoke up when the spirit moved her.

Although Truth may have been an unusual character in Akron, she was only one of several Black female preachers active in the antebellum North. They, too, published autobiographies: Jarena Lee in 1839 and 1849; Zilpha Elaw, who preached in England for five years, in 1846; and Nancy Prince in 1850, the year Sojourner Truth's *Narrative* appeared. Nancy Prince was no stranger to women's rights or antislavery circles; indeed, she spoke at the fifth national women's rights convention in Philadelphia in 1854. These Northern women came out of the African Methodist Episcopal (AME) Church and reached wide audiences with messages of conversion and sanctification similar to Sojourner Truth's. Rebecca Cox Jackson also began in the AME Church and went on to become a Shaker eldress. If not for Truth's residence in the Northampton Association and her well-publicized advocacy of what we now consider secular reforms, she would belong wholly to this tradition of Black women preachers.[5] She built an enduring reputation on the antislavery feminist circuit over the years, and White women rather than Black were her companions and filled her audiences.

Not only Truth's religious history but also her socioeconomic background would seem to contrast starkly with that of most other women at the Akron meeting. Whereas Truth had grown up as poor as could be, enslaved on a farm in upstate New York, many antislavery women leaders—White women like Lucy Stone and Abby Kelley, and Black women like Sarah Mapps Douglass and Frances Ellen Watkins Harper, both of Philadelphia—came from urban backgrounds. Also, like Stone, Kelley, Douglass, and Harper, leading antislavery women were from middle- and upper-middle-class families and consequently had a good deal more education and money than most of their female contemporaries, including Sojourner Truth. And like Frances Dana Gage, they had often grown up in reform-minded homes and had long been exposed to discussions of moral reform (e.g., temperance) and politics.[6]

Many feminist abolitionists came to advocate women's rights after experiencing frustration in their antislavery work, but they found that acting on their convictions did not come easily. Often antebellum women who became feminists were not able to move unimpeded into the public realm. As Elizabeth Cady Stanton discovered, women raised to stay at home had to overcome shyness, inexperience in public speaking and in presiding over meetings, familial and community hostility, and the pressures of housekeeping and child-rearing. These conditions explain Frances Dana Gage's nervousness chairing the 1851 Akron meeting where Sojourner Truth spoke up.[7]

In common with women preachers through the ages, Truth had surmounted these barriers long ago. In the 1820s she had left her husband and four of her five children in Ulster County; by 1851 all her children lived apart from her and consumed none of her time and energy. She had already addressed camp meetings by the score. As an independent and, as she said, self-made woman, Truth could speak out in 1851 with the self-confidence that came from long experience. But did these experiences truly distinguish Truth from other women's rights abolitionists? Not necessarily, and not entirely.

A closer look at other antislavery feminists and at the 1851 meeting in Akron blurs easy distinctions. Two of the most salient figures at the Akron convention, Gage and the journalist Jane Swisshelm, were better educated than Truth, but had, like Truth and many other early nineteenth-century Americans, grown up on farms. But if access to formal education separated Truth, who was unlettered, from other women who were journalists and schoolteachers, religion united them. Quakers, who recognized the right of women to preach, often supplied the common thread. Abby Kelley, Amy Post, and Sarah and Angelina Grimké, among feminist abolitionists, were or had been Quakers. Others, particularly those who lectured in public, shared with Truth a penchant for Quaker dress and close association with Quakers. Like Truth, other female leaders conceived of their mission in religious terms yet were deeply critical of organized churches and clergy. In 1854, Lucretia Mott spoke for all women's rights advocates: "It is not Christianity, but priestcraft that has subjected woman as we find her."[8] Their belief in the cause of the slave as a religious duty led antislavery feminists to lecture and write messages such as Angelina

ist friend of Sojourner Truth's named Marius Robinson, was president of the Western Anti-Slavery Society. He published lengthy accounts of the proceedings for the newspaper he edited, the Salem, Ohio, *Anti-Slavery Bugle*. Although his account acknowledges the power of Sojourner Truth's remarks, Robinson's lengthy reports also give voice to the other participants. Here is a fragment of Robinson's report on Truth's comments as it appeared in 1851 in his newspaper. NB: this is the report from 1851. Let me repeat: this is part of a report from 1851, not the one by Frances Dana Gage from 1863, which I will turn to momentarily. From June 21, 1851,

> May I say a few words? Receiving an affirmative answer, she proceeded; I want to say a few words about this matter. I am a woman's rights. I have as much muscle as any man, and can do as much work as any man. I have plowed and reaped and husked and chopped and mowed, and can any man do more than that? I have heard much about the sexes being equal; I can carry as much as any man, and can eat as much too, if I can get it. I am as strong as any man that is now. As for intellect, all I can say is, if woman have a pint and man a quart—why can't she have her little pint full? You need not be afraid to give us our rights for fear we will take too much, for we can't take more than our pint'll hold. The poor men seem to be all in confusion, and don't know what to do. Why children, if you have woman's rights give it to her and you will feel better. You will have your own rights, and they won't be so much trouble. I can't read, but I can hear. I have heard the bible and have learned that Eve caused man to sin. Well if woman upset the world, do give her a chance to set it right side up again. The Lady has spoken about Jesus, how he never spurned woman from him, and she was right. When Lazarus died, Mary and Martha came to him with faith and love and besought him to raise their brother. And Jesus wept—and Lazarus came forth. And how came Jesus into the world? Through God who created him and woman who bore him. Man, where is your part? But the women are coming up, blessed be God, and a few of the men are coming up with them. But man is in a tight

place, the poor slave is on him, woman is coming on him, and he is surely between a hawk and a buzzard.

This 1851 report is not well known, though it was published in the *Anti-Slavery Bugle* and republished in the authoritative twentieth-century reference collection *The Black Abolitionist Papers*. When historians apply tests for the authenticity of a source, this report stands up well. It was taken down at the time, and the reporter, Marius Robinson, knew Truth as her host in northern Ohio. Of paramount importance, Robinson's report does not include Gage's dramatic phrase "A'rn't I a woman?"

The report was not contested at the time and was corroborated by a brief mention in William Lloyd Garrison's official organ *The Liberator*. Gage's competing version appeared twelve years later. Yes. *Twelve years later.*

The picture of the Akron meeting emerging from the pages of the *Bugle* contradicts Gage in several regards, starting with the call to the conference, which ran in several reform newspapers in the spring of 1851 and appealed to "all the friends of Reform, in whatever department engaged." The call cited four evils that women's rights would combat: war, intemperance, sensuality, and slavery. Rather than fearing contamination by the antislavery cause, as Gage later asserted, the organizers deliberately reached out to abolitionists.[11]

Robinson reports the women's spirited discussions, citing particularly the frequent contributions of the fervent Pittsburgh journalist Jane Swisshelm and of Emma Coe, a popular women's rights lecturer from Michigan. At one point a Mr. Sterling protested that men were talking too much and recommended their restraint. Mary A. W. Johnson dissented, reminding everyone that men as well as women were welcome to the floor. Robinson sums up approvingly: "The business of the Convention was principally conducted by the women." He features the speeches of Gage and Truth in separate articles, for Gage had delivered an effective keynote, and Truth's was "one of the most unique and interesting speeches" of the convention, thanks to "her powerful form, her whole-souled, earnest gestures, and . . . strong and truthful tones." But according to Robinson, the other women in attendance were not, as Gage would have them, silent nor discomfited. The meeting included enough other women with public speaking experience that Sojourner Truth did not stand out only for that reason.[12] Accounts in other newspapers also emphasize the liveliness of the proceedings and mention Frances Dana Gage, Emma Coe, and Jane Swisshelm by name.[13]

Frances Dana Gage, who often published commentary and fiction under the pen name of Aunt Fanny, was a far more creative and experienced writer than Marius Robinson. She dramatized Sojourner Truth's presence much better than did he. In Gage's scenario, the featureless organizers of the convention "tremble" when Truth appears in all her physical strength. Whereas Robinson mentions merely Truth's "powerful form," Gage supplies a vivid image of "this almost Amazon form, which stood nearly six feet high, head erect, and eyes piercing the upper air like one in a dream," whose first words produce "a profound hush." Gage's Truth bares a tremendously muscular right arm, pulls herself up to her full six feet, and has a voice like thunder. The words that Gage quotes Truth speaking are commanding, and they emanate from a superhuman body.

Gage's sketch of Truth, first published in 1863, not in 1851, was influenced by another writer of far greater renown whose portrait of Truth had already reached a vast audience. By the time Harriet Beecher Stowe published "Sojourner Truth, The Libyan Sibyl" in the April 1863 issue of *The Atlantic Monthly*, she was famous as the bestselling author of *Uncle Tom's Cabin* and other novels and stories. Stowe made mistakes, such as that Truth was dead. Such errors did not prevent the essay from becoming the most popular rendition of Truth in the mid-nineteenth century. For the next twenty-five years, other Truth biographers, including Gage, repeated (sometimes with variations, as was the case with Gage) the Libyan Sibyl appellation that Stowe had used.[14]

Stowe places less emphasis than Gage on Truth's physical presence and creates an exotic Truth persona: "No pen, however, can give an adequate ideal of Sojourner Truth. This unlettered African woman, with her deep religious and trustful nature burning in her soul like fire, has a magnetic power over an audience [that is] perfectly astounding." Whereas Gage's Truth is a voice in a powerful body, Stowe's Truth is an amusing native, an African whose insight gushes, untamed, out of her nature. Stowe contrasts the untutored Truth with the eminent clergymen who are her houseguests. Gage uses a similar strategy of opposition, contrasting potent Truth with insipid White women. Both quote Truth speaking in dialect while White characters speak cultured, standard English. Truth emerges from both essays as a colorful force of nature profoundly different from lackluster (White) people like the authors.

Other descriptions of Truth also stress her singularity. Frederick Douglass called her a "strange compound of wit and wisdom, of wild enthusiasm and flint-like common sense." She was, he said, "a genuine specimen of the uncultured negro" who cared nothing for "elegance of speech or refinement of manners. She seemed to please herself and others best when she put her ideas in the oddest forms."[15] The newspapers reprinted in the second part of the 1875/78 and 1884 editions of *Narrative of Sojourner Truth* also underscore her differentness, portraying her as "this interesting and decidedly original character," "unique, witty, pathetic, sensible," "a child of nature, gifted beyond the common measure, witty, shrewd, sarcastic, with an open, broad honesty of heart, and unbounded kindness."[16]

Sojourner Truth's appeal was at once broader than race and deeply rooted in Americans' notions about the connection between Blackness and slavery. Educated Americans have long been attracted to naifs, whether or not of African descent. Truth's seemingly unaffected religiosity gave her access to large American audiences. The prophetic, evangelical style that Truth employed has struck Americans as embodying more authenticity and more fundamental truth than the more educated rhetoric derived from the law and from written sermons. Truth's mode of expression owes much to late eighteenth- and early nineteenth-century Methodists, who invented the art of preaching—as opposed to sermonizing—and within fifty years grew into the largest American denomination. Nineteenth-century Americans were susceptible to inspired preaching, and Truth was first and foremost a preacher who gloried in divine inspiration. Elaborating on the Bible more than on the news from Washington, Sojourner Truth's message was thoroughly and thoughtfully steeped in biblical imagery, and her text was intimately familiar to all her fellow citizens. To those numerous nineteenth-century Americans whose basic education had come from the Bible and whose religion was evangelical, Sojourner Truth would have been a persuasive purveyor of enduring, fundamental wisdom.

Truth was unforgettable for two reasons. First, she was a forceful speaker—like Frances Dana Gage, Frances Ellen Watkins Harper, Emma Coe, Nancy Prince, and Jane Swisshelm. Second, she presented herself as a woman who had been a slave; she made her persona as different from the educated White women who made her famous as they thought it possible to be. Even though the opportunities for women to speak in public were relatively circumscribed and always controversial in the first half of the nineteenth century, as a woman speaker, Truth had many peers. Actresses were seldom considered entirely respectable; spiritual mediums spoke only while in a trance. But women preachers, Quakers or not, spoke in churches and camp meetings. Women lecturers like Emma Coe talked about great American women in schoolhouses, churches, and meeting halls. Sojourner Truth had addressed audiences in each of these venues and had been recognized as a thrilling performer for twenty years before she went to Akron.

Truth had also crafted a persona that appealed enormously to educated White Americans. Her manipulation of the imagery of slavery and difference recommended her to talented publicists who guaranteed her place in the history of antislavery feminism. Gage's portrait, emphasizing Truth's body, reinforces notions that Truth herself asserted: that her experience in slavery—in which she worked like a man, suffered the loss of many children through sale, and felt a mother's grief but had no solace—lent her a potency that the White women at the meeting in Akron lacked, no matter how well they had been educated.

Unquestionably Sojourner Truth constructed her public persona to establish that what had happened to her—her enslavement, rather than her reason—lent her a unique wisdom. She always reminded audiences that she had been enslaved and that she remembered what enslavement meant. If Gage quotes her accurately in 1851 when she says she lost thirteen children, Truth had appropriated her mother's sad experience of bearing and losing to slavery more than ten children. In fact, Sojourner Truth had five children, one of whom was sold away from her but whom she recovered through an extraordinary use of the law. By the 1870s Truth had added a decade to her time as a slave. She knew full well that her experience in slavery authenticated her being and reinforced her message, whether she was speaking about antislavery, women's rights, or freedmen's relief. And indeed, taking their cue from Truth, most readers conclude with Gage that Truth embodied some fundamental characteristic of Blackness rooted in slavery, some power of race in rhetorically concentrated form.

Black slavery, Truth realized, was more memorable than Black freedom for most Americans. Even the relatively enlightened communities of abolitionists focused more easily on abuses against the enslaved than on discrimination against the free. Again and again, free Blacks in the antislavery movement had to remind their colleagues of their own situation, for the cause of the slave seemed so much more romantic and attractive. For many White abolitionists (William Lloyd Garrison, the Grimké sisters, and Abby Kelley were exceptions), free Blacks existed in a conceptual limbo in which they were unseen or uninteresting or distasteful. Whereas other Black women abolitionists spoke and dressed like educated Americans, Truth emphasized her otherness by reciting her experiences as a slave. Widening the distance between herself and her audiences, Truth took maximum advantage of being exotic.

Truth resisted or ignored the temptation, as Frederick Douglass did not, to create an educated persona to display the benefits of freedom. Douglass recalled her poking fun at him as he remade himself: "[Truth] seemed to feel it her duty to trip me up in my speeches and to ridicule my efforts to speak and act like a person of cultivation and refinement." Douglass, like most other African American abolitionists, made one choice; Truth made another. As the historian Carleton Mabee has noted, she remained illiterate despite many efforts to instruct her as an adult. Other formerly enslaved men like Douglass and J. W. C. Pennington associated literacy with freedom and presented themselves to the public as educated people.[17] Truth claimed that God inspired her, and she disdained formal education in lecturers or in clergy. By stressing the inspirational aspect of her speaking gift and downplaying self-conscious preparation, she dispensed with any need for literacy, the very attainment that many other Black abolitionists prized most.

Truth also used her body in ways that women who were not actresses did not dare. Old and Black and modestly dressed, she obliterated the sexual aspect of womanliness that youth, beauty, and lightness of skin would have accentuated. Yet Truth intentionally exhibited her body, and her American public recorded the occasions. She showed her arm in its full length in 1851 and bared her breast in 1858, defining her womanliness and, miraculously, representing the essence of worker and mother rather than that of whore. Here her age, color, and naivete served her well, for the figure of the light-skinned, ladylike Negro woman symbolized the enslaved fancy girl, whose sexuality—which could be bought and sold—was her most salient characteristic.

Sojourner Truth was not selling herself, at least not literally. But her gestures, sensational for the time, definitely enhanced her career. Truth followed a practice that was (and still is) common on American lecture circuits. Like Frederick Douglass and others who had published their autobiographies or other writing, she sold her books to reform-minded audiences whose curiosity had been whetted by her personal appearance. This tactic worked equally well for Frances Ellen Watkins Harper, a Black poet and teacher who joined the antislavery lecture circuit in the 1850s. The free-born Harper toured under the auspices of the Maine Anti-Slavery Society, selling not a slave narrative but two volumes of poetry, *Forest Leaves* (1845) and *Poems on Miscellaneous Subjects* (1854).

Harper gained considerable respect as both poet and lecturer before the Civil War. After emancipation she taught in the South, and after Reconstruction she headed the Colored Division of the Woman's Christian Temperance Union. In 1892 she published *Iola Leroy*, one of the earliest novels by an African American. For nearly half a century, Harper was active in the various reform movements that attracted the support of American women. Scholars like Hazel

Carby, Frances Smith Foster, and Bettye Collier-Thomas have investigated her life and work.[18] Besides Frances Harper, Sojourner Truth had several other Black women contemporaries in feminist abolitionism. Two pioneers of Black women's history, Gerda Lerner and Dorothy Sterling, have edited documents that illuminate the lives of antislavery feminists such as Sarah Mapps Douglass, the most active Black member of the Philadelphia Female Anti-Slavery Society and a correspondent of Sarah Grimké's for forty years, and Sarah Parker Remond, born into an antislavery family in Salem, Massachusetts, an antislavery lecturer in New England and Great Britain in the 1850s. Marilyn Richardson has republished the speeches and essays of the Boston lecturer Maria Stewart. A popular speaker in the early 1830s, Stewart formulated phrases that Sojourner Truth came close to echoing: "What if I am a woman; is not the God of ancient times the God of these modern days?"[19]

The names of Harper, Douglass, Remond, and Stewart occasionally appear in passing in histories of abolitionism and in the three volumes of *History of Woman Suffrage*. Although they are now becoming better known and their work is being reprinted, none has her portrait on a postage stamp, as has Sojourner Truth since 1986. Their lives and works remain the stuff of scholarly research, not of popular legend. Why this invisibility? On the one hand, as mostly light-skinned, ladylike women of African descent, they resembled too closely the stereotypical enslaved fancy girl; on the other hand, they were too much like their White women peers to seem memorable. But mostly, because they were very obviously free, the exotic character of the slave-woman victim has overshadowed their existence. Educated, free Black women have come very close, in fact, to vanishing entirely from the annals of antislavery and women's rights. To explain this near disappearance, we must return to the phrase associated with Sojourner Truth: "and ar'n't I a woman?" Truth—and Stewart, Harper, Douglass, and Remond—saw themselves as women; their own womanly identity was secure. But the culture in which they lived seldom accorded them complete female identity. Even Frances Dana Gage quotes Truth presenting her statement in the form of a question, which she does not answer straightforwardly. Gage does not let Truth proclaim, "Yes, I *am* a woman!" Instead, the rhetorical query leaves room for doubt. Most Americans in the middle of the nineteenth century would not even have thought to formulate such a question regarding Black women or poor women of any race; as *woman*, these figures would have been invisible.

Had the question been posed, however, the short answer would most likely have been no. One of the era's most prominent antislavery feminists provides an example. In 1863, as several antislavery feminists were launching a petition drive to enact an amendment to the United States Constitution prohibiting slavery, Susan B. Anthony wrote to Elizabeth Cady Stanton that she planned to field teams of lecturers who would rally public support. Each team would consist of three people: "a *White* man, *Black* man & a woman." Another women's rights advocate, Jane Swisshelm, followed the logic of her time when she spoke of "woman's rights" as opposed to the rights of "colored men." Swisshelm, like many of her colleagues in feminism, also deleted working-class women from the collectivity she called "woman." Certainly, White women's rights supporters were far from unified when they defined "woman," and Parker Pillsbury and Frances Dana Gage insisted on including women who were Black. By and large, however, the women who spoke up for "woman" did not have poor White women and women of color in mind.[20]

This way of thinking has proved amazingly durable. Nineteenth- and early twentieth-century human sciences like anthropometry and phrenology routinely paired White women and men of color, as though women of color did not, need not, exist. The White woman/ Black man parallel that ignores Black women inspired Gloria T. Hull, Patricia Bell-Scott, and Barbara Smith to include it in the title of their 1982 anthology of Black women's writing, *All the Women Are White, All the Blacks Are Men, But Some of Us Are Brave.* Describing her experiences in Harvard Law School in the 1970s, Patricia Williams recalls feeling utterly invisible.[21] With educated White women as *woman* and Black men as *the slave,* free, articulate Black women simply vanished. What little social category existed for the Black woman was reserved for the enslaved: if dark-skinned, as Mammy; if light-skinned, beautiful young sexual prey. Even to their compatriots in reform, educated free Black women were not engaging enough to attract publicists who had a keen eye out for drama, like Frances Dana Gage and Harriet Beecher Stowe.

Sojourner Truth, in contrast, purposefully anchored herself in slavery. She employed a naive persona, which until the second half of the twentieth century was the most certain means for a Black woman to secure individual recognition in American public life. In the twentieth century, Mary McLeod Bethune and Zora Neale Hurston used the naive persona to advance their interests with powerful White Americans in politics, education, and the arts. All three women came under criticism from other Blacks for reinforcing unfortunate stereotypes of the-Black-as-Other at the same time that they charmed educated Whites as quaintly picturesque.

Sojourner Truth presented herself as a woman at a time when the American *woman* could not be Black. Truth and other nineteenth-century Black women who employed feminist strategies did not succeed in destroying the barrier between themselves and *woman*. Not-*woman*, they seemed to be something else—authentic, powerful, native—that was memorable. To appear in the eyes of most nineteenth-century Americans to be both memorable and *woman* at the same time simply was not possible. Black women's individual experience had either to be reconstructed as something emblematically Negro—that is, as enslaved—or to be erased. In the nineteenth century, Frances Dana Gage did not let Sojourner Truth answer her own rhetorical question unequivocally, because for most of their compatriots, if not for themselves, Blackness was exiled from the category of woman.

June 1994

The Truth of the Matter

LETTER TO THE EDITOR OF *THE NEW YORKER*

I ADMIRED AMY DAVIDSON SORKIN'S FINE PIECE on the Republicans' shameful, bigoted manhandling of Judge Ketanji Brown Jackson's nomination to the Supreme Court (Comment, April 18). Sorkin quotes a phrase—"Ain't I a woman?"—that was long held to have been spoken by Sojourner Truth, in an 1851 speech in Akron, Ohio. Yet, as I revealed in my 1996 biography, *Sojourner Truth: A Life, A Symbol,* Truth never uttered those words. The phrase originated with Frances Dana Gage, a White abolitionist, women's rights advocate, and journalist, who, in an article written twelve years after the speech, put "Ar'n't I a woman?" in Truth's mouth. (Gage was rebutting a careless essay by Harriet Beecher Stowe, in the April 1863 issue of *The Atlantic Monthly,* which depicted Truth as quaint and, erroneously, as dead.)

Elizabeth Cady Stanton and Susan B. Anthony reprinted Gage's piece in their book *History of Woman Suffrage,* from 1881, which second-wave feminists would draw on as they forged the field of women's history in the twentieth century. By that time, the line had been reworked into a supposedly more authentic Southern Negro dialect, as "Ain't I a woman?" But a contemporaneous report of what Truth said, published by Marius Robinson, a White abolitionist minister, in the *Anti-Slavery Bugle,* does not include the line in any form. Although both Gage and Robinson were present at Truth's speech, Robinson was the designated amanuensis; it is hard to imagine that he would have omitted such a refrain. (Gage claimed that Truth repeated it four times.)

As a scholar, I find Robinson's account of Truth's speech more reliable than Gage's. "Ain't I a woman?" has nonetheless taken on a life of its own as a synecdoche for what we now term "intersectionality." The false quote flattens Truth into little more than a magical Negro savior of White women and obscures her identity as a New Yorker who spoke standard English (as well as Dutch). Unfortunately, I've found that, in our country's historical imagination, my academic research as a Black woman frequently loses out to a slogan that my sister citizens *want* Truth to have said, and to the national hunger for simplifying history.

May 2022

Humanity, Scholarship, and Proud Race Citizenship

THE GIFTS OF JOHN HOPE FRANKLIN

JOHN HOPE FRANKLIN died seven weeks after my mother, Dona Lolita Irvin, of the same cause: congestive heart disease. World renowned and universally mourned, he was two years older than my mother, she, a celebrity in her own right on a closely circumscribed, very local stage. They had just a little in common—both grew up in the Southwest in relatively privileged circumstances, steadied by the ballast that even relative privilege can provide. And he, with characteristic generosity, blurbed her first book. She adored him, but otherwise they lived widely separated lives. Yet in my emotion of grief, their deaths have merged. Giants in my life in very different ways, Franklin and Irvin, survivors of American apartheid, insisted on their personal uniqueness while situating themselves proudly as African Americans with much to contribute to the United States, as Black people and as individuals. Their stance demanded enormous intelligence and a constant expenditure of energy, not simply in the exercise of their vocation as authors.

In the segregated world, Franklin received accolades in abundance as the author of *From Slavery to Freedom,* first published in 1947 and still in print and flourishing. The handsome portrait on the John Hope Franklin Center website by Simmie Knox (who paints our society's eminences) situates him between a portrait of his beloved late wife,

Aurelia, and his namesake orchid. Franklin holds a copy of *From Slavery to Freedom* so that its title may be clearly read.

For all of us of a certain age, *From Slavery to Freedom* spoke a different language from that of our schools. There "the Negro" did not belong in America. He (and he was a he) appeared in public only briefly, and only in the guise of slavery, the feckless slave emancipated by the actions of other men, White men, if not exactly the crouching naked figure freed by Abraham Lincoln, then imprisoned within that iconography. A fleeting, passive, ridiculous figure, this mid-twentieth-century image then disappeared from history.

Like so many others before and after me, I underwent a quintessential Negro-child experience in Oakland, California, in the supposedly liberal and enlightened San Francisco Bay Area. Thank heaven I had John Hope Franklin and my parents as counterweights at home, for my junior high school homeroom pictured Henry Ford's Americanization ceremony across the top of one entire wall. On the left, myriad Europeans in traditional peasant dress lined up to enter the melting pot. They emerged on the right in suits, ties, and hats as Americans. Nary a dark figure among them. With knowledge of the true nature of American history on my side, I confronted my homeroom teacher. She stamped me as a troublemaker, a label I have yet to outlive.

John Hope Franklin, bless him, delivered a different image and a larger story, which evolved over the decades with the elaboration of history and of historiography. Were his greatness to have ended there, it would deserve my deepest gratitude.

As a scholar-citizen, Franklin very rightly deserves honors for the finest and most enduring history of African Americans. He also deserves recognition for a good deal else he has written. In addition to contributing a distinguished oeuvre in African American history, Franklin also thought and wrote across the color line to alter the meaning of American history, especially of Southern history, as a whole. A Southern historian from the outset, he wrote perceptively of White as well as Black Southerners and of all Americans. I'm thinking of his mid-twentieth-century works, notably *The Militant South: 1800–1861* (1956), *Land of the Free: A History of the United States* (1965), and *Southern Odyssey: Travelers in the Antebellum North* (1976). *The Militant South* analyzed the myriad ways the South's economy, based on personal violence and maintained through local militia, distorted its public realm and civil sphere, militarizing the society from top to bottom and, it might be added, contributing to a homicide rate that remains astronomical. How much richer history would have been if historians of all races had followed his lead and peered beyond their own allotments.

Much of Franklin's bibliography and citizenship contributes to a larger understanding of American society and the central place of Black people within it. Here again, in word and deed, is sufficient cause for thanks, from his work on *Brown v. Board of Education,* his policy analyses, his citizenship-based scholarship, and his Sisyphean chairing of "One America," President Bill Clinton's Initiative on Race. Were his greatness to have ended there, too, it would deserve our deepest gratitude.

Perhaps less noted are Franklin's works of biography, a concentration on the individual—on individual initiative and individual difference—that characterizes his thought. The same year he first published *From Slavery to Freedom* he also published *The Diary of James T. Ayers: Civil War Recruiter.* More familiar is his biography of his intellectual ancestor, George Washington Williams, which appeared in 1985 in a biographical series he edited with the University of Chicago Press. Then followed other personal studies: his edition of his father's autobiography, *My Life and an Era* (1997) and his own autobiography, *Mirror to America* (2005).

All these works evince a fighting spirit that John Hope Franklin never renounced. Gentleman that he was, this spirit never emerged abusively, but he also never let his own honors obscure the actual facts of American life and history. The generosity of his spirit tempted his colleagues into setting him apart from other Black people who could be dismissed as angry. They were wrong to do so, for John Hope Franklin never lost sight of the fundamental character of American White supremacy, no matter how much certain fans of his wanted him to demur.

On one of the many occasions in which he was invited to speak and thereby flatter an institution proud of its progress, he jolted a preening audience into remembering the depth of White privilege in America. His topic was the US Congress's first definition of national citizenship, the Naturalization Act of 1790, which drew a clear White color line. To undo so long and deep a history would require much more than short-range or easy remedies. When I thanked him for this much-needed dose of sobriety, he said, "The older I get, the madder I get."

My mother, like so many of her peers, performed that same balancing act between justified anger and personal warmth. Only her own circle read her books and saw the truth-telling gift she gave her country. But John Hope Franklin, a luminary on the world's stage, shared the beauty of individual humanity and proud race citizenship with millions.

Summer 2009

Long Divisions

———————————

THE HISTORY OF RACISM AND EXCLUSION in the United States is the history of Whiteness.

A generation ago, as the culture wars raged, Toni Morrison stood at the front lines demanding the desegregation of the American literary canon. In her Tanner Lectures in 1988, and later in her book *Playing in the Dark,* she argued against a monochromatic literary canon that had seemed forever to be naturally and inevitably all-White but was, in fact, she said, "studiously" so. She accused scholars of "lobotomizing" literary history and criticism in order to free them of Black presence. Broadening our conception of American literature beyond the cast of lily-White men would not simply benefit non-White readers. Opening up would serve the interests of American mental as well as intellectual health, Morrison said, since the White racial ideology that purged literature of Blackness was "savage." She called the very concept of Whiteness "an inhuman idea."

In her new book, *The Origin of Others,* Morrison extends and sharpens these themes as she traces through American literature's patterns of thought and behavior that subtly code who belongs and who doesn't, who is accepted in and who is cast out as "Other." She has previously written of how modernist novelists like William Faulkner (who saw race) and Ernest Hemingway (who did not) respected the codes of Jim Crow by dehumanizing Black figures or ignoring the connotations of Blackness in their non-Black figures. But the process of exiling some people from humanity, she observes here, also ranges beyond American habits of race: one need only look at the treatment of millions now in flight from war and economic desperation. Othering as a means of control is not just the practice of White people in the United States, for every group perfects its self-regard through exclusion.

Morrison anchors her discussion of these complexities in her personal experience, recounting a memory from her childhood in the 1930s: a visit from her great-grandmother Millicent MacTeer, a figure of enormous power whose skin was very black. On her arrival, MacTeer looked at Toni and her sister, two girls with light skin, and pronounced them "tampered with." Colorism ordinarily refers to Black people's denigration of dark skin and preference for people who are light, but in this case it meant, more broadly, a judgment based on skin color. "It became clear," Morrison writes, "that 'tampered with' meant lesser, if not completely Other." Deemed "sullied, not pure" as a child, Morrison finds that Othering, as well as the racial self-loathing of colorism, begins in the family and connects to race, class, gender, and power.

Morrison's history of Othering represents an intervention in history on several fronts. Although the theme of desegregating the literary canon reappears in *The Origin of Others,* times have changed since *Playing in the Dark.* Surely thanks to the more multicultural, multiracial canon that Morrison helped foster, no respectable version of American literature today omits writers of color. Morrison herself has received nearly all the honors a novelist can win: the Pulitzer Prize for Fiction, the Nobel Prize in Literature, the Presidential Medal of Freedom, and the French Legion of Honor, among many more. *The Origin of Others* is the result of her lectures in the prestigious Charles Eliot Norton series at Harvard University, where she is only the fourth woman and the second Black lecturer in the ninety-two-year history of the series.

Within the Norton Lectures' tradition of wisdom, and among its tellers, Morrison represents a novelty by virtue of her gender, her race, and her American subject matter. Historically the series has shown a preference for European topics and for British scholars as avatars of learning. Not until 2014, when Herbie Hancock addressed "The Ethics of Jazz," did the Norton recognize wisdom in the humanities as both pertaining to American culture and emanating from a Black body. Morrison's lectures and book are a historic achievement, as they confirm the impact of her intellectual tradition in American thought—a tradition that links her to James Baldwin, and in a younger generation Ta-Nehisi Coates, in the critique of Whiteness.

Morrison's earliest witnesses of Othering are two women who had been enslaved, Mary Prince and Harriet Jacobs, both of whom recorded their physical and mental torture at the hands of their owners. In her 1831 memoir, Prince described her owner's reinforcement of hierarchy through beating; her master "would stand by and give orders for a slave to be cruelly whipped . . . walking about and taking snuff with the greatest composure." Thirty years later, Jacobs wrote of how slavery made "the White fathers cruel and sensual; the sons violent and licentious." Within slavery, the process of Othering is physical and is meant to work in only one direction, from the enslaver to the enslaved.

Morrison asks instead, "Who are these people?"—focusing not on the victimized, the enslaved, but on the victimizing owners. "The definition of the inhuman describes overwhelmingly the punisher . . . the pleasure of the one with the lash." Rendering enslaved people "a foreign species," Morrison concludes, "appears to be a desperate attempt to confirm one's own self as normal." Humanity links the enslaved and the enslaver, no matter how viciously enslavers seek to deny the connection. Torture, the crucial ingredient of slave ownership, dehumanizes not the enslaved but the enslaver. "It's as though they are shouting, 'I am not a beast! I'm not a beast!'" Neither side escapes unscathed.

Physical force would seem to suffice to enforce dehumanization, but it does not. The people doing the Othering further bolster their self-definition through words. Thomas Thistlewood, an English planter and rapist who moved to Jamaica in 1750, documented his assaults on the women he owned, categorizing those that took place on the ground, in the fields, and in large and small rooms, whenever, wherever he wished, as he recorded. He noted the rapes in his journal in Latin. Harriet Beecher Stowe's novel *Uncle Tom's Cabin* takes a very different tone, defining the Other by making a romance of slave life. Stowe presents a slave cabin in dulcet description that Morrison calls "outrageously inviting," "cultivated," "seductive," and "excessive." Here, a White child can enter Black space without fear of the dark, the very sweetness of the language reinforcing the Otherness of places where Black people live.

Othering is expressed through codes of belonging as well as difference. Most commonly, pronouns convey the boundaries between "we" and "them" through the use of first- and third-person plurals. "We" belong; "they" are Other and cannot belong. Those who are "them" can be described in the negative language of disgust: Black as ugly, Black as polluting. Definitions of color, Morrison says, define what it means to be an American, for belonging adheres to Whiteness. The possession of Whiteness makes belonging possible, and to lack that possession is not to belong, to be defined as something lesser, even something not fully human. But neither possession nor lack is natural or biological. Something has to happen; a process needs to get underway.

Blackness remains the great challenge to writers of fiction on all sides of the color line, for the central role of race in American Othering affects us all, White and non-White, Black and non-Black, not just writers who are White. Morrison describes her own struggles with color codes in her work, notably in her novels *Paradise* (1997) and *Home* (2012), and her story and play *Recitatif* (1983). "Writing non-colorist literature about Black people," she writes, "is a task I have found both liberating and hard." Non-colorist literature does not make racial identity do the work of character creation. Characters may have racial identities—in the USA, race is too salient a part of experience to overlook. But race should not decide how a character acts or thinks or speaks or looks.

Morrison articulates her determination "to de-fang cheap racism, annihilate and discredit the routine, easy, available color fetish, which is reminiscent of slavery itself." But it is far from easy. The actors in

Recitatif, like editors and many readers, want to identify characters by race—a crucial ingredient of American identity, but one defined by generalizations rooted in the history of slavery and too facilely evoked through recognizable stereotypes. Racial identification, invented to serve needs of subjugation, can diminish a character's individual specificity, that hallmark of Morrison's brilliance.

Where Morrison identifies race, she struggles against the expectations of race. *Paradise* begins with color—"They shoot the White girl first." But she never says which of the women in the group under attack is White, and offers almost no clues. ("Some readers have told me of their guess," Morrison reveals in *The Origin of Others,* "but only one of them was ever correct.") *Paradise* turns to themes of Black colorism's purity requirements and misogyny, the deadly means of Othering that Morrison's characters employ. Colorism appears early on in the novel with wealth; in 1890 members of an established Black community turn away a group of freedmen deemed too poor and too dark. The freedmen go on to found the town of Haven and its successor, Ruby, and from that moment up to the novel's present in the 1970s, they pride themselves on their unadulterated Blackness. Nearby, a group of women, seeking refuge from traumatic pasts, move into an old convent. One source of the Ruby men's murderous hatred of the women is their racial heterogeneity—their utter lack of racial purity. But that is not the only source: in Paradise, *misogyny* fuels the hatred that kills.

Looking back on *Home,* Morrison admits to misgivings. It was a mistake, she concludes, to accede to her editor's request for color-coding the main character, Frank Money. A minor mistake, for Money's race only appears obliquely, after a two-page description of the hospital he is leaving. A reader would have to know that in the tiny AME Zion Church that succors Money, AME means "African Methodist Episcopal." A few pages later, the reader would need to grasp the meaning of he "won't be able to sit down at any bus stop counter." If Morrison lost the struggle between individual characterization and racial identification, which not only flattens out characters but also furthers racist habits of thought, it was just barely. Throughout her career, Morrison has confronted those habits and broken them down, not just in her own writing but also in her work as an editor.

44

In her nineteen years at Random House, Morrison made known the stories of a variety of specific lives and their individual identities. She published biographies of the writer Toni Cade Bambara, the activist-scholar Angela Davis, and the athlete Muhammad Ali. In 1974 she published a nonfiction anthology: *The Black Book*, a scrapbook of Black history drawn from the collection of Middleton A. Harris, who also served as its editor. There readers discovered photographs of Black soldiers in impeccable uniforms, Black families in their Sunday best, early Black movie stars, and patents for typewriters and laundry machines, along with postcards of smiling White people at a lynching. The abundance and variety of material relating to the history of people of African descent in *The Black Book* opened millions of eyes to diversity within Blackness, a crucial step in loosening the grip of American apartheid.

One of Morrison's major novels was inspired by an 1856 article she found in *The Black Book*. Titled "A Visit to the Slave Mother Who Killed Her Child," the article presented an interview with the fugitive Margaret Garner, who had murdered her youngest child after she and her family were captured in Ohio. Garner's mother-in-law did not condemn the infanticide. Rather she condoned an act that saved a child from enslavement. The figure of the supportive mother-in-law fascinated Morrison and formed the basis for the character Baby Suggs, the un-churched folk preacher of Black self-love, in her 1987 novel, *Beloved*. *Beloved* won the Pulitzer Prize for Fiction and the American Book Award; Oprah Winfrey made the novel into a movie. Embedding the emotional costs of enslavement in Morrison's powerful language, *Beloved* spoke American history at the level of heart and gut, transforming the institution of slavery into tragedy with resonance for every reader and moviegoer. The novel and the movie communicated to everyone who loved their family the anguish of enslavement, of knowing your children were not yours at all.

What places *The Origin of Others* in this very moment of twenty-first-century American history—a moment that, sadly, bears much in common with earlier awful times—are two texts Morrison quotes at length. One is a testimony of lynchings committed in America in the early twentieth century. The other comes from Baby Suggs's sermon to her people in *Beloved*.

The testimony of lynchings continues for the better part of two pages. This is only a small portion of it:

> Ed Johnson, 1906 (lynched on the Walnut Street Bridge, in Chattanooga, Tennessee, by a mob that broke into jail after a stay of execution had been issued).
>
> Laura and L. D. Nelson, 1911 (mother and son, accused of murder, kidnapped from their cell, hanged from a railroad bridge near Okemah, Oklahoma).
>
> Elias Clayton, Elmer Jackson, and Isaac McGhie, 1920 (three circus workers accused of rape without any evidence, lynched in Duluth, Minnesota; no punishment for their murders).
>
> Raymond Gunn, 1931 (accused of rape and murder, doused with gasoline and burned to death by a mob in Maryville, Missouri).

Here is Baby Suggs, the mother-in-law figure in *Beloved,* as quoted in *The Origin of Others:*

> "Here," she said, "in this here place, we flesh; flesh that weeps, laughs; flesh that dances on bare feet in grass. Love it. Love it hard. Yonder they do not love your flesh. They despise it. They don't love your eyes; they'd just as soon pick em out. No more do they love the skin on your back. Yonder they flay it. And O my people they do not love your hands. Those they only use, tie, bind, chop off and leave empty. Love your hands! Love them."

To these, I would add a list currently circulating on Facebook of police shootings for which no one has been convicted of murder. As of late summer, the list looked like this, but, as we know, it is tragically subject to additions at any time:

#PhilandoCastile = No Conviction
#TerenceCrutcher = No Conviction
#SandraBland = No Conviction
#EricGarner = No Conviction
#MikeBrown = No Conviction
#RekiaBoyd = No Conviction
#SeanBell = No Conviction
#TamirRice = No Conviction
#FreddieGray = No Conviction
#DanroyHenry = No Conviction
#OscarGrantIII = No Conviction
#KendrecMcDade = No Conviction
#AiyanaJones = No Conviction
#RamarleyGraham = No Conviction
#AmadouDiallo = No Conviction
#TrayvonMartin = No Conviction
#JohnCrawfordIII = No Conviction
#JonathanFerrell = No Conviction
#TimothyStansburyJr = No Conviction

These lists, and Baby Suggs's sermon, capture the physical peril of existing in the United States in a body that is Black, of the deep and long tradition of Black hating and Black murder. And in doing so, they address a persistent theme in the writing of two other authors who play a part in *The Origin of Others,* one by name, one as a presence.

Ta-Nehisi Coates, author of *Between the World and Me,* the phenomenally bestselling personal statement in the guise of a letter to his teenage son, provides the foreword to *The Origin of Others.* Toni Morrison had blurbed Coates's book: "I've been wondering who might fill the intellectual void that plagued me after James Baldwin died. Clearly it is Ta-Nehisi Coates." Coates says Morrison's endorsement was the only one he craved. Morrison recognized in Coates, the cultural critic Michael Eric Dyson has written, a quality that she prized in Baldwin, and that we can see in her own work: "a forensic, analytical, cold-eyed stare down of White moral innocence." Coates cites Baldwin's 1963 book, *The Fire Next Time,* as a crucial inspiration, in form and in tone, to *Between the World and Me.*

Born in 1924, Baldwin serves as the intellectual ancestor to both Morrison and Coates, as tribune of the themes of violence against Black people and of the process by which European immigrants came to see themselves as White people in America. Baldwin began *The Fire Next Time* with a letter to his fifteen-year-old nephew, James, accusing his fellow Americans of the unforgivable crime of having destroyed and continuing to destroy thousands of Black lives without knowing and without wanting to know. Coates in 2015 writes to his then fifteen-year-old son that "in America, it is traditional to destroy the Black body—*it is heritage.*" Morrison in 2017 adds, as I quoted above: "The necessity of rendering the slave a foreign species appears to be a desperate attempt to confirm one's own self as normal." Both echo Baldwin's 1984 short essay, "On Being White . . . and Other Lies," first published in *Essence,* a magazine for Black women. Refocusing Black discourse from Black subjects to Whites, Baldwin made an early contribution to what would become Whiteness studies.

It's perhaps inevitable that such prominent authors would come to be seen as representatives of the entire community of Black Americans, though Coates says he speaks only for himself. Still, his vast audience demands spokesmanship from him. Morrison embraced the responsibility and welcomed the message that her Nobel Prize belonged not only to her, but to Black women writers generally. Certainly Baldwin embraced the role of Black spokesman in the 1960s with a passion that sometimes moved his audiences profoundly—as in a Cambridge University debate with the conservative William F. Buckley in 1965. When Baldwin appeared, impassioned, on *The Dick Cavett Show* in 1968, the host and other guests remained stolid and inert, even looking away in discomfort. The video is painful to watch, but instructive in the history of White American willful unknowing.

American culture has changed: whether writing as oneself alone—Coates—or speaking for a people—Morrison—these two Black writers have reaped the named and remunerated honors that are their due. Baldwin did not share their good fortune, despite informal recognition of his work's fundamental importance and utter necessity.

Between Baldwin and Coates, Morrison forms the keystone in an arch from neglect to celebration. This is not by accident or automatic recognition of genius. Historical agency, the action of protest, disrupted the withholding that was Baldwin's fate. Activism hoisted Morrison's reputation into its rightful place.

In the aftermath of Baldwin's death in 1987, forty-eight prominent Black poets, novelists, and scholars took note of his fate and demanded redress. In a letter published in *The New York Times,* they protested Baldwin's neglect and insisted it not be repeated. They focused attention on the literary establishment's ongoing habit of ignoring Black writers and pointed to the need to support another distinguished Black author who had been denied commensurate honors: Toni Morrison, whose *Beloved* had recently lost the National Book Award. After the letter appeared in the *Times,* things did start to change. *Beloved* received the Pulitzer Prize, and Morrison's work was never again disregarded. Morrison, in that moment, became a historical event. With the recognition of her writing and her whole tradition, America was opening up and offering Black Americans and Black authors belonging.

In the history that connects Baldwin to Morrison and Morrison to Coates, much has been gained in terms of literary reception. At the same time, however, something that distinguishes Morrison's fiction has been diminished: women and gender. Not entirely lost, for in *The Origin of Others,* Morrison discusses her novels of women—notably *Paradise* and *A Mercy.* (She might well have added another of her major women-centered works, *Sula.*) She also cites the woman-to-woman relationship of motherhood that binds Sethe and Baby Suggs in *Beloved.* But to the extent that they complicate the racial Othering that the two male writers also treat, these themes lose sharpness.

In *Paradise,* Morrison touches on the scapegoating of the women who live in the Convent. But the murder described in the opening pages is a murder of women by men, a brutal act of woman-hating that cannot be explained purely by race or by the line—"They shoot the White girl first"—that opens the book so sensationally. *A Mercy* begins and ends with a mother's relinquishment of her daughter to the American domestic slave trade that tore more than a million people, many of them children, from their families. The mother's act can be partially explained by the history of the Atlantic slave trade, for the mother, an African captive, had been raped on her arrival in Barbados. Historical explanation, however, neglects the child's emotional meaning and the centrality of women in Morrison's work. In the novel, the child becomes the protagonist. Only at the end does she seem to understand the circumstances of her abandonment and drop the bitter thread running through the narrative.

Beloveds He Saw Her Pink, 2013, ink, graphite, and digital collage on paper, 6″ × 6″. One of four digital collages combining text and visual motifs from Toni Morrison's monumental novel *Beloved.* Two *Beloveds* appear in *Women's Studies Quarterly* 42, nos. 1 and 2 (Spring/Summer 2014).

Morrison's depiction of women, of motherhood, of misogyny, of hatred and self-hatred within and around race constitutes the foundation of her genius as a writer and thinker. Nearly all Morrison's protagonists are women whose identities and narrative trajectories fill entire fictional universes. A universe of women emerges most clearly in *Paradise,* in the community of lost and broken women who come together in the Convent and heal themselves, free of men's oversight. The women in the Convent are Othered through race, but as women, they create their own belonging, which proves their undoing. Free women enrage the men of Ruby, whose "pure oil of hatred" clarifies the "venom" they feel toward them. Bent on murder, the men attack with "rope, a palm leaf cross, handcuffs, Mace and sunglasses, along with clean, handsome guns."

The Origin of Others combines Toni Morrison's accustomed eloquence with meaning for our times as citizens of the world. But the breadth of her humanist imagination emerges most gloriously from her magnificent fiction, in which women play leading roles, in which social and racial identities influence but never determine individual character; her novels guide our understanding of how both race and gender inflect experience without diminishing psychological uniqueness. Although her lectures and the race-centered tradition of James Baldwin and Ta-Nehisi Coates are crucial to understanding her thought, they cannot contain her extraordinary vision of human Othering and belonging.

October 2017

"Introduction" in *Incidents in the Life of a Slave Girl, Written by Herself*

ARRIET JACOBS'S *Linda: Incidents in the Life of a Slave Girl, seven years concealed in Slavery, Written by Herself* (1861), the best-known nineteenth-century African American woman's autobiography, makes a marked contribution to American history and letters by having been written, as Jacobs stressed, "by herself."[1] Many other narratives by women who had been enslaved (for example, Sojourner Truth) had been dictated to amanuenses whose roles diluted the authenticity of the texts.[2] Jacobs not only wrote her own book, but as an abolitionist and ardent reader, she knew the literary genres of her time. Describing an African American family whose members cleave to one another against great odds, she skillfully plays on her story's adherence to and departure from the sentimental conventions of domestic fiction. In so doing, she used its difference to a woman's advantage. Her self-consciously gendered and thoroughly feminist narrative criticizes slavery for corrupting the morals and the families of all it touched, whether rich or poor, White or Black. She lays the groundwork for the analysis of Black womanhood.[3]

Incidents in the Life of a Slave Girl shows, first, the myriad traumas owners and their agents inflicted upon enslaved people. Bloody whippings and rapes constituted ground zero of their condition, but in addition, enslaved people were subject to a whole series of soul-murdering psychological violations: destruction of families, abandonment of children, sexual harassment, verbal abuse, humiliation, contempt. Jacobs details the physical violence so common in her Southern world, but she especially stresses the assault on enslaved

Incidents Through Window with $100 Reward, 2022, ink on paper, 12″ × 9½″. One of several drawings from 2022 using the motif of the shadow of a window in my Pigeon East bedroom at Yaddo, together with text from Harriet Jacobs's runaway-slave advertisement. The window projects the layered facts and visibility of this history.

people's psyches. Second, she denounces the figure of the "happy darky." While enslaved and later as an abolitionist, she was frequently confronted with this favorite American myth, which she knew to be false. In answer to this proslavery argument, she enumerates the miseries of the enslaved; in chapter 13 she shows precisely how Northerners were gulled into believing Black people liked being enslaved.[4] Third, and most courageously, Jacobs insists that enslaved people—

here, Black women—cannot be judged by the same standards as women who were free. Jacobs expounds the conditions of enslavement that deprived people of autonomy, denying them influence over their own and their children's destinies. While her enslaved friends and family took advantage of every possible loophole[5] in the fabric of an evil system, working the system allowed them only a modicum of self-determination. Because they literally belonged to other people, enslaved people lacked the power to protect their morals, their bodily integrity, and their children.

In sum, Jacobs delineates a system in which the enslaved and their enslavers (aided and abetted by Northern sympathizers) were totally at odds or, as she says, at war.[6] As she sees it, there could be no identity of interest between the two parties to the peculiar institution, even though lives and bloodlines commonly intersected. The frequent occurrence of similar names—for example, Margaret Horniblow (Harriet's first owner) and Molly Horniblow (Harriet's grandmother)—may confuse the reader but attest to these very intersections.

Harriet Ann Brent Jacobs was born in about 1813 in Edenton, North Carolina.[7] Her younger brother and best friend, John S. Jacobs, was born two years later. Their parents, Delilah and Elijah[8] Jacobs, were enslaved, but they lived together as a family with Delilah's mother, Molly Horniblow. Horniblow, the daughter of a South Carolina planter who emancipated her during the Revolutionary War and sent her to freedom outside the United States, had been captured, returned to American territory, and fraudulently reenslaved after her father's death. The head chef at the Horniblow Inn in Edenton, Molly Horniblow managed to earn and save money as a caterer even while enslaved. Her industry and clientele made her well known, well respected, and well connected in Edenton, and even before being freed again at the age of fifty, she had accrued as much standing as possible by one who was neither White nor free.

Enslaved, Horniblow could not marry, yet her daughter Delilah and her husband, Elijah, lived with Molly as a married couple: Delilah even wore a wedding ring, which she left to her daughter, Harriet. Horniblow's effective marital status, on the other hand, remains a mystery, as does the never mentioned existence or identity of her own children's father. These silences—in the historical record, in Harriet Jacobs's *Incidents in the Life of a Slave Girl,* and in John S. Jacobs's "A True Tale of Slavery"—speak volumes, given Horniblow's seemingly hypocritical attachment to the feminine ideal of chastity. Her insistence on premarital sexual purity, a condition that often eluded even free poor and working-class White women, would wreak havoc in her enslaved granddaughter's emotional life.

Neither Harriet nor John recalled much about their mother, who died when Harriet was about six and John about four years old, although Harriet later praised Delilah as "noble and womanly" in nature.[9] Their father, Elijah, the best house carpenter in the region, hired himself out from his base at home. Both Harriet and John recalled their father as a man of independent mind, whose slave status embittered and depressed him. John was convinced that his father died young—in 1826—precisely because he was enslaved: "My father, who had an intensely acute feeling of the wrongs of slavery, sank into a state of mental dejection, which, combined with bodily illness, occasioned his death when I was eleven years of age."[10]

By dint of their skills, values, connections, and ancestry, the entire Jacobs family had much in common with Edenton's elite. However, their African descent, legal status as slaves, and extreme vulnerability placed them firmly on the wrong side of a towering color bar. Molly Horniblow and her grandchildren experienced the ambiguities of their allegiances differently. The grandchildren admired, but could not share, her heartfelt Christian piety. The grandmother counted on the existence of conscience in the slave-owning class, another faith beyond her grandchildren's reach. She sought decent treatment through personal entreaty; they both followed the route of permanent escape. Horniblow's son Joseph shared her grandchildren's hatred of slavery; he ran away twice, the second time intending to leave the United States for good. Punning on the common term for whipping, he told his brother that he meant to "get beyond the reach of the stars and *stripes* of America."[11]

The Jacobses lived on the left bank of the Chowan River where it empties into Albemarle Sound. Connected through internal waterways with Hampton Roads, Virginia, and the Chesapeake Bay during the eighteenth and early nineteenth centuries, Edenton served as an administrative center for its own Chowan and surrounding counties and as northeastern North Carolina's main port. In 1820 the population numbered 1,261, of whom 634 were White, 499 enslaved, and 67 free Black.[12] During Harriet's and John's youth, Edenton was still vibrant enough as a trading center that the town's leading families would station members in the New York area. The Tredwells and Blounts in Brooklyn, New York, who made the Jacobses' later residence there unsafe, belonged to Edenton's merchant families. During the mid-nineteenth century, Edenton lost importance as the Albemarle Sound silted up and North Carolina's economy shifted away from the heavily slaveholding and agricultural east coast toward the diversified farming and industry located in the Piedmont farther inland.

In 1819 and 1820 Edenton rated two visits from President James Monroe; in 1820 the town offered him a banquet, prepared by none other than Molly Horniblow, the region's finest chef, at the Horniblow Inn, the local elite's gathering place. The inn sat on the main street, across an alley from the courthouse. Between the inn, the jail, and the courthouse stood the whipping post, where enslaved people's blood flowed. John S. Jacobs recalled seeing "men and women stripped, and struck from fifteen to one hundred times and more. Some whose backs were cut to pieces were washed down with strong brine or brandy . . ." He described one instrument of torture, the oak backing paddle, the blade of which was full of small holes that pulverized the body and left "the flesh like a steak." He himself had dressed the wounds of a woman whose back he "solemnly declare[d] . . . had not a piece of skin left on it as wide as my finger."[13]

The Edenton elite, small and inbred, was closely connected through ties of ownership and sentiment to the Jacobses and included the heads of the Sawyer, Tredwell, and Norcom families. Drs. Matthias Sawyer (d. 1835) and James Norcom (1778–1850) were longtime business and professional partners. An 1808 inventory of the value of their joint practice revealed a net worth of $8,000, half of which consisted of outstanding debts.[14] The financial precariousness of medicine, combined with the doctors' ostentatious standard of living, kept them constantly on the lookout for financial advantage. Both Sawyer and Norcom operated plantations that (usually) contributed to their income and where Harriet and John had occasion to work. During this same period, Samuel Tredwell Sawyer (1800–1863)[15] and John Norcom (1802—?) attended the Edenton academy together; the younger Norcom followed in his father's footsteps by graduating from the University of Pennsylvania with a medical degree. Samuel Tredwell Sawyer attended but dropped out of William and Mary College. With his family connections, neither his limitations as a scholar nor his feckless dandyism impeded his flourishing as a lawyer.[16]

After her mother's death in 1819, Harriet Jacobs went to the home of her owner, Miss Margaret Horniblow. Jacobs recalled Margaret Horniblow as a kind mistress "almost like a mother to me."[17] During her six years with Horniblow, Jacobs learned to read, sew, and generally to carry herself as a lady, a bearing others remarked upon for the rest of her life.

Reflecting the extreme vulnerability of enslaved people to the fates of those who owned them, Margaret Horniblow's death in 1825 made Jacobs the property of Horniblow's sister's three-year-old daughter, also the daughter of James Norcom, who became her de facto owner. The following year, Jacobs's father died, leaving the child with only her grandmother as protector. Molly Horniblow's stature and residence in the center of town did pose a counterweight to Norcom's power over the young woman he owned. Jacobs realized that both the town's gossip mill and her grandmother's standing offered her limited but tangible protection.

When her own mistress died in 1828, fifty-year-old Molly Horniblow, too, became the property of James Norcom and was put up for sale at auction. On account of her age and stature, the sight of Molly Horniblow on the auction block scandalized the good citizens of Edenton, but her sale, entirely legal, went through. According to *Incidents,* an older White woman bought Molly Horniblow, emancipated her, and made Horniblow the owner of her own older son, Mark Ramsey. John S. Jacobs's "A True Tale of Slavery" tells a different story. It says the grandmother entrusted her savings to a kindly White man, who carried out her wishes.[18] In any case, Horniblow's younger son, Joseph, ran away, was recaptured, jailed in Edenton, and sold to New Orleans. Joseph escaped again and met his brother, Mark Ramsey, in New York City, prior to disappearing forever. Mark Ramsey hired his time as a steward on a passenger boat, a position that made it possible for him to aid many a fugitive running toward freedom. Molly Horniblow bought her own seven-room house in the very center of the town with excellent access to her catering market of Edenton's elite.

At the same 1828 auction at which James Norcom sold Molly Horn-iblow, he bought Harriet's brother, John, then about thirteen years old. John worked in Norcom's medical office, where he learned the then common practices of cupping, leeching, and bleeding, and the manufacture and use of various salves and dressings. As a youth, John doctored the enslaved and later attracted the attention of a medical student, who attempted to buy him. His then owner, Samuel Tredwell Sawyer, refused to sell him even for the handsome price of $1,500.[19]

By 1829 Harriet Jacobs had fallen in love with a free Black carpenter, who wanted to marry her. James Norcom forbade the marriage and intensified his pursuit of her by threatening to place her in a small house outside of town—the isolation of concubinage. As a very young, enslaved, orphaned African American woman, Jacobs was virtually powerless to resist the obscene advances of her leading-citizen, middle-aged White male medical doctor owner.

The close relationship between the elder Norcom and Sawyer and their sons grew thornily incestuous around the person of young Harriet Jacobs. James Norcom, at fifty-two, was trying to seduce thirteen-year-old Jacobs, who lived in his house as property. He dared not exercise one right against her—exiling her to the plantation where his son John lived—for fear John would possess her sexually.

Jacobs found herself in a common quandary, for during the nineteenth century, young girls of all races and sexes were regarded as little more than prey: men saw even the most privileged mainly as rich potential wives. In *Incidents*, Jacobs attacks this dynamic, calling slavery "that cage of obscene birds." She chastises Northerners who married their daughters to Southern slaveholders, for the "poor girls" would soon find themselves victims of adultery, their homes scenes of "jealousy and hatred."[20] Conservatives like the South Carolina novelist Sue Petigru King and the Civil War diarist Mary Chesnut—both of whom accepted the justice of Negro slavery—deplored Southern husbands' habit of committing adultery with women they owned; it mattered less to Chesnut and Petigru King that the women under the husbands' control were mere girls. But girls they often were, vulnerable in both their status and their youth.[21] James Norcom had been following a Southern tradition of taking advantage of girls when he married a teenager situated to improve his financial situation. He had been a thirty-two-year-old divorcé in 1810, when he married Mary Matilda Horniblow, the barely sixteen-year-old daughter of the woman whose business affairs he managed. This marriage had brought him control of Harriet Jacobs's family.

Norcom's threats and Jacobs's distress alerted Norcom's partner's son, the unmarried young lawyer Samuel Tredwell Sawyer, to her sexual availability and made her quarry. He began courting her through letters and other expressions of sympathy. Finding herself trapped, Jacobs "made a headlong plunge" into a sexual relationship with Sawyer. Jacobs admits she knew what she was doing when she slept with Sawyer instead of Norcom: Norcom was building a cottage in which to hide her from the town whose gaze had lent her some meager protection. Harriet had "exhausted [her] ingenuity in avoiding the snares, and eluding the power of the hated tyrant." In *Incidents,* she says, "I tried hard to preserve my self-respect; but I was struggling alone in the powerful grasp of the demon Slavery; and the monster proved too strong for me . . . I saw whither all this was tending."[22] Caught between two older stalkers, Harriet gave in to the younger evil. As the peer of Norcom's son John, Samuel Sawyer belonged to a filial generation. In relation to fourteen-year-old Harriet, he belonged to a parental generation. When he impregnated her, he was nearly thirty years old.

Jacobs's difficulties increased when her pregnancy began to show. Already jealous of her husband's pursuit of Jacobs, Mary Matilda Horniblow Norcom assumed the child Jacobs was carrying was her husband's and threw her out of her house. Jacobs went to her grandmother, touching off a scene that scarred the younger woman for life.

At first reading, Molly Horniblow's reputation appears to have both protected Jacobs against Norcom and aggravated her vulnerability. On the one hand, Horniblow's standing among the Edenton elite made outright rape of her granddaughter too costly for Norcom and his reputation as a gentleman. The dozen or so slave women he had raped, impregnated, and sold had all lived outside of town on the plantation and lacked highly visible family connections. On the other hand, Jacobs held back from confessing Norcom's harassment to her grandmother, who, in a contradictory but time-honored pattern, would have blamed Jacobs for prompting the advances both women deplored. Jacobs's reticence forestalled her grandmother's confronting Norcom head-on and, perhaps, forcing him to desist.

A second look at *Incidents,* however, shows Molly Horniblow aware of her granddaughter's peril and taking all the steps open to her to warn Norcom off. Her approach—indirect, moral, and highly contingent—reflected the fundamental disparity of power between owner and grandmother. Although Horniblow could not afford a direct or angry confrontation with one of the town's first citizens, she had "high words" with him over Jacobs.[23] In the last analysis, she lacked means of retaliating against him materially; her puny weapons and the need to keep up appearances failed her on Edenton's sexual hunting ground.

Horniblow's staunch belief in the ideal of female chastity put her nearly as much at odds with her granddaughter as with her harasser. Jacobs addresses her reader directly in *Incidents:* "You never knew what it is to be a slave; to be entirely unprotected by law or custom; to have the laws reduce you to the condition of a chattel, entirely subject to the will of another."[24] But when she says that the prospects of the unfree are so "blighted by slavery" that chastity becomes an impossible goal, she speaks to her grandmother as well as the Northern reader she addresses as "you."[25]

Molly Horniblow accused Jacobs of disgracing her dead mother's memory after Jacobs had been turned out of the Norcoms' house. "I had rather see you dead than to see you as you now are," Horniblow exclaimed as she wrenched Harriet's mother's wedding ring from her finger and sent her away. Horniblow waited several days before answering Jacobs's plea to take her back home. Even on relenting, Horniblow pitied Jacobs but never forgave her. One critic wonders whether Harriet sinned chiefly by losing caste: becoming pregnant without marrying, she was acting just like all the other ordinary slave girls. Horniblow, after all, took pride in her and Harriet's superiority over the common run of the "degraded" enslaved."[26]

In 1831, two years after Harriet gave birth to her son, Joseph, Nat Turner led an insurrection in Southampton County, Virginia, some forty miles from Edenton. As in insurrection scares in 1807, 1819, and 1822, the Nat Turner insurrection fomented a pogrom in and around Edenton.[27] On the pretext of searching for insurrectionists, White men looted, beat, raped, murdered, and generally terrorized African Americans. For a moment, Southern legislators, particularly in Virginia, considered the possibility of saving their skins by abolishing slavery. They decided instead to tighten its controls, making manumission more difficult and the lives of free Blacks yet more precarious.

During the early and mid-1830s, Samuel Tredwell Sawyer launched his political career with service in the North Carolina state house and senate. He spent increasing amounts of time in Raleigh but fathered a second child with Jacobs, Louisa Matilda, born in 1833. Meanwhile, James Norcom flourished in Edenton as chairman of the town commissioners.[28] To punish Jacobs for rejecting his renewed advances, he sent her to one of his plantations. Upon learning in 1835 that he intended to send her children to the plantation to be "broken in," Jacobs panicked. She knew the breaking-in process entailed much physical and psychological abuse, which Jacobs had already witnessed to her sorrow. Several times in *Incidents* she mentions enslaved people who had been so "brutalized" as to lose all human feeling. We still recognize the behavior she described, now labeling it trauma and the effects of post-traumatic stress syndrome: depression, self-loathing, anger, violence against the self and/or others.[29] The plantation to which Norcom proposed sending her children was a place of bloodletting torture.

To divert Norcom from his plan and persuade him to let her children's father purchase them, Jacobs ran away, commencing the long process of self-emancipation that would entail spending several days

$100 REWARD

WILL be given for the apprehension and delivery of my Servant Girl HAR-RIET. She is a light mulatto, 21 years of age, about 5 feet 4 inches high, of a thick and corpulent habit, having on her head a thick covering of black hair that curls na-turally, but which can be easily combed straight.

$100 Reward 3, 2022, ink and tusche on paper, 7¼″ × 5″. This is a detail of the *$100 Reward Triptych,* inspired (if that word encompasses disgust) by Harriet Jacobs's 1835 runaway-slave advertisement. The *Triptych* appears in this book's coda.

and nights in a swamp full of snakes and nearly seven years hidden in a crawl space in her grandmother's house. Norcom imprisoned Jacobs's aunt Betty, her brother, John, and her children, but in the end, he would allow Sawyer to purchase their two children and Harriet's brother, John.

Sawyer was elected to one term in the United States House of Representatives in 1837. He took John S. Jacobs, whom he owned, to Washington and then with him on a wedding trip to Chicago, Canada, and New York. To travel in the North, Sawyer bade Jacobs pose as a free man working for wages, which Jacobs, who said he hated lies and hypocrisy, found repugnant. Toward the end of the journey, he left Sawyer in New York City and emancipated himself. Now free, John S. Jacobs quickly made his way to New Bedford, Massachusetts, a haven for fugitives where young Frederick and Anna Douglass had recently settled and where doubtless all three became acquainted as fellow workers and budding abolitionists.[30]

The early 1840s also brought the emancipation of Harriet Jacobs and her children, one by one. Sawyer had brought little Louisa from Edenton to Washington, D.C., to tend to her half sister, his and his wife's new baby. Once Sawyer's term ended, he sent Louisa to work for his Tredwell cousins in Brooklyn. Harriet finally escaped from Edenton to New York in 1842. Her grandmother sent Harriet's son, Joseph, to her, and Jacobs sent Joseph to her brother in New Bedford. Jacobs lived and worked in the Astor House, the favorite New York stopping place of wealthy White Southerners and the same hotel where John S. Jacobs had left Sawyer in 1839.

Jacobs served as the live-in baby nurse of Nathaniel Parker Willis, the popular poet, litterateur, and editor of the weekly *Home Journal*, and his English wife, Mary Stace Willis. They lived well, thanks to her father's £300/year subvention.[31] Willis was well known among New York's smart set and among its abolitionists; he had courted Lydia Maria Child, editor of the New York *National Anti-Slavery Standard*, who later became Harriet Jacobs's editor. Child described Willis in terms of his "aristocratic tastes, social snobbery, dandyism, and political conservatism."[32] Jacobs did not weigh in on the first three of these characteristics, but she knew Willis to be proslavery. In

1850 he wrote "Negro Happiness in Virginia,"[33] dismissing whatever doubts Jacobs might have harbored about his politics and, undoubtedly, inspiring a scene she includes in chapter 13 of *Incidents*. Here, a slaveholder seduces a Northern visitor, producing enslaved people who—because, as Jacobs explains, they would suffer violent reprisals if they spoke the truth—attest to their perfect contentment. While Willis was hobnobbing with apologists for slavery, Jacobs was attending abolitionist meetings on a regular basis.

During her years in antebellum New York, Jacobs always felt hunted. As the North's busiest seaport and one of fugitives' preferred destinations, New York harbored numerous slave catchers, whose numbers increased after the 1850 passage of the Fugitive Slave Act made the recapture of fugitives—or Black people alleged to be fugitives—even more lucrative. Jacobs always felt somewhat safer in Massachusetts. In 1843 she fled to Boston, later returning to New York City, but another scare in 1844 sent her back to Boston with her daughter, Louisa.

After the death of Mary Stace Willis in 1845, Nathaniel Parker Willis took his daughter, Imogen, and Jacobs to England to visit Imogen's grandparents. In London, Jacobs felt truly free—of slavery, of American White supremacy and racial oppression—for the first time in her entire life; she was thirty-two years old. But needing to make a living for herself and her children, Jacobs returned to employment in New York City and several subsequent recapture scares. Finally, Cornelia Grinnell (the second Mrs. Willis) bought Jacobs for $300 in 1852 and emancipated her.[34]

During Harriet Jacobs's years with the Willises, John S. Jacobs extended his activism in the abolitionist movement, serving as the corresponding secretary of Boston's Black New England Freedom Association. In 1848 and 1849 he toured as a paid lecturer of the Massachusetts Anti-Slavery Society, appearing with star speakers such as Frederick Douglass, who praised Jacobs's "calm but feeling manner."[35] In 1849 John S. Jacobs purchased the Rochester Antislavery Office and Reading Room, a bookstore located above Douglass's *North Star* newspaper offices. Harriet sent Louisa to school in Clinton, New York, and joined her brother's antislavery enterprise. The reading room failed, as did John's succeeding endeavor, an oyster restaurant.

Harriet roomed in Rochester for nine months with Amy and Isaac Post, a White feminist abolitionist couple unusual in their ability to deal with African Americans on a footing of equality. Through the Posts, Jacobs met another of their Black houseguests, the chatty young Bostonian William C. Nell, who worked in the offices of William Lloyd Garrison's *Liberator*. Jacobs had already left Rochester when the Posts hosted the itinerant antislavery activist Sojourner Truth. During their time together, Harriet Jacobs shared her life story with Amy Post, who encouraged her to write and publish it. Jacobs eventually acted on the suggestion, but not in the 1840s.

The Compromise of 1850 included a tough new Fugitive Slave Act. On the lecture circuit, John S. Jacobs exhorted his Black brethren and sisters to arm themselves for self-defense, then left the East for safer and potentially more lucrative fields. Always enterprising, he went to California to pan for gold.[36] Harriet returned to New York City; her son, Joseph, now twenty-one years old, joined her brother in California. Unbeknownst to her, her Edenton tormentor, Dr. James Norcom, died late in 1850.

During the 1850s, when she was in her late thirties, Harriet Jacobs worked for the Willises, who were now settled in their Hudson River estate, and wrote her book in secret. *Linda: Incidents in the Life of a Slave Girl, seven years concealed in Slavery, Written by Herself* was published in January 1861 under the pseudonym "Linda Brent." Such a firsthand account had never before appeared. Jacobs indicts the institution of chattel slavery for its physical torture, its debasement of family attachments among White as well as Black, its corruption of Southern White religion, and the prostitution of young women. Despite its uniqueness, *Incidents in the Life of a Slave Girl* failed to capture the attention of a public preoccupied with the breakup of the Union and the impending Civil War. John S. Jacobs, now living in London, published serially "A True Tale of Slavery" in the London magazine *The Leisure Hour* in February 1861.

Harriet Jacobs, like several other women abolitionists (including, later, Sojourner Truth and Maria Stewart), put her antislavery principles to work in 1862, moving to Washington, D.C., to volunteer in the freedmen's relief movement under the auspices of New York and Philadelphia Quakers. Her daughter, Louisa, now about thirty, joined Jacobs in 1863. They distributed food and clothing to "contraband"—Black people who had escaped slavery in Maryland and warfare in northern Virginia. Freedmen's relief took Harriet back to Edenton in 1865 and 1867, as a free woman able to succor the poor who had in the past shared her oppression. This relief mission also took her to Savannah, Georgia; she then traveled to England and raised £100 to build an orphanage and old-age home. (Harriet Tubman, in Auburn, New York, acted on a similar vision.) But Ku Klux Klan terrorism made the Savannah undertaking dangerous, and Jacobs finally recommended the home not be built. With the end of Reconstruction in Georgia and North Carolina, the Jacobses returned North. By 1870 they were running a rooming house for Harvard faculty and students in Cambridge, Massachusetts; by 1885 they were living in Washington, D.C., where Louisa taught at Howard University. Harriet accompanied Louisa to meetings in 1895 at which the National Association of Colored Women was organized. Harriet Jacobs died in 1897; Louisa died in 1917. Although Harriet and Louisa stayed together until the end of Harriet's life, Joseph, the son and brother, disappeared in Australia in 1863; his mother had been able to send him money but not to save his life. Harriet's brother, John S. Jacobs, died in 1875 and is buried beside his sister and niece in Mount Auburn Cemetery in Cambridge.[37]

Incidents in the Life of a Slave Girl is first and foremost a piece of engaged writing, a means of advancing the struggle against the institution of slavery by politicizing respectable Northern White women—as women. Jacobs agreed with her friend and sister abolitionist Amy Post that her story should be told in order to reveal gendered evils of slavery that—due to their sexual nature—were usually passed over in silence. Whereas many other ex-slave narratives presented testimonials against a vicious institution and also served as a means for their authors' financial support, Jacobs wrote purely out of her antislavery ideology. Well and gainfully employed, her children grown up, she was not in great need of money.[38]

Lacking formal education, Jacobs initially doubted her ability as a writer to strike the right balance between candor and prurient detail. She thought first to dictate her experiences to someone more comfortable with writing for publication, as Sojourner Truth had to Olive Gilbert in the 1840s.[39] The bestselling author of *Uncle Tom's Cabin* struck Jacobs as a potential amanuensis, but Harriet Beecher Stowe saw in Jacobs only grist for her own mill. She asked to print the whole of Jacobs's experiences in her *Key to Uncle Tom's Cabin,* but Jacobs allowed her only a brief sketch. Stowe not only sought to appropriate Jacobs's material; she also sent Jacobs's letter, containing details about her sexual history, to Jacobs's employer, without Jacobs's permission. Jacobs, perhaps naively, had also proposed to Stowe that Louisa accompany Stowe on a trip to England. Stowe's patronizing refusal offended Jacobs. Deeply chagrined, Jacobs decided to become an author in her own right. The death of her grandmother in 1853 removed the last obstacle to her writing her own story, "by herself."

Between 1853 and 1858, Jacobs wrote in secret, certain her employer would oppose her mission. She also honed her skills by writing letters to the editors of New York newspapers.[40] Once the book manuscript was complete, her daughter, Louisa, who had the advantage of formal education, recopied the manuscript, standardizing the spelling and punctuation. Jacobs took the recopied manuscript to England to engage a publisher; she did not succeed. In Boston in 1859 she found Phillips and Sampson, but the firm went bankrupt before the book could be printed. Meanwhile, like many other abolitionists, Harriet Jacobs was deeply inspired by John Brown's 1859 raid on the federal arsenal at Harpers Ferry, Virginia. She added a final chapter to her book on Brown's visionary attack.

A new publishing firm in Boston, Thayer and Eldridge, agreed in 1860 to publish *Incidents,* provided the experienced abolitionist author and editor Lydia Maria Child would add a preface. William C. Nell, whom Jacobs knew as a fellow abolitionist and Post family friend, introduced Jacobs to Child. Child agreed, further, to edit the manuscript in the late summer of 1860.

The two women's correspondence shows that Jacobs had completed her book before meeting Child and that Child made only two substantive changes, minor cuts, and one act of reorganization. Child suggested that Jacobs delete the chapter on John Brown and end with her purchase by Cornelia Grinnell Willis and subsequent emancipation. Jacobs complied. Child also gathered together the stories of physical torture, placing them in one chapter, "Sketches of Neighboring Slaveholders." In addition to Child's authenticating preface, Jacobs's friends Amy Post (a White woman) and John Lowther ("a highly respectable colored citizen of Boston," according to the *National Anti-Slavery Standard*[41]) appended endorsements.

Thayer and Eldridge went bankrupt in December 1860, having stereotyped the plates but not printed the book. Jacobs bought the plates and published the book herself using a Boston printer, a recourse Sojourner Truth had also used in 1850 with her *Narrative*. Lydia Maria Child continued to help with publishing and promotion. She had arranged for a subvention so that Thayer and Eldridge could print 2,000 copies (it is unclear whether 1,000 or 2,000 were finally printed), and she wrote friends such as John Greenleaf Whittier, urging them to have their local booksellers stock copies of *Incidents*.[42]

Linda: Incidents in the Life of a Slave Girl, seven years concealed in Slavery, Written by Herself appeared in Boston in January 1861. Although the name "Linda" appeared on the book's spine, its title page omitted it. As a result, the book is better known today without "Linda."[43] (W. Tweedie published the English edition, entitled *The Deeper Wrong: or, Incidents in the Life of a Slave Girl, Written by Herself*, in September 1862.[44] Child used parts of *Incidents* [citing Jacobs as author] in *The Freedmen's Book*, an anthology she compiled for freedpeople in 1865.)

The earliest notices of the publication of *Incidents in the Life of a Slave Girl* amounted to far less than sustained book reviews. Jacobs's old friend William C. Nell puffed the book in a letter to the editor in the Boston *Liberator*. Nell acknowledged that *The Liberator* overflowed with news of secession and impending civil war, but he wanted to alert readers to the existence of a newly published book, *Linda: Incidents in the Life of a Slave Girl, seven years concealed in Slavery*, which he thought certain to "render a signal and most acceptable service" in a time of crisis. Nell praised the book as more useful than most ex-slave narratives because it was straight fact, with no fiction: "This record of complicated experience in the life of a young woman, a doomed victim to America's peculiar institution—her seven years' conceal-ment in slavery—continued persecutions—hopes, often deferred, but which at length culminated in her freedom—surely need not the charms that any pen of fiction, however gifted and graceful, could lend. They shine by the lustre of their own truthfulness . . ." Nell expressed the hope that all mothers and daughters would read it and "learn yet more of the barbarism of American slavery and the charac-ter of its victims."[45]

The New York *National Anti-Slavery Standard* published the book's "Preface by the Author," signed "Linda Brent," as well as Lydia Maria Child's introduction and the accompanying notes from Amy Post and George W. Lowther in its New Publications column on February 23, 1861. The editor, claiming to have read the book, added a paragraph assuring readers that it "will not disappoint the expectation which these testimonials are so well adapted to excite. It casts a strong light upon the system of slavery, revealing features too often obscured by a mistaken delicacy. If this narrative of the terrible experiences of a noble woman in slavery could be read at every fireside in the free States, it would kindle such a feeling of moral indignation against the system and its guilty abettors" that Northerners would no longer coddle Confederate secessionists.[46] Several months later, the *National Anti-Slavery Standard* columnist Richard D. Webb briefly noted the publication of both Jacobses' narratives, calling hers "one of the most interesting and affecting in the whole compass of anti-slavery litera-ture."[47] The New York *Anglo-African* ran an unsigned review prais-ing *Incidents* for portraying "the true romance of American life and history" and showing a "more revolting phrase . . . because it is of the spirit and not the flesh." The reviewer condemned the sexual dynamics of American slavery and said the book would strike a telling blow against this "cursed system." As though anticipating twentieth-century interpretations of the provenance of the text, *The Weekly Anglo-African* review stressed the circumscribed nature of Child's role as editor.[48]

Lydia Maria Child deplored the antislavery press's lack of inter-est in *Incidents in the Life of a Slave Girl* as early as February 1861, and unfortunately, that interest hardly picked up.[49] Jacobs's publication date, coinciding with the furor preceding the outbreak of the Civil War, practically consigned the book to obscurity; the demise of the institution Jacobs attacked diminished its interest for American readers for more than a century. Only in the aftermath of the civil rights, Black Power, and Black studies movements did *Incidents in the Life of a Slave Girl* begin to find a larger readership. The growth of the fields of women's history and women's studies has further elevated it to the status of a classic American text. The narrative of an enslaved woman is being recognized as a story of a representative American woman.

July 2000

Martin R. Delany

ELITISM AND BLACK NATIONALISM

IKE MOST NINETEENTH-CENTURY Black leaders, Martin R. Delany's influence did not flow from the usual prerogatives of leadership. He could not reward his friends with patronage jobs or call out the militia against his enemies. His leadership lay instead in his ability to express what many Americans believed. As an abolitionist writer and lecturer in the 1840s and early 1850s, he insisted that Black people deserved the American citizenship they were denied. But as racial discrimination worsened in the 1850s and increasing numbers of Black Americans contemplated expatriation, Delany acted. Prizing Black self-reliance, he refused White American philanthropy, traveled to Africa, signed a treaty permitting African American immigration, and called for a Black nation with Black men to govern it. Although the Civil War rekindled Delany's faith in the United States, and he ended the war as a major in the US Army, he was not able to translate his impressive credentials and symbolic leadership into political power during Reconstruction. His last organization was an emigrationist venture that failed. After his death in 1885, he remained virtually forgotten until his resurrection three-quarters of a century later as the father of Black nationalism and the epitome of proud Blackness.

The Black revolution of the 1960s recast the study of African American history by reaching for antecedents of the sentiments and

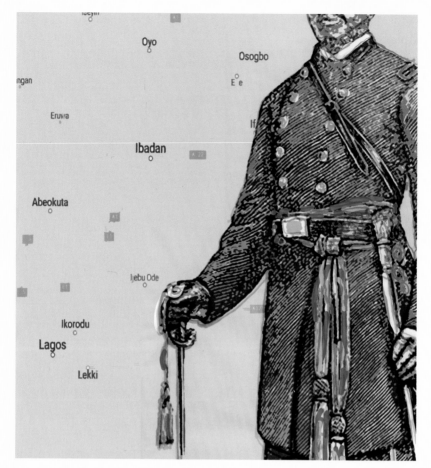

Delany Colored with Map, 2022, ink and digital collage. This drawing was inspired by a Civil War carte de visite of Martin Delany's that sold at auction in December 2020 for more than $59,000, when the presale estimate was $6,000–$8,000, a testament to the recent—and, to auctioneers, surprising—increase in value of images of Black Americans. See www.liveauctioneers.com/news/auctions/auction-results/black-civil-war-officers -portrait-tops-59k-at-cowans.

movements that arose in that decade. Shunting aside the decorous, light-skinned integrationist idols of Negro history—the Booker T. Washingtons and the Ralph Bunches—men and women who considered themselves Black nationalists rushed to find ancestors who, like modern Black revolutionists, turned their backs on White America and spoke for their African nation in both America and Africa. Black college students found Martin Delany, prominent abolitionist and emigrationist, an ideal ancestor, for not only had he concretely advocated Black American emigration to Africa, but he had also studied at Harvard.

Any examination of the career of this symbol of Black pride and racial integrity exposes contradictions between the man of the 1840s, 1850s, 1860s, and 1870s and his role in the late twentieth century. True, Delany strenuously rejected any notion of Black inferiority on racial grounds, and in the 1850s and 1870s he proposed emigration rather than submission to racial humiliation. But beyond his willingness to consider expatriation to Africa, which he came to see as a solution for only a select few, Delany's thinking about race, class, and "elevation" was thoroughly American and right in step with that of his African American peers; and, with the important exception of his repudiation of racial inferiority, it was as conventional as that of Henry Grady, White Southern apologist for the aggressively capitalist New South vision of the 1880s.

As a Black thinker Delany was not unique in embracing American ideals like leadership by elites (e.g., W. E. B. Du Bois's Talented Tenth) or in his faith in private enterprise that also appears in the thought of Booker T. Washington. As with his friend Frederick Douglass, the secret of Delany's leadership lay in his eloquent espousal of purely American ideals purged of racism and racial subjugation. Delany spoke for men and women who considered themselves the best of the race, fitted through relative wealth and education to lead the Black masses. As long as the class interests among Black Americans did not seem to differ, Delany's conviction that what was good for Black elites was also good for Black masses held up. But when class interests diverged, as in Reconstruction South Carolina, the foundations of Delany's claim to leadership of all Blacks crumbled.

Happily for the reputation of Martin Delany, his misadventures after the Civil War were ignored by the Black nationalists of the 1960s, so the elitism of his brand of Black nationalism did not attract scrutiny. Without knowledge of Delany in Reconstruction, Black nationalists of the 1960s could read their own Black nationalism, centered on the masses, into Delany.

. . .

Martin Robison Delany was born in Charles Town, in what is now West Virginia, on May 6, 1812. He claimed that his paternal grandfather was a Golah (Angolan?) chieftain, a captive of war enslaved and transported to Virginia; his maternal grandfather was, he said, a Mandingo prince, also a war captive, who, after a period of servitude in the US, somehow gained his freedom and returned to Africa. Thus Delany boasted not only pure African ancestry but noble blood as well.

Delany's mother, Pati (Peace) Delany, was free; his father, Samuel Delany, enslaved. The Delany children learned quickly, and their mastery of reading produced threats from Whites that forced Pati to move with them to Chambersburg, Pennsylvania, in 1822. Samuel purchased his freedom and joined them the following year.

In Chambersburg and later in Pittsburgh, where he moved in July 1831 at the age of nineteen, Martin Delany pursued his education at the Reverend Lewis Woodson's school for Negroes and later in the offices of abolitionist medical doctors. A trip down the Mississippi River to New Orleans, Texas, Louisiana, Mississippi, and Arkansas in 1839, made under circumstances that are not known, constitutes a curious chapter in Delany's larger education. By his own admission, Delany had something to say about everything, yet he never elaborated on this journey into the slavocracy. Neither slaves, slaveholders, nor the institution of slavery seems to have impressed him in a concrete way. In his abolitionist writings of the 1840s, all three remained abstractions, as they would in the mind of a writer who had never observed them firsthand.

As a well-educated young Black man in Pittsburgh, Delany joined voluntary associations promoting temperance, gentlemanly culture, and antislavery. He served as recording secretary of the Temperance Society of the People of Color of the City of Pittsburgh and secretary of the executive board of the Philanthropic Society, which helped fugitives to freedom in the North and Canada, and was one of the founders of the Theban Literary Society. In 1843 Delany married Catherine Richards, the light-skinned daughter of one of several relatively prosperous and educated Blacks with whom he associated in church and antislavery work. By then he had completed enough medical study to qualify as a cupper, leecher, and bleeder and could make a comfortable living as a medical practitioner. But given his interest in public affairs, he was fortunate that his wife was skilled as a seamstress. Catherine supported the family by sewing when Delany gave more of his time to public activities than to medical practice, which was often the case.

Delany's mentor in antislavery work in Pittsburgh was John B. Vashon, a well-to-do barber, a veteran of the War of 1812, and, until his death in 1854, a friend and supporter of William Lloyd Garrison. With Vashon's encouragement, Delany began publishing *The Mystery* in 1843, the first Black newspaper west of the Alleghenies. In 1847 lack of money forced him to suspend publication of the abolitionist paper, but he was not long out of journalism. At the end of the year he joined Frederick Douglass in Rochester, New York, as coeditor of the newly founded weekly *The North Star.* Delany traveled throughout the mid-Atlantic and Midwestern states, speaking and raising money for the paper, reaching a national audience for the first time.

Delany's letters to Douglass, printed in *The North Star*, analyzed all he encountered. He criticized racists and praised Whites who helped him; he enumerated the property holdings and business ventures of successful Blacks and castigated those content in domestic service, encouraging and admonishing his readers by using the people he visited as object lessons. Echoing the Jacksonian ideal of the self-made man, which was also a staple of the contemporary Black convention movement, Delany rejoiced when he found prosperous Black communities of farmers and tradespeople. Business, not domestic service, he constantly repeated, held the key to success for the colored people as a whole. Delany's formulas for racial uplift reappeared in his books written in the 1850s and 1860s, as did the elitism that characterized his thought throughout his life.

Delany believed that Blacks deserved liberty as a human right, but he also believed in "elevation," which a people had to earn. He exhorted Blacks to elevate themselves so as to close the gap between themselves and Whites, by becoming skilled workers and landowning farmers. Elevation, one of Delany's favorite concepts throughout his life, meant more than mere material success and upward mobility. His definition of elevation included the acquisition of gentlemanly culture and correct speech, of upright morals, independent thought, and "manly" religion (as opposed to religiosity, which he disdained as servile). Elevation meant achievement that would earn the world's applause, such as owning a successful business or governing a prosperous nation. Delany wanted for his people the sort of collective self-respect that he thought only education, wealth, and recognition would secure.

"Elevation" offered a self-reliant strategy for racial improvement, for Delany despised what he saw as his people's dependence on Whites. Though writing primarily to free Northern Blacks, he included the enslaved people of the South in his self-reliant vision. Just as Northern Blacks must earn their elevation through success in business, enslaved Blacks must "dare strike for liberty." Only by acting on his own behalf would the American slave rise up "disenthralled—a captive redeemed from the portals of infamy to the true dignity of his nature—an elevated freeman." The alternative for Delany was retrogression, a sinking "inevitably down to barbarism and obscurity, worse by far, if possible, than the present."

Even as a member of the African Methodist Episcopal Church, Delany castigated African Americans for trusting too fully in religion. He believed that human affairs were regulated by three immutable, invariable "laws of God": the Spiritual, the Moral, and the Physical. Black people erred by turning spiritual means toward moral or physical ends, Delany said, but they should instead borrow a leaf from Whites, who used wealth, not prayer, to improve life on earth.

In the *North Star* letters Delany denounced Liberia as the creation and ward of the American Colonization Society, a White organization. Like most of his Black contemporaries, he accurately judged the society and its scheme to remove free Blacks from the United States so as to make slavery more secure, thereby serving the needs of slaveholders, not free Blacks. From the society's founding in 1816, free Blacks had condemned colonization as forcible exile, and Delany, too, saw the society's aims as degrading to Blacks.

African Americans were part of the United States, Delany argued, instructing them in American politics. He condemned the annexation of Texas, which he said made slave territory of what had been a land of freedom (slavery had existed in what became Texas before annexation, however), and he warned against Southern expansionists' ambitions in Cuba. At the Free Soil convention in Buffalo in 1848, which nominated Martin Van Buren for the presidency, Delany helped block the nomination for vice president of a judge who had convicted Underground Railroad workers for aiding fugitives seeking freedom.

Participating in the political ferment of the 1840s as an editor of *The North Star* suited Delany perfectly, but the Douglass-Delany collaboration suffered from financial and intellectual strains. Despite Douglass's prominence and Delany's untiring fund-raising tours, *The North Star* ran short of money. In June 1849 Delany resigned as coeditor, although he continued to lecture for some months. The parting reflected a growing philosophical divergence between Delany and Douglass, for Douglass welcomed the support of White abolitionists while Delany criticized them for racial prejudice and preferred that Blacks help themselves. Although Delany's views were not unique, Douglass's position was more popular among American Blacks in the late 1840s.

Delany grew discouraged in 1849–50. He had done his best to ameliorate the condition of his people, yet he did not feel appreciated. "I have labored for naught and received nothing," he wrote in the fall of 1849; indeed, he believed that he had borne more than his fair share of sacrifice for the elevation of his race. Political events compounded his sense of frustration. In September 1850 Congress tightened the Fugitive Slave Act to include fines and prison sentences for anyone aiding fugitives. Now the burden of proving free status fell on Blacks, not on those attempting to reenslave purported runaways. Delany declared his hostility to the act, swearing that he would shoot anyone entering his house in pursuit of a fugitive from slavery. While continuing to help fugitives reach Canada, Delany pulled back from full-time public service and returned to medical study and practice. He also applied to several medical schools, only one of which admitted him.

Delany's application to the Harvard Medical School was supported by eight positive letters of recommendation, some signed by medical doctors, others by ministers. All agreed that he was an intelligent man of unimpeachable moral and religious character, a leader of the Pittsburgh community. His application reached the medical school at the same time as those of two other Black men, sponsored by the American Colonization Society and destined to practice only in Liberia, as well as that of a White woman. The female applicant bowed to pressure and did not enter Harvard, but Delany and the other Black men began attending lectures in November 1850. When several students demanded their removal, they became a source of controversy. After other students rallied to their support, the brouhaha itself became the issue. Dean Oliver Wendell Holmes decided that the controversy was distracting to education and asked the Black students to withdraw at the end of the winter term. Delany left Boston in March 1851 and reentered public life in Pittsburgh.

The early 1850s saw a heightening of racial feeling in the North. Hundreds of Black people, free and fugitive, including the abolitionist Henry Bibb of Detroit, immigrated to Canada to escape the slave catchers' grasp, and fugitives continued to escape from the South. Crowds in Boston, Detroit, Chicago, and other cities tried to prevent their return, making the enforcement of the Fugitive Slave Act impossible without federal troops. Sectionalism increased with the publication of Harriet Beecher Stowe's *Uncle Tom's Cabin*, in serial form in 1851 and as a novel the following year. Objecting to Stowe's paternalism and to her use of colonization to solve the race problem, Delany decided to write his own book. On a trip to New York City he hurriedly summarized his thinking on citizenship, race, emigration, and racial destiny, including much that had appeared in *The North Star* in the late 1840s. In the spring of 1852 he published in Philadelphia *The Condition, Elevation, Emigration, and Destiny of the Colored People of the United States, Politically Considered.* The book presented the first full-length analysis of the economic and political situation of Blacks in the United States, though it suffered from the haste in which it was written. It is remembered today for its nationalism and its advocacy of emigration to Africa.

Delany assumed that Black Americans were not uniquely oppressed. Every society contained an oppressed group that the dominant population considered inherently inferior, an imputation that grew from the condition of oppression, not from any natural, inherited deficiency of African Americans or any other subordinate people. Delany argued that instead of being inferior, Blacks were a superior people of especially resilient African stock who functioned well under conditions in America that debilitated Europeans and Native Americans. Thus Blacks had been foremost among the original developers of what became the United States and had earned United States citizenship through investment of their blood and sweat in their native land. But should these investments not suffice, Delany listed scores of examples of prosperous, educated Blacks who already had further reinforced the race's claims.

Vindication of the race is the book's central purpose. Delany pursued his logic, arguing that although Black people were willing and able to play a constructive role in the affairs of their country, racism denied them a part in American nationality. Not recognized by Whites as citizens and subject to kidnapping and reenslavement, free Blacks now had no more rights than the enslaved—an intolerable predicament. Taking a sober look at race relations in the United States, Delany concluded that African Americans should immigrate to Central or South America or to the Caribbean islands, where they could become useful citizens and create a United States of South America. Development of tropical America was therefore the "great and glorious work" destined for the colored people of the United States, an opportunity to reach their final goals of elevation and self-respect.

Delany's central arguments seem commonplace today, as ideas he mentioned in passing continue to resonate. The famous phrase, in which he called Black Americans "a nation within a nation . . . really a *broken people*," appears only in an appendix in which he explained his plans to forge a true African American nation in Africa, which contradicted the call for emigration within the Americas in the book's main text.

In *The Condition . . . of the Colored People* Delany's main concern was elevation rather than nationalism, and his argument resembles what came to be known later in the century as Zionism. Contending that a successful (i.e., prosperous and commercially developed) Black nation would elevate its own citizens and also free the enslaved people in the American South, he formulated an argument made famous half a century later in Theodor Herzl's *Der Judenstaat* (1896), which argued that Jews would only be able to defeat anti-Semitism in Europe through the establishment of a strong Jewish nation-state. Delany's vision of a Black nation depended on a vanguard, and as his first step toward implementing his national project, he called a secret national convention of colored men "of the highest grade of intelligence." He assumed that such men would adopt his plan to send commissioners to explore Africa and locate a suitable place to settle, despite the obvious and influential example of Frederick Douglass, who flatly opposed emigration. Delany made no provision for anti-emigration or for any other divergent opinions.

Having formulated what he took to be the single intelligent course of action, Delany supposed that the correctness of his views would silence dissent. Not only would the convention of intelligent colored men accept his emigrationist remedy, but all Black Americans would in turn follow the commissioners' advice. He never questioned his assumption that the most intelligent of the race—however defined— should decide what the masses should do, and he saw unquestioning acceptance of "intelligent" leadership as the duty of the masses. As a prime example of colored intelligence, Delany saw his role as instructing the rest of the race.

"Intelligent" was the most common adjective in Delany's vocabulary, and, like many other educated mid-nineteenth-century Americans, he used it to connote common sense, leadership, education, cultured deportment, and independence of mind, the same qualities that characterized a people who had achieved "elevation." Intelligence was the means of acquiring elevation on the individual level; it was the psychological precondition for elevation. Intelligence and elevation ensured the respect of others, which Delany valued tremendously. By 1852 he had come to see emigration as the only way in which African Americans might gain world respect, for as poor and oppressed as they were in the United States, elevation at home was unlikely. As conditions worsened in the 1850s, increasing numbers of Black Americans agreed with Delany, but his position was never accepted universally among them.

In the early 1850s emigration was a controversial solution to the race problem because many Blacks associated emigration with colonization, which they opposed as forced expulsion—as "ethnic cleansing." Delany himself opposed colonization. Even those, like Frederick Douglass, who drew the distinction between expatriation and exile, still thought that the United States was the best place for Black Americans.

During the 1850s Delany deepened his involvement with emigration, moving from advocacy to actual planning. One of the conveners of the first emigrationist convention in Cleveland, Ohio, in 1854, he wrote a pamphlet, *The Political Destiny of the Colored Race* (1854), depicting American race relations as hopeless enough to prompt emigration. Meeting shortly after Douglass's convention in Rochester had denounced emigration, Delany's Cleveland meeting did not attempt to convert non-emigrationists. All delegates were required in advance to support emigration, but none could advocate settlement outside the Americas at the meeting.

Two years later Delany called a second emigration convention in Chatham, Canada West (now Ontario), where he had moved with his family earlier in the year. He had visited Canada in 1851 at the invitation of Henry Bibb, a fellow emigrationist and editor of the Windsor, Canada, *Voice of the Fugitive*. Delany had resisted emigration to Canada for several years, but by 1856 he was ready to sacrifice his standing in the Pittsburgh Black community and his established medical practice. Joining the 50,000 to 60,000 Black Americans who fled to Canada before the Civil War, Delany left the city that had been his home for a quarter of a century.

In Chatham, Delany was immediately recognized as a leader. He contributed regularly to the local newspaper, took part in politics, and voted for the first time. Although the Delanys called Chatham home for eight years, Martin was there for only three years at a stretch in the late 1850s. Enjoying an unusually long stay with his family in Canada, he did not withdraw from the public activities that he saw as serving the interests of his race.

In the spring of 1858 John Brown visited Canada West, and Delany arranged a one-day convention of Blacks to hear Brown present his antislavery "Provisional Constitution and Ordinances for the People of the United States." The convention elected Brown commander in chief of guerrilla forces, then Brown went on his way. When his actual raid occurred the following year, Delany was in Africa. Before departing, however, Delany wrote the first half of his only novel, *Blake, or the Huts of America;* he completed the second half after his return from West Africa and Great Britain. The novel appeared in serial form in *The Anglo-African Magazine* in 1859 and in *The Weekly Anglo-African* in 1861–62.

Blake, the fourth novel written by an African American, featured a Delany-like hero, Henry Holland/Henry Blake/Henrico Blacus, a free African Cuban who had been kidnapped and taken to Mississippi. "Intelligent," manly, handsome, and educated, Blake is one of only two slave characters in the book who speak Standard English. The other is Blake's wife, Maggie, who like Blake represents Delany's racial ideals. Blake is of pure African ancestry; the equally dignified and "intelligent" Maggie is a beautiful mulatto. Both are Christians, but neither participates in the slave religion instilled by the oppressors.

When Maggie and Blake's master sells her to Cuba, Blake decides to organize an insurrection in the whole American South and Cuba. He travels throughout the United States and even to the west coast of Africa, painstakingly constructing what the novelist Sutton Griggs later called an imperium in imperio—an underground government ready to take control of a Black American nation—after Blake and his fellow revolutionaries have overthrown slavery and killed all slaveholders.

The book ends before the revolution begins, but it is already clear that the insurrectionist leadership includes women and men of every stratum of the Negro race. They are Black, mulatto, and quadroon; slave and free; rich and poor; Muslim, Catholic, and Protestant (no animists, however); Creole and African-born. They constitute a vanguard party reminiscent of John Brown's band, and they plan an uprising "for the sake of our redemption from bondage and degradation." As in *The Condition . . . of the Colored People,* the aims of collective action are abolishing slavery, establishing self-respect, and gaining the respect of others for people of African descent.

Delany's insurrectionist Blacks are unified, well organized, and thoroughly independent in their thinking. They formulate their own solutions, cooperate among themselves in the interests of the race, and are free of even the slightest hint of prejudice or ill feeling. They are dignified in demeanor and have a native sense of good taste. Delany shows them as revolutionaries with the lofty goals of elevation and racial redemption. In their gatherings, he explains, "there was no empty parade and imitative aping, no unmeaning pretensions." This was Delany's vision for enslaved Blacks, nature's noblemen and noblewomen poised to claim their own freedom. Such people would rather leave the land of their birth than succumb to prolonged degradation. In his own life Delany found in emigration a practical form of insurrection.

At home in Chatham, Delany helped organize the third emigration convention in 1858, by which time he was the leading advocate of emigration. The convention identified him with Africa, and on his own recommendation he was designated a commissioner to investigate the continent. Delany's decision to explore West Africa represented a shift in his views. In 1852 he had contemplated settlement in eastern Africa for reasons he did not explain, but it is likely that he realized the tremendous distance and logistical problems that emigration to East Africa would entail. While West Africa was far more accessible, Delany faced competition there that probably persuaded him to act immediately. In 1858 the Reverend Henry Highland Garnet of New York, also a Black abolitionist, had joined with several wealthy Whites, including the American Colonization Society's Benjamin Coates of Philadelphia, to form the African Civilization Society, with aims like Delany's. Delany condemned the African Civilization Society's reliance on Whites and objected particularly to Whites associated with the suspect colonization society. The rivalry intensified when the African Civilization Society announced plans to explore West Africa; Delany would have to act quickly or be overtaken. He sailed to Liberia on a ship owned by three African American emigrants, arriving in July 1859.

Delany had long criticized Liberia's relationship with the American Colonization Society and its dependence on American Whites. Yet he shared the fundamental premises of this settler society, did not perceive African American immigrants as oppressors of native-born Liberians, and enjoyed himself in Liberia as the contented guest of a distinguished American, the Reverend Alexander Crummell. Delany delivered several well-received speeches that ambiguously urged both selective emigration of Black Americans and the emigration of all free Blacks. In Monrovia he argued that as a small minority of the population of a country in which the majority rules, Blacks in America could never become a political force, even with the demise of slavery. He favored the immigration of Northern free Blacks to Africa, where they would join the native population, "their degraded brethren, [and] assist to elevate them." This Black nation in Africa, led by African American settlers, would exert what Delany called a "reflex influence upon America" that would improve the lot of the Black people who remained, whether enslaved or free.

Delany accompanied Alexander Crummell fifty miles up the Cavalla River to his Cape Palmas mission school, which for Delany represented Crummell's civilizing mission in Africa, a prime example of racial redemption and elevation. Delany reported that the school had changed the pupils from "dirty, ragged, barefooted Black boys, feeding on nothing but rice and palm oil, eating on the ground, sleeping on naked mats on a bare floor—*because they would have it so,* and no teacher could prevent it—to that of cleanly, well-dressed, polite young gentlemen, assembling in the ordinary at meal time, and occupying neat and comfortable bed-chambers."

Crummell's mission and Delany's projected Black American settlement in Africa were very similar. Both were thoroughly elitist and based on a supposed mandate to propagate civilization (i.e., Western culture). Although Delany sometimes envisioned a mass emigration of African Americans out of the land of their oppression, by the late 1850s he stressed "a select migration of intelligent persons (male and female) of various vocations." These chosen few would eventually effect the "regeneration" of Africa, morally, religiously, and educationally. But more immediately, and for Delany, more importantly, African Americans would develop Africa economically and make it prosperous.

As in his articles of the 1840s, Delany saw commerce and farming as the means of regeneration. His settler nation would grow cotton for export, with Black Americans supplying the management and Africans the labor. "Intelligent" Americans would make all the decisions, political and economic. When Delany called for "Africa for the African race and Black men to rule them," he did not imagine that Africans would rule themselves. This was a paternalistic, not a democratic, scheme.

Although his settlers would be identified racially with the indigenous population, in other respects Delany's notion of an African nation differed little from those of British settlers in East Africa or Jewish settlers in Palestine. In all three cases, settler spokespersons took for granted that their presence meant development and subsequent prosperity that would automatically benefit the local people, who in turn would appreciate the arrival of foreign settlers without resenting their loss of independence. The locals, it was assumed, would understand that they were degraded people and would welcome the opportunity to be civilized, and in West Africa, Christianized, trading their autonomy for a cash economy.

Leaving Liberia in November 1859, Delany traveled to Lagos and Abeokuta in Nigeria. He probably picked Yorubaland because its people already lived in cities, which he would have seen as proof that they were further civilizable, and because of Alexander Crummell's ties with the African Anglican missionary Samuel Crowther. Crowther would provide Delany an opening to the local aristocracy that he would have lacked elsewhere.

In Abeokuta, Delany met his fellow commissioner, Robert Campbell, for the first time. Campbell, a twenty-seven-year-old, light-skinned Jamaican, taught science at the Institute for Colored Youth in Philadelphia. Together Delany and Campbell visited the other Yoruba cities of Ijaye, Oyo, Ogbomosho, and Ilorin; by himself Delany also went to Iwo and Ibadan. The climax of the expedition came on

December 27, 1859, at Abeokuta, when Delany and Campbell signed a treaty with the *alake* (king) of Abeokuta and several nobles. Samuel Crowther and his son, a surgeon, served as witnesses.

The treaty permitted African Americans associated with Delany and Campbell to settle unused tribal lands in exchange for sharing their skills and education with the Egba (part of the larger Yoruba people). The Americans were to be subject to their own laws, but in cases concerning both Egba and African Americans, commissions of equal numbers from each side would settle the differences, the laws of the Egba to be respected by the settlers. Delany was satisfied with the treaty, although it did not spell out his American hegemony and commercial expansion, which the *alake* most certainly would not have accepted. For Delany the specific wording of the treaty was less important than the very existence of a signed agreement between representatives of African Americans and African rulers. No one questioned him closely on the incongruity of his plans for African American exploitation of African land and labor and the treaty provisions regarding Egba land and laws.

The cordial welcome that he and Campbell received in Yorubaland delighted Delany, for the king of Ilorin called them "his people" and the king of Oyo lent his "kinsman" a special guard of honor. These and other signs of friendship reinforced Delany's conviction that Black Americans were destined to play a special role in Africa. Happy with his contacts and findings, Delany departed for Britain in April 1860, ready to put into place the second half of his plan.

Like British and American advocates of free trade, supporters of the free produce movement, and his rivals in the African Civilization Society, Delany assumed that the cotton produced in his African American nation would undercut slave-grown cotton from the American South in European markets. He imagined that African production costs would be lower because land would be free, the growing season would be longer, and that free labor would naturally prove more efficient than forced labor. In Glasgow he spoke with cotton dealers and international merchants; in London he met with philanthropists and businesspeople interested in supporting the implantation of Christian colonies in Africa to compete with the slave South. His findings encouraged the founding of the African Aid Society, which would have lent two-thirds of the money needed by the first group of settlers, who were expected to leave the United States for Yorubaland in June 1861. A phenomenal success in Great Britain, Delany had realized all his goals.

In Britain, Delany attended social functions and the meeting of learned societies where aristocrats treated him with respect. His invited paper on his African explorations at a meeting of the International Statistical Congress chagrined the White American delegation, led by Augustus Baldwin Longstreet, president of the University of South Carolina, who walked out as soon as Delany was introduced to the congress. The matter became a public issue in Britain and finally reached the columns of the American antislavery press, where Frederick Douglass drew the contrast between race relations in Britain and America: "Delany, in Washington, is a *thing*! Delany in London is a *man*."

Abraham Lincoln's election and the beginnings of secession did not instantly convert emigrationists from their belief that Black Americans would be better off outside the United States. With American race relations still dismal, the Reverend J. T. Holly, a Black abolitionist, continued to advocate emigration to Haiti; Alexander Crummell toured Liberia to stimulate interest in immigration there; and Martin Delany wrote his *Official Report of the Niger Valley Exploring Party* (1861) and gave lectures on Africa dressed in Yoruba robes. But as secession provoked hostilities, Delany's attention gradually turned away from West Africa to the United States. He canceled the departure of the first group of settlers.

In 1862, after the War Department reversed its refusal to enroll Black volunteers in the Union army, Delany became a full-time recruiter of colored troops for the state of Massachusetts, which organized two Black regiments, the Fifty-Fourth and the Fifty-Fifth. One of the Fifty-Fourth's first recruits was Toussaint L'Ouverture Delany, Martin Delany's oldest son. (Delany had named each of his seven children after famous Black figures.) During the war he also recruited for Rhode Island and Connecticut, which appealed to him in terms of both racial destiny and business sense. (Recruiters received a bounty for each man enrolled.) Delany felt he was performing a service that only he and a few others were suited to provide. "Intelligent competent Black men adapted to the work [of recruitment] must be the most effective means of obtaining Black troops," he wrote in 1863, "because knowing and being of that people as a race, they can command such influences as is required to accomplish the object."

After the Confederacy considered the use of Black troops early in 1865, Delany wanted to broaden the use of Blacks in the Union army. He proposed to Secretary of War Edwin M. Stanton that he be permitted to organize a Black army with Black officers (with the exception of the Louisiana Native Guard, existing Black regiments had White officers). Such a force would "penetrate through the heart of the South, and make conquests, with the banner of Emancipation unfurled, proclaiming freedom as they go, sustaining and protecting it by arming the emancipated, taking them as fresh troops, and leaving a few veterans among the new freedmen . . . keeping this banner unfurled until every slave is free."

This was the grand gesture Delany had wished for in *The Condition . . . of the Colored People,* a realization of Henry Blake's insurrection, action that would command the respect of the rest of the world. After nearly four years of bloodshed, Delany's idea appealed to the secretary of war and to President Lincoln, who endorsed the plan. On February 26, 1865, Delany was commissioned a major in the Union army, the first Black American field officer, and he began to compile his list of officer candidates. Before taking up his duties in South Carolina, he visited Wilberforce, Ohio, where he had moved his family in 1864. But before he had been in South Carolina long, the war ended.

Delany remained in South Carolina, where, as in Chatham, he was immediately recognized as an important public figure. His three and a half years of government service in South Carolina proved controversial, beginning with a speech delivered shortly after surrender, as he began his work with the Bureau of Refugees, Freedmen and Abandoned Lands, the Freedmen's Bureau. He was already known as a popular public speaker when St. Helena Blacks invited him to speak at the Brick Church on July 23, 1865. The army considered him sufficiently provocative to warrant planting informers in the audience, and one of them, a White army officer, reported to the War Department and the commander of the Freedmen's Bureau in South Carolina that Delany was encouraging the freedpeople "to break the peace of society and force their way by insurrection to a position he is ambitious they should attain to."

Delany had told his audience of freedpeople that they would not have been freed "had we not armed ourselves and fought for our independence." In warning them not to believe the Northern teachers and planters in the Sea Islands, he said, "Believe none but those Agents who are sent out by Government to enlighten and guide you," and seemed to be telling freedpeople to trust only Blacks, not Northern Whites. Such phrases, applauded by the freedpeople, initially earned Delany a reputation as a race agitator. One informant called him "a thorough hater of the White race [who] excites the colored people unnecessarily." But Delany's anti-White reputation subsided quickly, as he gained planters' grudging respect by proving himself a skillful arbitrator between workers and employers in the South Carolina low country. Before long a planters' newspaper praised him for being "on the right track" and cited his "wonderful influence for good over the freedmen. He tells them to go to work at once; that labor surely brings its own reward; and that after one more good crop is gathered, they will find their condition much better than at present."

A Freedmen's Bureau report reached similar conclusions, calling his advice to the freedpeople "sensible" and entirely in agreement with the bureau's own policies. Delany had not changed his views. He simply shared the economic assumptions of many Southern planters and White Northerners in South Carolina, the same ideas that had informed his plans for African American settler nationality in Africa. In South Carolina, however, the laborers in question were freed Americans, not Africans.

Like many conservative nineteenth-century Americans, Delany thought that all classes of society shared a common interest and that in a properly adjusted social order everyone's needs would be met equally. He did not believe in the inevitability of social or class conflict and was well disposed toward the planters he met in the low country, whom he took to be the region's natural leaders. They impressed Delany as being anxious to develop what he called "our common country—the South." To bring prosperity back to the area, he proposed a system that was essentially sharecropping on thirds: one-third of proceeds to labor (freedpeople), one-third to landowners (planters), and one-third to capital (Northern furnishing merchants). He called this a "Triple Alliance" that would bring all parties into a fair-minded partnership, for he believed that "a union of the Whites and Blacks is an essential industrial element for the development of the wealth of the South."

Delany saw no contradiction between his belief in the need for Black/White and labor/employer unity and his ability to represent his race, most of whom worked for others and at whose expense such unity would be achieved. Without realizing it, he took a class position that soon put him at odds with large numbers of Blacks. As early as 1865, according to a biographer who worked closely with him, he noticed that freedpeople were beginning to think that "he was opposed to their interest and in that of the planters" and that "his advice to them only served to arouse their suspicions." To Delany, their distrust merely proved that slavery had made them incapable of taking good advice when it came from a Black man. When freedpeople disagreed with him, he concluded that they were dupes of White planters or White carpetbaggers. Throughout his stay in South Carolina, Delany took a patronizing view of Southern freedpeople, who failed to measure up to his idealized Black folk in *Blake*. He never hesitated to tell freedpeople what was good for them and what they should do. But the longer Delany remained in South Carolina, the more clearly his views of what was proper for freedpeople coincided with the convictions of the "better class" of the state, who were also likely to be employers.

Delany's work with the Freedmen's Bureau—overseeing contracts, handing out blankets and clothes to freedpeople and White refugees—ended in early 1869, marking a watershed in his career. Leaving Hilton Head to seek a new career at the age of fifty-seven, he failed to realize his ambition of becoming the first Black minister to Liberia. (Not until 1871 did President Ulysses S. Grant appoint a Black to that post, J. Milton Turner, a lawyer from Missouri.) Without a federal appointment, Delany returned to South Carolina, while his family remained in Wilberforce.

Settling in Charleston, Delany went into the real estate business. He was an active Republican, and the governor appointed him one of seven lieutenant colonels of the South Carolina militia. In 1871 he received an appointment as jury commissioner of Charleston County, and in 1872 he served as a member of the state Republican executive committee. Yet he grew increasingly disaffected with Radical Reconstruction, criticizing Republican officeholders for corruption, carpetbaggers for demagoguery, freedpeople for disorderliness, and the Republican Party for withholding offices from Blacks. Conditions in South Carolina, he said, were "most disgraceful . . . all in the name of Republicanism."

By the early 1870s Delany had soured on Reconstruction, which he thought had ruined race relations and divided Blacks among themselves. He wrote a bitterly accusatory open letter to Frederick Douglass that said Southern colored people used to be "polite, pleasant, agreeable, kindly common people, ever ready and obliging . . . proverbial for their politeness." But now they were "ill-mannerly, sullen, disagreeable, unkind, disobliging . . . seemingly filled with hatred and ready for resentment . . . these people are despoiled of their natural characteristics and shamefully demoralized." Delany laid the blame squarely on White carpetbaggers who had misled the Blacks and turned them against the intelligent colored people—like Delany— who ought to have been their leaders. It did not occur to him that carpetbaggers might have been saying what the freedpeople wanted to hear or that he was a carpetbagger himself. Instead, Delany summed up the influence of carpetbaggers in South Carolina as "menacing, threatening, abusing, quarreling, confusing and frequently rioting."

He also accused Blacks of serious errors: prejudice against different shades of color—the lighter refusing to associate with the darker— and discrimination against Northern Blacks by Southern Blacks. Delany called these distinctions a "shameful evil" that weakened the race even more than White demagoguery. Douglass also regretted divisions within the race, but he chided Delany for his other criticisms. "Were you not M. R. Delany," Douglass retorted, "I would say that the man who wrote thus of the manners of the colored people of South Carolina had taken his place with the old planters." Delany would not have analyzed his thoughts in that way, but Douglass discerned the drift of his friend's sentiments.

Increasingly estranged from Republican Reconstruction and its constituency of poor Blacks, Delany came to prefer what he called intelligence, respectability, and honesty. In his shift from the Republican camp of the freedpeople to the Democratic camp of the planters, Delany joined a small but prominent group of politically active Blacks in several Southern states (as well as some prominent White Republicans who saw themselves as reformers). In Louisiana this tendency was called "Southernizing," as Black conservatives criticized carpetbagger-Negro-scalawag Reconstruction regimes and softened on Democrats. P. B. S. Pinchback of Louisiana, W. A. Pledger of Georgia, and the Reverend Richard H. Cain, Francis L. Cardozo, and Joseph H. Rainey of South Carolina all joined Delany in deploring the corruption they thought characterized Republican Reconstruction.

Southernizers advised Black voters to alter their habits, turn unscrupulous Republicans out, put honest Southern men into office, or be disfranchised. Lamenting the split of the electorate along racial and partisan lines that isolated Blacks from their fellow Southerners, Southernizers argued that carpetbaggers had never done anything for Blacks. Southernizers advised freedmen to overcome their suspicion of Democrats and vote for those who represented the wealth and intelligence of their state—the elites who had ruled before and during the Civil War, conservative Democrats for the most part. This line of reasoning, based on what Delany saw as an identity of interest, represented an elaboration of the views he espoused in his "Triple Alliance" of the immediate postwar years.

For Delany "it was easy to see that it was [in] the interest of both races to go hand in hand together," because Whites monopolized the land and education in South Carolina, Blacks the ability to work. He envisioned a one-party political order without dissent, convinced that unless Black voters broke with their enemies (carpetbaggers) and sided with Southern White elites, Blacks would lose their civil rights.

By 1874 Delany was prepared to go beyond the rhetorical phase. He resigned his position as customs inspector and entered the gubernatorial campaign.

Delany ran for the office of lieutenant governor on the Independent Republican ticket, which represented less a party than a coalition of moderate and conservative Republicans who were distressed by the corruption and taxation policies of the regular Republicans or who had lost battles over patronage, and moderate Democrats who accepted Black suffrage. (The Democratic Party did not field a slate in South Carolina in 1874.) The Independent Republican ticket represented several strands of long-simmering opposition. In 1871 and 1874 taxpayers' conventions had denounced the state's mounting debt and the new basis for calculating representation in the state legislature. In 1868 the constitutional convention had apportioned seats according to total population only, whereas the antebellum legislature had keyed representation to White population and amount of taxes paid. In Reconstruction, people, not wealth, became the sole basis for representation, annoying the well-to-do. Besides issues of taxation and apportionment, several prominent individuals also denounced the corruption of the Reconstruction government. Some Republicans, like Robert B. Elliott, a Black congressman, leveled their criticisms from within the Republican fold. Others, like Delany, moved to the opposition.

Delany's gubernatorial running mate was Judge John Green, a Democrat who had held office before the war. Due to Green's poor health, most of the burden of campaigning fell on Delany, who spoke throughout the state on themes he had voiced since 1871: Republicans had done nothing for the freedpeople; Republicans had arrayed Blacks against Whites and pitted Blacks against each other. Delany attracted other Black supporters like Congressman Richard H. Cain to the Independent Republicans, but his campaigning in the largely White up-country attracted more attention. In Spartanburg and Chester, he spoke to mixed meetings that welcomed him enthusiastically. Blacks remarked upon a dark-skinned Black man who spoke like a gentleman; Whites marveled at the combination of Delany's Blackness and his support of conservative positions. A Democratic newspaper praised his good work in "strengthen[ing] the cause of Honesty and Reform."

Despite defeat at the polls, Delany was delighted with the company he was keeping. Assuming that his nomination meant that Whites of the better classes honored and respected him, he flattered himself that they had proven their good intentions toward Black people in general by taking him in. In the following electoral campaign, Delany felt justified as a Black man in supporting the Democratic gubernatorial candidate Wade Hampton III, the richest man in the South before the Civil War and a former Confederate general. Like Delany, Hampton was not experienced in the everyday give-and-take of democratic politics and believed in the identity of interest of all the people, whom he promised to serve equally.

Delany, like Hampton, disregarded the armed rifle clubs that were using violence and intimidation against Black voters in the name of the Democratic Party; he also paid more attention to Hampton's words, which resembled his own. Both men espoused what Delany termed "*a union of the two races,*" in which Black as well as White civil rights would be respected "*in one common interest in the State.*" Both men deplored racial hostility, and Delany repeated his warnings of the early 1870s that unless harmony was restored between the races, Blacks would have "but one terminal destiny, political nonentity and race extermination."

Delany supported the Democratic redeemers in 1876 for what he saw as the good of his race and all South Carolina. He was convinced that a union of Blacks and Southern Whites, under the Democratic banner, would produce a state government "that would have respectability, and possess the confidence and respect of the people." This was particularly important in the depression of the 1870s, for Delany—among others—believed that government by the best people would ease hard times by reestablishing peace and prosperity.

Seeking to attract Northern capital, Delany reasoned in 1876 much as did the New South spokespeople of the following decade, and for many of the same reasons. His was the New South formula in which native White elites would lead a united following of Blacks and Whites, respect everyone's civil rights, and know best how to serve their state and region. This apolitical, elitist, Southernizing/New South position attracted many respectable Blacks in the South. But Delany discovered on the campaign trail that his identity-of-interest argument did not fit every reality. On Edisto Island he encountered workers on rice plantations whom hard times had brought into conflict with their employers.

The rice plantations of the low country south of Charleston were the scene of labor disturbances during the depression of the 1870s, when rice planters, short of cash, had taken in 1876 to paying their workers in what they called "checks," or scrip, redeemable in goods at plantation stores that charged exorbitant prices, or in cash in 1880. Useless as a medium of exchange, checks provoked a strike by plantation workers who were also staunch Republicans. Their employers, the rice planters—including at least one who was Black—were Democrats.

Being a Democrat in South Carolina in 1876 meant not only opposing corruption and prizing prosperity but also identifying oneself with the interests of planters and employers. In addition, hard times aggravated existing racial and partisan tensions, as planters and other employers pressured employees to proclaim themselves Democrats in order to get or keep jobs. Many strikebreakers had bowed to this pressure and called themselves Democrats, so that being a Democrat meant even more than being pro-Confederate and pro-planter in the low country; it also meant being a scab. Ignorant of these conditions and unaware of the nexus of class, race, and partisan bitterness he would encounter, Martin Delany went to Edisto Island in support of Wade Hampton, a Democrat, for governor.

As soon as he mounted a wagon to speak to a crowd of Black people, they beat their drums and refused to listen to what they called a damned "nigger Democrat." As men marched away, women pressed around Delany to call him names and threaten him. Order returned after half an hour, and Delany began to scold his audience. He told them that "he had been in the presence of the nobility [of] many countries and Black as he was he had never been insulted as he had been to-day by the people of his own race." With his speech frequently interrupted by jeers, he "reminded them of the fact that he had come to South Carolina with his sword drawn to fight for the freedom of the Black man; that being a Black man himself he had been a leading abolitionist ... He was a friend of his own race, and had always held the position that it was the duty of those who had education to teach them that their best interests were identical with the White natives of the State."

The following day Delany spoke alongside several White Democrats in the village of Cainhoy, ten miles inland from Charleston and, like Edisto, in the low country. Black Republicans again gave Delany a hostile reception. When the Negro militia and other Republican partisans fired on the speakers, Delany and his White comrades sought refuge in a White church. After Edisto and Cainhoy, Delany left the campaign. He did not speak for Hampton again, not even in ward meetings in Charleston, where he retained a measure of popularity. Despite his foreshortened campaigning, Delany was rewarded with the office of trial justice after Hampton's victory, a position he kept until the South Carolina legislature elected Hampton a United States senator in 1879 and purged Black officeholders throughout the state. By this time Delany was sixty-seven years old, and he had identified himself once again with emigration.

As Reconstruction ended and White Democrats quickly consolidated their position in South Carolina and the rest of the region at Black expense, many African Americans doubted their future in the South. As in the trying 1850s, West Africa seemed to offer a field in which Black men and women could work out their destinies. For many African Americans in 1877, emigration extended a last hope for true freedom, and Liberia fever swept through the Deep South.

That spring Harrison Bouey of Edgefield and George Curtis of Beaufort had persuaded the Reverend B. F. Porter of Charleston to join them in organizing Black emigration from South Carolina to Liberia. Porter accepted the office of president of the Liberian Exodus Joint Stock Steamship Company, and by the end of the year Delany had joined the company's board of directors, with the charge of negotiating with the Liberian government for land grants for African American settlers. Enthusiasm for emigration outstripped the company's planning, however, and thousands of would-be emigrants converged on Charleston early in 1878. The company hastily acquired a ship and carried more than two hundred immigrants to Liberia in a passage plagued by delay, deaths, and unexpected expenses. As chairman of the committee on finance, Delany was responsible for sorting out the company's debts, but he failed to raise the $5,000 owed in early 1879, and the ship was sold at auction.

The Liberian Exodus Joint Stock Steamship Company's legal and financial problems persisted into the mid-1880s, but by that time Martin Delany had left South Carolina. In the early 1880s he still cherished dreams of taking his family to Africa or of securing a government position in Washington or of managing a fruit plantation in Central America or of realizing a profit from his last book, *Principia of Ethnology: The Origin of Races and Color, with an Archaeological Compendium of Ethiopian and Egyptian Civilization*. After a lecture tour selling *Principia of Ethnology*, Delany went home to Wilberforce in late 1884. He died in January 1885, nearly seventy-three years old.

Leaving no papers, money, or fashionable ideas, Delany seemed to disappear after his death. A few historians, like Carter G. Woodson, knew of him and discussed his work. But with this scholarly exception, Delany's only memorial for decades was a Pittsburgh drill team called the "Delany Rifles," organized by a Black veteran of the Spanish-American War. Then, in the 1960s, Delany reemerged as a symbol of Black nationalism, but transmogrified to fit the tastes and politics of the mid-twentieth century.

Because the Black nationalism of the 1960s and 1970s was egalitarian and democratic, inspired by anti-imperialism and emphasizing self-determination for ordinary Black people in the United States and Africa, many assumed that as a Black nationalist Delany must also have held ordinary Black people in high regard. Few of his twentieth-century admirers realized that his nineteenth-century Black nationalism was a settler, not a democratic, creed. His chosen constituency was what he called "intelligent colored men and women," and he saw the masses as no more than a mute, docile workforce to be led by their betters—their *Black* betters, but their betters nonetheless.

Delany could not conceive of policies that would benefit one group of Blacks but not others, and he never understood why he had offended working-class Black audiences in 1876. He saw always one entity, "the colored people," with one true course, and he did not realize (nor did Wade Hampton) that his thinking was class-bound. He did not see that as a medical doctor, real estate agent, and trial justice his concerns were not those of the great mass of freedpeople, who were landless plantation workers. As one of the "intelligent," he thought it his duty to point out what was right, whether or not his truths were popular or even relevant. When his views were unpopular, he concluded that the masses were wrong, not that they might have been reasoning from different premises.

Delany's outspoken love for his people, his praise of unmixed Blackness, and his Pan-Africanism made him a leader in the nineteenth century and an attractive figure in the twentieth. But some of his convictions have been jettisoned by his later admirers, such as his embrace of the settler ideal, which has caused such bloodshed in Algeria, Zimbabwe, and the Middle East and which now seems more to resemble these examples of colonial mentality rather than an enlightened plan to regenerate a homeland. Also forgotten is his insistence that everyone follow him or a small handful of designated, not elected, leaders, which now seems more authoritarian than philanthropic.

A claim to leadership in his own times lay in Delany's eloquence and activity in pursuing his ideals, which many other Blacks shared. His was not the most popular position, but he never stood alone. Delany's unquestioning elitism was typical of his times, as was his patriotism. Before the Civil War his allegiance was to a nation of race; after the war his field broadened and his elitism and patriotism enfolded all the people of South Carolina, Black and White. As a nationalist, he could not tolerate internal conflict, whether the "nation" in question was an African American settler society in West Africa or the biracial commonwealth of South Carolina. Never seeking material gain in politics, he lived up to his ideals of a gentleman in public life.

February 1988

HISTORY

Who Decides What Is History?

IF HISTORY IS THE INTERPRETING OF THE PAST, then everyone who has a hand in making the past or shaping its interpretations decides what history is. Most people influence history by generating primary sources. They give their ages and incomes to the census taker, correspond with their creditors, write in their diaries, and make their wills. Heirs decide what history is when they deposit the letters of a Confederate great-aunt in the state archives (perhaps ignoring the scrapbook of her half brother, the barber). Historians read in the archives and fashion their interpretations of the past. Then comes the winnowing process of publication, reception, and incorporation. Editors decide which manuscripts by which authors to publish; publishers publicize what they like best; reviewers accept this book or that and recommend it to readers; readers favor some interpretations over others; then, textbook writers incorporate acceptable interpretations into their syntheses, which may or may not be adopted by school boards. The steps are many and varied. Without belittling any part of the complicated process of deciding what history is, I'm going to look closely at the part that follows upon publication and begin with the two groups of people Herbert Gutman named in *The Nation*: historians and ordinary readers.

Gutman asked, "Whatever happened to history?" and he noted that historians and nonhistorians have very different conceptions of American history. Characterizing the failure of the groundbreaking historical scholarship of the 1960s and 1970s to affect the way ordinary citizens view American history, Gutman observed, "It was as if the American history written in the 1960s and 1970s had been penned in a foreign language and had probed the national experiences of Albania, New Zealand and Zambia."

While historians have come to see a plural of American pasts that include the many histories of Black people, workers, and women, nonhistorians seem still to carry around a chronicle of campaigns and administrations of great White men. This chronicle is part of the older synthesis traditionally taught in schools—a synthesis that stresses consensus and assimilation, notions by now largely discredited among professional historians. But textbooks haven't caught up with the new historical writing. And textbooks teach most Americans what they know and believe about American history. For most nonhistorians, textbooks decide what history is and is not.

At the same time that textbooks decide what history is, they also provide a powerful version of the collective past and usually end by validating the present. Many historians would like textbook history to reflect the varied experiences of different races, classes, and sexes in America, but the difficulty of doing so is as much ideological and economic as it is historiographical. The more textbooks speak of Black people, the more likely they are to mention the great American failing, racism. The more they mention failings, the less attractive they are to school boards. What publisher would commission a textbook that no school board would buy? If new historical interpretations, no matter how accurate, are to change how large numbers of Americans think about their history, they must gain acceptance and incorporation.

Although what I'm about to say also applies, to some extent, to both women's history and labor history, I am going to concentrate on the issue of African American history.

The field of African American history grew at a tremendous rate in the last decades of the twentieth century, and that writing has altered the way most professional historians think about American history. Black people are no longer invisible in American history, and even White undergraduates are likely by now to have heard the name of Frederick Douglass.

Yet most nonhistorians still have little idea of what Black people thought in the past or that they thought at all. Donald Trump called

Douglass "an example of somebody who's done an amazing job and is being recognized more and more." Knowing nothing, for instance, of the debate that took place among free Blacks in the 1850s about appropriate responses to slavery and their own deteriorating situation, White nonhistorians are likely to assume that it never took place. In fact, the questions that these discussions posed reappeared later in the nineteenth century and again in the early twentieth. The issues are fundamental to Black political thought. In its simplest terms, the 1850s debate matched Frederick Douglass against Martin Delany. Douglass leaned toward forging coalitions with well-meaning yet prejudiced Whites. Delany favored self-reliant action, even though Blacks were terribly poor. He explored the possibility of voluntary expatriation, a solution to the race problem that has had several vogues despite its impracticality.

In *There Is a River: The Black Struggle for Freedom in America,* a 1981 book on the history of Black Americans, Vincent Harding rightfully gives a good deal of attention to this debate. His treatment of both positions is accurate and sensitive. By probing the debate in depth, Harding makes a valuable contribution to the understanding of Black American intellectual history and politics. On this issue and throughout this book, Harding puts Black people at the center of his attention and discusses their concerns fairly and completely. It is this focusing squarely on Blacks, I suspect, that has thrown White readers and reviewers off-balance.

Harding's narrative begins in Africa, with a second-person-plural evocation of the African homeland, "where the verdant forests and tropical bush gave way gradually to the sandy stretches of the Guinea coast." Chapter names resonate with mythic phrases—"Beyond the North Star," "On Jordan's Stormy Banks"—and they divide according to a Black-centered periodization. Ending on a hopeful note in 1865, the last chapter closes with newly emancipated Black people thanking the God "who had made it possible for them, and all who lived before them, to come so far and stand so firm in the deep red flooding of Jordan."

Despite its impeccable scholarship, *There Is a River* has failed to gain approval in important reviews. Books win acceptance in a variety of ways, but easily the most visible of these is by means of positive and well-placed reviews. The reviewers are usually senior historians at major universities whose views on the past are accepted by large numbers of readers and incorporated into textbooks. These historians enjoy access to the influential book pages such as *The New York Times Book Review* and *The New York Review of Books.* (In the case of Harding's book, however, *NYRB* is not a good example, for few reviews of books about Blacks and no Black historians—not even the few dazzling exceptions who are over fifty, productive, and otherwise suited to grace its pages—ever appeared there.) In the scholarly journals where younger historians have more of a say, Black historians will doubtless review *There Is a River*. But the big time remains beyond the reach of most Black historians, if only because of their relative youth.

This means that the important early reviewers of *There Is a River* have not been Black, and they have found the book hard to take. Its celebratory tone is not to their taste, and they dislike what they call its lack of objectivity. They fault it for downplaying differences among Blacks, for favoring racial separation, and for relegating Whites to a shadowy backdrop. They see the book as a call to arms and its author as a relic of the 1960s. They want Harding to speak less about widespread resistance among Blacks and more about why there were so few slave revolts in the antebellum South. Their criticisms point not only to their troubles with this particular book but to a basic problem in Black history: Black and White historians sometimes differ as to what is important and to what counts as history.

Here I wish my vocabulary contained more nuanced terms to describe shades of opinion, for "Black" and "White" are far too simplistic to be accurate. Not all Black people, most notably the neoconservatives, share the orientation that I'm calling "Black." And not all Whites hold what I'm calling "White" views; Lawrence Levine and Herbert Gutman, for instance, are able to think about history in what I'd call "Black" ways. With that caveat, I'm going to say that Black historians and White historians are receiving *There Is a River* in different ways, and that these differences are instructive.

The Black historians I have spoken with seem fairly comfortable with Harding's interpretation. They accept his central metaphor, the river of struggle that unites all Black Americans and makes them a people. They agree that Blacks generally resisted rather than acquiesced in slavery and inferiority. Black historians quibble little with Harding's virtual identification of *the* Black experience with *the* Black struggle or with his use of the singular in both phrases. Pleased with Harding's focus on Black people as historical actors, they seem not to mind the absence of detailed discussions of contemporary Whites in his book. They have reservations about the book's heroic tone, but those are reservations, not fundamental objections. By and large they are pleased with the book because it speaks of what Blacks were doing and saying instead of picking away at supposed shortcomings and deviations.

For the last several years, Black scholars, not just historians, have felt that Whites tend to concentrate on three aspects of Black life: inferiority, deviance, and dependence on Whites. Whether or not this is a fair charge to level at historians, it is most certainly an accurate reading of the way Black people appear in American history as most non-historians know it, and Harding's White reviewers definitely seemed to share such assumptions. They are uncomfortable with Harding's book because his interpretation of the river of Black struggle runs counter to what they and most Americans take for granted about race.

That is why I doubt that Harding's explanation of Black life will gain currency or be incorporated into textbooks. Even if Harding's interpretation were to appear miraculously overnight in textbooks, school boards steeped in traditional assumptions about Black people would reject the texts. If the great majority decides what history is, then *There Is a River* is not history, at least not in the short run.

But the state of race relations and the writing of textbooks are not static, or *There Is a River* would be history only for Black readers and the saving remnant of Whites. Things do change and so do textbooks. Already, some efforts such as *A People and a Nation*[1] have incorporated new historical writing, including African American history (but not yet Vincent Harding). If such textbooks reach wide audiences, the present generation of high school students and undergraduates may well take the next step and decide that history includes Harding's autonomous and resisting Black people. But as much as I would like

White assumptions about race to more nearly approximate Blacks', I'm afraid that the present political climate tends in the opposite direction. Historians and nonhistorians are likely to continue to decide that history is vastly different things, at least until the political mood changes and pluralism comes back into favor.

March 1982

French Theories in American Settings

SOME THOUGHTS ON TRANSFERABILITY

*T*HE JOURNAL OF WOMEN'S HISTORY opens volume 1, number 1 by reprinting an essay by several French historians connected with the prestigious French historical journal *Annales,* which has long stimulated the thinking of historians working in several fields. A lively debate should ensue, further encouraged by the responses by American historians that accompany the French essay. Although its style may challenge American readers, we enrich our own thinking through exposure to that of other intellectual worlds.[1] In the last generation, for example, Europeans have contributed analytical subtlety and concepts of class formation and revolutionary potential to American scholarship.

The *Annales* piece says much that is either new or bears repeating: that the field of women's history began with militants rather than with scholars; that habits of thought and action are fundamental components of women's culture; that women's culture is a basic part of society; that violence and vengeance pervade relationships between women and men; that women got the vote later than men—on purpose; that political (or public) history ignores women. Yet not all here translates smoothly into the American context.

Even as I remain mindful of the frustrations that feminist historians continue to face in the United States, I suspect that feminist theory may well have made more headway here than in France. Many of our colleagues ignore our insights, but at the same time, others heed our messages, and in many intellectual circles in the US, feminist history has become exceedingly influential. Much remains to be done, but feminist theories of history are altering the writing of history in general and have spawned the controversial new field of men's history. If part of the message of the *Annales* essay now seems somewhat stale, it should be remembered that it was first published in 1986, at about the same time that Joan Scott was offering an appropriate paper on the subject at the annual meeting of the American Historical Association.[2]

My main concern, however, is that Europeans sometimes provide Americans inappropriate, or should I say incomplete, models. In my field of labor history, for example, the enormous contributions of European styles of analysis must be balanced against their silence on fundamental facts of American history: the existence of race as a potent social and economic category and the relationship between race and class. It is true that Europeans like Johann Friedrich Blumenbach invented the scholarship of race in the late eighteenth century, but until quite recently race has not figured as an important theme in European social thought. In the United States, however, race and labor have gone hand in hand ever since the institutionalization of chattel slavery.

Despite the salience of race and racism in American history, they have been difficult for American historians who were not Black to confront. (Genocide, gays and lesbians, and, of course, women also have long histories of oversight. These are topics that have been, as the French would say, *occultés*.) The civil rights movement and the concomitant Black studies movement would have seemed to have ended the silence on race: most certainly the field of African American studies has grown tremendously, with many of its most active participants being non-Black scholars. Yet the very vigor of African American studies provided historians of labor a pretext for continuing to produce lily-White analyses—race, they could say, belonged exclusively to Black studies. Turning their backs on African American studies, many labor historians took the further step of embracing paradigms from European history that seemed more sophisticated theoretically than American analyses but that have disregarded race.

The result has been an outpouring of interesting yet flawed labor history that pretends that non-Black workers are not affected by the existence of a workforce segmented by race.[3] Although they know that non-Black as well as Black workers have been affected by racism in the US, labor historians sometimes only admit to this fact when the question is put to them directly. They often prefer to wrap themselves in fashionable Europeanisms and to write as though their favorite Northern, European American workers lived out destinies divorced from matters of slavery and racism, as though, say, Chartism meant more in the history of the American working class than slavery.

With such struggles over American labor historiography in mind,[4] I confess the fear of having to start all over again with historians of women. My nightmare is that this *Annales* article, with the customary European blindness to matters of race, will play the E. P. Thompson role in women's history, with historians of women adopting the myopia along with the genius of European thought.

Perhaps things ought also to be going the other way around. As we read them, French scholars should be consulting Americans who recognize the importance of race, for late-twentieth-century European populations, including the French, now include large numbers of southern European, Arab, and African working-class immigrants. A glance at French newspapers reveals the popularity of demagogues like Jean-Marie Le Pen, whose xenophobia has begun to alert Europeans to the power of race right there at home. Le Pen is the best-known racist now active in Europe, but the continent is full of racists and proto-racists of the sort familiar to Americans. It would be a pity if European historians remained blind to the importance of the relationship of race and class in their own societies, several of which were imperialist, continuing instead their traditional preoccupation with peasants and shopkeepers of European ethnic backgrounds. In one sense, Americans who came of age intellectually in the 1960s have the advantage of thinking about heterogeneous populations. For the movement in the United States that spawned the New Left and modern feminism was a movement of people of color. French historians of our generation, in contrast, look back to *mai* 1968. They have nothing like our civil rights movement unless they adopt the Algerian war of independence, which does not figure as a moment of intellectual awakening in the *Annales* piece. We know that we can still learn from Europeans, but they may also stand to learn a good bit from us.

American historians also have another contribution to offer the *historiennes* of *Annales* concerning class. Years ago, it was fashionable in this country to write, as they do (mutatis mutandis), as though American women formed an undifferentiated mass, assumed to be White, educated (i.e., relatively wealthy), and Northern. After a good deal of debate, many of us writing in women's history have come to expect a series of adjectives to precede the word "women." Realizing that much unites women (i.e., subordination to men within the same context), much also divides. Class has split American women just as has race, with race and class, or religion and class, often reinforcing each other. We now recognize that many common generalizations about women, such as that women are relegated to the private sphere, are shortsighted. In this case, it is because large numbers of poor women have always worked for wages, usually outside their homes. Further, masses of American women have worked for wages as household workers or domestic servants inside other women's homes. Employers of household workers have nearly always been women, so that in the widespread phenomenon of domestic employment, women have been engaged on both sides of a cash transaction, an aspect of public life that cannot be reduced to "maternal power."

To ignore the kind of employer-employee relations that characterize household work is to overlook the most widespread economic relationship in which women have been engaged and to ignore the most fundamental class relationship between women. In the American situation, such blindness is particularly crippling theoretically, for household workers have been distinguishable from their employers by religion, ethnicity, and race as well as class. Over the decades, the practice in the United States of employing household workers of another identity—Irish Catholic in the Northeast, Scandinavian in the Midwest, Chicana in the Southwest, African American in the

South—reinforces the distance between women at the two ends of the employer-employee relationship. Change over time has widened the divide, as Euro-Americans have left household work and women of color have not. In the mid- and late-twentieth century, household work has been identified mostly with racial-ethnic women.

To neglect household labor as women's work, therefore, is to make women of color disappear from women's history. I would add that with household labor as the most important women's occupation in the nineteenth century and with women of color as the mass of household workers, no historical generalization about women workers in the United States that overlooks this occupation or these workers is valid.

I am encouraged by the phenomenon of professional organizations'—such as the American Studies Association, in 1988, and the Berkshire Conference, in 1990—taking diversity of race, class, and gender as the theme of their annual meetings. The French historians writing in *Annales,* male and female, might see their own society in a new light, were they exposed to this aspect of American discourse. Meanwhile, we should not be tempted to adopt uncritically any analysis that ignores fundamental themes that have shaped both the experiences and the interpretation of experiences of Americans of all classes and races.

Spring 1989

Hill, Thomas,
and the Use of Racial Stereotype

J UST NOW I HAVE HAD A TEACHING EXPERIENCE with Princeton graduate students who were reading a lot and thinking hard, which
reminds me of the difficulty of seeing class and gender, as well
as race, in matters African American. The assignment challenged
even thoughtful young people who had an entire semester to work
things out. The Thomas-Hill hearings presented a spectacle of senatorial unknowing, for the scenario played itself out on live television
before a congressional audience unaccustomed, even unable, to think
about gender and race simultaneously. Because the protagonists of
this American theatrical production were Black, race stayed in the
forefront nearly all the time. Even so, viewers realized, however fuzz-
ily, that something else was going on. The unusual cast of characters
made the viewers' task novel and hard: to weigh the significance of
race in an intra-racial drama. But the exercise proved too daunting,
and stereotype, almost inevitably, became the medium of exchange.
Even before the second part of the televised hearings began, Clarence
Thomas had shown me that he would rework issues of gender into
racial cliché.

As troubled as I was by what happened to the person and the persona of Anita Hill in the hearings, I had begun to have doubts about
Clarence Thomas's manipulation of gender issues well before she
entered the scene. My own difficulties with Thomas regarding women
began when I learned that he had portrayed his hardworking sister,
Emma Mae Martin, as a deadbeat on welfare. In a speech to Republicans (who invented the persona of welfare queen), he had made

Martin into a stock character in the Republican scenario of racial economics. His point was to contrast her laziness with his hard work and high achievement to prove that any Black American with gumption and a willingness to work could succeed. Thus, a woman whom he had presumably known and loved for a lifetime emerged as a one-dimensional welfare cheat, one of the figures whom Black women cite as an example of the pernicious power of negative stereotype. For Thomas, it seemed, all the information that needed to be known of his sister compared her with him: she was a failure on welfare and he was a high-ranking official. He left it to others—who were his critics—to describe his sister more completely.

Other people, like Lisa Jones in *The Village Voice*, had more to say about Emma Mae Martin. It turns out that she was on welfare only temporarily and that she was usually a two-job-holding, minimum-wage-earning mother of four. Unable to afford professional help, she had gone on welfare while she nursed the aunt who had suffered a stroke but who normally kept her children when Martin was at work. Feminists noted that Martin belonged to a mass of American women who were caregivers to the young, the old, and the infirm. She had followed a trajectory common in the experience of poor women, regardless of race; this pattern Clarence Thomas did not acknowledge.

That his life and the life of his sister had differed by virtue of their gender was not included in Clarence Thomas's rendition of contrasting destinies. He seemed not to have appreciated that he was the favored boy-child, protected and sent to private schools, and that she was the girl who stayed behind, married early, and cared for an ailing relative. If he realized how common his family's decisions had been, he gave no indication of seeing those choices as gendered. His equation balanced one thing only, and that was individual enterprise. Even though as a hospital worker his sister was a symbol of Jesse Jackson's masses of Black folk who work every day, her life as a worker counted for naught in Thomas's story. His eagerness to shine on a conservative stage allowed him to obscure the actual circumstances of her life and her finances and to disregard her vulnerabilities as a poor Black woman. If he were ignorant of how very characteristic of poor women's her life's course had been, he would seem to have performed his job heading the Equal Employment Opportunity Commission in a perfunctory manner; if he were aware of how often families in need engage in such triage and distorted her situation to satisfy a Republican audience, he is guilty of outright cruelty.

Clarence Thomas's wielding of stereotype against his sister—a woman whose identity was already overburdened by stereotype—foreshadowed his strategy in the hearings that pitted him against another Black woman, both in its heartlessness and its exploitation of racial imagery. Both times he distorted his relative position vis-à-vis a specific Black woman.

Comparing his sister's failings to his own achievements, he spoke as though the two of them had played with the same advantages and handicaps, as though he had seized his chances while she had unaccountably kicked her own equal opportunities aside. Later, as he confronted Anita Hill, his translation of the power relations of gender was similarly skewed. This time he ultimately portrayed himself as the person at the bottom facing terrible odds. His older adversaries were his favorite cardboard-cutout bogey-people: the (Black, male) civil rights establishment and organized (White) feminists who persecuted him for being of independent mind. Squared off against his bogey-people, he saw himself as an underdog symbol of integrity.

Thomas's version of American power dynamics reversed a decade's worth of his own rhetoric, in which he had castigated Black civil rights advocates for whining about racist oppression. The haughty dismissal of claims that racism persisted had previously been his stock-in-trade. But once a Black woman accused him of abusing his power as a man and as an employer, he quickly slipped into the most familiar role in the American iconography of race: that of the victim. Accused of misuse of power, he presented himself as a person with no power at all. It mattered not that the characterization was totally inappropriate, in terms of gender and of race.

In a struggle between himself and a woman of his same race, Thomas executed a deft strategy. He erected a tableau of White-Black racism that allowed him to occupy the position of *the race*. By reintroducing concepts of White power, Thomas made himself into *the Black person* in his story. Then, in the first move of a two-step strategy, he cast Anita Hill into the role of *Black woman as traitor to the race.*

The Black woman as traitor to the race is at least as old as *David Walker's Appeal* of 1829, and the figure has served as a convenient explanation for racial conflict since that time. Although Thomas did not flesh out his accusation, which served his purposes only briefly, it should be remembered that in the tale of the subversion of the interests of the race, the Black female traitor—as mother to Whites or lover of Whites—connives with the White man against the Black man. Such themes reappear in *Black Skin, White Masks,* by Frantz Fanon; in *Black Rage,* by William Grier and Price Cobbs; and in *Madheart,* by LeRoi Jones (later and better known as the activist poet Amiri Baraka), in which the figure of "the Black woman," as "mammy" or as "Jezebel," is subject to loyalties to Whites that conflict with her allegiance to the Black man. Unable to extricate herself from Whites, the Black-woman-as-traitor misconstrues her racial interests and betrays Black men's aspirations to freedom. Freedom, in this particular instance, meant a seat on the United States Supreme Court.

Although she is well known among African Americans, *the Black woman as traitor to the race* is less familiar to White Americans and thus is not a useful trope in the televised shorthand of race through which Clarence Thomas communicated. Having made Anita Hill into a villain, he proceeded—wittingly or not—to erase her and return to a simpler and more conventional cast. By the end of his story, Anita Hill had lost the only role, that of villain, that his use of stereotype had allowed her. She finally disappeared, as he spun out a drama pitting the lone and persecuted figure of Clarence Thomas, *the Black man,* against an army of powerful White assailants. Democratic senators became the lynch mob; Thomas became the innocent lynch victim. As symbol and as actual person, Anita Hill was no longer to be found.

Hill's strategy was different from Thomas's. But had she not stood on the ground of personal integrity and the truth of her own individual experiences, she might have sought to work within the framework of racial typecasting. To do so would have tested the limits of the genres of senatorial testimony and televised hearings, for she would have needed at least a semester to reveal, analyze, and destroy the commonplaces of American racism that Thomas manipulated so effectively. Her task could neither be undertaken nor completed in sound bites and within a matter of days. Simply to comprehend Hill's identity as a highly educated, ambitious Black female Republican imposed a conceptual burden on American audiences, Black and White, that they were unable—at least at that very moment—to shoulder. With breathtaking cynicism, Thomas evoked the pitiable image of the victimized Black man, and his exploitation of the imagery of race succeeded. Such images, such stereotypes, of Black women as well as of Black men, bear closer inspection.

Black people of both sexes have represented the American id for a very long time, a phenomenon rooted in our cultural identities of race and class. The stereotypes are centuries old and have their origins in European typecasting of both the poor and the Black, for sex is the main theme associated with poverty and with Blackness. Even where race is not at issue, the presence of the poor introduces the subject of sex. William Shakespeare's characters provide a handy reminder across spectra of race, class, and ethnicity: the nurse in *Romeo and Juliet* speaks of sex purposefully and unintentionally, so that her every other utterance is characterized as bawdy; Caliban, in *The Tempest*, is a playfully uninhibited savage; and, of course, there is Othello the Moor in a tortured saga of desire.

Sexuality, in the sense of the heightened desirability of working-class characters, figures centrally in the diaries of Arthur J. Munby and Hannah Cullwick, in *My Secret Life,* in D. H. Lawrence's *Lady Chatterley's Lover,* and, homoerotically, in Hermann Hesse's *Demian.* In each case, members of the middle and upper classes seek sexual titillation or fulfillment with lovers of a lower class. Sigmund Freud, describing the complex family dynamics of bourgeois households, spoke of women in domestic service as people of low morals because they were so likely to become entangled sexually with the men of the families that employed them. More recently, Susan Brownmiller has noted that women who are particularly vulnerable to sexual violence by token of their ethnicity or race—Jews in Europe, Blacks in the United States—are viewed as especially provocative by potential assailants.

Over and over in European imaginations, the poor epitomize unfettered sexuality, and this convention has come to serve in the United States as well. American writing not only echoes the sexualization of the poor (Stephen Crane's *Maggie: A Girl of the Streets,* Wilbur Cash's *Mind of the South*), but, reflecting a history in which masses of workers were enslaved, also adds the ingredient of race. In American iconography the sexually promiscuous Black girl—or more precisely, the yellow girl—represents the opposite of the White woman on the pedestal. Together, White and Black women stand for woman as Madonna and as whore.

Today, as in the past, race and class are hopelessly intertwined in the United States. This is so even generations after the end of legal segregation and the confusion of usages related to race and usages related to class. In eighteenth- and nineteenth-century England, it was the lower classes who were expected to show deference toward the aristocracy by bowing their heads, doffing their hats, tolerating the use of their first names, entering by the service entrance, and, above all, revealing no sign of independent thought. In the era of American segregation these habits became the patterns of racial subordination that all Black people, no matter their class standing, were expected to observe. For most Americans race became and remains the idiom of expression of differences and characteristics of class. Just as enslaved people were the most exploited of workers, so Blacks in the United States have become the sexiest of the American poor.

The imagery of sex in race has not and does not work in identical ways for Black women and men, even though figures of educated Black people, whether male or female, are not well enough established for quick recognition on TV, where the Thomas-Hill saga played and where so many American stereotypes are reinforced. Aside from Bill Cosby, there is no handy Black character in our national imagination, male or female, who has strayed very far from the working class. And Cosby constitutes less a symbol than an individual phenomenon. If Clarence Thomas could not reach for a stereotypical Black man who would be educated and respectable, Anita Hill (had she succumbed to the temptation) could not have done so either. To silence his questioners quickly, Clarence Thomas had to draw on older, better-known formulations of racial victimization, and he had to reach across lines of class and privilege to do so.

Thomas appropriated the figure of the lynch victim despite glaring differences between himself and the thousands of poor unfortunates who, unprotected by White patrons in the White House or the United States Senate, perished at the hands of White Southern mobs. As though education, status, and connections counted for nothing, Thomas grasped a chain of reference that begins with the stereotypical Black-beast-rapist, as depicted in D. W. Griffith's *Birth of a Nation*. As Thomas knew well, however, those associations do not end with the rapist; they extend into meanings that subvert Griffith's brutalized invention.

The Black-beast-rapist connects to the Black man accused of rape, who, in turn, is only one link in a chain that also casts doubt on the validity of the charge of rape when leveled against Black men. Ida B. Wells began to undermine the credibility of the accusation in the 1890s, and the NAACP and the Communist Party helped to discredit lynching even after trials, as in the case of the eight young Black men summarily sentenced to hang in Scottsboro, Alabama, in 1931. Since that time the presumption (among non–Ku Klux Klansmen, at least) has been that the quintessential lynch victim was innocent, that like the Scottsboro boys, he was a casualty of a racist miscarriage of justice. To mention the figure of the Southern Black lynch victim is to cite a man unjustly accused, and this was the meaning that Clarence Thomas summoned. Had the sexualized figure of the Black man not evolved past *Birth of a Nation*, he could not have served Thomas's purpose.

Anita Hill, on the other hand, had no comparable tradition of a stereotype that had been recognized, analyzed, and subverted to draw upon. The mammy image is in the process of being reworked, while the welfare queen and the oversexed Black Jezebel are still unreconstructed. Considering that Hill is a beautiful young woman who was leveling a charge of sexual harassment, adapting herself to stereotype and then reworking the stereotype would not have been a simple matter. (No odder, perhaps, than assimilating the figure of a lynch victim to the person of a nominee for the United States Supreme Court.) Stereotypes of Black women remain fairly securely in place, and the public discussion that would examine and dislodge them has only begun to occur around the mammy image. The oversexed Black Jezebel is likely still to be taken at face value.

The depiction of the oversexed Black Jezebel is not so salient in American culture as that of the Black-beast-rapist lynch victim, but she has sufficient visibility to haunt Black women to this day. This stereotypical Black woman not only connotes sex, like the working-class White woman, but unlike the latter, is assumed to be the instigator of sex. Theodore Dreiser's Sister Carrie may have been seduced by a fast-talking city slicker she met on a train, but Rose Johnson, in Gertrude Stein's *As Fine as Melanctha,* positively revels in sexual promiscuity.

Overdetermined by class and by race, the Black-woman-as-whore has appeared nearly as often as Black women are to be found in representations of American culture. Mary Chesnut, in her Civil War diary, pities the virtuous plantation mistress surrounded by Black prostitutes anxious to seduce White men and boys. The figure of the oversexed Black Jezebel has had amazing longevity in movies made in the 1980s and 1990s—*She's Gotta Have It, Jungle Fever, City of Hope*—in which Black female characters are still likely to be shown unclothed, in bed, and in the midst of coitus.

Mammy, welfare cheat, Jezebel, period. These were the roles available to Anita Hill. Hill chose not to make herself into a symbol Americans could recognize, and as a result she seemed to disappear, a fate reserved for Black women who are well educated and are thus doubly hard to see. Mammy and Jezebel and the welfare queen may be the most prominent roles for Black women in American culture, but even these figures, as limited as is their range, inhabit the shadows of American imagination.

As commentators like Darlene Clark Hine and Patricia Hill Collins have noted, silence and invisibility are the hallmarks of Black women in the imagery of American life. The most common formula for expressing minority status is "women and Blacks." As the emblematic woman is White and the emblematic Black is male, Black women generally are not as easy to comprehend symbolically. Barbara Smith, Gloria Hull, and Patricia Bell-Scott noted in 1982 that while all the women seem to be White and all the Blacks seem to be men, some of us are brave.

Because Black women have been harder than men to fit into clichés of race, we often disappear. Few recall that after Bigger Thomas, in Richard Wright's *Native Son*, accidentally killed rich White Mary Dalton, he committed the brutal, premeditated murder of his girlfriend, the innocent Black Bessie. *Native Son* is generally summed up as the story of a racial crime in which a White woman dies and a Black man emerges as the victim of society. Two generations later Eldridge Cleaver said in *Soul on Ice* that he raped Black women for practice; he was honing his skills before attacking White women, who were for him real women. The poet Audre Lorde remembered and grieved for the twelve Black women who were murdered in Boston in the spring of 1979, but their remembrance grows shadowy beside the figure of the Central Park jogger.

Disregarded or forgotten or, when remembered, misconstrued, the symbolic history of Black women has not functioned in the same way as the symbolic history of Black men. If the reality of the Scottsboro boys and other Black men accused of rape showed that the charge was liable to be false and thereby tempered the stereotype, the meaning of the history of Black women as victims of rape has not yet penetrated the American mind. In the absence of an image equivalent to that of the Scottsboro boys, Black women's reputed hypersexuality has not been reappraised. It is as though silence and invisibility had entirely frozen the image of Black men at the Black-beast-rapist stage. Lacking access to the means of mass communication, Black women have not been able to use our history of abuse as a corrective to stereotypes of rampant sexuality.

Since the seventeenth-century beginnings of their forcible importation into what would become the United States, Black women have been triply vulnerable to rape and other kinds of violence: as members of a stigmatized race, the subordinate sex, and people who work for others. The history of sexual violence against Black women is rooted in slavery, but as bell hooks points out, it did not end there. Despite two centuries' worth of Black women's testimony, as exemplified in Harriet Jacobs's *Incidents in the Life of a Slave Girl*, Alice Walker's *The Color Purple*, and the St. John's University rape case of 1991, our vulnerability to rape has not become a standard item in the list of crimes against the race. When the existence of rape is acknowledged, it is, as often as not, to name a crime of which the Black man, rather than she who was raped, is the victim. Unable to protect "his" woman, the Black man suffers the loss of his manhood when a female family member is assaulted. The belief persists that Black women are always ready for sex and, as a consequence, cannot be raped. Introducing the specter of sex, Hill made herself vulnerable to Virginia Thomas's doubly stereotypical retort: Hill—as both the oversexed Black Jezebel anxious for sex and as the rejected, vindictive woman who trumps up a charge of sexual harassment—really wanted to sleep with Clarence Thomas. The injury, then, is to him, not to her.

More, finally, is at stake here than winning a competition between Black men and Black women for the title of ultimate victim as reckoned in the terms of White racism, as tempting as the scenario of Black-versus-White tends to be. Anita Hill found no shelter in stereotypes of race not merely because they are too potent and too negative to serve her ends. There was no way for Hill to emerge a hero of the race, because she would not deal in Black and White. By indicting the conduct of a Black man, Hill revealed the existence of intra-racial conflict, which White Americans find incomprehensible and many Black Americans guard as a closely held secret of the race. Keeping that secret in the interest of racial unity has silenced Black women on the issue of sexual abuse, for our attackers have been Black men as well as White, as *The Black Women's Health Book* poignantly reveals. Because discussions of the abuse of Black women would not merely implicate Whites, Black women have been reluctant to press the point. Our silence, in turn, has tended to preserve intact the image of oversexed Black Jezebel. Who knows how long Anita Hill would have held her tongue had not circumstances forced her to go public?

As things turned out, in the short run at least, Clarence Thomas and his allies managed once again to disappear Black women and to stage a drama of race. But the gender issue that Anita Hill raised, despite its potential for deep divisiveness, looks toward the future of racial politics in the United States (unless the David Dukes of the world force us back into a terrorized, defensive, androcentric unity). Ironically, Black conservatism, which is not very hospitable to feminism, initially staked the claim for diversity within the race. Black feminists are enlarging this claim in the name of our history as Black women.

Black women, who have traditionally been discounted within the race and degraded in American society, are becoming increasingly impatient with our devaluation. Breaking the silence and testifying about the abuse, Black feminists are publishing our history and dissecting the stereotypes that have been used against us. So far, the discussion has not engaged large numbers of Americans, but I trust that Anita Hill will have helped us reach many more. If my experience with earnest and hardworking Princeton graduate students offers any guidance, the process, though ultimately liberating, will prove to be intellectually demanding. We will know we have succeeded in taking a first step when Americans greet the images of the mammy, the welfare queen, and the oversexed Black Jezebel with the skepticism they turn toward the figure of the lynch victim accused of raping a White woman. Our work, however, cannot end there, for both the Black-beast-rapist and the oversexed Black Jezebel would still survive with enough vigor to dog both our tracks. The next step, just as necessary, will examine and subvert stereotypes.

October 1992

What Eighteenth- and Nineteenth-Century Intellectuals Saw in the Time of Trump

AMERICAN UNIVERSITIES, MONUMENTS, AND THE LEGACIES OF SLAVERY

THOSE OF YOU WHO KNOW ME and my work know my long-standing interest in what Germans call *Vergangenheitsbewältigung,* coming to terms with the past. And you know that what I—what we—consider "the past" is often broader and deeper than the prevailing sense of what constitutes the American past. Only in recent years, in this twenty-first century, have non-Black American allies joined Black Americans in opening up the American past. Only now are more than a saving remnant of Americans engaging in the *Vergangenheitsbewälti-gung* that was forced on Germans after the end of the Second World War. After National Socialism and defeat in the war, Germans have engaged in a long-term reckoning with their past, in terms of the writing of history, but also in terms of culture—monuments, commemorations, and who counts as a great German (formerly as a great man).

Just now non-Black Americans have become engaged in *Vergangenheitsbewältigung,* most obviously in the reconsideration of monuments to the heroes of the Confederacy. As we think about the meaning of various Confederate generals, we rethink the meanings of American history, especially in the South. I've been doing this work as a historian for decades. Only now, as an artist, has *Vergangenheitsbewältigung* entered my art.

For a long time I assumed that going to art school and making art separated me from my former vocation as historian. The suite of prints I'm showing you now was my first time of addressing American politics and history head-on in my art. Usually I let my history books speak for me with regard to history. Art I reserve for imagination, for visual fictions. The last two years changed that for me.

Winter 2017 and my reconsidering the relationship between the present time and the past. My Brodsky Center suite of prints, *You Say This Can't Really Be America,* was prompted by conversations in the aftermath of Donald Trump's election and inaugural.

The back and forth between me and a friend ends with my saying I do, indeed, recognize this America, which I know from American history—"Look South. Look West."

Here and now, I want to concentrate on the "look South" part of the equation, looking at Trump's America, the slave-owning South, through the eyes of four observers:

Harriet Jacobs,
Hector Saint John de Crèvecoeur,
Thomas Jefferson, and
Charles Dickens.

I could have shared the views of many others, such as Frederick Douglass, Sojourner Truth, David Walker, Hosea Easton, Alexis de Tocqueville, Gustave de Beaumont, William Lloyd Garrison, Frances Kemble, and even Ralph Waldo Emerson, to name just nine writers who testified to slavery's harm to American political character as a whole. Bear with me here, please, and let Crèvecoeur, Jefferson, Dickens, and Jacobs stand in for the many.

Let me begin the body of my remarks with my conclusion:

Americans need to face the enduring social and political consequences of slavery, which can most simply and conveniently be summed up as Trumpism's White supremacy and sexism. I am not the first to notice that Trumpism's White supremacy and sexism inspire a political enthusiasm that is, at heart, a tribalist rather than a democratic persuasion.

Trumpist White supremacy and sexism subjugate governance—notably important political and economic issues such as public health, education, and the environment—to the preservation of White supremacy and the disempowerment of women. I include sexism, the subjugation of women, in the spirit of what the twentieth-century Georgian writer Lillian Smith (1897–1966) termed the spiral of sex, sin, and segregation. I recommend to you a perusal of the nonfiction works of Lillian Smith on your own.

We can still see White supremacy and subjugation of women in the extreme in the Deep South and especially among White evangelicals, but it exists throughout the USA.

Now, why look to White people to comment on the effects of slavery on American society? The usual way of thinking about slavery is to look at Black Americans and ask what slavery did to them. This is a very sound way to proceed, and this is the way we have pursued our research since the mid-twentieth century. This research has produced a valuable body of scholarship that has remade American history and literature. But there is more.

What the time of Trump does for us now is make White Americans visible as raced Americans, as raced counterparts to Black Americans. Long-standing assumptions—that only non-Whites have racial identities, that White Americans are individuals who only have race if they're Nazis or White nationalists—those assumptions no longer hold. I'm turning the glass around to focus on what living in a slave society did to non-Black Americans and to the society as a whole. For me now, *Vergangenheitsbewältigung*—reckoning with history, here with slavery in American history—now means acknowledging slavery's distortion of the American public sphere. The riveting issues of

OVERLEAF, AND FOLLOWING THREE PAGES *You Say This Can't Really Be America,* 2017, digital and silkscreen print on Sunset Cotton etching paper, eight parts, 17″ × 17″ each. Exclamations following the inaugural of Donald Trump inspired this series' self-portrait conversation in which I hear surprise and reply with the weariness of a historian of the United States.

You say This is the worst thing ever.

You say We've never seen anything like this before.

I say Yes This is the America I know.

I say Yes This is America too.

You say This isn't really America. Not the America you know.

You say This can't really be America.

I say Yes This is the America I know from history.

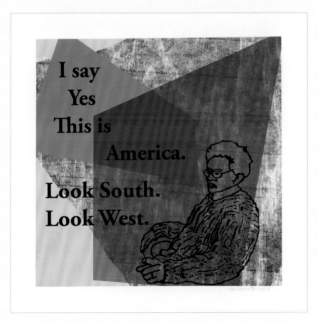

I say Yes This is America. Look South. Look West.

our own time now—sexual harassment of working women and gun violence—are old themes in observances of American society as a whole.

I start with Harriet Jacobs (1813–1897), whom you probably already know.[1]

Jacobs wrote her narrative, *Incidents in the Life of a Slave Girl, Written by Herself,* in New York in the early 1850s and published it in 1861. Jacobs's autobiography is the urtext of sexual harassment. In addition to describing how sexual harassment corrupts the workplace, it also corrupts non-enslaved women's own intimate lives—their own marriages. (This is witnessed in detail in *The Secret Eye: The Journal of Ella Gertrude Clanton Thomas, 1848–1889.*) Jacobs's chapter 5, "The Trials of Girlhood," provides a classic description of sexual harassment in the workplace. As Jacobs was enslaved at the time (the early 1830s), her workplace was wherever she was. Unlike today's working women, Jacobs had no non-workplace. She found only provisional shelter in her grandmother's house, where she hid for years from her owner. Jacobs says her male owner "peopled my young mind with unclean images . . . He told me I was his property; that I must be subject to his will in all things . . . where could I turn for protection? No matter whether the slave girl be black as ebony or as fair as her mistress . . . there is no shadow of law to protect her . . . If God has bestowed beauty upon [the slave girl], it will prove her greatest curse. That which commands admiration in the white woman only hastens the degradation of the female slave."

The chapter that follows Jacobs's experience of being treated as sexual prey is called "The Jealous Mistress." Here Jacobs describes her mistress before turning to the larger question of what sexual harassment and rape of enslaved women does to non-enslaved women's marriages. It spoils them: "[Northerners] are not only willing, but proud, to give their daughters in marriage to slaveholders. The poor girls have romantic notions of a sunny clime, and of the flowering vines that all the year round shade a happy home. To what disappointments are they destined! The young wife soon hears that the husband in whose hands she has placed her happiness pays no regard to his marriage vows. Children of every shade of complexion play with her own fair babies, and too well she knows that they are born unto him . . . Jealousy and hatred enter the flowery home, and it is ravaged of its loveliness."

Jacobs adds that Southern women marry knowing their husband to be the "father of many little slaves." Slave-owning women sell these children "without a twinge of regret . . . this bad institution deadens the moral sense, even in white women, to a fearful extent."

Adultery and broken marriages are generally considered the purview of women and women writers. Let me turn to three male writers who pondered the evil effects of slavery on American society.

The French soldier-diplomat Michel-Guillaume-Jean de Crève-coeur (1735–1813) is best known for contrasting class-riven Europe, the land of opulent aristocrats and destitute peasants, with the egalitarian United States, home of mobility and democracy, in his quickly translated, widely read, and endlessly quoted *Letters from an American Farmer* (1782).[2]

Crèvecoeur was for a while the most widely read commentator on America. His reputation was further increased in the 1920s when a bundle of his unpublished English essays was discovered in an attic in France. These were brought out as *Sketches of Eighteenth Century America, or More Letters from an American Farmer* (1925).

Letter 3 is where we find Crèvecoeur's American. This "new man"—of mixed but totally European descent—constitutes "a new race" who has escaped old Europe's oppression and embraces new opportunity. He glories in freedom of thought and economic mobility. Such are the thoughts most often associated with Crèvecoeur and his notion of "the American" as a "new man."

Those generalities, though widely quoted and lauded, hold only when Crèvecoeur was speaking of New England and the North. Crève-coeur also went to Charleston, South Carolina, where ugly scenes of slavery broke his heart. His pessimism arose most from the shock of his wealthy hosts' callousness. The rich slaveholders entertaining Crèvecoeur are the "gayest" people in America, but gay at the cost of their humanity. His chapters on Charleston, South Carolina, and slavery are utterly bleak, with a bleakness extending past the enslaved to their enslavers and to human nature in general.

According to Crèvecoeur, his hosts "neither see, hear, nor feel the woes" of the people they own or the bloodcurdling violence of their social arrangements. Crèvecoeur can only marvel at such insouciance: "Can it be possible that the force of custom should ever make me deaf to all these reflections [of the realities of slavery and the slave trade], and as insensible to the injustice of that [slave] trade, and to [slaves'] miseries, as the rich inhabitants of this town [Charleston] seem to be." He meant the diminished humanity of all Americans, diminished on account of habits of tyranny and cruelty created by the ownership of people.

Crèvecoeur was a European thinking in terms of rampant poverty and obscene wealth and seeing the enslaved as the poorest members of American society, not counted as American people on account of race.

Writing a few years after Crèvecoeur, Thomas Jefferson (1743–1826) missed the class dimension that so alarmed Crèvecoeur. Jefferson, a slave owner, never questioned that American society was structured according to race. He assumed that the poor people who served, including most prominently the people he owned, belonged to a naturally servile race. Jefferson's thinking was straight-out racist, insulting Black people with an all-too-common mean-spiritedness. For Jefferson, in "Query XVIII: Manners," in *Notes on the State of Virginia* (1787), slavery had an "unhappy" influence on the slave-owning class, although he scarcely mentions the suffering of the enslaved. In "Query XVII" Jefferson dwelled on the price paid by the South's White slave owners, whose children mimicked the parents' abuse of the people they owned, coarsening their character and, thereby, their entire society. The White child, "thus nursed and educated, and daily exercised in tyranny," Jefferson warned, "cannot but be stamped by it with odious peculiarities. The man must be a prodigy who can retain his manner and morals undepraved by such circumstances."

In *Notes on the State of Virginia,* Jefferson spent more time on the meaning of slavery in the future of American politics than on Black or White people. For him, the relation between slavery and the future of the United States was extremely close. In letters in 1820 and 1824, Jefferson said, "But, as it is, we have the wolf by the ear, and we can neither hold him, nor safely let him go. Justice is in one scale, and self-preservation in the other." Yet by the 1820s, Jefferson the slaveholder had given up earlier hopes that slavery might be abolished.

Jefferson died in 1826, a decade and a half before the popular English novelist Charles Dickens (1812–1870) toured the USA.[3]

In the United States, Dickens was at first welcomed, but as he voiced his disapproval of American institutions—slavery, above all, but also solitary confinement and spitting tobacco juice everywhere—his American audience soured on him. His observations, especially for us here today, still can sound familiar, as he ends *American Notes* with a harsh chapter entitled "Slavery." This chapter excoriates Americans in general for tolerating the continued existence of enslavement by shrugging their shoulders, saying nothing can be done on account of "public opinion." After repeated outpourings of protest against American gun violence, Dickens's condemnation of the excuse of "public opinion" as a bulwark against reform echoes loudly: "Public opinion! What class of men have an immense preponderance over the rest of the community, in their power of representing public opinion in the legislature? The slave owners. They send from their twelve States, one hundred members, while the fourteen free States, with a free population nearly double, return but a hundred and forty-two. Before whom do the presidential candidates bow down the most humbly, on whom do they fawn the most fondly, and for whose tastes do they cater the most assiduously in their service protestations? The slave owners always . . ."

There follow three pages of runaway advertisements of fugitives with scars and brands and instruments of torture.

After speaking of the wounds visited upon the enslaved, as testified in runaway advertisements, Dickens turns to non-enslaved Americans, who beat, shoot, stab, and kill one another according to the passions encouraged by slavery. He includes instances in slave and non-slave territory, on the ground that Americans even outside the slave states are "brutalized by slave customs."

A fatal political shooting in Wisconsin, a fatal shooting on the street in Iowa, a fatal shooting in Louisiana, a fatal knifing in Arkansas, a political assassination in Missouri, a fatal knifing in New Orleans, &c.,

&c. for three more pages: "Do we not know that the man who has been born and bred among its wrongs . . . that fine mode of training which rears up such men; should we not know that they who among their equals stab and pistol in the legislative hall, and in the counting-house, and on the market-place, and in all the elsewhere peaceful pursuits of life . . ."

Dickens says Americans can't criticize the supposed brutality of others, like the Irish, the Indians, the Spanish, and the Italians. "Liberty in America doth hew and hack her slaves; or, failing that pursuit, her sons devote them to a better use, and turn them on each other."

As though foreseeing the election of Donald Trump, Dickens accuses Americans of loving "'smart' dealing: which gilds over many a swindle and gross breach of trust; many a defalcation, public and private; and enables many a knave to hold his head up with the best . . ."

And as though he were watching Fox News, Dickens blames the "licentious Press" in the United States, which fosters and reflects Americans' "Universal Distrust."

In sum, I don't mean to collapse earlier eras into our own—that would not be thinking like a careful historian. What I do mean to say is that over the course of the last century and a half, observers have commented on certain inhumane American characteristics that they blamed on slavery, characteristics they saw as intimate, moral, and political, and the persistence of those characteristics help explain the legacies of slavery and the state of American public and intimate lives today.

Further, I want to loop back to my prints *You Say This Can't Really Be America,* in which an innocent American in early 2017 knows nothing of the unsavory parts of American history. It is easy to conclude that the fault lies in not knowing the past. I want to complicate that not knowing and call it "willful unknowing" (phrase from Eve Kosofsky Sedgwick). Each of the four authors I mentioned—Harriet Jacobs, Hector Saint John de Crèvecoeur, Thomas Jefferson, and Charles Dickens—addressed the larger meanings of slavery in American society. But the conversation around them, the historical and literary criticism, has omitted those observations.

Harriet Jacobs's thinking has been seen as commentary on enslaved women only.

Hector Saint John de Crèvecoeur has been pictured as the originator of the idea of the American as a new man, better, different from his European forebears.

Thomas Jefferson, revealed as the intimate partner of a young woman he owned, is now seen as a hypocritical patriarch, but not as an observer of American society as a whole as shaped by slavery.

Charles Dickens, when remembered as a commentator on Americans, appears as one deeply critical of the role of public opinion and lying news media in American public life.

All of them saw slavery as an undemocratic source of tyranny in the whole of American society, whose force was not limited to people personally involved in the institution.

To move past the unknowing in my *You Say This Can't Really Be America* print, we need to undertake a continuing *Vergangenheitsbewältigung* that does not stop at the color line. My eighteenth- and nineteenth-century observers recognized and wrote that slavery implicated all Americans, enslaved or not, slave owning or not. Now, in the time of Trump, we can read them more thoroughly than ever and take to heart all they have to say about what slavery meant and still means in American life.

March 2018

Reparations

BE BLACK LIKE ME

ANDALL ROBINSON IS ABSOLUTELY RIGHT about the need for reparations for the unpaid labor extorted from the enslaved before 1865 ("America's Debt to Blacks," *The Nation*, March 13, 2000). But I have two further suggestions along reparations lines, which are meant to address the continuing racism of American culture. First, every Black person should have his or her own therapist for life, because dealing with this society is enough to make you crazy. Second, every White person should have to live two months as Black. (No less, because you'd have to experience it at length; no more, because not having been brought up with the necessary protective strategies, too many of you would lose your minds.) How can a White person live as a Black person? It's more or less simple: (1) By taking a leaf from the 1947 classic about anti-Semitism, *Gentleman's Agreement,* and letting drop a hint about race. Once a doubt is planted, one's physical appearance need not change. (2) If one is ambitious, one can apply dark makeup and not accept the way out as offered, e.g., accepting the assignment of South Asian background. (3) By carrying about a Black periodical, book, or other talisman, listening to Black music, wearing a T-shirt from a Black college, or otherwise engaging in Black-identified behavior. Just being seriously interested in Black stuff. (4) By being seen on a regular basis with a Black person. (5) By protesting against racism out loud, without the disclaimer "I'm not Black, but . . ." (6) This is absolutely necessary: read everything pertaining to Black people you can get your hands on. While one of the privileges of Whiteness is that of "unknowing" (to quote Eve Kosofsky Sedgwick), finding out what goes on in this country with regard to race changes a person of any racial persuasion.

So there. It is possible and has been done. Remember *Black Like Me* and *Soul Sister*, from the 1960s. Maybe it's time someone tried that again.

May 2000

Art School + History History

MY HISTORIAN'S LIFE seemed to recede while I was in art school, disconnected from art as a foreign country with its own foreign, native tongue. Values that governed my work as a historian—clarity, coherence, and representativeness—looked all wrong in art. If not wrong, then not very useful, almost as bad as "academic." The two halves of my brain, one orderly, the other spontaneous, connected only tenuously, the remnants of connecting tissue more hindrance than help. Frowning on historical subject matter, my teachers encouraged the disconnect. Leaving history seemed like what I absolutely had to do because history was dragging me down. I knew with certainty that historians' attachment to scientific truth was cramping my painting hand and misleading my eye.

Publication of my book *The History of White People* while I was in graduate school disrupted an already uneasy coexistence, for my tasks as an author competed with art school. Starting with an appearance on *The Colbert Report* the very week *The History of White People* was published, book promotion took me away from Providence on a regular basis. In that instance, absence increased my standing, for arm wrestling Stephen Colbert gave me impressive RISD cred. What was that like? Fun, like doing improv. Undergraduate RISD students in my digital tools class watched the video together and applauded my return to Providence. RISD's hip young president posted my *Colbert* clip on his blog.

The History of White People had been favorably reviewed on the front page of *The New York Times Book Review,* along with a stunning

Caesar's paragraphs
on the Germani
provide only
brief and pat-
ronizing ac-
counts of
the
barbarians
north of
Roman Gaul.
For instance,
Caesar
de notes
the largest
of the German
tribes, the
Suebi
Germans
east of the
Rhine, as
"ignorant
and unciviliz-
ed." Only one
German char-
acter rates
an appearance by

Alternator Self-Portrait, 2007, graphite and colored pencil on paper, 33″ × 23¼″. While I was studying at Mason Gross School of the Arts at Rutgers I was also writing *The History of White People*. The person in the drawing holds a book and a brush in front of text from the book's manuscript. My modes of production were an alternator in the place of a heart and one of Marcel Duchamp's bicycle wheels.

graphic image of the tangled taxonomy of the idea of White people. That review awed some New York–based RISD faculty—some, but hardly all—for reviews of history books didn't count for much in the art world. I certainly did not feel any increased stature in the MFA painters' club in the Fletcher Building. Between book promotion talks and interviews, I drew and painted with the purposeful resolve of my inner worker bee, drawing and painting and painting and drawing with the discipline that was ever my forte. Immersion in work always transported me to a better place, a higher plane, a truer zone. I enjoyed every moment, all right, but beyond my studio, I still felt like an alien.

While I bore down on my work over solitary hours in the studio, I imagined my fellow painters lolling about together, pleasuring themselves in Matisse-like *volupté*, drinking, smoking, turning up late, and schmoozing from one studio to another. They were making the work the teachers applauded, painting with knowing hands, seeing with clever eyes. They knew what I didn't. They could drink and drug without paying a price—or so I thought. They were young enough for exemption, fresh enough not to owe alcohol's tax in sleeplessness and looking totally rotten in the morning.

We weren't supposed to eat or drink in our studios, but what the hell. Eno Fine Wines and Spirits, a combination wine bar–corner liquor store on Westminster Street, facilitated our drinking. Its sophisticated décor, expensive liquors, and wine tastings gave it upscale cachet, while its long hours and stock of cheap beers made it an all-hours convenience store. I wouldn't know about *all* hours, but I wasn't the only one fueling my art with alcohol. Well, I ate, too. Tazza, a self-consciously cool art-school hangout on the corner of Eddy and Westminster Streets, projected obscure European movies on ceiling monitors with music the cognoscenti recognized. Tazza served pretty good food as well as drink. Food and drink nearby, I worked steadily in my pitiful isolation. By the time of my crit with Teacher Irma, I had too many drawings to fit on my studio walls.

For her studio visit, I had put up a score of new drawings inspired by Ingres's *Grande Odalisque*, Michael Jackson, and Apollo Belvedere, with two large paintings and some etchings. Much of it was just regular drawing, regular painting, not objects of great beauty. But some was ambitious. I was trying to make paintings that exceeded my skill, drawing on art history and history history and trying to cram too much into my images. I might have been away from Providence a great deal, but I made up for it with a lot of work. No one, not even Teacher Irma, could accuse me of slackness. She did not accuse me of slackness. Quality, not quantity, was my defect.

She walked in as usual, reminding me,

You can't draw, and you can't paint.

I fell for it every time: she had plumbed the truth of the matter; she knew the real deal; I couldn't draw, and I couldn't paint. It didn't occur to me that she might be saying exactly the same thing to other students, that other students might be torturing themselves as I tortured myself. I should have grasped the possibility that it was all psychological-warfare poppycock. She was probably one of those dia-bolical people who can sniff out each person's particular insecurity. I had a history colleague at Penn who could do that. He'd pass on a comment impugning the teaching of one who was insecure in the classroom and whisper a critique of his book to one worried about publication. It's a gift some people have. Maybe she had it. She tor-tured me, and she knew it. She did it on purpose, I just know. In my pathetic insecurity, I felt her judgment applied to me alone and feared she was right. Some of it *was* just for me, because I was the one jug-gling so many lives. Teacher Irma hastily looked around my studio, pausing over nothing. She dismissed all but one small, light-colored print as,

The only interesting thing in here.

She wasn't there to talk about my work; she was there to complain: Why did you choose to go to graduate school when the biggest book of your career was coming out?

That's what she said.

I heard, You stupid fart! You never should have gone to art school!

The terrible painter in me flinched.

The nincompoop that I was struggled to answer.

During undergraduate art school, I had managed more than one thing. I finished my book . . .

Actually, I *thought* I had finished my book. I really hadn't.

My plan had been to finish *The History of White People* before starting art school. I had made tremendous progress the year before, then Glenn broke my writing rhythm by dragging poor little me to Paris for the month of May, where I griped about how hard it was to work there. A chapter that had practically been writing itself in April bogged down in June. No one, not one single friend of mine, empathized. Oh, jeez! I'd been finishing this book for what felt like forever; it had, in fact, gone on for years and years. I wrote steadily all summer, but I started at Mason Gross with my book still in pieces and an intention to finish the following summer. A historical organization presidency disrupted my writing for an entire year.

Teacher Irma saw *THWP* as an obstacle, a fatal distraction from art school, and she was right. But she didn't know about the obstruction that had *truly* disrupted my plan to complete my book before graduate school. I tended also to sublimate the obstruction because it was so ridiculously, agonizingly, enragingly time-consuming. My book was a screen memory repressing the real distraction in my second year at Mason Gross, the real absurd drain of time and energy that dragged me down. I was president of the Organization of American Historians—OAH, the international professional organization of scholars of American history—a test in the guise of an honor.

I had belonged to the OAH for thirty years before being elected president, as I had belonged to the Southern Historical Association, of which I was also elected president; the American Studies Association, of which I was defeated in an election for president; the Association of Black Women Historians, of which I served as director; the American Historical Association, which gave me an award for distinguished graduate teaching; the Southern Association for Women Historians; the Berkshire Conference of Women Historians; the Association for the Study of African American Life and History; and organizations you had to be elected to, such as the Society of American Historians, the American Antiquarian Society, the American Academy of Political and Social Science, and the American Academy of Arts and Sciences. I felt it was important to be active in the historical profession, so for thirty years I faithfully attended annual meetings, served on committees, and wrote my share of reports. I did not mind taking part in professional organizations, not at all. It was the right thing to do. I was a good citizen of my profession.

Along with my History Department and programs in African American Studies and Women's Studies, professional organizations had comprised my intellectual community, where I was known and respected. Some colleagues became close friends. We became leaders in our fields, and our students grew up to write important scholarship. The history profession, history history, was my intellectual home. This home opened the jaws of a trap.

Only now do I recall the year when my book fell off schedule, for my memory had thrown out the endless conference calls, the wrangling, the verbal struggles, the hand-to-hand combat with only the dull bayonet of my presidency to fend off my adversary, the executive director, a man whom the sweetest of historians called "a sleazy son of a bitch." The saving grace of that time was the comradeship of struggle forged between me and the presidents before and after me, solid historians with a sense of humor, stick-to-itiveness, and guts. We proclaimed ourselves a Gang of Three forged in combat. Thank heaven for my dear presidential comrades.

The closest metaphor I can think of to describe my OAH presidency is the boulder Sisyphus had to push up the hill every day, only to have it roll back down in the night.

Here's the morning, sunny, warm, and clear, and here's the day's boulder, a financial plan. You roll it up the hill. It rolls back down. The next day the boulder is a conference call. You roll it up the hill. It rolls back down. The next day the boulder is a mission statement. You roll it up the hill. It rolls back down. The next day the boulder is a strategic plan. You roll it up the hill. It rolls back down. The next day the boulder is another conference call. You roll it up the hill. It rolls back down. The strategic plan was no mere boulder. It was an eagle pecking out my liver every night.

In art school I didn't talk about the Organization of American Historians. No one had ever heard of it, so even if I had bragged about being OAH president, people would have rolled their eyes at me in a netherworld of No Interest Whatsoever, a totally uncool realm of squares.

So I have suppressed that time of travail. My presidency ended, and with its ending, the history profession passed, I assumed, into my anterior life. For years I proclaimed myself a *former* historian, and when asked how art school influenced my thinking about history, I maintained I no longer thought about history. Which was *so very wrong.*

Tongue-lashed in my studio crit by Teacher Irma, I forgot the OAH but countered with my ability to juggle several tasks at once:

I finished my book . . .

And I looked after my parents in California as my mother was dying and my father disintegrated.

That was undergraduate, Teacher Irma countered. Graduate school is different. You're hardly ever here.

This I disputed, though I had to admit to all the entanglements of my life. I felt like I'd been in Providence a lot. I knew I'd done a lot of work, more than some other painting students. Like a chump, I carried on explaining myself as though exculpation were needed in a moment of surpassing triumph. I'm embarrassed to admit that I even sent Irma an email with the abject subject line "It Came as a Surprise." None of my other books had attracted so much attention, even though they'd been favorably reviewed in *The New York Times* and done well. At a dinner at President Ruth's at Brown, Novelist John noted my new celebrity. He said I had finally found the right people to write about. Technically this was not true, as two of my other books had been about Americans in general. But he was right in the spirit of the thing.

A total ninny with scolding Teacher Irma, I was actually achieving a height of accomplishment. I had not only survived the devilish OAH, I had parented my parents and published a book that came in at five hundred pages in hardcover and gotten the review of a lifetime. Back at Mason Gross, I had already turned my multiplicity into art, as a collage, *Chapter Revised,* based on a page of my book manuscript. The ground was a wash of dark green under a page of manuscript I had shaped according to lines of text. On top of the shaped manuscript, I had sewn by hand in thick orange thread hand-cut strips of a dark red man's tie bought at Newark's Salvation Army. Basting the tie's strips to the manuscript at angles to lines of typing, I obscured the text and

Chapter Revised, 2006, manuscript page, fabric, and thread on paper, 12″ × 9″. Another visualization of the tension? coexistence? of discourse and image.

created competing lines and conflicting narrative messages in lines as though to be read. The black-and-white manuscript, though edged organically, expressed the orderliness of scholarship; the strips of red tie, unraveling and adhered by an unsteady hand, talked over the type, posing the old riddle, What's black and white and red/read all over?

So, yes, I had held it all together for years now. But, just as true, I was exhausted all the time—pressed, harried, rushed, squashed, smashed, and impossibly stretched all over the place, barely hanging on.

Wait, now. I was also all-powerful. Omnipotent, practically. I didn't question whether I could balance book and art school. I even made a three-foot-high drawing in charcoal and pastel of myself doing both, with text from my book manuscript beside me, a brush in one hand, a book in the other, a Duchampian bicycle wheel for power, and a precisely drawn red alternator in place of a heart for converting one form of energy into another.

I had and would continue to balance book, art school, and declining parents. I'd already proven my powers. If only I had stood up to Irma with the conviction of the abilities I really had! As for mollifying her, that was pissing into the wind. Even as her hostility was turning me against graduate school, she was right about at least one thing: *The History of White People,* my seventh authored book, was the biggest book of my career.

Art school influenced *The History of White People,* but art's influence on my writing of history had originated years earlier. When did my turn toward the visual begin? When I was faced with Sojourner Truth, a biographical subject who did not read or write. My book *Sojourner Truth: A Life, A Symbol* did not turn to art history out of respect for the image. No, I was grappling with a failure of written language, a deficiency of text. The paucity of Truth's own words documenting her life, not pure attraction to pictures, led me to art. Focusing on image in its own right came later, with art school.

The History of White People is a visual book. In the first instance because human taxonomy, though fetishizing bodily measurement, usually turns on how people look. In the second instance because race scientists have used what they call science to prove racial superiority, and racial superiority often rests on the claim that the superior

146

race is the most beautiful. Desire is all over beauty, as in the classical judgment of Paris.

What became *The History of White People* sprang from a simple question prompted by a photograph on the front page of *The New York Times* in 2000. It showed bombed-out Grozny, the capital of Chechnya, in another round in the endless wars between Russia and the Caucasus, and looking like Berlin in 1945. Wikipedia says, "In 2003, the United Nations called Grozny the most destroyed city on Earth." It certainly looked that way. Knowing that Chechnya was part of the Caucasus, I couldn't help connecting devastation over there to a common notation in the United States. Why on earth, I wondered, are White Americans called "Chechens"?

You recognize the name Caucasian maybe not every day, because calling White people "Caucasian" is like calling your car your "vehicle." "Caucasian" proclaims an elevated purpose, like scientific truth. Medical researchers and sociologists are prime users of "Caucasian," and they don't use it sardonically. How, I wondered, did we get from the Caucasus, between the Black and Caspian Seas, just barely in Europe and thousands of miles from the Western Hemisphere, to "Caucasian" in American usage?

The great thing about having already written many books is that you can pursue whatever question sticks in your mind. So I pursued "Caucasian" as a euphemism for the too bald-faced label of White people. Answering my question took me to Göttingen, Germany, where I found Johann Friedrich Blumenbach, an eighteenth-century professor who picked out five skulls as embodiments of what he called the "varieties" (rather than the "races") of mankind.

Let me repeat that: Professor Blumenbach, working according to scientifically recognized methods, picked out five skulls—skulls from five individuals—and turned them into *varieties* of mankind. It was as though I lost my head, you boiled all the flesh off it and the brains and eyeballs out of it, and you called it "New Jersey Variety of Mankind." I would stand for all nine million people in New Jersey. My husband, Glenn, whom I love dearly and who lives in the same house with me, would not count. It would be my skull, not his, and not yours, that personified New Jerseyans as a whole.

Blumenbach's prettiest skull—no dings, all its teeth, nicely symmetrical—came from a young woman from Georgia in the Caucasus, a part of the world subject to slave raids over several millennia. Blumenbach (in translation) called hers "the really most beautiful form of skull, which my beautiful typical head of a young Georgian female always of itself attracts every eye, however little observant." The Georgian who had possessed the head that became the skull had been enslaved, brought to Moscow, and raped to death. I kid you not. Her skull, the skull of a young Georgian woman raped to death, became the emblem of White people as Caucasian.

Blumenbach's beautiful Georgian sex slave's skull stood for a figure that art history calls the "odalisque." This is where art history and art school deeply influenced my writing. At RISD I drew by hand in colored ink a small map of the land of the odalisques, a work of conceptual rather than terrestrial geography and color. Violet and green made conceptual sense for the two seas, Black and Caspian. Bleached-out yellow and orange came purely from imagination.

From art history I knew the countless museum paintings of odalisques, the most famous by Jean-Auguste-Dominique Ingres, *Grande Odalisque*, who is not wearing clothes, followed by countless others, more and less clothed, by painters like Jean-Léon Gérôme and Henri Matisse. Their titles allude to slavery, slave markets, and harems, with young, mostly female beauty the constant. In the nineteenth-century United States, Hiram Powers's *The Greek Slave* allowed viewers to ogle a naked White girl in the interest of high art. There is no such thing as an ugly odalisque or an old odalisque. Tipped off by art history, I chronicled the way themes associated with the odalisque, enslavement and beauty, made their way into science. I began my chapter 5, "The White Beauty Ideal as Science," with the pioneering eighteenth-century art historian Johann Joachim Winckelmann, who established the hard White aesthetic for the art of ancient Greece.

Having answered my original question of why White Americans are called "Chechens," I needed thousands more words and nearly a decade to complete my book. In order to refute the all-too-common but mistaken notion that ancient Greeks and Romans thought in the

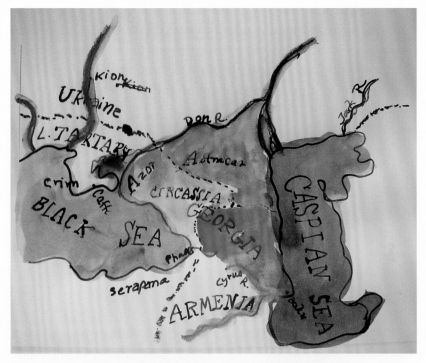

Wonky Black Sea Map, 2009, ink on paper, 14″ × 17″. This map expresses the mysteries of the terrain of the Caucasians of *The History of White People*.

same racial terms as we use today, I began in antiquity. Yes, yes, the ancients could see that some people had darker and lighter skin than others. But they didn't turn those distinctions into race, which wasn't invented until the Enlightenment of the eighteenth century. Upper-class ancient Greeks, who staged their manly games in the nude, derided their Persian enemies for being pale. In Greek eyes, Persians' lack of suntan presented physical evidence that they spent too much time indoors; paleness impugned Persians' manhood.

After correcting errors about the ancients, my book had to come up to the present time to explain how we got to where we are now. This all took much longer than I had planned. Mounting travail exacted its toll on my own body, whose writing machine demanded peanuts and wine. I was getting fatter and fatter. My body could stand the puffing up, but the gain, oh no! made my face look its age, its old age. Either

I push on with the book or I slow down, rest up, do my exercises, and, once rested up, eat right. I pushed on with everything.

During my time at Mason Gross, my own art made its way into *The History of White People* as four graphite drawings on page 26, images of the so-called monstrous races of people thought to exist in the Middle Ages.

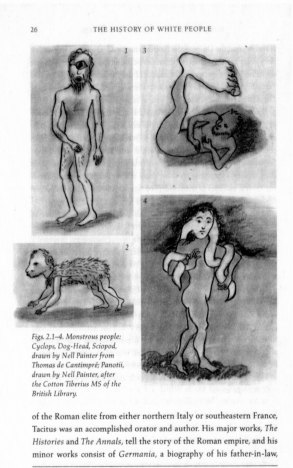

26   THE HISTORY OF WHITE PEOPLE

Figs. 2.1–4. Monstrous people: Cyclops, Dog-Head, Sciopod, drawn by Nell Painter from Thomas de Cantimpré; Panotii, drawn by Nell Painter, after the Cotton Tiberius MS of the British Library.

of the Roman elite from either northern Italy or southeastern France, Tacitus was an accomplished orator and author. His major works, *The Histories* and *The Annals*, tell the story of the Roman empire, and his minor works consist of *Germania*, a biography of his father-in-law,

nationalist websites, such as that of the Aryan Nations: "It's not a matter of White Supremacy it's about Racial Purity!"

Page 26 of *The History of White People,* 2010. These four 2008 drawings of medieval monstrous human races I came across in my research for *The History of White People* are ink and graphite on Yupo, 12″ × 9″.

TOP *Dog-head,* 2009, hand-colored lithograph, approx. 5″ × 7″ × 2″. Inspired by medieval monstrous human races I came across in my research for *The History of White People*. BOTTOM *Golda's Sciopod,* 2009, hand-colored lithograph, approx. 5″ × 12″. Inspired by the medieval monstrous human races I drew for *The History of White People*.

At Mason Gross, I turned two of those drawings into lithographs, one three-dimensional in dark forest colors, one a Warhol-esque multiple in Warhol-esque brightness.

History into art.

June 2018

On Horseback

BLOODY NEWS from April laid me low—murders worse than sense-less, purposeful slaughter of the sort my country seems to reserve for my people, Black Americans. The murders hadn't occurred in geographical or temporal proximity. They were in the Midwest, Upper South, and Deep South. One had been concealed for weeks; none of the perpetrators had been punished. The murders of George Floyd, Breonna Taylor, Ahmaud Arbery, Eric Garner, Trayvon Martin, Michael Brown, and the needless loss of Sandra Bland were themselves hard to stomach. Worse was their terrible inevitability, a never-ending history of carnage defined by Emmett Till's nauseating sacrifice to White supremacy in 1955. An old anguish bound me to these most recent victims.

Then all across the country, Americans rose up for George Floyd, in Black Lives Matter protests against police brutality and Confederate statuary that spread to other countries, where multiracial protest-ers tore down emblems of colonialism and the Atlantic slave trade. Insurgent masses filled the streets—city streets, suburban streets, little White country town streets, even roads in my outdoor tourist playground of northern New York State's Adirondacks. The images of protest were glorious, and some took me by surprise by giving me pleasure.

From my hometown of Oakland, California, there came photographs of Brianna Noble on her huge, seventeen-hand horse, Dapper Dan,

George Floyd Uprising 2020: From Slavery to Freedom, page 4, 2020, ink and collage on paper, 12″ × 9½″. I savored the national outpouring of indignation over the murder of George Floyd in Minneapolis and the persistent pattern of police brutality against Black people. I wish I could track down the originator of the apt phrase "great White awakening" for 2020, an important dimension of the year that proclaimed that Black Lives Matter.

Juneteenth 1865: From Slavery to Freedom, page 12, 2020, ink and collage on paper, 12″ × 9½″. In 2020 the previously local (Texas, California) Black holiday commemorating the date when enslaved people in Texas finally learned of emancipation received national recognition. Rooted in the history of Texas, Juneteenth celebrations prominently featured people on horseback.

leading protesters and bearing a Black Lives Matter sign. Noble knew what she was doing, saying, "No one can ignore a Black woman on top of a horse." Her image reappeared nationally, internationally, as above the caption, "*Aktivistin Noble bei einer Demonstration gegen Polizeigewalt in Oakland,*" in Germany's *Der Spiegel* newsmagazine.

Additional photos of Black demonstrators on horseback from Los Angeles and Houston quickly followed, along with quotes from the Compton Cowboys and Cowgirls confirming their decades-long history. There's even a Federation of Black Cowboys in New York City, founded in 1994, at the border between Brooklyn and Queens.

Most Americans don't know the history of Black cowboys, even though in the heyday of cattle drives from Texas to Midwestern meat processors, Black cowboys represented about a quarter of the workers on horseback. After railroads replaced overland cattle drives early in the twentieth century, Black cowboys like Nat Love and Bill Pickett turned to the rodeo circuit, where you're most likely to encounter professional Black cowboys and cowgirls today. Cleo Hearn founded the American Black Rodeo Association in 1971, which became the more inclusive Cowboys of Color in 1995. In 1984 Lu Vason founded the annual Bill Pickett Invitational Rodeo, named in honor of the turn-of-the-twentieth-century inventor of rodeo bulldogging, or steer wrestling. The Oakland Black Cowboy Association is nearly half a century old. Black rodeos are far older than Lil Nas X's blockbuster hit "Old Town Road," but the hit record broke color barriers in country music and stirred curiosity about Black cowboys.

An attraction to Black people on horseback is something I share with millions of others, as an expression of this moment's protests and perhaps, I dare add, of hope. There's more, though, for me, as my anti-racist solidarity turned intensely personal. Black Lives Matter photos of Black people on horseback brought my autobiography to the surface of my consciousness, as images elicited a memory of my late father.

When I was a girl in the 1950s, my father would take me horseback riding in San Pablo, which was still totally rural at the time. For him, these outings recalled the joy of boyhood, riding his own blue roan horse in rural Spring, Texas. Both my parents were Texans, united early on by their determination to leave Texas's mean-spirited segregation. In Oakland they brought me up as a Californian, never sending me back to Texas for summers to reinforce my Texan roots. Of course there were their old friends, also migrants from Texas and Louisiana, their love of certain foods—crab gumbo, head cheese, Texas-style barbecue, and little hot Texas tamales—but little else to make me identify with Texas. Like my mother, I was bookish as a girl. But for my father and me, horseback riding was every Saturday's treat.

In art school many years ago I made an etching and spit bite print about my horseback riding. And then, I once again forgot my tie to this Texas of the West and to my father's equestrian identity. My claim on this Western identity has been something I barely feel, for simply being Black imposes a sectional identity that is Southern. Since my youth, a generation of immigrants has added the Caribbean and Africa as places of recognizable Black roots. But the West? Not much. Texas is Western, but the Blackest part of Texas in historical memory is Juneteenth, the folk holiday (on its way to official recognition) commemorating the 1865 date when Texans learned of their emancipation. When my parents' Texan origin comes to mind, I usually think Texas = South. Yet horseback riding is Texas = West. No matter where they were born, the legendary Black cowboys of history, of cattle drives and rodeos, came out of Texas.

For me now, to recall my father on horseback, my father as a cowboy, is to reclaim my own personal San Pablo–Californian–Texan past. My reawakening faces down the Whitewashed history of Americans—Native Americans as well as African Americans—on horseback. Like so many facets of US history, cowboy history has been lily-Whited-out, via the movies' exaltation of the cowboy as a White man.

In so many ways, too much of US history reads as a story of White men. This is about to change. Although the current upheavals have begun with reforming policing, that's only a start. History is being remade, including the history of the West. This new history, visualized in images of Black women and men on horseback, brings me into more personal, more intimate connection with the political pro-

Memory Piece, 2007, etching and spit bite on paper, 12″ × 8¼″. I made this print at
SUNY Plattsburgh in the fall after we had moved my parents into their continuing care
facility in Oakland. I was thinking of them a lot and remembering our lives together in
the Bay Area in the twentieth century. Juneteenth in 2020 brought the memory and
my print back to mind.

tests that demand wide-ranging, far-reaching improvements in our national life. If the United States can move away from institutional racism and police brutality, millions of my fellow and sister citizens will savor their own complex identities within the comradeship of community.

June 2020

It Shouldn't Be This Close.
But There's Good News, Too.

In the long lines of 2020's voters, I see hope.

M Y PEOPLE ARE WRINGING THEIR HANDS and tearing their hair out over the early presidential election returns: How could it be so close?

After all we've been through, with the lying and the White nationalists and the children in cages and the 230,000-plus dead from Covid-19, how could tens of millions of our fellow citizens still have voted for Mr. Trump?

I don't know, though I nod along with some of the guesses: White resentment, evangelical Christianity, macho-masculinity, anti-abortion, the fate of retirement accounts and restaurant jobs.

This question and its possible answers were not upmost in my mind's eye just now, for I focused on images of voters of all political beliefs, queuing up in circumstances as varied as rain in Georgia, cold in Montana, and heat in Arizona. Old people with their walkers standing patiently for hours. Indigenous Americans on horseback riding ten miles to vote. Parents, their kids on their shoulders. Lines stretching for blocks, nearly as long as the lines of cars at food pantries a few months ago. The vertical shapes of Americans standing in wait to vote one after another, in their masks and, for the most part, socially distanced. An estimated one hundred million voters cast their votes early, with rounds of applause often greeting first-time voters.

These images of this US election seemed familiar to me, but foreign, recalling other elections in other places, such as South Africa in 1994 at the ending of apartheid. South Africans stood with stunning patience, outdoors in the elements, as though voting expressed an existential need that overrode bodily comfort.

What was I witnessing now? Americans in 2020 reenacting the South African voters of 1994?

In my visual imagination, images of such determined voters come mostly from other places. The important exceptions are Southern— the American South in the 1960s, where Black voters stood in bunched-up lines in Birmingham and Selma, Alabama, to cast votes after the bloody, yearslong campaign for civil rights and the enactment of the Voting Rights Act of 1965. In serried ranks, the opposite of our Covid-19 distancing, they squeezed into newly accessible civic spaces.

The American historian in me can reach further back to envision determined voting, to Reconstruction, to the image on the cover of *Harper's Weekly* of November 1867, with A. R. Waud's illustration of Black men lined up to deposit ballots into partisan urns. At the front of the line stands an old graybeard in ragged clothing, workingmen's tools in his pocket. He is dark-skinned, evidently formerly enslaved. Behind him stands a light-skinned dandy in curls and cravat, and behind him, a decorated Union soldier. These three lead a line of voters of varied classes and darkness of skin. This *Harper's* image used to seem so time-bound to me, so clearly belonging, with the 1960s images, to our American past, assuming the United States is not like that anymore.

The congratulatory notion of American exceptionalism doesn't usually tempt me. There's just too much bloodshed and antidemocracy to make me think that Americans somehow avoided the perils of class conflict and hereditary aristocracy. What is White supremacy if not a hereditary aristocracy based on the ideology of race? Nonetheless, I take pride in what my fellow Americans have now pulled off, so far at least. An upwelling of faith in the epitome of citizenship, voting.

Despite the erection of walls around businesses and even the White House, this election and its reckoning are unrolling peacefully. This is not to be taken for granted in the world we live in. Other countries routinely experience political violence. In the United States, we don't expect that, and our exemption is not to be taken for granted. Americans should be proud of the marvel of peaceable elections.

I realize that quoting a taxi driver is a tired journalistic trope, but let me share the observation of my most memorable taxi driver, who was taking me home in the fall of 2000. He was listening to *All Things Considered* and said he was following the outcome of the presidential election, whose settlement in Florida seemed interminable to us both. The driver, who was new to America, was following this story with admiration, struck as he was by its character, its lack of resorts to arms. I hadn't thought of it that way, having taken for granted this feature of American democracy.

But what about now? As I write, the outcome of the 2020 presidential election has not been determined. People are afraid. Walls have gone up. Some are rattling their automatic weapons and telegraphing their readiness to take to the streets. Will our exemption from fear hold? Or will these armed protesters—like those invading the Michigan State Capitol in April, May, and September—waving Confederate flags reappear? Will those advised to stand down no longer stand back? So far, we remain within my taxi driver's scenario of settlement according to law. But much depends upon leadership. As I write, President Trump has falsely claimed victory, cited voter fraud, and promised legal challenges to official state results.

A wink toward Proud Boys and Boogaloos might well end this current run of American exceptionalism and take us back not only to the practices of other, less democratic countries, but also to our own shameful past of violent disfranchisement.

November 2020

After the Riot

SOME FORTY YEARS AGO I was a Harvard graduate student research-ing the dissertation that became my first book, *Exodusters: Black Migration to Kansas after Reconstruction* (1977). My field was nineteenth-century Southern history, my topic the conditions at the end of Reconstruction that prompted tens of thousands of Southern-ers to leave their homes for Kansas, the state they knew as Free Kan-sas. These Louisianians, Mississippians, Texans, Tennesseans, and Kentuckians were refugees from the terrorism that, quote, unquote, *redeemed* Southern states and restored the power of Democrats. My dissertation and book were considered Black, not American, history.

"Redemption's" tools were murder and intimidation, what we call terrorism, for Redeemers were well organized and well armed. As a Black Republican Louisianian testified to the US Senate,

The white people in Louisiana are better armed and equipped now than during the war, and they have a better standing army now in the State of Louisiana than was ever known in the State . . . You see them parade the streets of New Orleans with their gray uniforms on, and with their improved Winchester rifles and their Gatling guns, and they have now got everything

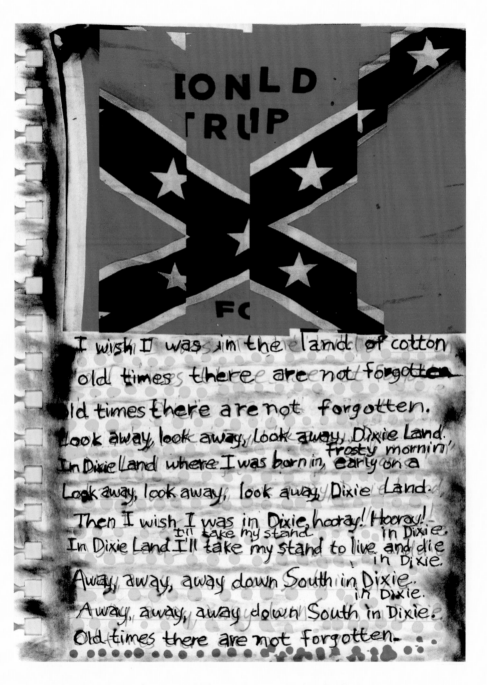

Trump in Dixie: From Slavery to Freedom, page 8, 2020, ink and collage on paper, 12″ × 9½″. Page 8 of my artist's book on protest, memory, and celebration during 2020's year of upheaval.

except the rebel flag—even to the gray uniform. (*Exodusters,* p. 23)

I find it interesting that at this point, Redeemers were not parading under a Confederate flag. That would come later, even much later.

I won't take you through the gruesome scenes of carnage in my book, but before I leave *Exodusters,* let me quote part of its flap copy, words of my editor at Knopf, Ashbel Green, saying that my account draws "on neglected primary sources" and that it testified to "the spirit of a movement that has previously been denied its rightful place in American history." The historical record existed, but it had not previously been publicized. And even after I publicized it, my book was exiled from American history and Southern history, relegated to the then minor field of Black history. This, after all, was the 1970s.

I researched my dissertation in Widener Library in the aftermath of upheaval—no, not the aftermath, for upheaval was all still going on. Upheaval around the right to vote in states like Mississippi and upheaval over the Vietnam War. No sooner had the Civil Rights Act of 1964 and the Voting Rights Act of 1965 seemingly assured Black Americans full citizenship than carnage in Vietnam divided the country anew. Much of the opposition to the war revolved around the draft and the colonial nature of the conflict. Less often noted was the near novelty of fully integrated American armed forces.

Until President Harry Truman's Executive Order 9981 in 1948, the US armed forces had been either exclusionary or segregated. The very new fact of multiracial forces attracted attention, notably from Thomas A. Johnson (1928–2008), a pioneering Black journalist who covered Black service members for *The New York Times.* In 1968 and 1969 Johnson published several articles on the Negro in the Vietnam War. He noted the troops' spirit of interracial comradery. He also took note of the presence of outright racism and White supremacy.

White racial animus appeared in journalism as a racial problem, therefore as something to be thrown onto the Black pile, where it remained with my sources and analysis of the White political violence that ended Reconstruction. Neither the White political violence of the 1870s nor White nationalism in the armed forces in the 1960s made its way into the broader national consciousness as American—as opposed to Black—political issues.

We are now nearly a century and a half from the end of Reconstruction and a generation or two from the Vietnam War. In the intervening years, politics in the US has become ever more subject to media attention, as the media have become more varied and pervasive.

The French language has a word for the intensification of visibility and attention paid to current events: French says politics has been *médiatisé*. An awkward translation speaks of politics' being mediatized.

Our recent public life has indeed been intensely mediatized, so that we see not only images of current events, but we hear their soundtracks accompanying moving images. Mediatization has crystalized images into indices of our recent past—of the 2020 election, of the 2021 runoffs, of the Capitol riot—into emblems carrying symbolic meaning. The intense mediatization of the politics of recent months has recolorized American politics, has recolorized American democracy, by exposing to the great American public the American-ness of issues that used to be hidden away as uniquely Black history and uniquely Black concerns.

So on the one hand, my 1970s sense of writing ancient political history has proven false. Militarized political violence is not a relic of the American past. Here it is with us again, in not only the Capitol riot of January 6, but also the besieging of state capitols in Oregon and Michigan.

But in another way, what we are living through now is new; the intense mediatiziation of the twenty-first century has emblematized American democracy and colorized it with striking intensity. On the one side, we have the exercise of voting rights crystalized in the symbol of the state of Georgia, where a grass-roots movement personalized in the figure of one Black woman, Stacey Abrams, turned out thousands of voters standing in long lines to vote in November and again in January. Those voters were not exclusively Black, but the passionate determination of Black voters colorized as Black the fundamental act of democratic citizenship: voting.

On the other side was an insurrectionist mob intending to overturn the results of the presidential election through an assault on the home of American representative democracy, the Capitol. The face of this insurrection was not only angrily White, but also militarized through its remarkable cohort of White veterans.

In short, the highly mediatized events of the last few months have colorized American democracy around voting. Voting is Black. Pro-democracy is colorized Black. Overturning the results of voting is White. Antidemocracy has been colorized White. What, in a nation whose history is intensely racial and racist, is the future of democracy when it's colorized Black?

February 2021

From 1872 to 1876 in the Space of One Year

DURING THIS YEAR OF 2021, I've been going around smiling, telling my friends that I feel like I'm living in 1872. As a historian, I know that 1872 was a high point of Reconstruction in the South, a moment when it looked as though true democracy had arrived in a region that before the Civil War had had the greatest disparities of income and wealth—between immensely wealthy planters and enslaved workers without wages or possessions—and the greatest political polarization: not only were all women disfranchised, but also men identified as Negro could not vote. Reconstruction promised to turn much of that around by enfranchising Black men.

Reconstruction legislatures did try some good policies, such as public schooling and, through the Freedmen's Bureau, enforcing employment contracts. For the first time in the South, race did not bar men elected to office from taking their places in local and state legislatures. Promising indeed.

During this year of 2021, I had been basking in the anti-racist upheaval of 2020. Yes, the pandemic saddened me, the illness, the death, the economic crisis that left hundreds of thousands hungry and threatened with homelessness. But the largest public demonstrations in memory brought Americans into the streets against police brutality and for racial justice. Unlike the civil rights manifestations of the 1950s and 1960s, this time it wasn't just Black people and a few of our non-Black allies in the streets. This time it was Americans of all races and ages, all over the country.

In its apparent depth and breadth, the anti-racist reckoning that followed also felt new to me. By now even the overpowering Robert E. Lee monument in the capital of the Confederacy has come down, part of a nationwide questioning of the meanings of the symbols we have chosen to embody our civic identity. No longer can the champions of a nation dedicated to the permanence of slavery dominate public spaces of Americans of many races and ethnicities.

In national politics, the Biden-Harris administration has been seeking to enact policies that I favor, from protecting voting rights to addressing climate change to supporting the well-being of children. I haven't noticed a widespread application of the term "Reconstruction," or "Third Reconstruction" (the "Second Reconstruction" had been applied to the civil rights legislation of the 1960s). Nonetheless, in the arenas of business and culture, diversity and equity seemed to be meaningfully addressed. Here I was, feeling as hopeful as 1872, even though I know what came after 1872.

We know now what came after 1872. In nineteenth-century prevailing parlance, it was "Redemption." "Redemption" was the work of terrorists on the ground, of bloodshed and intimidation. On the national level, it was the Tilden-Hayes compromise after the contested election of 1876 that withdrew the last federal troops from the still reconstructed states of Florida, South Carolina, and Louisiana. In the US Supreme Court, it was also the *Slaughterhouse* cases of 1873, which reoriented the protections of the Fourteenth Amendment from people to corporations, from voting rights to property rights.

We are at a pivotal point in our Third Reconstruction, as Democrats, now the party of civil rights, are being urged to jettison voting rights in order to court White voters without college degrees. As in the presidential election of 2016, the argument is couched in terms of class, not race, when class is interpreted in terms of education and applies only to White people. It's not said that White people without college degrees don't care about Black people's access to the ballot. It's not said that White people without college degrees prefer to keep the pre-2020 racial order intact. In pundit language, "class" means the mass of White people.

But what happens if Democrats don't stress the causes that Black voters care about? Would Black voters turn out massively, as they did in 2020 for the Biden-Harris ticket (and, as Biden acknowledged, Black voters had delivered his margin of victory)? Between the disregard of White voters without college degrees and declining enthusiasm from Black voters of all classes, national Democrats are doomed. Once again, just to make sure, the forces of Redemption are resorting to terrorism, as at the Capitol on January 6, 2021. Emboldened by congressional Republicans, the Redeemers promise a return, in the states and in the nation.

We may not be in 1877 yet, but pundits are preparing its way, reinterpreting "class" to mean not upsetting White people's place in the racial/cultural order. Our "Third Redemption" aims to undermine voting rights, a foundation of American citizenship whose history is racialized. For now, though, I'm savoring my 1872, with its promise of multiracial, multicultural American citizenship.

January 2022

Improving American Democracy Means Working Locally for the Common Good

---

WHEN I THINK OF THE FATE of American democracy in 2050, I can't help showing my roots as a historian, but at the same time I'm not able to look past the behemoth overshadowing our future as humans: global warming and its attendant climate disasters. The genocide of Indigenous Americans, a series of assaults and democratic failures, has contributed to our climate's endangerment. Had Indigenous Americans been able to influence the nature of democracy in the United States, we may well have avoided the excessive development of and reliance on fossil fuels that imperil the environment today. Before the lost role of Indigenous Americans in the American environment was recognized, I remember mid-twentieth-century visions of the future that imagined superhighways to everywhere and cars that could fly. Highways and cars looked better before the cost of those highways to people whose homes and businesses were demolished was widely known, as they are more likely to be now. We're no longer able to regard the future as myopically as we did before the horrors of climate change became obvious and the disasters of Trump-time prompted fears for the future of American democracy. So when *The New Republic* asks whether continued union is really possible, I hear dread. I hear it stopping short of what comes next, the scary phrase "civil war."

I know people who fear civil war as ultimate disaster. Not me. I look back at the Civil War of 1861–1865, which killed at least 620,000 combatants, as a human calamity. But death is not the Civil War's entire meaning. The Civil War got rid of slavery, and war was probably the only means of ending the crimes of enslavement. The Civil War also added three Amendments—the Thirteenth, Fourteenth, and Fifteenth—to the United States Constitution, thereby improving an American democracy that definitely needed improvement. Today's American democracy, even though further improved since the mid-nineteenth century, can still stand improvement, so long as Republicans can lose the popular vote but still hold the presidency and appoint a majority of justices to the Supreme Court. The resulting Republican Supreme Court is about to finish off one of the twentieth century's signal democratic improvements: the 1965 Voting Rights Act. Nonetheless, at no point can we look backward to a time when US democracy was more robust or complete than it is now, threatened though it be by the kinds of armed attacks and election denial not seen since the nineteenth century.

In the year and a half since the January 6, 2021, assault on the United States Capitol, an overwhelmingly White riot, Republicans have solidified their embrace of the assault, just as they embrace former president Donald Trump's profoundly antidemocratic lies about a "stolen election." It's as though Republicans are bent on reminding us of their ever more obvious rejection of democracy's crucial symbol and central act: voting.

In November 2020, millions of Americans voted, with images widely broadcast of voters, especially voters of color, standing in long lines in order to do so. In Georgia, the contest for US senator was between a Trump-endorsed White Republican and Raphael Warnock, a Black Democrat allied with Stacey Abrams's New Georgia Project for voting rights. The right to vote is closely associated with the Democratic Party, and voting rights are widely considered a Black, not a White, issue, even though universal suffrage is not supposed to be limited by color.

As long as we have a party of Republicans perceived as White and a party of Democrats perceived as Black, as we do now, politicized versions of race remain a threat to American democracy, especially given the well-armed and fanatically loyal nature of the Republican base. I can easily envision more antidemocratic actions from Republicans to come in the near future, for their hold on state, local, and national offices seems secure for now. It is also possible that massive climate-disaster-induced migration will encourage the kind of antidemocratic responses that have occurred in Sweden (see the success of the Sweden Democrats) and eastern Germany (see the success of the AfD, Alternative für Deutschland). At the same time, I see important countervailing tendencies in the United States that by 2050 could very well make this country's democracy stronger than it is now.

I take my cues from Heather McGhee's revealing 2021 book, *The Sum of Us: What Racism Costs Everyone and How We Can Prosper Together*. Starting from the swimming pools that twentieth-century racist localities preferred to fill in rather than desegregate, McGhee reminds us that paved-over swimming pools penalized everyone, not just aspiring swimmers who were Black. Those bigoted actions deprived "the sum of us" access to a public good. In more recent years, McGhee finds something new, a recognition of that loss. She tells of people who have done something that seems hard in our racialized public sphere: overcome racial barriers to work locally toward results that benefit "us all."

McGhee finds her examples in places like Lewiston, Maine; Richmond, California; and New Haven, Connecticut, where local actions, the foundation of democracy, provide a "solidarity dividend" that benefits everyone. Immigrants from several African countries regenerated the dying town of Lewiston, and the Maine People's Alliance, founded in 1982 and now 32,000 members strong, spearheaded the ballot provision that brought universal Medicaid to the state in 2017, after the governor had refused to do so. The environmental movement that began in the South in the 1980s gave rise to organizations such as Just Transition Alliance; the Poor People's Campaign; Dallas Truth, Racial Healing & Transformation; the Florida Rights Restoration Coalition; Fight for $15; California's Richmond Progressive Alliance; and so many other local and state-wide coalitions that work across racial and ethnic boundaries for public ends such as environmental justice and an expanded safety net. McGhee concludes that "when people have a chance to create a bond that's not based on skin color or culture, what they actually connect on are the things they value in common."

Unfortunately, given the central role of entertainment value in US news, it's far easier to learn about QAnon, Oath Keepers, and election deniers than about peaceful, multiracial coalitions for the public good. One nation-wide, multiracial, multiethnic coalition is in full view, however, and that's the Democratic Party, which has won the popular vote in seven of the last eight presidential elections. Joe Biden and Kamala Harris campaigned on a promise to defend voting rights and pursue environmental justice; in 2021, they established the White House Environmental Justice Advisory Council. Federal policy has included the term "environmental justice" since the 1990s. At this point, however, the severity of global warming's wildfires, droughts, and floods have made the need all the more visible and all the more deserving of being addressed equitably.

Although climate disaster can threaten democracy, climate may play a pro-democracy role by forcing us to see that we are all in this together and encouraging collaborative work toward environmental ends. The example of the Richmond Alliance's work for environmental justice may well say more about the future of a multiracial US democracy than the actions of a group of heavily armed White nationalists.

Am I "hopeful" or "optimistic" about the future of our democracy? No, I am not. I have lived as a Black American too long to dare to be hopeful about my country's politics, for hopes are bound to be dashed on the rocks of racial violence and discrimination. At the same time, I don't expect a future civil war or a steep, long-term destruction of US democracy. I lived through the era of McCarthyism, and my studies in history taught me about the slave and Jim Crow eras. I do fear more antidemocratic assaults in the near future, as long as the cult of Trump entrances the White party. Meanwhile, masses of Americans are learning to work together to spread what Heather McGhee calls the "solidarity dividend" that accrues to Americans working together locally for their common good. The "solidarity dividend" is good for democracy, good for us all.

December 2022

HISTORY—SOUTHERN HISTORY

Soul Murder and Slavery

TOWARD A FULLY LOADED COST ACCOUNTING

WE ALL KNOW ON AN INTUITIVE LEVEL that violence is insepara-
ble from slavery, but historians rarely trace the descent of that
conjunction. On another level, journalists have taken note of
regional differences in homicide rates. In a 1998 article in *The New
York Times,* the journalist Fox Butterfield addressed the South's permanently high murder rate: the states of the former Confederacy all
figured in the top twenty states for murder, with the highest rate in
Louisiana: 17.5 murders per 100,000 people. Overall, the Southern
murder rate nearly doubled that of the Northeast.[1]

Butterfield advanced several explanations, based on the views of
nineteenth-century observers such as Alexis de Tocqueville and Frederick Law Olmsted, who blamed the prevalence of guns and a frontier mentality. Historians pointed to the Scotch-Irish culture of many
Southerners, which disposed them toward whisky drinking and family feuding, a system of "primal honor," and a touchiness that slavery
reinforced. None indicted the long-standing ideals of obedience and
submission, the values of slavery, and the acceptance of violence as a
means of enforcement.

In this essay I accept the unhappy task of probing slavery's legacy
of violence. My aim is to examine the implications of soul murder (a
phrase to which I will return momentarily) and use them to question
the entireness of historians' descriptions of American society during

the era of slavery. My hope is that a more complete accounting—what bookkeepers would term a "fully loaded cost accounting"—of slavery's costs, most notably the tragic overhead costs that were reckoned in the currency of physical abuse and family violence, will yield a fuller comprehension of our national experience. With the broad geography of American slavery in mind, I take as my theme "Soul Murder and Slavery."

This work is interdisciplinary, drawing on the history of American slavery, on feminist scholarship on women, the family, and the workplace, and on the thought of sociologists and psychologists regarding children. My questions have their roots in second-wave feminism of the 1960s, which influenced the rewriting of history generally. By focusing attention on women's lives, feminist scholarship has made women visible rather than taken for granted and queried the means by which societies forge gender out of the physical apparatus of sex. While some feminist thinkers have analyzed women's writing and gender, other intellectuals and activists have turned a spotlight on a protected, potent social institution: the family. Even though families, as the site of identity formation, shape the elaboration of politics, and even though public policy profoundly influences families, family dynamics have generally been treated as private and separate from the public realm and have not traditionally figured prominently in the writing of history.

Historiographical blindness toward families still persists, even though the source material is abundant. Turning new eyes on evidence that has been at hand forever, feminist historians are able to hear subaltern voices and recognize phenomena that had not previously been investigated seriously.[2] What were long termed "discipline" and "seduction" of the young and powerless, who were described as feckless and oversexed, we can now call by their own names: child abuse, sexual abuse, sexual harassment, rape, battering. Psychologists aggregate the effects of these all-too-familiar practices in the phrase "soul murder," which may be summed up as depression, lowered self-esteem, and anger.

Soul murder has a long genealogy, going back to folk beliefs in Europe and Africa about the possibility of stealing or killing another person's soul. Soul murder appeared in connection with the 1828 story of Kaspar Hauser, who, having spent his childhood imprisoned alone in a dark cellar, emerged as an emotionally crippled young adult unable to talk or walk. Before emerging into the light, Hauser had glimpsed only one other person, his jailer, to whom he wished to return. Within psychoanalytic literature, the classic, anguished phrasing of "soul murder" as the violation of one's inner being, the extinguishing of one's identity, including sexual identity, comes initially from Anselm von Feuerbach's 1832 account of Hauser and from Daniel Paul Schreber's 1903 *Memoirs of My Nervous Illness,* inspired by Feuerbach and commented on, in turn, by Sigmund Freud and Jacques Lacan. Schreber's memoir made him the world's most famous paranoid.[3]

"Soul murder" also appears in the title of a book by a professor of psychiatry at the New York University School of Medicine, Leonard Shengold (*Soul Murder: The Effects of Childhood Abuse and Deprivation,* 1989). The "abuse" in the subtitle can be violent and/or sexual, which presents children with too much sensation to bear. "Deprivation," as in the case of Kaspar Hauser, refers to neglect that deprives children of enough attention to meet their psychic needs.

Sexual abuse, emotional deprivation, and physical and mental torture can lead to soul murder, and soul-murdered children's identity is compromised; they cannot register what it is that they want and what it is that they feel. Like Kaspar Hauser, they often identify with the person who has abused them, and they may express anger toward themselves and others. Abused persons are more at risk for the development of an array of psychological problems that include depression, anxiety, self-mutilation, suicide attempts, sexual problems, and drug and alcohol abuse.[4] Victims of soul murder do not inevitably turn into abusers—there is no direct or predictable line of cause and effect—but people who have been abused or deprived as children grow up at risk psychologically.

We surely cannot translate contemporary psychology directly into the mentalities of eighteenth- and nineteenth-century societies, because many aspects of life that we regard as psychological were, in earlier times, connected to religion. Spirituality then, as now, varied considerably from person to person and from group to group; with the passage of time, religious sensibilities were subject to fundamental alterations. American religion generally changed in the aftermath of the Great Awakening of the early eighteenth century and the Second Great Awakening of the early nineteenth century. The various evangelicals, especially Methodists and Baptists, deeply influenced what we would call the psychology of Americans, as well as the terms in which they envisioned and communicated with their gods.

Despite differences of mentality wrought by greater or lesser religiosity, psychology—when used carefully, perhaps gingerly—provides a valuable means of understanding people and families who cannot be brought to the analyst's couch. Ideally historians could enter a kind of science fiction virtual reality in which we could hold intelligent conversations with the dead, then remand them to their various hells, purgatories, and heavens and return to our computers. Lacking this facility, we can only read current practitioners and enter the archives with our eyes wide open.

Even without the benefit of an esoteric knowledge of psychology, we readily acknowledge the existence of certain conventions associated with slavery: the use of physical violence to make the enslaved obedient and submissive, the unquestioned right of owners to use the people they owned in whatever ways they wished. But we may need to be reminded that these habits also translate into a set of ideals that were associated with White women in middle- and upper-class families and into another set of ideals identified with evangelical religion. Submission and obedience, the core values of slavery, were also the key words of patriarchy and piety.

Because the standard of slavery calibrated values in other core institutions, slavery deserves recognition as one of the fundamental influences on American family mores and, by extension, on American society as a whole. Religion, democracy, the frontier, patriarchy, and mobility are all recognized as having played their part in the making of American families and American history. Slavery also counted, and not merely for Americans who experienced it as captive, unpaid laborers.

No matter how much American convention exempts Whites from paying any costs for the enslavement of Blacks, the implications of slavery did not stop at the color line; rather, slavery's theory and praxis permeated the whole of slaveholding society. Without seeking to establish one-to-one relationships or direct lines of causality, I will pose questions and suggest answers that may foster more comprehensive and feminist thinking about American history. Ironically, perhaps, names that have only recently been coined help reinterpret the past.

The fields of study focusing on child abuse, sexual harassment, and sexual abuse were born in the 1960s and 1970s. Over the decades, these fields have grown and supplied therapists, medical doctors, recovering victims, lawyers, and feminists, some of whom were looking for the roots of women's impaired self-esteem, others of whom were seeking to right the wrongs that women have suffered in patriarchal families and in the workplace. I suppose the appearance of professionals who profit from suits over child abuse, sexual abuse, and sexual harassment is inevitable in a capitalist society. Nonetheless, the profit-making aspect of the phenomenon of recall has provoked a good deal of commentary about suppressed memory and false memory. The debate came to center mainly on women who could afford therapists and lawyers and whose family mores and career chances encouraged the suppression rather than the reporting of unacceptable memories. Much commentary on child sexual abuse—usually the most discussed form of violence against the young—involves what the skeptical philosopher Ian Hacking terms "memoro-politics." His and the psychologist Carol Tavris's doubts are institutionalized in the False Memory Syndrome Foundation, founded in Philadelphia in 1992.[5] With all its visibility, the controversy over false memory obscures the subjectivity of enslaved people, whose victimization is well documented and uncontested.

American habits of thought—what the Marxist philosophers and critics Louis Althusser and Pierre Macherey call "ideology"—have rendered the experience of the enslaved virtually invisible in the literature of child abuse. No one at all disputes the fact that these children and women endured hurts that they did not forget, yet these victims do not currently figure in the consideration of the effects of child abuse and sexual harassment. An example is to be found in the widely acclaimed work of Judith Herman, one of the premier analysts of sexual abuse. Herman includes a chapter entitled "Captivity" in her second book, *Trauma and Recovery* (1992). Here the captivity in question is figurative rather than literal. Herman does not acknowledge the history of the literal captivity of millions of enslaved Americans over several generations.[6] Actual slavery is not there.

For most scholars of child abuse and sexual abuse, slavery possesses neither a literal meaning nor consequences; it serves only as a potent, negative metaphor. As a historian familiar with the institution that existed throughout most of American territory into the early nineteenth century, I *do* want to think literally: I want to investigate the consequences of child abuse and sexual abuse on an entire society in which the beating and raping of enslaved people was neither secret nor metaphorical.

The first step is to think about the enslaved as people with all the psychological characteristics of human beings, with childhoods and adult identities formed during youthful interaction with others. As ordinary as is the assumption that White people evolve psychologically from childhood to adulthood, to speak of Black people in psychological terms can be problematical. This history has a history. Much of scholars' and readers' reluctance to deal with Black people's psychology goes back to the 1960s debate over Stanley Elkins's *Slavery: A Problem in American Institutional and Intellectual Life* (1959), which provoked extensive criticism and revision.

Acknowledging the "spiritual agony" inherent in American slavery, Elkins compared slavery in the American South with Nazi concentration camps, in which, he thought, an all-encompassing system of repression infantilized people who had been psychologically healthy. Elkins wrote that on Southern plantations and in Nazi concentration camps, inmates "*internalized*" their owners' attitudes. Drawing a flawed analogy between concentration camps, which existed for a few years, and enslavement, which persisted over many generations and was psychologically more porous, Elkins argued that the closed system of slavery produced psychologically crippled adults who were docile, irresponsible, loyal, lazy, humble, and deceitful; in short, who were Sambos. With regard to both enslavement and concentration camps, Elkins's methodology was more psychological than archival, and he also overlooked resistance in both contexts. In the American South, Elkins ignored the significance of enslaved families and communities and the long tradition of resistance and revolt, as chronicled in Herbert Aptheker's *American Negro Slave Revolts* (1943).[7]

The scholarship appearing in the 1970s and 1980s provided a more complete view of the enslaved and their families than Elkins had presented in the broken-up character of Sambo. Yet since the thunder and lightning of the Elkins controversy—even after the appearance of extensive revisionist writing—scholars and laypeople have avoided, sometimes positively resisted, the whole calculation of slavery's psychological costs. The Sambo problem was solved through the pretense that Black people do not have psyches.

Prevailing wisdom says that strong Black people functioned as members of a group, "the Black community," as though Black people shared a collective psyche whose only perception was racial, as if race obviated the need to discuss Black people's subjective development as individuals. Within this version of the Black community, the institution of "the Black family" appears as preternaturally immune to the brutality inherent in enslavement. Black patriarchy with a human face appears in much of this post-Elkins writing, particularly in the case of the well-intentioned work of Herbert Gutman, which refuted a 1965 report by Daniel Patrick Moynihan that blamed poverty and criminality on Black families.[8] In family groups or as individuals, the enslaved emerge from historians' pages in the pose of lofty transcendence over racist adversity. Any analysis hinting that Black people suffered psychological trauma as a result of the vicious physical and emotional practices that slavery entailed seemed tantamount to recapitulating Elkins and admitting the defeat of the race at the hands of bigots.

Rejecting that reasoning is imperative because denying enslaved people psychological personhood impoverishes the study of everyone in slaveholding society. Historians already realize that including enslaved workers as part of the American working classes recasts the labor history of the United States; similarly, envisioning the enslaved as people who developed psychologically sheds new light on the culture of violence in which they matured.

Societies whose economic basis rested on slave production were built on violence, and the calculus of slavery configured society as a whole, as nineteenth-century analysts realized. When proslavery apologists spoke of owners and slaves as belonging to the same family, they were acknowledging the relationship between modes of production, politics, family, and society that three other nineteenth-century European social analysts and commentators, Karl Marx, Friedrich Engels, and Alexis de Tocqueville, also perceived. From very different vantage points and with quite different emphases, Tocqueville in *Democracy in America* and Marx and Engels in *The German Ideology* recognized the influence of the political economy on civil society. For Marx and Engels, "the production of ideas, of conceptions, of consciousness, is at first directly interwoven with the material activity and the material intercourse of men," which they totaled up as "the language of real life." Material existence, they said, shapes the relationships between husbands and wives and between parents and children that we term "family" and that they underlined in the original.[9]

Peering through the lens of political economy, Marx and Engels spoke in the interest of workers, but Tocqueville, who was more comfortable with people of his own privileged class, unabashedly admired the democracy of the United States. Moving among Americans who had flourished since the American Revolution, Tocqueville in his appraisal of the consequences of American institutions was generally positive. He credited American political arrangements with the creation of more democratic relationships within American families, but he also traced democracy's limits. Where there was slavery, he noted, democracy could not do its salutary work. Slavery was "so cruel to the slave," but it was "fatal to the owner," for it attacked American society through opinions, character, and style and devalued the ideals that undergird democratic society.[10]

Marx and Engels may have overestimated the ramifications of the dominant mode of production, and Tocqueville may have held too sanguine a view of the consequences of political democracy within the household, but all three remind us that political and economic life shapes families and households. This point has been rephrased by more recent theorists. Twentieth-century commentators like Louis Althusser modify Marx and Engels's analysis of relations between the economic base and the social superstructure but nonetheless relate the institutions of civil society, including the family, to the political economy. The psychoanalyst Jacques Lacan indicates the crucial role of the family—the role of the father, in particular—in reproducing on a subjective level the power relations of the political economy.[11] When the household was also a work site, the influence of labor relations within families would have been magnified.

Child Abuse and Slavery

Slaveowners, the enslaved, jurists, abolitionists, and historians have all recognized personal violence as a component of the regulation of owned labor; as Charles Pettigrew, a slaveholder, wrote to his son: "It is a pity that . . . Slavery and Tyranny must go together and that there is no such thing as having an obedient and useful Slave, without the painful exercise of undue and tyrannical authority." Tyrannical authority there was in abundance, and enslaved children's parents, even when they were present, could not save their babies. It was as though an enslaved mother's children were not her own. A formerly enslaved man recalled, "Many a day my old mamma has stood by an' watched massa beat her chillun 'till dey bled an' she couldn' open her mouf."[12]

From an entirely different vantage point, Southern judiciaries acknowledged that owners needed and should lawfully exercise total power over people they owned. The central legal tenet of slavery was summed up by a Southern judge: "The power of the owner must be absolute, to render the submission of the slave perfect." Kenneth Stampp entitled the fourth chapter of *The Peculiar Institution* "To Make Them Stand in Fear."[13]

On the personal level, the evidence of this kind of discipline is heartbreaking, whether between owner and owned, enslaved parent and child, or across the generations. When the fugitive narrator

William Wells Brown was a child, he witnessed the harrowing scene of his mother being flogged for going late into the fields. Years later Brown recalled that "the cold chills ran over me, and I wept aloud." Sojourner Truth, who was beaten while enslaved in New York's Hudson Valley in the early nineteenth century, beat her own children—to make them obedient and to stop their hungry cries when her work prevented her from feeding them.[14]

One of the most vivid testimonies of the intergenerational effect of child beating in slavery appears in oral testimony gathered one hundred years after the abolition of slavery. In Theodore Rosengarten's *All God's Dangers,* an old Black Alabamian, Ned Cobb (alias Nate Shaw), laments that his father, Hayes, who had been enslaved for his first fifteen years, beat his children and his wives as he himself had been beaten.[15] Cobb testifies to two kinds of hurt, for in addition to himself having been flogged, he was haunted by his father's brutal attacks on his mother and stepmother.

Owners beat enslaved children to make them into good slaves. Enslaved parents beat children to make them regard obedience as an automatic component of their personal makeup that was necessary for survival in a cruel world, a world in which they were to be first and always submissive. In other words, enslaved parents beat enslaved children to make them into good slaves. The underlying motives of parents and owners did not overlap, but in practice, their aims coincided.

Parents and owners taught enslaved children to quash their anger when they were beaten, for anger was a forbidden emotion for enslaved people to display before owners. A Virginia owner summed up the prevailing wisdom among his peers in these phrases: "They Must obey at all times, and under all circumstances, cheerfully and with alacrity." Suppression of this kind of anger is one of the characteristics of what the psychologist Alice Miller terms the "poisonous pedagogy" of child abuse, and it has certain fairly predictable effects on its victims: feelings of degradation and humiliation, impaired identity formation, suppression of vitality and creativity, deadening of feeling of self, anger, hatred, and self-hatred on the individual level and violence on the social level.[16]

186

Enslaved children, particularly those whose mothers worked in the fields, were also very likely to suffer physical and emotional neglect because their mothers were allowed only a minimum of time off the job with their children. Childcare by people other than mothers could be adequate, as in the case of the young Frederick Douglass, who began his life in the custody of his maternal grandmother. But in other situations, the caretakers of children might be too old, too young, or too infirm to provide adequate supervision. Ex-slave narratives illustrate child-rearing patterns that forced hardworking parents to neglect their children, and that, as a consequence, often denied babies the opportunity to attach securely to a parent or parental figure.[17]

The slave trade, which disrupted an estimated one-third of all enslaved families in the antebellum South, weighed heavily on children and young adults under thirty, when they were most likely to be the parents of young children. Such trauma took a devastating emotional toll, as antislavery writing and iconography illustrate.[18] As a young child in New York State, Sojourner Truth lived with her own parents, but they were chronically depressed as a result of having sacrificed their children to the market, one after the other. Such forfeiture would have been tantamount to having one's child die, and Truth's grieving parents lost ten children to this callous trade.

In slave societies, neglect was routine, abuse was rampant, and anger was to be suppressed. The question regarding the neglect and physical abuse of enslaved children is not whether they took place—everyone agreed that they did—but rather what they meant to the children and adults who experienced them. Did the whipping that was so central a part of child-rearing and the enforcement of discipline among the enslaved affect them and their families as child abuse traumatizes contemporary victims?

There is evidence that the child abuse of slavery imposed enormous costs. The relationship between abuse and repercussion is not simple or predetermined, but the damage is frequent enough to be recognizable. For countless women and children, these injuries were magnified by the intimate nature of the abuse.

Sexual Abuse and Sexual Harassment

Like child beating in slavery, the sexual torment of enslaved women and children has been evident for more than a century. Some of this mistreatment occurred in situations that we now recognize as sexual harassment on the job, and some occurred within households—which were work sites for hundreds of thousands of enslaved women—and with overtones of incest. One well-known figure exemplifies both patterns.

While many ex-slave narratives mention owner-enslaved sexuality, the most extended commentary on the sexual harassment of enslaved women comes from Harriet Jacobs, who was enslaved in Edenton, North Carolina. Writing under the pseudonym "Linda Brent," Jacobs published a narrative in 1861, entitled *Incidents in the Life of a Slave Girl*. Jacobs's character, Linda, becomes the literal embodiment of the enslaved as sexual quarry in the literature of enslavement. We know from the work of the critic Jean Yellin that *Incidents in the Life of a Slave Girl* is autobiography, and that Jacobs's owner harassed her sexually from the time she was thirteen. Her narrative is a story of pursuit, evasion, and, ultimately, escape, although in order to evade her owner, Jacobs had to spend seven years closed up in her grand-mother's tiny attic crawl space, unable to stand up straight, sweltering in the summer, cold in the winter. As portrayed in *Incidents in the Life of a Slave Girl,* much of Jacobs's life in North Carolina revolved around avoiding her owner's advances.

Jacobs says that without her owner's having succeeded in raping her, he inflicted injuries that young women frequently suffered and that we would consider psychological. As she became nubile, she says, her owner began to whisper "foul words in my ear," which robbed her of her innocence and purity, a phenomenon that psychologists call inappropriate sexualization, which encourages a child to interpret her own value primarily in sexual terms. Describing the effect of her own-er's "foul words" and the angry and jealous outbreaks from his legal wife, Jacobs's "mistress," Jacobs says she became, like any enslaved girl in her position, "prematurely knowing in evil things," including life in a household cum work site that was suffused with predation, infidelity, and rage.[19]

Jacobs commits an entire, highly charged chapter of *Incidents in the Life of a Slave Girl* to "The Jealous Mistress." The angry figure of the jealous mistress, frequently ridiculed, seldom seriously investigated, is so common in the literature of slavery as to have become a Southern trope. Perhaps because I have my own jealous mistress, so to speak, I am certain that the figure deserves a longer, much longer look. My jealous mistress is Gertrude Thomas, of Augusta, Georgia, who kept a journal from the time she was fourteen years old in 1848 until 1889, when she was fifty-five.

Although she was a jealous mistress, Gertrude Thomas may also be understood as a victim of adultery. According to the ostensible mores of her community, she stood near the pinnacle of society (as a woman, she was denied space at the very top). She was a plantation mistress in a society dominated by the minuscule proportion of White families who qualified as planters by owning twenty or more people; she was an educated woman at a time when only elite men could take higher education for granted; and she was White in a profoundly racist culture. Yet neither Gertrude Thomas's economic or educational advantages nor her social status protected her from what she saw as sexual competition from inferior women. She knew, as Mary Chesnut and her friends knew, that they were supposed to pretend not to see "what is as plain before their eyes as the sunlight."[20] The deception did not ease the discomfort, for Thomas knew and wrote that White men saw women—whether enslaved or free, wealthy or impoverished, cultured or untutored, Black or White—as interchangeable. She and other plantation mistresses failed to elevate themselves sufficiently as women to avoid the pain of sharing their husbands with women who were owned.

Preoccupied by the issue of competition between women, Thomas realized and recorded with tortuous indirection a central fact of her emotional life: that enslaved women and slaveholding women were in the same sexual marketplace and that in this competition, free women circulated at a discount due to the ready availability of women who could be forced to obey. The existence in the same market for sex of women who were literally property lowered the value of Gertrude Thomas and her mother as sexual partners. The concept of women as property has long been evident to feminists as a powerful means of keeping women subjected.

"The traffic in women," a phrase coined by the early twentieth-century American anarchist Emma Goldman, is shorthand for cultural practices that anthropologists (such as Claude Lévi-Strauss) and psychoanalysts (such as Jacques Lacan) have seen as basic to human nature but that feminists have identified with patriarchy and considered devastating to women. The phrase reappears in a classic 1975 essay by the feminist anthropologist Gayle Rubin, who analyzes the sex/gender system of several different cultures.[21]

Rubin uses the concept of the traffic in women allegorically when she turns to American society, but the notion of such a traffic is useful both literally and metaphorically with regard to American society during its nearly three centuries of slavery. Once again, American history holds a massive, literal traffic in women—and children. Over the course of those ten or more generations, rich White women saw themselves in competition for the attention of husbands whose Black partners were ideal women: enslaved women had to be present when summoned and were conceded no will of their own. Gertrude Thomas knew moments of despair over her husband's infidelities, but if she contemplated suicide, she censored the thought. Testimony from Kentucky captures marital strife more vividly.

Andrew Jackson, an ex-slave narrator (not the president of the United States), had belonged to a fiery preacher he called a "right down blower." Though the owner's preaching moved his congregation to tears, at home he and his wife quarreled bitterly over his attraction to their enslaved cook, Hannah. Jackson recalled hearing the wife accuse the preacher of having gone into the kitchen expressly to be with Hannah, which the preacher denied. "I know you have, you brute," Jackson quotes the wife crying, "I have a great mind to cut my own throat!" To this, Jackson says, the preacher replied, "I really wish you would." The wife understood his meaning: "Yes I presume you do, so that you could run to the kitchen, as much as you please, to see Hannah." Andrew Jackson concluded that slaveholders "had such bad hearts toward one another" because they treated the people they owned so brutally.[22]

At the same time that jealous mistresses were angry over their husbands' adulterous conduct, enslaved women like Harriet Jacobs who were the husbands' prey realized fully that mistresses saw themselves (not the women who were owned) as the victims in such triangles. Enslaved women resented what they envisioned as their mistresses' narcissistic self-pity, and they returned their mistresses' anger in kind. Jacobs's outrage at her mistress is part of a larger phenomenon, for other ex-slave narrators, like Sojourner Truth, and historians, like Kenneth Stampp, Elizabeth Fox-Genovese, and Eugene Genovese, corroborate the existence of a good deal of resentment at jealous mistresses on the part of enslaved women. Enslaved women's anger has etched yet more deeply the unsympathetic portrait of women who owned them. Today we can see that more was at stake than contention over the ultimate title of victim.

What the enslaved could seldom acknowledge and historians have not seen is that attachment often lay at the core of enslaved women's resentment. With enslaved families constantly subject to disruption, mistresses often functioned as mothers—good or bad—to the young women they owned. In this sense, the bitterness that Linda Brent felt as the prey of her owner emerged against her mistress, just as victims of incest often hate their mothers for not saving them from the sexual advances of fathers and stepfathers. The psychiatrist Judith Herman says that many sexually abused children feel deeply betrayed because their mothers or mother figures are not able to protect them. Victims who do not display anger at their abusers may displace their rage on to non-abusing but impotent parental figures: mothers.[23] The psychological dynamics of the heterogeneous households of slavery explicate attitudes and behaviors that cannot be explained if we deny to the enslaved the personhood that we grant to our own contemporaries.

It has been difficult for historians to view interracial households as families and the enslaved as workers and as people, but such understanding places the sexual abuse of enslaved women and children (including boys) within categories that are now familiar and that we now term sexual harassment and assault. One of the founders of the field, Catharine A. MacKinnon, noted in the 1970s that poorer women seem more likely to suffer physical harassment than middle-class and career women, whose abuse is more often verbal.[24] This should alert us to the triple vulnerability of enslaved women; they were among the poorest of working women and members of a race considered inherently inferior, and, if they were domestic servants like Harriet Jacobs, they spent long hours in the company of the men who held ultimate power over them.

Psychologists say that children and young women who are sexually abused, like children who are beaten, tend to blame themselves for their victimization and consequently have very poor self-esteem. They may also see their sexuality as their only means of binding other people to them as friends or allies. Scholars list a series of long-term psychological repercussions of sexual abuse and incest: depression, difficulty sleeping, feelings of isolation, poor self-esteem, difficulty relating to other people, contempt for all women including oneself, revictimization, and impaired sexuality that may manifest itself in behaviors that can appear as frigidity or promiscuity.[25] I doubt that the enslaved possessed an immunity that victims lack today.

It is tempting to see all the enslaved as strong people who recognized the injustice of their treatment and were therefore able to transcend the savagery to which they were subjected from very early ages. However, ex-slave narratives also bear witness to much psychological hurt. What today's psychologists call anger, depression, and problems of self-esteem come through ex-slave narratives and attest to enslaved people's difficulty in securing unqualified trust. The theologian Benjamin Mays discerned the theme of personal isolation that pervaded Black religion and that spiritual songs expressed so movingly. Their titles are embedded in American memory: "Sometimes I Feel Like a Motherless Child," "Nobody Knows the Trouble I've Seen," "I'm a Long Way from Home."[26]

We are used to hearing such sentiments as poignant artistry, but they are also testimonies of desolation. Enslaved people's situation within a system built on violence, disfranchisement, and White supremacy was analogous to that of contemporary victims of abuse, and, as primary documents indicate, some of the enslaved, like people today, responded with self-hatred, anger, and identification with the aggressor. As understandable as such responses would have been, they are not all there is to the story.

Were this analysis to stop here, it might seem to invite a rerun of the controversy over Stanley Elkins's *Slavery*, for I might seem to be saying, like Elkins, that slavery inflicted psychic wounds so severe that the enslaved were massively disabled psychologically. This is *not* a recapitulation of Stanley Elkins, because my arguments exceed Elkins's in two important ways: I insist, first, that enslaved people had two crucial means of support that helped them resist being damaged permanently by the assaults of their owners and their fellows; and second, that owners also inflicted the psychic damage of slavery upon themselves, their White families, and, ultimately, on their entire society.

Enslaved People's Means of Survival

Since the 1959 publication of Elkins's *Slavery*, historians such as John Hope Franklin and Earl E. Thorpe have presented evidence of the ways in which the enslaved seized the initiative and found "elbow-room" within a system that was meant to dehumanize them.[27] Once historians began to seek it, confirmation of enslaved people's resistance and survival appeared in abundance. The testimony comes from enslaved people and from owners, and it affirms that most enslaved women and men were able to survive bondage in a human and humane manner, particularly if they lived where they were surrounded by people who were actual or fictive kin. Historians have concentrated their attention on the half or so of enslaved people in the antebellum South who lived on plantations with twenty or more bondspeople, the people more likely to belong to a community. Enslaved people on plantations did not, however, represent the totality of Americans who were enslaved. So far, unfortunately, the other half of enslaved Southerners and virtually all those in the North, who were surrounded by mostly White people, have received little scrutiny.[28] Enslaved people living in isolation would hardly have benefited from the psychological support that a community of peers could provide.

John Blassingame sees enslaved families as a source of psychic protection from slavery's onslaught and considers families "an important survival mechanism." (Had he been critiquing Elkins's whole argument, Blassingame might have extended this insight to concentration camps, where actual and fictive kin and comrades helped inmates resist their dehumanization.) Deborah Gray White, writing as a feminist, is more explicit, and she explores enslaved women's own community in far more detail. White entitles one chapter of her book *Ar'n't I a Woman? Female Slaves in the Plantation South* (1985) "The Female Slave Network," in which she shows how enslaved women working together created their own internal rank ordering. Although their owners and other Whites might dishonor and mistreat them, enslaved women forged "their own independent definition of womanhood" through their own web of women's relationships, which functioned as an antidote to slavery's degradation.[29]

White and Blassingame are supported by psychologists such as Gail Wyatt and M. Ray Mickey, who explain that the existence of a countervailing value system helps people who are abused resist internalizing their oppressors' devaluation of their worth.[30] Ex-slave narratives from the nineteenth and twentieth centuries make it clear that the enslaved rejected their owners' assumptions that enslaved people were constitutionally inferior as a people and that they deserved to be enslaved.

Historians like Deborah Gray White and John Blassingame have shown that the psychic health of people enslaved on plantations depended largely on another essential emotional counterweight to owners' physical and psychological assaults besides the enslaveds' own families. That second bulwark consisted of a system of evangelical religious beliefs that repudiated the owners' religious and social ideology of White supremacy and Black inferiority. Slave religion also buttressed a countervailing belief system by promising that equity would ultimately prevail in God's world.

During and after slavery, religion was an important means through which powerless people preserved their identity. Scholars such as Albert Raboteau, Gayraud S. Wilmore, and James Cone have shown how Black people forged their own evangelical religion, which could be apocalyptic and reassuring. Wilmore, especially, indicates that a belief in the impending apocalypse, a perennial theme in American evangelicalism, served the particular needs of the Black poor by promising that there would soon come a time when God would judge all people, that he would punish the wicked, who were the slaveowners, and reward the good, who were the enslaved. Cone stresses enslaved people's identification with the crucifixion, which symbolizes Jesus's concern for the oppressed and his repudiation of the hierarchies of this world.[31]

Psychologists have noted that in situations where the individual is totally powerless, faith in a greater power than the self becomes a potent means of survival. Enslaved people with a firm religious belief were able to benefit from this nonmaterial source of support, which we also recognize today in the methodology of twelve-step programs for overcoming addiction that begin by putting one's fate in the hands of a greater power than the self.[32]

In their appeal to countervailing ideologies, supportive communities, and spirituality, the enslaved were, in a sense, behaving like good feminists seeking means of lessening the power of oppression and sexual abuse in their lives. Having been identified and set apart as a despised race, enslaved people found it easier to create alternative ideologies than the White people—including women—who owned them and who told them what to do. There is no denying that White ladies were able to oppress those whom they owned, but even so, the ladies lacked access to much of their society's other kinds of power. Of all the people living in slaveholding societies who might have benefited from an alternative system of values, rich White women were least likely to forge one. In the words of Catherine Clinton, plantation mistresses, unlike enslaved people, "had no comparable sense of community."[33]

Damage across the Color Line

Owning as well as owned families paid a high psychological and physical cost for the child and sexual abuse that was so integral to slavery. First, despite what Black and White people may assume about the rigidity of the color bar, attachment and loss often transcended the barriers of race and class and flowed in both directions. The abuse of enslaved people pained and damaged nonslaves, particularly children, and forced those witnessing the abuse of the enslaved to identify with the victim or the perpetrator.

Second, the values and practices of slavery, in particular the use of violence to secure obedience and deference, prevailed within White families as well. The ideals of slavery—obedience and submission—were concurrently and not accidentally the prototypes of White womanhood and of evangelical piety, which intensified the prestige and reinforced the attraction of these ideals. Caroline Howard Gilman, for instance, wrote in the antebellum era as both a "New England bride" and a "Southern matron." She recommended that the former "reverence" her husband's wishes; to the latter she advised not only "submission," but also silence when self-defense was called for. The White Southern matron may mourn her subjugation or suffer painful illness, but she must always smile, smile no matter what the circumstances.[34]

Nineteenth-century evangelical religion meant various things to its many believers. It could compel them toward startlingly different ideological conclusions, as exemplified in the North in the Jacksonian era. After the abolition of slavery in the North, evangelicalism fostered a profusion of convictions, including abolitionism and feminism; in the region still committed to slavery, however, evangelicalism produced no reforming offshoots that were allowed to flourish. Instead, unquestioning evangelical piety was more valued, and "piety" was another word for "submission" and "obedience," terms that also figured prominently in the language of the family.

The imageries of religion and family have much in common, rhetorically and structurally, and scholars have repeatedly stressed the crucial role of human families as structural models both in religion and in slavery. Christians speak of God the Father, the Son, and the Holy Ghost, and Christians, Jews, and Muslims trace the origin of human-kind to the family of Adam and Eve. Religions routinely evoke the language of kinship when sketching out holy relationships between gods and people.

Slavery and the family are just as inextricably intertwined, for the etymology of the word "family" reaches back to the Latin words *familia,* meaning a "household," and *famulus/famula,* meaning "servant or slave," deeply embedding the notion of servitude within our concept of family. As the ideals and practices of servitude, family, and religion are so firmly linked in this cultural system, a search for cause and effect is bound to prove frustrating. Even without recourse to relations of causality, however, the confluence of values is noteworthy.[35]

Slavery accentuated the hierarchical rather than the egalitarian and democratic strains in American culture, thereby shaping relations within and without families and polities. Patriarchal families, slavery, and evangelical religion further reinforced one another's emphasis on submission and obedience in civil society, particularly concerning people in subaltern positions.

Despite the existence of a wide spectrum of opinion on slavery and feminism, agreement exists on the close relationship between the concepts of the White woman and slavery. Proslavery apologists often insisted that the maintenance of slavery depended on the preservation of patriarchy within White families, arguing that White women, especially rich women, must remain in their places and be submissive to their fathers and husbands so that enslaved people would not conceive notions of equality. Similar motives prohibited White men from acknowledging publicly that White women commonly labored in Southern fields at tasks that the culture reserved rhetorically for women who were enslaved.[36] The reasoning of proslavery apologia ran from women's honor to gender roles to Black men–White women sex, skipping over the reality of White men's sexual use and abuse of Black women in a manner that I find remarkable for its silences, its intertextuality, and its unabashed patriarchy. Of course, there is nothing at all contradictory between family feeling and hierarchy, between attachment and the conviction that some people absolutely must obey others.

Hierarchy by no means precludes attachment. Just as enslaved youngsters attached to the adults closest to them, White as well as Black, so the White children and adults in slave-owning households became psychologically entangled with the enslaved people they came to know well. When Peter, Sojourner Truth's son, was beaten by his owner in Alabama, his mistress (who was Sojourner's mistress's cousin) salved his wounds and cried over his injuries. That story concluded with Peter's mistress's murder by the very same man, her husband, who had previously abused Peter. Like Peter's murdered mistress, other slaveowners, especially women, grieved at the sight of enslaved people who had been beaten.[37]

The abolitionist Angelina Grimké recalled scenes from her life as a privileged young woman in Charleston, South Carolina. When Grimké was about thirteen and attending a seminary for wealthy girls, an enslaved boy who had been severely battered was called into her classroom to open a window. The sight of his wounds so pained Grimké that she fainted. Her school was located near the workhouse where enslaved people were sent to be reprimanded. One of her friends who lived near it complained to Grimké that the screams of the people being whipped often reached her house. These awful cries from the workhouse terrified Grimké whenever she had to walk nearby.[38]

As slave-owning children grew into adults, their identification with victims or victimizers often accorded to gender. Elizabeth Fox-Genovese shows that mistresses could be cruel tormentors.[39] But in comparison with male owners, White women were more likely to take the side of the enslaved, while White men nearly unanimously identified with the aggressor as a requisite of manhood. Becoming such a man did not happen automatically or painlessly. Playing on the patriarchy inherent in Western cultural institutions, which are also rooted in Christian religion, Jacques Lacan terms this socialization "the name-of-the-father."

Fathers ordinarily did the work of inculcating manhood, which included snuffing out White children's identification with the enslaved. In 1839 a Virginian named John M. Nelson described his shift from painful childhood sympathy to manly callousness. As a child, he would try to stop the beating of enslaved children and, he said, "mingle my cries with theirs, and feel almost willing to take a part of the punishment." After his father severely and repeatedly rebuked him for this kind of compassion, he "became so blunted that I could not only witness their stripes with composure, but *myself* inflict them, and that without remorse."[40]

The comments of Thomas Jefferson on this whole subject are revealingly oblique. Thomas Jefferson, Founding Father, slave owner, author of the Declaration of Independence, and acknowledged expert on his own state of Virginia and the United States generally, wrote *Notes on the State of Virginia* in response to a questionnaire from François Marbois, the secretary of the French legation at Philadelphia. Between 1780 and 1785 Jefferson codified his social, political, scientific, and ethical convictions. Jefferson did not have a very high opinion of Africans, though American Indians, he thought, would display their real and substantial worth when afforded decent opportunities. Jefferson found African Americans stupid and ugly, a people more or less well suited to the low estate they occupied in eighteenth-century Virginia. Contrary to facile assumption, Jefferson's appraisal of the capacities of Africans did not make him an unequivocal supporter of slavery. Nonetheless, as a gentleman whose entire material existence depended on the produce of people he owned, he was never an abolitionist. In fact, his reluctance to interfere with slavery hardened as he aged. By 1819, as the Missouri Compromise was being forged, Jefferson was warning American politicians not, under any circumstances, to tamper with slavery, even though he realized that by preserving slavery, the United States was holding "a wolf by the ears."

Jefferson's reservations about slavery pertained to the owners, not to the enslaved. Being the property of other people was not noxious to Blacks, he thought, but owning people entailed great drawbacks for Whites. Jefferson recognized that the requirements of ownership of people "nursed, educated, and daily exercised" habits of tyranny, and he observed that "the man must be a prodigy who can retain his manners and morals undepraved by such circumstances." In this part of his discussion, Jefferson's customary verbal talent and intellectual suppleness turned into obfuscation. He veiled his explanation of the bad things that slavery did to slave owners and was only able to write, intriguingly, of slavery's breeding "odious peculiarities."[41]

Jefferson's phrasing does not appeal to today's family systems theorists and psychoanalysts, who use instead the language of triangles to explain family relationships, including those that are violent. Children who are observers of abuse are likely to assume the position of the other members of the triangle: either by becoming victims themselves or by abusing others, especially younger siblings or children in positions of relative weakness.[42] This is the kind of repercussion that eighteenth- and nineteenth-century observers like Thomas Jefferson were deploring through euphemism.

So far in this discussion, mainly enslaved people have figured as the victims of physical and psychological abuse. But the ideals of slavery affected families quite apart from the toll they exacted from the bodies and psyches of Blacks. Thanks to the abundance of historical scholarship that concentrates on antebellum Southern society, it is possible to reach some generalizations regarding Whites. But even in the slave South, historians have been much less aware of the abuse of White women than of the oppression of enslaved Blacks. Abuse there was, as the diary of Baltimorean Madge Preston indicates.[43]

Petitions for divorce and church records show that wife beating was a common motive for the attempted dissolution of marriages and the expulsion of men and women from church membership. Doubtless this was true in nonslaveholding regions as well. What is noteworthy in this context, as Stephanie McCurry shows for the South Carolina low country, is that legislators and church leaders routinely urged women to remain in abusive unions and to bear abuse in a spirit of submission.[44] In the hard-drinking antebellum South, which was well known for rampant violence against enslaved people and between White men, White women had little recourse when their husbands beat them, for, in general, the Southern states were slow to grant women the legal right to divorce or to custody of their children in cases of separation. Until the 1830s, Southern states lacked divorce laws, and state legislatures heard divorce petitions on a case-by-case basis. The result was a small number of divorces granted inconsistently and according to the social and economic status of the petitioner.

The disposal of the small number of cases of incest that came before judges also illuminates the reasoning of the men who exercised power in the slave South. As in instances of wife beating, so in cases of incest judges preferred to investigate the flaws of the female petitioner, who, even despite extreme youth, usually came to be seen as consenting. Not surprisingly, incest seldom became public, but when it entered the criminal justice system, the girls in question were likely as not seen as accomplices in their own ravishment. In the interests of preserving patriarchy, victims of incest, like victims of wife abuse, were abandoned by law and sacrificed to the ideal of submission. Legal historians like A. Leon Higginbotham Jr. and Peter Bardaglio have discovered that Southern lawmakers and judges anxious to regulate racialized sexuality were loath to punish White men for sexual violence against White or Black women and children.[45]

Incest and wife beating do not usually appear in general studies of the antebellum South, where the received wisdom, as in histories like Daniel Blake Smith's study of eighteenth-century planter society in the Chesapeake, is that planter families came to be child-centered and companionate.[46] Such a vision fails even to allow for the level of familial abuse that psychologists see as usual in contemporary households, where, according to the American Medical Association, one-quarter of married women will be abused by a current or former partner at some point during their lives.[47] Were planter families more straightforwardly loving than we? I doubt it.

Keeping Secrets from Historians

Aristocrats were skilled at keeping secrets and preserving appearances, as I know from experience with Gertrude Thomas. Only by reading her 1,380-page journal repeatedly was I able to discover her secrecy and self-deception. In this case, the secret I discovered was adultery, for both her father and her husband had outside wives and children. Her journal never reveals her other family secret, her husband's alcoholism, which was only preserved orally in family lore.

Then and now, family violence and child sexual abuse are usually concealed, and the people with the most privacy, the wealthy, are better at preserving their secrets than poor people, who live their lives in full view of the world. Scholars have connived with wealthy families to hide child sexual abuse among people of privilege, which one psychologist concludes is "most conspicuous for its presumed absence."[48] This is an old, old story.

In the 1890s Sigmund Freud discovered the prevalence of incest as a cause of hysteria; when his professional colleagues objected to what he had found, he reworked his theory into fantasy and the Oedipus complex. In 1932 Freud's friend and protégé Sandor Ferenczi reestablished the facts that childhood sexual trauma was common in the best of families and that it was devastating to emotional development. A few months after he presented his paper "Confusion of Tongues between Adults and the Child" to the International Psycho-Analytic Congress in Wiesbaden, Ferenczi died, and his theory died with him. In the 1980s Jeffrey Masson revealed Freud's about-face and was drummed out of psychoanalysis.[49] Historians who have taken their sources at face value have missed the family secrets of slave-owning households, but in their unwillingness to see, they find themselves in distinguished psychological company.

Some historians are ready to examine their sources more critically. Works by Richard Bushman and the critic Jay Fliegelman alert us that by the late eighteenth and early nineteenth centuries, wealthy Americans had come to prize gentility so highly that they spent enormous amounts of time and energy creating pleasing appearances. Bushman and Fliegelman say, and I concur, that the letters, speeches, and journals that historians have used as the means of uncovering reality and gauging consciousness ought more properly to be considered self-conscious performances intended to create beautiful tableaux. People with sufficient time, space, and money modeled themselves on characters in novels and acted out what they saw as appropriate parts. What was actually taking place at home was another story entirely, which was not necessarily preserved for our easy investigation.[50] If historians are to understand the less attractive and deeply buried aspects of slave society, the scales will have to fall from their eyes. They will have to see beyond the beauty of performance and probe slavery's family romance skeptically.

Once we transcend complete reliance on the written record, deception clues are not hard to see. They include the murderous rage Fox Butterfield highlights in his 1998 *New York Times* article, but also the eloquent alcoholism and invalidism of the eighteenth- and nineteenth-century South that could not be concealed. Murder, alcohol, and illness hint at the existence of compelling family secrets. In the 1940s the Southern author Lillian Smith summed up the society in which she lived in a phrase that applies to slave societies. Smith said that her thoroughly segregated South, with its myriad instances of bad faith, was "pathological."[51]

Historians need to heed the wisdom of psychologists, take Lillian Smith to heart, look beneath the gorgeous surface that cultured slave owners presented to the world, and pursue the hidden truths of slavery, including soul murder and patriarchy. The task is essential, for our mental health as a society depends on the ability to see our interrelatedness across lines of class and race, in the past, as in the present.

1995/2002/2021

Of *Lily*, Linda Brent, and Freud

A NON-EXCEPTIONALIST APPROACH TO RACE,

CLASS, AND GENDER IN THE SLAVE SOUTH

IN MY WORK ON SEXUALITY in the nineteenth- and twentieth-century South, I return often to what the late Herbert Gutman used to say about Karl Marx, but with application to Sigmund Freud: "He raises some very good questions." While I have plenty of feminist company in my turn toward psychoanalysis, the Freud I am using here is not quite the Freud who has been making recent appearances.[1] As a historian of the nineteenth- and early twentieth-century American South who remains tethered to a history project grounded in the archives, I find that Freud is valuable mainly as an acute observer of nineteenth-century bourgeois society, as an analyst (pun intended) who recognized the relationship between sexuality and identity. His writing permits unusually clear views into the ways in which social, economic, and ethnic hierarchies affected households and families, for he was accustomed to dealing with people in households that encompassed more than one economic class. Such vision enriches Southern studies, which is still impoverished by exceptionalism and a tendency to see race as an opaque obstacle blocking feminist investigation.

My subject is the family relations that affected the richest and the poorest of antebellum Southern daughters. The tragically tiny number of Black daughters who would have been actually or nominally

Incidents Through Window with Freud, 2022, ink, graphite, and digital collage on paper. Visualizing Harriet Jacobs of North Carolina, motifs of Southern history, and Freud as author of a classic paper on sexual harassment.

free, and the large cohort of White daughters who would have lived beyond the reach of the aristocracy, belonged to families who were able to shelter them from predatory wealthy men and were more likely to escape the fate of the daughters under discussion here. But whether Black or White, if young women lived in households where men had access to the poorest and most vulnerable, these daughters ran gendered risks related to sexuality that did not respect barriers of class and race.

It has been no secret, then or now, that in the plantation South, owners and the people who were owned lived on terms of physical closeness and often engaged in a lot of sex. Yet historians have followed the lead of privileged nineteenth-century Southerners who, though well aware that sex figured among the services owners demanded of enslaved people, briskly pushed the matter aside. Even psychoanalysts like Abram Kardiner and L. Ovesey pass quickly over the repercussions of interracial sexuality in Southern White families and hence on Southern society generally.[2] Virtually by default, the conclusion in Southern history was that owner-enslaved sex was a problem for the enslaved, not the owners; thus, as a social phenomenon, interracial, interclass sexuality as a topic has been relegated to African Americans alone. This is not the position I hold. Because intimate relations affected White as well as Black families, I argue that such sexuality and its repercussions belong not to one race or the other, but must reside squarely in Southern history.[3]

One needs only to read the works of class- and gender-conscious historians of Great Britain and Europe to recognize the parallels between nineteenth-century European bourgeois societies and that of the antebellum South.[4] Such usefulness is not limited to historians' insights. Though very much in vogue with literary critics, Freudian psychoanalysis also offers thought-provoking assistance to historians, particularly on the formation of individual identity. Specifically, Sigmund Freud's "Dora" case history raises fundamental questions about the dynamics of elite families in a hierarchical society where the employment of servants (and here I concentrate on female servants) is routine. This essay addresses the pertinence of three pieces of Freud's writing to Southern society, as reflected in two mid-nineteenth-century Southern literary figures known as "Lily" and "Linda Brent."

Lily is the title character of an 1855 novel by Sue Petigru King (Bowen) (1824–1875). King was a daughter of the very respectable Charlestonian Thomas Petigru. Having been educated in Charleston and New York, she had returned to South Carolina to pursue her career as a writer. Her character Lily is the quintessential young plantation mistress: hyper-White, wealthy, and beautiful. Much better known today, thanks largely to the work of Jean Fagan Yellin and others, is Linda Brent, who, in contrast to Lily, was enslaved. Brent is both the central character and the pseudonym that the Edenton, North Carolina, fugitive Harriet Jacobs (1813–1897) used in her autobiography, *Incidents in the Life of a Slave Girl,* originally published in 1861.[5]

If rich, White, and free Lily represents the top of the antebellum South's economic and racial hierarchies, then poor, yellow, and enslaved Linda Brent represents the near bottom. Linda, after all, has some free relations, and her grandmother, nominally enslaved, lives in her own house in town. Things could have been much worse for Linda Brent. Both Linda's and Lily's stories are about very young women and sex, and taken together with Freud's "Dora," they tell us a great deal about Southern family dynamics in slaveholding households. As both texts are about sex and race, a word about the phenomenon of owner-slave sex, as I discovered it in Gertrude Thomas's journal, precedes the discussion of Lily, Linda Brent, and "Dora."

It is clear that sexual relations between male slave owners and enslaved women were exceedingly common in the antebellum South—as in any other slave society, as Orlando Patterson points out.[6] Nineteenth-century fugitive slave narratives, such as those of Frederick Douglass and Moses Roper, and the Fisk and WPA ex-slave narratives from the 1930s are full of evidence that owners did not hesitate to rape enslaved women, despite the marital status of either party. I suspect that about 10 percent of owners also slept or wanted to sleep with enslaved men and boys; some mistresses likely also regarded the women they owned as objects of desire.[7] On the other side of the class and racial continuums from the Frederick Douglasses and Moses Ropers, White women—Southerners and observers—penned and sometimes published criticisms of the institution of slavery based on what they perceived as the demoralization of White men who engaged in adultery and/or polygyny.

I began to draw my own conclusions as I concentrated on the journal of Ella Gertrude Clanton Thomas (1834–1907), published in 1990 as *The Secret Eye*.[8] Thomas, wealthy, educated, and White, lived in and around Augusta, Georgia, for most of her life. She began keeping a journal in 1848, when she was fourteen years old, and stopped writing definitively in 1889, when she was fifty-five. Although she was born into an immensely wealthy, slave-owning family, Thomas married a man who was a poor manager. Her husband, Jefferson Thomas, succeeded financially as a planter before the Civil War, thanks to unpaid labor and continual financial support from Gertrude's father. But her father died in 1864, and the people they had owned were emancipated in 1865. After the war the Thomases entered a long cycle of debt that sent Gertrude into the paid labor force as a teacher. Her earnings kept the family afloat economically, but poverty imposed great strains. This journal, therefore, chronicles a life of privilege before the Civil War, the trauma of supporting the losing side, the loss of the labor and prestige that slavery had assured her, and the chagrin of downward mobility. Thomas joined the Woman's Christian Temperance Union in the 1880s and became a suffragist in the 1890s. She died in Atlanta at seventy-three.

Initially I appreciated this journal as a valuable primary source for Southern social history, for which Thomas was an excellent witness. Extraordinary as her record is, however, it works on yet another level, which psychoanalysis is well equipped to explore. The journal contains a veiled text, characterized by the keeping of secrets, lack of candor, and self-deception. Whereas the surface of this text presents a Southerner of a certain class at given historical junctures, a less straightforward message also emerges. The veiled text, less bounded chronologically, is about families and gender, and it contains and reveals a great secret that is relatively timeless: adultery. I know from the "deception clues" and leakage in the journal that most certainly by the 1860s, probably by the 1850s, Thomas was painfully aware but unable to admit that her father had had children with at least one of the women he enslaved.[9] By the 1870s, possibly as early as the 1850s, Thomas also knew that her husband had fathered at least one child by a woman who was not White.

This should come as no surprise. Harriet Martineau in the 1830s spoke of the plantation mistress as "the chief slave of the harem." Fredrika Bremer in the 1850s coined a famous phrase that Thomas quotes in her journal, "these White children of slavery." And Mary Chesnut wrote of the mulatto children in every slaveholding household.[10] Gertrude Thomas was hardly alone.

Some of the most interesting evidence comes from fiction, which, considering the subject, should not be surprising. Most respectable nineteenth-century people retreated—or attempted to retreat— behind the veil of privacy, rather than reveal their actual patterns of sexuality. The very ability to conceal the rawer aspects of the human condition, an ability that we sum up in the term "privacy," served as a crucial symbol of prosperity when the poor had no good place to hide. Nonetheless the topic of interracial sexuality was of enough fascination to reappear in fiction under various disguises. Taking my cue from Gertrude Thomas, who was hypersensitive about sexual competition between women, I began to pursue sexuality through the very theme of competition. Tracked in that guise, Southern fiction reveals some interesting manifestations.

Sue Petigru King sounded themes that occur in the works of several White Southern women writers, such as Caroline Lentz, Grace King, and Willa Cather. For example, Cather's final novel, *Sapphira and the Slave Girl* (1940), is precisely and openly about a White woman's perception of sexual competition between herself and a Negro woman. In its racial candor, *Sapphira* is exceptional. More often the competition between women is not about individuals with different racial identities, but about two White characters who are color coded in Black and White. While I realize that European writers such as Sir Walter Scott and Honoré de Balzac used light (blonde) and dark (*la belle juive*) female characters symbolically, Anne Goodwyn Jones, Mary Kelley, and Jane Pease, scholars familiar with Southern writing, corroborate my view that nineteenth- and early twentieth-century White Southern women writers were singularly fascinated by competition between light and dark women. While most publications by these women followed the usual theme of a young woman's quest for autonomy and her eventual marriage to a good man, they also very much echoed Gertrude Thomas's fixation on female rivalry.

Sue Petigru King is no longer very well known, but she loomed large in Gertrude Thomas's literary world and was known in Great Britain. William Thackeray, one of Britain's most celebrated authors, visited her on a trip to the United States. In the mid-nineteenth century King published several novels that repeatedly stressed themes of jealousy and competition between women, the best known of which is *Lily*.

Very briefly, *Lily* is the story of Elizabeth Vere, whom her father calls "Lily" because she is "as White as any lily that ever grew." Over the course of the novel's plot, Lily goes from age seven to seventeen. King describes her heroine with words like "White," "pure," "innocent," "simple," and "lovely." The character with whom King pairs Lily is her cousin, Angelica Purvis. Angelica is also a rich White woman, but King focuses on the blackness of her dresses and the intense blackness of her hair. At one point, King contrasts Lily, who "seemed made up of light and purity," with Angelica, who "was dark, designing, distracting." Angelica is exotic; King describes her as an "Eastern princess" and calls her looks "Andalusian." Whereas Lily is pure, Angelica is passionate, evil, voluptuous. Angelica says of her attractiveness to men: "I am original sin . . ."[11] At the age of seventeen, Lily is engaged to her first great love, Clarence Tracy, a childhood friend and graduate of Princeton University. Despite all her goodness, however, Lily is not rewarded, for Clarence is crazy in love with Angelica, who is married.

On the face of it, the most obvious theme in *Lily* is competition between two White women, which the less virtuous is winning. But race hovers in the very near background. First, these ostensibly White competitors are color coded in Black and White. Then, as though to make the point unambiguously, King abruptly introduces a new character, Lorenza, at the very end of the novel. Lorenza is Clarence's African American mistress. On the night before Lily's wedding, Lorenza murders Lily out of jealousy over her impending marriage.

King leaves nothing to guesswork in this novel, and to hammer home her message, she also addresses her readers directly with a point made by Mary Chesnut in her Civil War diary: that Southern planter husbands repaid their wives' faithful virtue with base infidelity. Wealthy Southern men married young, pure, rich White girls like Lily, then left them for mistresses tinged by Blackness, whether of descent or intimation. King sums up Mary Chesnut's conviction and Gertrude Thomas's fears: "It is not the woman most worthy to be loved who is the most loved." This conclusion is echoed in the writing of Sigmund Freud.

In 1912 Freud discussed exactly that phenomenon in his second contribution to the psychology of love: "On the Universal Tendency to Debasement in the Sphere of Love." Freud appraised the practical results of "civilized morality" and the sexual double standard from the standpoint of middle- and upper-class men who were susceptible to psychosomatic impotence with women of their own class. Freud said, making King's point: "Where such men love they have no desire and where they desire they cannot love."[12]

In *Lily*, the pure, young, rich White daughter is the most dramatic loser in the Southern sexual sweepstakes. In this interpretation of Southern sexuality, the motif is competition between women and the victims are wealthy White women. Writers from the other side painted a disturbingly similar, yet differently shaded portrait.

While many ex-slave narratives discuss owner-slave sex, the most extended commentary comes from Harriet Jacobs, who, writing under the pseudonym "Linda Brent," told of being harassed by her owner for sex from the time she was thirteen. Her character, Linda, becomes the most literal embodiment of the enslaved as sexual prey in the literature of slave narratives.

Harriet Jacobs depicts puberty as a "sad epoch in the life of a slave girl." As she became nubile, Linda Brent's owner began to whisper "foul words in my ear," which is the kind of act whose consequences Freud understood. Jacobs generalized from Linda's predicament that "whether the slave girl be Black as ebony or as fair as her mistress"— she, the slave girl, is sexually vulnerable.[13]

Incidents is of great interest in this discussion because Jacobs confronted the sexual component of servitude so straightforwardly. She recognized, too, that enslaved and enslavers interpreted the situation very differently. Jacobs dedicated an entire chapter of *Incidents in the Life of a Slave Girl* to "The Jealous Mistress." Here and elsewhere, Jacobs maintained that mistresses whose husbands betrayed them felt no solidarity whatever with the girls and women being abused.[14]

Like other ex-slave narrators, Jacobs could ascertain the view of slave-owning women but repudiate their conclusions. Jacobs supplies the key word, "victim," and recognizes that it was a matter of contention between the women who were owned and the women who owned them.

White women, Black women, and Black men all resented deeply White men's access to Black women. But the comments from the two sides of the color line are contradictory: where White women saw sexual competition—with connotations of equality—Black men and women saw rank exploitation rooted in grossly disparate levels of power. Moses Roper, his owner's child, relates the story of his near murder, shortly after his birth, by his father's jealous wife. Frederick Douglass also saw that slave-owning women were distressed by the bodily proof of their husbands' adulteries.[15]

For Jacobs, as for other ex-slave narrators, the prime victim was the enslaved woman, not the slave-owning woman, no matter how the latter perceived the situation. Slave owners' sexual relations with the women they owned—already a monstrous human relationship—constituted one of several varieties of victimization by men whose power was absolute. Enslaved people of both sexes were oppressed by class and by race, but women suffered a third, additional oppression stemming from their gender. Extorted sex belonged to the larger pattern of oppression embedded in the institution of slavery.

Harriet Jacobs and Gertrude Thomas provide examples of the family dynamics of cross-class, interracial sex. Located in very different places within the complicated families of slavery, each explicates the deleterious effects of adultery. Like Jacobs and Thomas, Sigmund Freud, in his analysis of "Dora," recognized the damage that a father's adultery causes a daughter.[16]

"Dora" was eighteen-year-old Ida Bauer, whose father took her to see Freud in October 1900 after she threatened suicide. Phillip Bauer hoped that Freud would cure his daughter's mental and physical ailments and stem her wild accusations of sexual harassment. Ida had claimed that a close family friend, "Herr K" (Hans Zellenka), had made several sexual advances toward her, and she told Freud that in one instance, Herr K had approached her with the same phrases he had used to proposition a servant woman. The entanglements ran deeper, for it was revealed that Herr K's young wife, "Frau K," was Phillip Bauer's lover. In this adulterous game between her father and the Ks, Ida felt like a helpless pawn, attached emotionally to Frau K and the female servant, as well as to her estranged mother and father. Freud diagnosed the distraught young woman as hysterical and used her case to put certain theories to the test.

Freud had been thinking about hysteria for several years and had worked out his notions in letters to his close friend and regular correspondent, Wilhelm Fliess. These comments are exceedingly helpful to me, particularly in observations that Freud enclosed with a letter dated May 2, 1897. Here Freud notes that children, even very young babies, hear things that later become the raw material for fantasies and neuroses. Accompanying this letter was "Draft L," which includes a paragraph on "The Part Played by Servant Girls."[17]

In Draft L, Freud echoes his society's assumption that the poor young women who worked in bourgeois households were "people of low morals" because they were likely to become sexually involved with the men and boys of the household. Here Freud was echoing the most common of assumptions about Black people in the South. But whereas Freud identified morals with class, White Southerners saw low morals as a racial characteristic of African Americans. For my purposes, however, this is not the crucial insight that Freud took from his failed analysis of Ida Bauer. For me, Freud's most useful observation relates to the critical importance of servants in the psychological and, hence, the social dynamics of the families in which they work. Although Freud thought mainly of the ramifications of the situation on the family of the employers, as we saw in the case of Linda Brent, employed people, too, felt the effects of adulterous—should I add incestuous?—family dynamics.

Freud wrote Fliess that in households in which servant women are sexually intimate with their employers, the children (here I believe he means female children) develop an array of hysterical fantasies: fear of being on the street alone, fear of becoming a prostitute, fear of a man hidden under the bed. In sum, said Freud, "There is tragic justice in the circumstance that the family head's stooping to a maidservant is atoned for by his daughter's self-abasement."[18]

Freud underscored the degree to which women in a household are emotionally intertwined. "Dora" identified with the servant that her would-be seducer had tried to seduce. Observing situations in which race was not a factor, Freud understood that the very structure containing class and gender power dynamics is virtually Foucauldian in its leakiness. No class of women remained exempt from a degradation that aimed at the least of them. Just as Gertrude Thomas saw that her adulterous father and husband treated rich and poor and Black and White women as interchangeable sexually, Freud saw there was a "part played by servant girls" and an object connection between "Dora" and her father's mistress. The Freud scholar Hannah Decker put her finger on the phenomenon that poisoned young women's lives in Freud's Vienna and that also characterized the nineteenth-century South: the careless sexual abuse of *das süsse Mädel*—the sweet young thing.[19]

Freud's letters to Fliess, his "On the Universal Tendency to Debasement in the Sphere of Love," and especially the "Dora" case analysis show that "Dora's" predicament is reflected in both *Lily* and *Incidents in the Life of a Slave Girl,* but in somewhat different ways. Linda Brent is more directly comparable with "Dora," for she was the object of unwanted sexual advances, as was young Ida Bauer. The case of Lily Vere is less obvious, for she is the daughter of "Draft L," of "The Part Played by Servant Girls." Lily is the daughter whose affective value is lowered by the existence of the sexually vulnerable servant class and the allure of enticing dark/Negro women like Angelica and Lorenza. While Linda Brent is a clear victim of her society's hierarchies of race and gender, Lily, unloved by her fiancé, and murdered by his servant lover, is victimized as well. Her fiancé, Clarence, is the very figure of the Freud patient suffering from psychically induced impotence.[20]

Examining these Southern women's stories and taking Freud to heart leads to two conclusions: First, that historians of the United States

South, sheltered too long in Southern exceptionalism, have let an intellectual color bar obstruct their view of the complexity of gender roles within households that were economically heterogeneous. Lily and Linda Brent, two examples of a spoliation of young women that was no respecter of race or class, underscore both the sexual vulnerabilities and the psychological interrelatedness of Southern daughters. Second, Freud contributes to our understanding that families and societies cannot designate and thereby set apart one category of women as victims. The victimization spread, in different ways and to different degrees. But where historians have been prone to construe Southern family relations within watertight racial categories, the stories of these three daughters pose complicated new questions whose answers do not stop at the color line.

Historians have wanted to reach a single conclusion that would characterize the relationship between slave-owning and enslaved women in the antebellum South: *either* enslaved women were at the bottom of a hierarchical society, as the ex-slave narrators testify, *or* all Southern women were, finally, at the mercy of rich White men. The relationship between Black and White women through White men deserves to be named, for slavery often made women of different races and classes into co-mothers and co-wives as well as owners and suppliers of labor. The question is whether there should be one name or, reflecting the number of races involved, more than one.

If feminist history has taught us anything, it is that important private matters become important historical matters. The example of the South Carolina fire-eater James Henry Hammond makes the point. Hammond's emotional turmoil following his wife's desertion when he took a second, enslaved wife so incapacitated him psychologically that he missed an important secessionist meeting that would have bolstered his sagging political career.[21] Hammond's wife serves as a reminder that Gertrude Thomas's preoccupation—competition—needs to reenter the equation, or historians risk missing much of the psychodrama of Southern history. Focusing on one part of the picture, even if more compatible with present-day understandings of power relations, flattens out the inherent complexity of Southern history. If historians do not acknowledge that wealthy White women saw themselves in competition with women who were Black and poor and powerless, they miss a vital dimension of Southern history that helps explain the thorniness of women's contacts across the color line well after legal segregation ended. We must acknowledge the existence of two ways of seeing, even while we keep our eyes on fundamental differentials of power.

What my approach means for Southern history is a renunciation of a "the South" way of thinking. For me there is seldom a "the South," for simple characterizations eliminate the reality of sharp conflicts over just about everything in Southern culture, slavery most of all. Saying that "the South" was proslavery (or, later, pro-segregation) equates the region with its ruling race and annihilates the position of at least one-third of its inhabitants. As a labor historian with a keen sense of the historical importance of all groups of people within a society (not simply the prestigious, published, and politically powerful), I insist on going beyond lazy characterizations in the singular. Recognizing the complex and contradictory nature of Southern society, I can rephrase my conclusions about the study of Southern history succinctly: Southern history demands the recognition of complexity and contradiction, starting with family life, and therefore requires the use of plurals; and though Southern history must take race very seriously, Southern history must not stop with race.

Summer 1992

Labor Relations in the Post–Civil War US South

WANT TO TALK ABOUT WORKING PEOPLE in the United States South immediately after emancipation, beginning with some general comments about the postwar labor market and ending with the experiences of an elite White Georgian, Gertrude Thomas, who before the war had owned many people. Thomas lived in the Black belt, and what I have to say today pertains to areas of the South in which Blacks were an important part of the workforce, but Whites (men and women) also belonged to the workforce. Thomas's experiences took place in and around Augusta, Georgia, and the workers with whom she dealt came, in part, from the town.

In areas of the United States South in which a significant portion of the workforce had been enslaved and emancipated, relations changed between the employing classes and the employed in 1865, not merely between former owners and the people formerly owned. Emancipation reordered relations between Black workers and White employers; emancipation also affected others in the economy, notably Whites in the workforce. The ways in which the end of the war unloosened poor Whites as it emancipated Blacks is not easily accessible, for witnesses' lack of interest in non-elite Whites and enormous class prejudice embedded in elite testimony obscure the activities of working-class people who were not formerly owned. As employers, planters were more obviously concerned with Black workers, complaining endlessly that the freedpeople would not work or would not work properly. Such accusations are familiar to students of Southern history. But what about relations between employers and White workers? In order to make some sense of labor relations among Whites, I have collected historians' asides and, in the primary sources, done some reading against the sources, following clues that also appear in Northern employers' disparagement of working people.

Although historians have hardly taken into account the immediate effect of the end of the war on non-elite Whites, particularly in areas where they lived among people who were formerly enslaved, some contemporary witnesses dwelled on the idleness of poor White men. The reporter John Richard Dennett said that he had seen hundreds of White men in rural Virginia, but not more than ten "engaged in labor of any sort." Black and White officials of the Freedmen's Bureau also commented on the prevalence of vagrancy among Whites. Observers generally reported that poor White women, on the other hand, were hard at work—at home, in the fields, or in the roads. Contemporaries frequently contrasted indolent White men with earnest, hardworking freedpeople.

The historian Joel Williamson cites the planter David Golightly Harris of the Spartanburg, South Carolina, district. Harris was attempting to hire White women as live-in servants, evidently as replacements for people he had owned and did not have to pay, an effort in which he did not succeed. With a bitterness against workers common to his class, Harris wrote that these White women resisted the idea of becoming live-in domestic servants. He relished the prospect of their comeuppance, when hardship would make them give up what he saw as inappropriate notions of independence.

The 1865–1866 correspondence of Harris and others used to having immobile, unpaid employees reveals much indignation. Women and men who had never had to give much thought to workers' considerations resented having to seek laborers and to take workers' demands into account. Planters and their families had work to be done, but workers (White and Black) refused it or held out for better terms, both of which raised planters' hackles. Some observers singled out Whites as especially idle while others concentrated on Blacks. Even though complaints of vagrancy were common on both sides of the color line, criticism was usually presented as though vagrancy were at once a unique racial characteristic of the freedpeople and a unique racial characteristic of poor Whites. The whole matter of defining idleness became important ideologically and legally, as Northerners and Southerners argued about the efficiency of free labor and Southern legislatures passed laws punishing people who did not work for other people for pay.

Given the contemporary habit of discussing labor relations in racial terms, it is difficult to estimate what proportion of planters and observers realized at the time that they were witnessing an upheaval in labor relations that implicated poor Whites as well as poor Blacks, that is, that implicated working people. But a preliminary review of the sources turned up at least one employer, a member of the Alabama legislature named Smith from Choctaw County, who was anxious to propose a sweeping set of labor laws (along the order of what soon became the Black codes) that would subject the whole of the Southern working class to tight control.

The struggle between would-be employers and reluctant employees extended to the terms of employment, to contracts between freedpeople and employers, and to wages as well, as though (again in the eyes of elites) poor Whites, on their side, and poor Blacks, on theirs, were making extraordinary demands. Historians have devoted a great deal of attention to the tug-of-war between Black employees and White employers over terms of employment (sometimes mediated by officers of the Freedmen's Bureau, often not). But historians have not realized that a similar struggle was going on between White employers and White employees demanding higher wages, even though it seems clear that Whites who worked for wages and who were in the same wage pool as Blacks were demanding more than they had before or, at any rate, more than employers wanted to pay.

It may be that much of the demand for increased wages was a response to the inflation that accompanied the war, although the historian Armstead Robinson believes that the switch away from Confederate currency entailed deflation. Economic historians such as Roger L. Ransom, Richard Sutch, and Gerald Jaynes advance an argument that I find persuasive: with emancipation, Black people participated less fully in the workforce and thereby created a labor shortage. Freedwomen exercised a new right not to work for anyone but their families; Black children entered school instead of employment; and people who remained in the workforce did not work as long or as intensively as when they had been supervised by whip-toting drivers and overseers. In short, wages rose as they would have in any other setting when the labor market tightened up.

Archival evidence shows that at least two changes occurred in postwar labor relations. First, overseers expected to be paid more to manage free workers, as in the case of the Greene County, Alabama, overseer of North Carolina planter Paul Cameron, who straightforwardly demanded a raise to accommodate the new labor arrangements. Second, emancipation gave White workers more leverage in the labor market because many planter families now preferred White to Black help. In a tight labor market, employers realized that reliable workers could demand and should be paid unusually high wages.

Although I have not yet found sources that present the employees' side of the story, the correspondence of elites is full of complaints about White labor. For example, in the Mississippi Delta, Samuel Agnew's father failed to engage Black household help on his terms. Approaching a White woman, Agnew's father found that she disdained as servile the work he offered. From eastern Tennessee, one woman employer wrote to another that after the Black workers left she had attempted to hire White women whose interests turned out not to coincide with hers. Her complaint echoed an age-old exasperation with (low-wage) workers: that they would quit as soon as they made enough money to "buy them a little *finery*." An employer in North Carolina expressed similar aggravation with White women workers, said to have "got a wrong kink in their heads some way, and I don't believe it will come out soon." Employers evidently were not offering wages high enough to attract and retain workers.

There can be no doubt that in 1865 relations between the various classes of Whites changed in ways that were relatively advantageous to those with less money and prestige. The term "emancipation" is too strong in this context, for even the poorest Whites had not been enslaved, and the White animus against Blacks seems to have been stronger than class feeling. Poorer Whites, not having been slaves, were not emancipated, but their positions improved so as to unloosen them. But there is no question that the end of the Civil War brought about an upheaval in the relations between the class of Whites who worked for wages and those used to employing hired help. The unsettling of the old hierarchy discomfited those used to being on top, whose correspondence betrays anger, confusion, and depression.

Contemplating a new set of class relationships, W. W. Lenoir, a wealthy North Carolinian, was in a troubled state of mind. While his peers were predicting the extermination of poor Blacks, Lenoir envisioned a radical reordering of White society in the South, including the creation of two new White upper classes and the disappearance of those whom he knew and of whom he approved, including his own.

First, Lenoir predicted that the distance separating Whites of different classes would widen dramatically. His own class of White elites, who, presumably, were cultured but not haughty, would disappear. In its place would arise two new White upper classes that are difficult to distinguish from each other. Their very similarity underscores the intensity of Lenoir's distaste for the new rich, whom he calls a "shoddy aristocracy," on the one hand, and the "very wealthy and extravagant devotees of fashion," on the other. He thought the former, previously poor, now suddenly rich, would have gained their wealth too quickly to have become refined. Anxious over marking a distance from their White servants, this new "shoddy aristocracy" would grind down their servants through mistreatment and miserable wages. The "devotees of fashion" would seek mainly to dazzle those below by aping the manners of European aristocrats and employing liveried European servants. In Lenoir's eyes, the ill-paid White poor at the bottom of the society would fall deeper and deeper into poverty and misery. Ultimately they would become so malnourished that they would "perish from want when unable to work." This former Confederate general despised what he saw as the new rich who profited from the war and its aftermath, but he reserved his death wish for the poor.

The former ruling class—faced with what seemed to them a topsy-turvy world of emancipated former slaves and angry poor Whites refusing to work or demanding more pay—rued the future. Lenoir said he was "gloomy, gloomy, gloomy," as others toted up the casualties of the new order. The strain of standing firm broke many who seemed to be the best of men, while accommodating to the new order appeared dishonorable. In Florida, E. Phillips saw the new commercial order, in which planters became merchants and lowered themselves by trading with Blacks, as a "vile and ominous portent." Defining such behavior as "low and contemptible," he concluded that "our race has already past [*sic*] its prime and is entering on its age of decline."

Gertrude Thomas belonged to the class I have just quoted in their despair. But where they left fragmentary commentary in letters, she left an enormous, candid journal that she kept from 1848 to 1889. Her comments on the years after 1865 provide a fascinating glimpse into the meaning of emancipation for Black and White women. The Thomas journal is particularly valuable because emancipation from the point of view of employers is so often discussed as though only men—who either routinely worked in the fields producing crops for the market or supervised such workers—experienced emancipation and, in the United States, Reconstruction.

In her prewar journal entries, Gertrude Thomas describes work as being accomplished by invisible hands, so that she *has* a fire made or her husband, Jefferson, *has* piles of brush burned. Thomas was the focal point in her household, and as a slave owner, she never had to give much thought to the needs of the workers she owned, which were automatically subordinated. Only one set of interests counted in her household, her own. Emancipation abolished what had seemed to her to have been frictionless labor relations. For the first time Thomas had to contend with employees who pursued interests of their own.

The spring of 1865 introduced Thomas to new, bilateral labor relations that were doubly complicated. Of itself, emancipation would have plunged Black families into turmoil, throwing issues of power and residence into question. But emancipation also occurred in the wake of a war that had further complicated gender relations between Black men and women as it had among Whites. Just as Southern White women had seized the opportunity to write, speak, and work for wages, so Black women in and around Augusta also moved into openings that had never existed before. They could withdraw from the paid workforce to stay home to care for their husbands and children, or they could sell food in the streets and railroad stations as well as keep other women's houses and babies for money. At the same time, Black men and women were not only adjusting to individual and familial autonomy but also were establishing and reestablishing relationships within their families that affected domicile and authority. The resulting upheaval tested Thomas's limits as an employer and housekeeper.

Freedwomen's increased opportunities inside and outside the workforce caused a shortage in household labor that Thomas found disadvantageous. White workers seemed to her a natural resort, and in 1865 Thomas predicted that Black labor would soon be displaced by White. Experience proved otherwise, and after experimenting with White workers, at least some of whom were Irish Catholics, she concluded that Whites were no improvement. In the house and in the fields, workers pursued their own interests, and Whites were no more selfless or reliable than Blacks. To make matters worse from the point of view of an employer used to a permanent, captive workforce, household workers now engaged to work only one month at a time and took advantage of workplace mobility.

Free labor presented Thomas with a number of frustrations, the greatest of which was workers' mobility into and out of the workforce and between employers. Considering that emancipation coincided with financial loss, Thomas found the second kind of mobility most trying. Chronically short of cash, she complained for years that she could afford to employ only young, inexperienced, or careless workers, who were particularly annoying within the household. Jefferson Thomas, who was acutely aware of the difficulty of keeping efficient workers, worked less intimately with his employees and disagreed with his wife on the extent to which employers should make concessions. Whereas he saw the necessity for conciliating first-rate workers, she insisted that workers meet her standards of employee-employer etiquette, which for her meant deference.

Gertrude Thomas describes the degree to which deference was touchy on both sides. Formerly enslaved workers sought to reinforce the distinction between slavery and freedom by dropping extreme forms of submission, as between an older servant and a younger member of the employer household. On the other side, Thomas tried as much as possible to preserve older forms of etiquette and to widen the social distance between employers/Whites and employees/Blacks. Deference counted for more in her scheme of labor relations than efficiency. She wrote that "hands are scarce but respect is a quality I demand from servants even more than obedience. I can overlook neglected work but cannot tolerate disrespect."

In the long run, Thomas won the battle for deference by paying for it. In the five years following emancipation, however, the only period in which she reports the wages she is paying, a labor shortage (of farm as well as household workers) drove wages steadily upward. In 1865 Thomas paid a mere twenty-five cents per week to a full-time worker in her house, who seems, not surprisingly, to have departed quickly, for Thomas not only offered minuscule wages. She put little importance on prompt payment. Wages quickly increased from thirty cents per day to wash to fifty cents per day to iron and $5 per month for a cook. By late 1868 wages had increased to $7 per month plus board. In 1870 she paid two young girls $9 per month for the work that in 1865 she offered one $1 per month.

Thomas may have paid better wages, but her management style never became very steady. She jawboned her employees and hinted that they should leave, then was surprised when they actually quit. Others she told to leave without actually meaning for them to do so. She expected that workers would discern her wishes through intimation or overhearing. Lacking the wherewithal to pay wages that first-rate workers could demand and insisting on an etiquette that workers found demeaning, Thomas shouldered more and more of the burden of her own household work. Keeping the house in perfect order wore her out, and eventually her standards fell. She began to wonder whether she was making the best use of her own energy, for she found housework "utterly uncongenial." Her decision to take up teaching related not only to a need for money but also to a realization that she was already performing a great deal of unpaid labor. Considering her level of education, she concluded that she could make more efficient use of her time in another line of work.

The conjunction of emancipation and impoverishment made

Thomas a working woman; Reconstruction, in her experience, meant a hitherto unimaginable burden of work, whether paid or unpaid, whether she supervised it or carried it out herself. Because women could neither vote nor hold office, the politics of Reconstruction was not the stuff of Thomas's day-to-day life. Nonetheless she resented the economic ramifications of Reconstruction: unintimidated free laborers who pursued better wages and working conditions. This meant that while her husband's adjustment to emancipation and Reconstruction took place largely in the more public worlds of politics and farm employment, hers was far more intimate, in the private world of house and yard, and unmediated by the power of the state. No laws regulated household employment, in which there were no contracts, liens, or prosecutions for debt.

For Gertrude Thomas as for her female peers, Reconstruction represented not so much a political revolution as an upheaval in labor relations. For the first time, she was not assured the help of reliable and experienced workers. For women like Thomas, emancipation not only meant downward economic mobility; it also changed their relation to work, in this case, to household work. Having been securely at the top, where they never had to be conscious of workers' concerns, much less adjust to them, women like Gertrude Thomas fell into a less privileged rank in which their needs competed with those of their workers, who had been formerly enslaved women and poor White women.

We more easily think of the post–Civil War era as remaking race relations, but remembering enslavement as a system of captive labor relations lets us see how a change in the Southern political economy empowered Southern working people on both sides of the color line—if only in the short run.

November 1989

Eric Foner's *Reconstruction*

AMERICA'S UNFINISHED REVOLUTION

I N A DEMOCRACY LIKE THE UNITED STATES the jarring presence of race and racism has been with us since before its very beginnings. Thus a topic like Reconstruction after the Civil War comes to acquire a long historiographical lineage, which I will not rehearse for you here. By now I think we will all agree that the continued salience of racism in American life lends the history of Reconstruction an enduring attraction as well as a string of varying and contradictory interpretations. Published in the spring of 1988, Eric Foner's *Reconstruction* marks a watershed in that historiography, succeeding brilliantly in its aim of presenting a comprehensive and modern treatment of its subject, embedded within a national context.

Erected upon a mountain of primary sources, Foner's book graciously pays tribute to other historians in chapter headings and subheadings that echo book titles of W. E. B. Du Bois, John Hope Franklin, Eugene Genovese, Willie Lee Rose, and others. Such abundant and self-conscious documentation cuts at least two ways, however, for while this method lends the book enormous historiographical resonance, it simultaneously produces take-no-prisoner footnotes. At two inches of notes per page, such aggressive footnoting humbles the reader and discourages impertinent queries.

Foner's periodization reflects one of his fundamental themes: the centrality of what he calls "the Black experience," to which I will return. This emphasis doubles the book's scope, however, for *Recon-*

struction intends to be more than a history of Reconstruction after the Civil War. It strives, as well, to present a history of the meaning of emancipation, and I will return to what I see as an unresolved tension in this regard as well. Suffice it here to note that Foner's focus on Black people affects the shape of the book from the outset. Instead of beginning in 1865 with Presidential Reconstruction, as it would have a generation ago, Foner's *Reconstruction* starts in 1863 with the Emancipation Proclamation.

The first four chapters deal largely with the emancipated people in a manner that is both clear and nuanced. This section of the book ripples with key words such as "ambiguity," "tension," and "conflict," indicating the many contradictions between postwar realities and the free labor ideology that Foner knows so well and the occurrence of unintended consequences that flowed from conflicting interests and competing claims. Explaining the meaning of freedom, Foner says that the very term was subject to multiple interpretations that were conflicting and that changed over time. Similarly he recognizes the contradictions buried in elite Southern economic thought. While capitalist development required a mobile workforce, free labor was anathema to employers determined to immobilize Black workers. Weaving together economic and racial matters, Foner very rightly sees much of what has been called race relations as labor relations. He pursues his insights north of the Mason and Dixon line to improve on current labor historiography that pretends that Northern workers were immune to their country's characteristic failing.

Foner recognizes that slavery was fundamentally a labor system (from the point of view of the employers/owners, at least, although he does not supply the conditional phrase). This means that he does not confuse racism and White supremacy with class bias. It also means that he understands how violence and fraud could serve broad economic as well as racial ends. Building on the comparative history that characterized his insightful Fleming lectures,[1] Foner is also alert to the uses (and abuses) of taxation policies. Considering that this book dwells on so many conflicts and ambiguities, I find its clarity to be one of its great beauties.

Foner's *Reconstruction* is a smart book of enormous strengths. Sensitive to local variations, it is coherent on issues of general importance. Foner takes race and racism seriously but is able nonetheless to discern their economic and political uses.

To my mind *Reconstruction* represents an intelligent, broad-gauged discussion of the postwar era, at least as such histories might have been written up to the mid-1980s. It is a masterpiece of its genre, the consummation of what used to be called neo-abolitionist or revisionist writing about Reconstruction. Even though I will be spending more time here on *Reconstruction*'s shortcomings than on its strengths, I do wish it to be understood that I deeply respect the book as a whole and appreciate the extraordinary sophistication and sensitivity that characterize it throughout.

For all its building from scratch (as indicated in the notes), *Reconstruction* remains oddly tethered to older histories. Its implicit definitions, which since the early 1980s have come to be questioned, and its virtual neglect of gender lead me to conclude that in its heart of hearts, *Reconstruction* is a mid-1960s book.

Unlike several newer histories of the South that deal with Blacks and Whites simultaneously—I'm thinking here of books that have appeared since 1984 by historians such as Suzanne Lebsock, Vernon Burton, Barbara Fields, and Dolores Janiewski—*Reconstruction* sticks mainly to the older concentration on Blacks and their former owners.[2] For Foner, "labor" means Black labor, unless the discussion concerns the North. Periodically non-planter Southern Whites appear, but peripherally and in general terms, as on pages 297–99, where they are scalawags, and 393, 396, and 596, in which they are yeoman farmers forced into cotton production. One realizes only vaguely that yeoman Whites and formerly enslaved Black people belonged to the very same economic system and that in the Black belts, non-slave-owning Whites would have been affected socially and economically by the revolution of emancipation. When, after the end of the Civil War, a labor shortage gave Southern workers something of an advantage vis-à-vis employers, in this book it is Black, but not White, workers who receive that bonus. Foner's myopia toward Whites of modest wealth perpetuates older conceptions of class and race in the South, in which Blacks are the poor and Whites the rich (although in fairness I should add that he is sensitive to gradations of wealth among Blacks), and as though poor Whites were not members of the same region at the same time. Foner's concentration on Blacks obscures the experiences of the majority of Southerners who experienced Reconstruction.

In a related definition that also remains implicit, Foner's delineation of work follows what he sees as the truly important economic relations in the South. Turning most often to the economic units that exerted such enormous influence, Foner concentrates on plantation agriculture. This means that in this book, "work" means primarily the agricultural work that produces commodities for national and international markets. While Foner does mention work that is not field work, it seems to me that in these nearly seven hundred pages, the work that really counts is done in the fields, particularly on plantations. Hence the wage work of women—particularly household work that produces no marketable product—figures hardly at all.

Foner's version of Southern economics overlooks the workplace experiences of many Southerners—women—who were employers and employees. This view of the Southern economy leaves no place for the White women employers who, after emancipation, found themselves at a disadvantage as they attempted to hire household workers. White women workers seeking household wage work saw their wages increase and their terms of employment improve during the postwar period of labor shortage, an improvement that was directly related to Black women's increased economic opportunities. New alternatives suddenly opened to Black women, who might withdraw from the paid labor force or drastically reduce their participation in it. They might go into business for themselves, as did Mary Chesnut's household maid, Mollie, whose egg and butter business helped them both financially.[3] Or they might bargain with employers for household work, which was not regulated by the state and was subject only to month-by-month employment.

In any case, many Southern women experienced Reconstruction within the bosom of families that were their own and/or those of their employers. The whole matter of employing and employment was far more intimate for women than for men for whom agricultural employment, away from home, was the norm.

By paying little heed to gender, Foner construes the public realms of the market economy and politics narrowly. Spending only the minimum of time on Black families and on the personal meanings of his period for Black people, he easily conflates two incongruent themes, which he defines at the end of the book as the "implications of emancipation" and the "political and social agenda of Reconstruction" (page 612). Foner writes as though the two were coeval, which is possible if slavery is defined mainly as a system of labor and enslaved people are defined primarily as workers for other people. Enslaved people *were* workers, and from the point of view of their employers, they were workers first and foremost. Yet enslaved people were also human beings whose lives meant more to them than employment. The lives of enslaved women, in which sexual victimization, loss of children, and lack of protection and support loomed so large, reminds me that they were also people whose emancipation had consequences that did not play out merely in the production of staples for the market or participation in electoral politics.

There was a considerable area of overlap of the "implications of emancipation" and the "political and social agenda of Reconstruction," especially in what Foner rightly calls the "politicization of everyday life" (page 122), including atrocious violence that was gendered. But the implications of emancipation were also personal and familial, which are two areas in which the enormous new strength, here neglected, of women's history can come into play. Most obviously, much of the meaning of emancipation for women who had been enslaved was not merely individual; it was familial, focused first of all on children.[4] Beyond neglecting much of the basic (and gendered) description of the meaning of freedom, Foner's failure to take women seriously leads him into questionable generalizations.

Overlooking gender permits the repetition of phrases popular in the 1960s and 1970s about "the" Black community and "the" Black experience, which Foner undermines in some places and reinforces in others. On the one hand, he is fully able to delineate instances in which Black men differed, as in Louisiana, in which free men of color sometimes reached different political conclusions from freedmen. But this acuity of vision stops at the cabin door, and Black families fall into line behind their men, à la the 1970s, male-centered Black worlds of John Blassingame and Herbert Gutman.[5] As in the histories of the 1960s and 1970s, Blacks are admirable men, cut on the patterns of images familiar from Montgomery in 1954, Birmingham in 1963, and Selma in 1965. These Black men exhibit, as on page 122, "quiet dignity in the face of assault." Few angry, enraged Blacks appear in Foner's pages, although a brief, veiled comment raises suspicions that I wish to pursue.

On page 88, Foner writes a long, pregnant, foreclosed paragraph that ends with these sentences, which I beg your patience while I read them in full:

> Not all Black women placidly accepted the increasingly patriarchal quality of Black family life. Indeed, many proved more than willing to bring family disputes before public authorities. The records of the Freedmen's Bureau contain hundreds of complaints by Black women of beatings, infidelity, and lack of child support. "I notice that some of you have your husbands arrested, and the husbands have their wives arrested," declared Holland Thompson, one of Alabama's leading Black politicians, in an 1867 speech. "All that is wrong—you can settle it among yourselves." Some Black women objected to their husbands' signing labor contracts for them, demanded separate payment of their wages, and refused to be liable for their husbands' debts at country stores. And some women, married as well as single, opened individual accounts at the Freedman's Savings Bank. Yet if emancipation not only institutionalized the Black family but also spawned tensions within it, Black men and women shared a passionate commitment to the stability of family life as a badge of freedom and the solid foundation upon which a new Black community could flourish.

This closing is very nice, but it presents a partial and a retouched picture of the enormous agitation that was taking place within Southern families, Black as well as White, after the war.

Contemporary sources attest to the outbursts of anger that characterized the postwar years. This anger came from Blacks and Whites, and among Blacks it came often from women. One historian of Black working women, Jacqueline Jones, sees Black women as "particularly outspoken and aggressive" and willing to "confront White authority figures." She also notes that after emancipation, freedwomen exchanged the drab, unattractive clothing of enslavement for fancier and more colorful garments. Black women's outspokenness and flamboyance, which were hardly the sort of characteristics that pious Americans encouraged in women, seem to have attracted vicious and violent attacks that Jones calls an important phenomenon in American women's history.[6] This aspect of emancipation—the freedom to be loud and tacky—does not fit in Foner's scheme. In fact, the whole nasty, fertile world of noise and sin and liquor and fighting that gave rise to the secular music of freedom and that has long characterized one part of African American life (especially urban life), Foner does not mention. He writes of churches and stability, not of the women we recognize in the blues.

Women as autonomous actors with their own interests separate from their husbands or the market economy pretty much disappear from *Reconstruction*. While Foner can delineate with marvelous clarity the conflicts of interest that bedeviled relations between employers and employees and between Blacks and Whites, he draws a veil over relations within Black families, even though his sources (and other historians) point to considerable turmoil that probably had much in common with relations within poor White households. In a book published just after *Reconstruction*, Linda Gordon traces the sources of family violence to "power struggles" between individuals that times of upheaval exacerbate.[7] Foner could hardly have consulted Gordon's book, but he might have been more attentive to what his infinite primary sources were saying about conflicts within Black families, to discover that the interests of "the family," even "the Black family," as a single entity were not always the same as those of particular women and children. Although historians are examining wealthy White families during the Civil War, very little published material concerns Black families at that time. Nonetheless the primary sources, such as the Freedmen's Bureau records, indicate that emancipation created conflicts as well as reconciliations for Black families that had been sundered. After four years of war and generations of slavery, it would have been extraordinary if Black families had been able to settle effortlessly into patriarchal orderliness in which all members meshed into a single, shared identity.

Politics in Foner's *Reconstruction* remains stuck in a pre–women's history definition, so that politics is still what legislatures and office-holders and political parties do. In the fashion of pre-1970s histori-ography, women enter this story primarily as proponents of woman suffrage. Politics here is neither so relentless nor so narrowly defined as in E. Merton Coulter's 1947 *South during Reconstruction,* and Foner shows throughout how public policies intentionally produced eco-nomic ends. Despite this enormous improvement, Foner neglects the gendered aspects of politics, notably by failing to pursue the salience of sex and marriage in Reconstruction politics. He mentions twice that the specter of interracial marriage was a staple of anti-Black and anti-Republican rhetoric but makes only the most tenuous connec-tion to antebellum and wartime patterns of Southern sexuality.[8] Fon-er's allusion to the use of interracial marriage in White supremacist politics hints at the salience of sex in American race relations. But the fertile field of marriage and sexuality in Reconstruction politics remains untouched.[9]

In veering away from intimate matters, Foner is following a long tradition in liberal and Marxist writing of defining power in political and economic terms and of sweeping the personal and familial under the rug. Since the days of abolitionism, well-intended writers have avoided discussions of Black sexuality and family relations out of fear of reinforcing ugly, racist stereotypes. In the last decade, however, feminist historians have marched into the thickets of family life and sexuality, even Black family life and Black sexuality. Investigators like Martha Hodes are going behind the silences and discovering that sex and sexuality were deeply intertwined with race and slavery.[10] As in the 1960s and 1970s, the friends of the Negro in the 1860s were reluc-tant to delve into the crucial but messy issues of sexual intimacy. But their reluctance does not make such issues any less crucial. A gen-dered approach to Southern history is now revealing that Reconstruction and emancipation were not quite the same thing, but also that gender and families were of crucial importance, in both experience and political ideology. Attention to gender is not more important than examining the free labor ideology as it applied to freedpeople. But since the mid-1980s, a truly current synthesis must include investigations of women and gender.

November 1989

The Shoah and Southern History

S OMEDAY AFRICAN AMERICANS and Jewish Americans may disentangle ourselves from one another, but that time hasn't arrived quite yet. I won't talk here about all our sundry engagements and exasperations, but one subject draws us together: Old Country trauma. For Blacks, the worst Old Country is the slave and segregationist South; for Jews, it is Europe, encapsulated in the Shoah (Holocaust) of the Nazi era.

Usually slavery and the Shoah keep their distance. But in the mid-1990s a bestselling young author's highly publicized comments brought European and Southern history together. The controversy swirling around Daniel Jonah Goldhagen, a Harvard political scientist, riveted my attention. Building on the work of historians such as Christopher Browning, Goldhagen's 1996 book, *Hitler's Willing Executioners: Ordinary Germans and the Holocaust,* disputes the common wisdom that a few evil men or bureaucratic automatons caused the Nazi genocide of European Jews.[1] Instead, Goldhagen insists that ordinary Germans willingly slaughtered Jews. Goldhagen attributes this willingness to kill to the steady stream of what he calls "eliminationist" anti-Semitism circulating in Germany since the late nineteenth century. By World War II, he argues, "ordinary" Germans killed Jews openly and shamelessly, convinced that they were doing the right thing. Even as the war was ending in obvious Nazi defeat, Goldhagen points out that German soldiers forced starving, moribund Jewish prisoners on otherwise purposeless "death marches."

Hitler's Willing Executioners describes face-to-face murders in graphic detail and includes such intimacies as a photograph of a policeman shooting point-blank a mother holding her child. Germans from all walks of life, Goldhagen says, "tortured and degraded Jews with zeal and energy." As though proud of the slaughter, assailants photographed the carnage, creating images that sometimes capture wives and girlfriends looking on.

Gory souvenirs remind me of similar but Southern images: the charred, tortured Black body, often naked, often burned beyond recognition; the proud perpetrators, posing like big-game hunters beside their victim; the crowd staring at the body or looking straight into the camera, sometimes bearing the smiles that greet a camera in happier circumstances. Like Goldhagen's ordinary Germans, these ordinary White Southerners documented their deeds for the benefit of lovers and friends.

I read *Hitler's Willing Executioners* with one eye on the American South, where White supremacy found its own willing executioners. The parallel between Nazi Germany and the American South also occurred to Daniel Goldhagen, although he was defending himself historiographically. Criticized for his portrayal of German culture as rooted in anti-Semitism, Goldhagen replied that writing about the mechanics of the Holocaust without focusing on the virulence of German anti-Semitism "would be like writing a book about American slavery without writing about racism and saying, 'So let's write about the way the plantations were organized.'"

Hmmmm. Unfortunately, that is precisely the way too many books on Southern history deal with slavery: all too often, American authors can still write as though slavery were incidental, not central, to the American past. Considering how rarely racism appears in scholarship as a fundamental constituent of American and Southern society, it seems clear that both the history and the historiography of the Shoah can illuminate the history and the historiography of the American South. These two great tragedies of the modern era share a host of horrendous similarities: the racialization of vulnerable people, dehumanization, legal discrimination, segregation, captivity, forced labor, humiliation, cruelty, gratuitous violence, intense bodily and psychic torture. In the aftermath of the Shoah, these resemblances struck Stanley Elkins and inspired his adventurous analysis, *Slavery.*[2] Deeply influenced by Freud, Elkins advanced some excellent points and opened up new interpretive possibilities for Southern history. But he made uncritical use of the Sambo stereotype and disregarded Black people's own strengths and coping mechanisms such as families and religion. On Elkins's prototypical Southern plantation, the master/father—not the enslaved child's own parents—shaped the enslaved/child's psyche. Elkins's depiction of an ego-less enslaved Sambo quite rightly provoked enormous outcry—against both his conclusions and his methodology. *Slavery* not only doomed psychoanalysis as a tool for Southern history; it also made anathema comparisons with the Holocaust. To this day, neither the theory nor the comparison has recovered from *Slavery.* This is a pity.

In my work on Gertrude Thomas, Sojourner Truth, and Southern violence, I have tried to bring some of the intensely personal attributes of Holocaust historiography—real hurt, real blood, real trauma—into the history of American slave society. After much excellent scholarship on post-traumatic stress disorder, child abuse, sexual abuse, and personal violence, historians are in a stronger position than a generation or two ago to make sense of the psychological and physical injuries of slavery. Both Freud and contemporary psychological theory can help us write better Southern history. Once we can write the words "trauma" and "slavery" in the same sentence, we will have enriched our understanding of slavery's human costs, for enslaved, enslavers, and bystanders. Already Wilma King, in *Stolen Childhood: Slave Youth in Nineteenth-Century America,* has made excellent use of late-twentieth-century Balkan conflicts to illustrate the costs of enslaved children's lives in the perpetual war zone of slavery.[3]

When historians and other Americans face the fact that violence undergirded Southern society after emancipation as before, we will be better able to measure the weight of institutionalized hatred. Racism will no longer appear as an individual, personal flaw, but rather as a way of life, as an ideology. The everyday racism of ordinary people will come into view. The very ordinariness of racism—in this case, Southern racism—needs to be faced and admitted. When this omnipresence penetrates Southern historiography, our overall estimation of the basic meaning of Southern history will change. Southern history will look more like the history of the Shoah.

November 2000

How We Think about the Term "Enslaved" Matters

THE YEAR 1619 IS MOMENTOUS in American history, as a recent visit by the current US president attests. In July, Donald Trump visited Jamestown, Virginia, to commemorate two events in 1619: the July creation of the colony's representative government, the House of Burgesses, and the August arrival of people he termed "enslaved Africans."

This phrase improves upon a commonplace in American discourse, the one-word "slaves." But the term "enslaved," in and of itself, merits further comment, as history and as ideology. How we use these words makes a crucial difference when we think about the meanings of our past. In that phrasing, the people from Africa disembarking in Virginia were always and already "slaves." Even if slavery had been common in early seventeenth-century Virginia, those Africans had not left their homes as slaves.

People were not enslaved in Virginia in 1619; they were indentured. The twenty or so Africans were sold and bought as "servants" for a term of years, and they joined a population consisting largely of European indentured servants, mainly poor people from the British Isles whom the Virginia Company of London had transported and sold into servitude.

Enslavement was a process that took place step by step, after the mid-seventeenth century. This process of turning "servants" from Africa into racialized workers enslaved for life occurred in the 1660s to 1680s through a succession of Virginia laws that decreed that a child's status followed that of its mother and that baptism did not automatically confer emancipation. By the end of the seventeenth century, Africans had indeed been marked off by race in law as chattel to be bought, sold, traded, inherited and serve as collateral for business and debt services.

This was not already the case in 1619.

Even in 1700, Africans were hardly the only unfree colonists, for a majority of those laboring in Virginia were people bound to service. They were indentured Whites. Population numbers are crucial in understanding the demography of labor in early Virginia. By 1680 only about 7 percent of Virginians were of African descent; 20 percent of Virginians were of African descent by 1700, and by 1750 the 100,000 enslaved Virginian men and women accounted for more than half the population. Here lies the demography of enslavement.

In short, the 1619 Africans were not "enslaved." They were townspeople in the Ndongo district of Angola who had been captured by Imbangala warlords and delivered to the port of Luanda for shipment to the Americas. Raiding, capturing, and selling people was not an exclusively African practice.

Raiding for captives to sell belongs to a long human history that knows no boundaries of time, place, or race. This business model unites the ninth-to-twelfth-century Vikings, who made Dublin western Europe's largest slave market (think of Saint Patrick, who had been enslaved by Irish raiders in the fifth century), and tenth-to-sixteenth-century Cossacks, who delivered eastern European peasants to the Black Sea market at Tana for shipment to the wealthy eastern Mediterranean. The earliest foreign policy of the new United States of America targeted the raiders of the Barbary Coast, who engaged in a lively slave trade in Europeans (think Robinson Crusoe). Sadly, as I said above, the phenomenon of warlords who prey on peasants knows no boundaries of time or place.

There's more to Virginia history, of course, than bondage. There's freedom, not only after the American Civil War, but also in the seventeenth century, when an Angolan man called Antonio, arriving in Virginia in 1621, became Anthony Johnson, a wealthy free farmer and slave-owning planter in Northampton and Accomack Counties. His immediate descendants prospered. His eighteenth-century descendants, living within a hardened racial regime, sadly did not. It is in the eighteenth century that we find the more familiar, rigid boundaries of racialized American identity.

In Jamestown in July 2019, the president of the United States spoke within a post-eighteenth-century American ideology of race. He dedicated some 688 words to the "settlers" who "worked hard. They had courage and abundance, and a wealth of self-reliance. They strived mightily to turn a profit." These "settlers" were hardy Christians who "forged what would become the timeless traits of the American character."

But what, in presidential discourse, of the "enslaved Africans" arriving the following month of August? They received sixty-seven words that did not include working hard, and the history they "forged" was different. Here lies an emblematic version of the American ideology of race.

Within this ideology of race, the Jamestown Africans of 1619 are always already enslaved, so that seeing the 1619 Africans and their descendants as slaves seals them within the permanent identity of enslavement. It says Africans and their descendants are the same as slaves.

Scholars call this kind of thinking "essentialist"—you are intrinsically what you always must be. When enslavement is the essence of Black identity, Black people cannot figure as American working men and women who play an active role in American history. It is the "settlers," that is, non-Africans, who forge "the timeless traits of the American character." They, not African workers, belong to the crucial core of this version of American history. The Africans are an afterthought, so that the president can skip quickly to the Reverend Martin Luther King Jr. and, finally, to twenty-seven words on how Black people have also contributed to the United States of America.

Why is this history of 1619 important now, at a time when versions of American society compete politically, when one fraction of the citizenry plots a return to an America whose image was White, and another fraction of the citizenry embraces an evolution into a multiracial, multicultural democracy? Because how we envision our past shapes how we see ourselves today. One of the favorite objectives of White pride makes this point.

People proud to be White occasionally argue they should be able to celebrate their White heritage during a "White History Month." But what, exactly, would a White History Month celebrate? The president's version of Virginia history would say the "settlers" who "forged what would become the timeless traits of the American character. They worked hard. They had courage and abundance, and a wealth of self-reliance." As though only White people worked hard, as in an unfortunate but prevalent trope of proud White American identity. A history for our present times is not so myopic.

A multicultural, multiracial version of US history is broader than easily categorized heroes, insiders, and outsiders. The history that can serve us now recognizes racial identity as a process in which identities are shared, shaped, and changed over time and place. This kind of history understands that statuses of freedom and servitude are not permanent, essential identities that never change over time. It can see identity as processes that continue as we speak, as we continue to forge it.

August 2019

WHITENESS

What Whiteness Means
in the Trump Era

DONALD J. TRUMP CAMPAIGNED on the slogan "Make America Great Again," a phrase whose "great" was widely heard as "White." Certainly the 2016 presidential election has been analyzed as a victory for White Christian Americans, especially men. Against Mr. Trump were all the rest of us: professionals with advanced degrees and the multiracial, multiethnic millions.

Though White Americans differed sharply on their preferences for president, the 2016 election marked a turning point in White identity. Thanks to the success of "Make America Great Again" as a call for a return to the times when White people ruled, and thanks to the widespread analysis of voters' preferences in racial terms, White identity became marked *as a racial identity*. From being individuals expressing individual preferences in life and politics, the Trump era stamps White Americans with race: White race.

I don't mean that Americans suddenly started counting people as "White." This has been going on since the first federal census of 1790, which enumerated three categories of White people ("Free White Males of sixteen years and upwards, including heads of families," "Free White Males under sixteen years," and "Free White Females"). That census also tabulated two other categories: "All other free persons" and "Slaves." Period. Black was not marked. Since 1790, population statistics have faithfully recognized a category of "White" people, sometimes more than one, especially native and non-native born. So I don't mean that Americans suddenly discovered the category of White in 2016.

American Whiteness Since Trump, page 10, 2020, ink and graphite on paper, 12″ × 9½″.
In the early spring of 2020, before coronavirus turned the world upside down and before
January 6, 2021, I made the artist's book *American Whiteness Since Trump* in residence
at the Bogliasco Foundation in Liguria, Italy. Since *American Whiteness Since Trump*
predated the national George Floyd protests and the rise of Trump-inspired vigilantism,
I had to draw another book in the summer of 2020 taking them into account: *From
Slavery to Freedom*.

I'm saying that what it means to see yourself as White has fundamentally changed, from unmarked default to racially marked, a change now widely visible: from *of course* being president and *of course* being beauty queen and *of course* being the cute young people selling things in ads to having to make space for other, non-White people to fill those roles.

We have been seeing this change in popular culture and in higher education over the course of the last decades. Black and Brown and Asian people now sell you financial instruments and clothing. The president and first lady are Black. Your college literature course includes Toni Morrison and Junot Díaz. But if you haven't gone to college, where multiculturalism has been making its way for a generation, and if your version of America was formed in school in the twentieth century, and that twentieth-century image remains in your consciousness, you may feel you have a lot to lose.

In our racially oriented American society, this change marks a demotion for White people. From assumed domination, they now take their place among the multiracial American millions. For Trump supporters embracing the social dimension of "Make America Great Again," their vote enacted a visceral "No!" to multicultural America. As if to say, "Take us back to the time of unmarked Whiteness and racially unmarked power," power that everyone just automatically assumed to be White.

In the Trump administration, White men will be in charge (virtually his entire transition team, and practically every name offered for a potential cabinet post, is a White man). You could say that's nothing new, that White men have been in charge forever. This is true, but now with a gigantic difference. This time the White men in charge will not simply *happen* to be White; they will be governing as White, as taking America back, back to before multiculturalism.

Mr. Trump's presidential campaign's leadership and support complicate making America great again, on account of the campaign's tilt toward White nationalism. Here lies a snare that has entrapped White identity for decades. White nationalism scares many ordinary White people away from embracing Whiteness, which White nationalism makes appear bigoted and terrorist. Given the people who emphasize their White racial identity—White nationalists, Nazis, Klansmen, and so on—Whiteness is a spoiled identity. Embracing Whiteness would seem to enmesh one in a history of slave owning and all the discrimination flowing from it. What righteous person would want to embrace that? Up to now, there's hardly been a pressing need to do so, for a fundamental dimension of White American identity has been individuality.

Conveniently, for most White Americans, being White has meant *not* having a racial identity. It means being and living and experiencing the world as an individual and not having to think about your race. It has meant being free of race. Some people are proud White nationalists, but probably not many of the millions who voted for Donald Trump. Thinking in terms of community would seem to be the job of Black people. The Trump campaign has disrupted that easy freedom.

By elevating Steve Bannon of Breitbart News into its leadership and not vigorously forswearing White nationalist support, the Trump campaign enmeshed "Make America Great Again" with White nationalism. As Whiteness emerges as an American racial identity, this constitutes a problem. Who defines American Whiteness right now? Does Mr. Bannon define what it means to be White, a definition not as an individual in the default category of American? How will White people who didn't support Mr. Trump in 2016 construe their identity as White people when Trumpists, including White nationalists, Nazis, Klansmen, and Mr. Bannon, have posted the markers?

Here's a further question about White American identity in the wake of "Make America Great Again." Mr. Trump did not win a majority of popular votes. Even if he had, the population he will have to govern far exceeds his supporters. Given this minority basis of support, what might a Trump administration portend?

The federal government's jurisdiction encompasses a country of more than 320 million multicolored, multireligious people in rural areas, towns, and cities, spanning 3.8 million square miles. If President Trump is to govern all of us, he will have to take on issues he never imagined and unimaginable complications, even on his pet issues of bringing back jobs. Whose jobs? Where? At what cost, and who's paying? What happens if Mr. Trump does try to address his supporters' economic grievances, even if only among White people? There are millions of them all over the place, with interests that hardly align with those of Republican elites.

What happens if Mr. Trump's people discover you can't just give away public lands and trash Native American sacred grounds without a huge pushback? What if Mormons won't go along and get along, morally and ethically, with Mr. Trump's agenda? As president, Mr. Trump's going to have to move beyond his White and heavily male electorate and face up to conflicts of interest even within his core. A Trump supporter in Atlanta warned the president-elect: break your promises at your peril.

I will not be surprised if the need to govern all of us alienates his base. And I will not be surprised if being president of a huge, multiracial, multiethnic democracy turns many of his supporters against him as a traitor to their values—perhaps, even, as a traitor to their race.

November 2016

American Whiteness Since Trump, page 7, 2020, ink and graphite on paper, 12″ × 9½″.
Years later, Steve Bannon still exerts pernicious power in American politics.

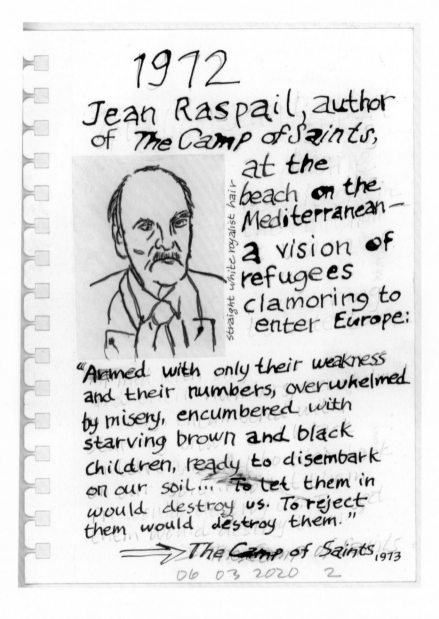

1972

Jean Raspail, author of *The Camp of Saints,* at the beach on the Mediterranean —

straight white royalist hair

a vision of refugees clamoring to enter Europe:

"Armed with only their weakness and their numbers, overwhelmed by misery, encumbered with starving brown and black children, ready to disembark on our soil.... To let them in would destroy us. To reject them would destroy them."

⟶ *The Camp of Saints,* 1973

06 03 2020   2

American Whiteness Since Trump, page 14, 2020, ink and graphite on paper, 12″ × 9½″.
One of the main inspirations of replacement theory is this pornographic French work.

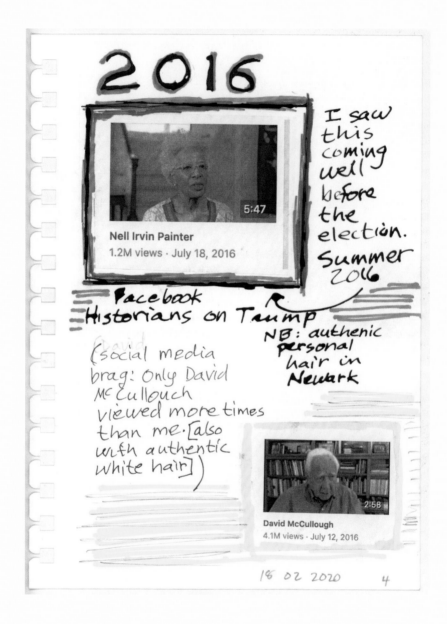

2016

I saw this coming well before the election. Summer 2016

Nell Irvin Painter
1.2M views · July 18, 2016

Facebook
Historians on Trump

NB: authenic personal hair in Newark

(social media brag: Only David McCullouch viewed more times than me. [also with authentic white hair])

David McCullough
4.1M views · July 12, 2016

18 02 2020   4

American Whiteness Since Trump, page 9, 2020, ink and graphite on paper, 12″ × 9½″.
In the summer of 2016, even before Trump was elected president, I understood his malicious influence in American politics and said so on Facebook's *Historians on Trump.*
Sadly, events have borne me out.

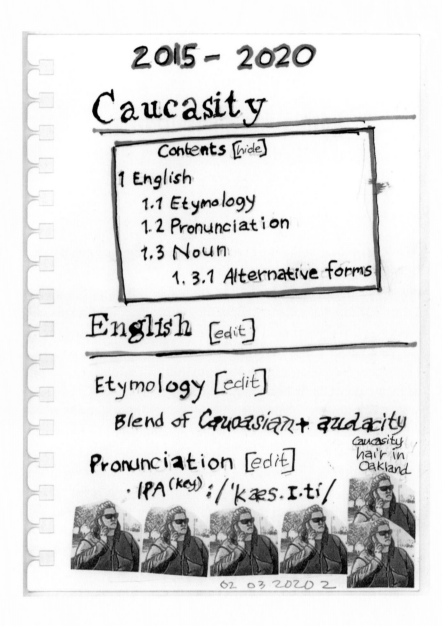

2015 - 2020

Caucasity

Contents [hide]

1 English
  1.1 Etymology
  1.2 Pronunciation
  1.3 Noun
    1.3.1 Alternative forms

English [edit]

Etymology [edit]

Blend of *Caucasian* + *audacity*

Pronunciation [edit]

· IPA (key): /ˈkæs.ɪ.ti/

Caucasity hair in Oakland

02 03 2020 2

American Whiteness Since Trump, page 23, 2020, ink and graphite on paper, 12″ × 9½″.
The year 2020 made Americans newly aware of the meanings of White race that
surveilled non-White people's access to public space presumably but not actually
open to all.

Rethinking Capitalization

S O MOMENTOUS, SO DARK YET HOPEFUL, these times have turned our world upside down.

Police brutality brought into the light. Masses in the streets confronting American history, toppling the Confederacy after years—decades—of well-mannered but vain protest. We are left to grapple with the conventions of American public life.

Restructuring policing in ways that matter will take months, years, and many more Confederate monuments remain standing than have come down. But one change has been implemented quickly: translating this social upheaval into print has suddenly and all but unanimously restored a capital "B" to "Black." I say "restored" because that capital "B" appeared in the 1970s. I used it myself. Then copy editors, uncomfortable with both the odd combination of uppercase "Black" and lowercase "white" and the unfamiliar, bumpy "Black and White," took off both capital letters. In one of many turns in the history of racial capitalization, "Black" returned to "black." There's a history to issues of capitalization.

"Spell It with a Capital," exhorted the Chicago *Conservator* in 1878. This pioneering Black weekly newspaper was founded by Ferdinand Lee Barnett, the husband of the crusading anti-lynching journalist Ida B. Wells. For the *Conservator*, as for journalists in the succeeding half century, the letter in question was "N," for "Negro," the then progressive name for Americans of African descent. As part of an extensive letter-writing campaign, W. E. B. Du Bois asked *The New York Times* in 1926 to capitalize "Negro" because the lowercase "n" inflicted "a personal insult." *The Times* refused, although *The New Republic* had agreed years earlier. By 1930 all Black and several important White newspapers, including the *New York World, New York Herald Tribune,* the *Chicago Tribune,* and *The New York Times,* had adopted the capital "N." Capital "N Negro" was standard usage by the 1950s.

In the 1960s "Black," formerly considered derogatory, gained acceptance as a sign of race pride, thanks to Malcolm X, the Nation of Islam, and Black Power coming out of the civil rights movement. In the 1970s capital "B Black" emerged in Black writing, sometimes but not always along with a corresponding capital "W White." In 1988 the Reverend Jesse Jackson, presidential candidate, changed names once again, deeming "African American" to be the correct terminology. The new phrase was accepted, with both adjectives in its phrasing conveniently capitalized. African American—at first with a hyphen, then without—went well with Asian American, Native American, and Hispanic, then Latino and Latinx, all capitalized.

By the early twenty-first century, "African American" was no longer working so smoothly, as African immigrants and their children became a sort of African African Americans. "Black" returned as a more inclusive term with the added attraction of roots in Black Power and James Brown's "Black + proud."

In the wake of massive George Floyd and Black Lives Matter protests, Black people and their allies now regard capitalizing "Black" as a badge of honor. By mid-June 2020 prominent newspapers and journalists' associations were embracing the capital "B." Even Fox News has joined the crowd. The most common motive for change was summed up as *respect.* As I started thinking about racial capitalization, I asked my multiracial, multiethnic Facebook friends for their views. They variously mentioned cultural identity, pride, and a shared "ethnicity," meaning Black American ethnicity, skipping over the various cultural backgrounds of Black people from around the Western Hemisphere and beyond. The case for capitalizing "Black" seemed obvious, whether as an ethnicity (a minority view) or a racial designation.

Which raises the question of capitalization for the other two currently recognized racial groups: "bBrown" and "wWhite."

I sense little sentiment for capitalizing "bBrown." As a demographic category, bBrown is scattered geographically, ethnically, and taxonomically. The US census considers Hispanics/Latinos an ethnicity rather than a racial group, pointing once again to the unwieldiness of trying to enumerate people according to concepts lacking clear boundaries like congressional districts, household wealth, or life expectancy. Do people from Latin America—Brazil, Mexico, El Salvador—go together in one category? Are people from Algeria, Iraq, and South Asia bBrown? "Brown" presents an exaggerated case of the universal imprecision of racial terminology. The Hispanic/Latino category, whose roots lie in the 1965 Immigration and Nationality Act, lacks the historical and emotional depth of Black, the subject of exhausting attention for some three hundred plus years. For now the media seem to have settled on lowercase "b" for "brown."

So what about "wWhite"? Perhaps the lowercase "w" for "White" mainly signals an unwillingness to poke the fiery hornet's nest of White nationalism of people like the Charleston church assassin, who capitalized "White." Besides, says *The New York Times,* White "doesn't represent a shared culture and history in the way Black does." *The Washington Post* continues to deliberate racial capitalization.

When I compare the cultural, intellectual, and historical heft of the three categories, Black comes out well ahead of the other two. We have whole libraries of books and articles about Blackness, world-beating traditions of Black music and literature, even entire academic departments thirty to fifty years old specializing in African American/Black studies. Compared with Blackness, Whiteness and brownness are severely under-theorized. Facebook friends' lowercasing of "white" and "brown" seems to prevail, at least for now. For a while I inclined toward the new formula: capital "B" for "Black"; lowercase "w" for "white"; lowercase "b" for "brown," but with serious reservations.

The National Association of Black Journalists prompted my first reservation. Its June 11, 2020, statement on racial capitalization says, "NABJ also recommends that whenever a color is used to appropriately describe race then it should be capitalized, including White and Brown." This recommendation from the leading organization representing Black journalists gave me pause.

A second reservation arose as I considered the asymmetry of

racial identities of Blackness and Whiteness that function differently in American history and culture. These two identities don't simply mirror each other, for one works through a very pronounced group identity; the other more often is lived as unraced individuality. However much you may see yourself as an individual, if you're Black, you also have to contend with other people's views. This is what Du Bois summed up as "twoness," as seeing yourself as yourself, but also knowing that other people see you as a Black person. You don't have to be a Black nationalist to see yourself as Black. Until quite recently, however, White Americans rarely saw themselves as raced, as White.

The people who have embraced White as a racial identity have been White nationalists, Ku Klux Klansmen, and their ilk. Thanks to President Trump, White nationalists are more visible than ever in our public spaces. Yet they fail to determine how masses of White people see themselves. In terms of racial identity, White Americans have had the choice of being either something vague—the paltry leavings of Blackness—or as Klansmen, which few have embraced. Those of my Facebook friends who said White should be capitalized were challenging the freedom to consider oneself as an unraced individual rather than subscribing to the preferences of White nationalists. "White" should be capitalized in order to unmask Whiteness as an American racial identity as historically important as Blackness. No longer should White people be allowed the comfort of racial invisibility; they should have to see themselves as raced. These Facebook friends said being racialized makes White people squirm, so, yes, racialize them with a capital "W." Make them squirm.

The good that might come from seeing White people squirm aside, persuasive Black scholars who have given the issue careful thought have prompted my own rethinking. In June 2020 Kwame Anthony Appiah of New York University said "White" should be capitalized, just as "Black" is capitalized, in order to situate "White" within historically created racial identities that have linked the two terms over the very long run. For intellectual clarity, what applies to one should apply to the other.

More emphatically, Eve L. Ewing, a poet and sociologist of education at the University of Chicago, recently started capitalizing "White" in order to emphasize the presence of Whiteness as a racial identity: "Whiteness," she says, "is not only an absence." For Ewing, the capital "W" stresses White as a powerful racial category whose privileges must always remain in sight. As an example, she compares the fate of the McCloskeys in Saint Louis, who pointed loaded firearms at peaceful protesters and faced the lightest of legal consequences, with that of young Tamir Rice, playing with a toy gun in Cleveland, who lost his life. Ewing may have been thinking of James Baldwin, who said at Wayne State University in 1980, "White is a metaphor for power." The capital letter can underscore the existence of an unjust racial power imbalance.

In the thinking of Appiah, Ewing, and my Facebook friends, Whiteness is less saliently linked to White nationalism than to racial neutrality or absence. Their reasons for capitalizing "White" are quite separate from White nationalism. We should capitalize "White" to situate Whiteness within the American ideology of race, within which Black, but not White, has been hypervisible as a group identity. Both identities are products of the American ideology of race. One way of remaking race is through spelling—using or not using capital letters. A more potent way is through behavior. Capital letters can remind us all of being a part of the American ideology of race, and for this reason I have now come around to capitalizing all our races, Black Brown, and White. Spelling may not change the world, but it signals a willingness to try.

July 2020

When Poverty Was White

C ARRIE BUCK, or rather only her last name, appears just once in the books of Charles Murray, the conservative sociologist and author of *Coming Apart: The State of White America, 1960–2010*, his portrait of the decline of poor White Americans. To find it, you have to look through the endnotes for the introduction to his most famous book, *The Bell Curve*, in which he cites *Buck v. Bell*, the 1927 Supreme Court case that approved Ms. Buck's involuntary sterilization. It's a striking omission, because her case highlights the historical blindness of Mr. Murray's narrow focus on the cultural and policy changes of the 1960s as the root of White America's supposed decline. The story of White poverty, as Ms. Buck's story illustrates, is much longer and more complex than Mr. Murray and his admirers realize or want to admit.

In 1924 Virginia ordered Ms. Buck, eighteen years old, unmarried, and pregnant, to be forcibly sterilized. Her legal guardian appealed, and the case made it to the Supreme Court. The winning argument blamed her pregnancy on hereditary weaknesses—in particular, her presumed feeblemindedness. Justice Oliver Wendell Holmes Jr.'s majority opinion entered history: "Three generations of imbeciles are enough." Involuntary sterilization was the early twentieth century's remedy for what Mr. Murray blames on changes in the 1960s. But it was precisely the changes of that later era—for Black civil rights, women's rights, poor people's rights—and socially committed Catholicism that ended this inhumane practice.

Something got lost in the discourse along the way. Ms. Buck, ster-

Carrie and Emma Buck in Window with $100 Reward, 2022, ink, tusche, and collage on paper, 12″ × 9½″. Carrie Buck was the defendant in *Buck v. Bell* in 1925, which made involuntary sterilization legal in the United States. Virginia had argued that Carrie Buck and her mother, Emma, were both feebleminded and had become pregnant, bringing generations of feebleminded people into being. The Bucks were poor White Virginians.

ilization, White poverty—this older history disappeared in the mid-twentieth century, when prosperity isolated the stigmata of poverty in Black Americans. In 1965 Daniel Patrick Moynihan's *The Negro Family: The Case for National Action* laid blame on a Black "tangle of pathology" of "ghetto culture." Mr. Moynihan voiced a logic widespread at the time that translated the disarray associated with poverty into a racial trait.

And so when Mr. Murray faults poor Whites' morals today, he unwittingly joins an earlier tradition of blaming the poor for their condition, whether they be Black in the 1960s or White in the early twentieth century.

The roots of the movement for the involuntary sterilization of poor Whites—the policy that Ms. Buck embodied—reach back into nineteenth-century social-betterment circles and an abundant social science literature on poor families.

The movement's pioneer was Richard L. Dugdale, corresponding secretary of the Prison Association of New York and secretary of the National Prison Association. He took up the scientific study of crime after the economic panic of 1873, which he blamed on unmarried sex, drunkenness, and crime. After visiting county and state jails, Mr. Dugdale published a report destined for greatness: *The Jukes: A Study in Crime, Pauperism, Disease and Heredity, Also Further Studies of Criminals.* By Mr. Dugdale's calculation, the "fornication," "crime," "prostitution," "bastardy," "intemperance," and "disease" of generations of the pseudonymous Jukes family had cost New York State a then staggering $1.3 million.

"The Jukes" found favor among penologists, social workers, and social gospelers, who combined a humanitarian commitment to the poor with a scientific approach to charity. One admirer was the Reverend Oscar Carleton McCulloch of the Plymouth Congregational Church in Indianapolis. Inspired by Mr. Dugdale, the Reverend McCulloch sought to make his own philanthropy scientific through research on Indiana's poor, some of whom came through his church doors.

One result was *The Tribe of Ishmael: A Study in Social Degradation* in 1888. In it, Mr. McCulloch answered a gigantic question in the burgeoning field of heredity at a time when the concept of "race" divided not just White and Black, but White people themselves: How could Americans of supposedly the finest of White racial stocks—English, Saxon, and Anglo-Saxon—engender a long history of pauperism and crime?

The answer, Mr. McCulloch said, still lay in blood, but in blood of the wrong kind. He wasn't being original when describing the English ancestors of the Ishmaelites as the "old convict stock which England threw into this country in the 17th century," but he was among the first to put it into a social-scientific context.

That logic was largely superseded in the 1910s by a seemingly more advanced approach to the persistence of White poverty: IQ testing. Such techniques to quantify intelligence aligned perfectly with an interventionist approach to social betterment, thanks to Charles Benedict Davenport, head of the Eugenics Record Office. Mr. Davenport stood at the hard end of a continuum of eugenic thinking, beside so-called negative eugenicists like Madison Grant, who proposed the literal elimination of people he thought inferior.

Though genes were not yet fully understood, Mr. Davenport had something like them in mind when he argued that intelligence was passed on as a single "unit trait." That unit trait could be quantified, in the words of an enthusiastic tester, as "the value of a man." (Mr. Murray made a similar argument in *The Bell Curve,* though he has since moved away from IQ hereditarianism.)

Mr. Davenport urged Henry H. Goddard, head of research at the Training School for Backward and Feeble-Minded Girls and Boys in Vineland, New Jersey, to test his charges. Mr. Goddard found the perfect resident, a twenty-two-year-old he called Deborah "Kallikak." His results, published in 1912 in the bestseller *The Kallikak Family,* invented the name "Kallikak" by joining the Greek *kalos* (goodness) and *kakos* (badness).

Her forebear, he deduced, had engendered two families: one upstanding, from a legitimate union, and Deborah's degenerate one, from sex with a feebleminded barmaid. Rating Deborah a "moron," Mr. Goddard concluded that she would lack moral judgment, and he blamed her mental handicap on her ancestry. According to Mr. Goddard, Deborah's degenerate branch counted 36 illegitimate children, 33 sexually immoral persons (mainly prostitutes), 3 epileptics (epilepsy was considered solely hereditary), 82 dead babies, 3 criminals, and 8 brothel keepers. How to block the propagation of hereditary social ills? Sterilization.

States had started sterilizing in 1907 to prevent crime, idiocy, and imbecility, in the parlance of the day. But some governors vetoed sterilization laws; in other states, courts invalidated the laws as cruel and inhumane, for lack of due process and for lack of equal protection. Were sterilization to prevail, expert guidance was needed, and Mr. Davenport's Eugenics Record Office supplied it in the form of a model sterilization law devised to withstand court challenge. Virginia passed the first such act in 1924.

The first person slated for sterilization under Virginia's new law was Carrie Buck, the daughter of an unmarried mother living in the State Colony for Epileptics and Feeble-Minded. Since both mother and daughter had been designated as feebleminded, her sterilization was deemed necessary to halt the propagation of "the shiftless, ignorant and worthless class of anti-social Whites of the South." After her sterilization, she lived an otherwise normal adult life.

Along with Ms. Buck, some 65,000 Americans were sterilized before 1968. Virginia repealed its sterilization law in 1974, and in 2002 the state placed a commemorative marker to *Buck v. Bell* in Ms. Buck's hometown of Charlottesville. The governor issued a formal apology.

Involuntary sterilization is no longer legal, and intelligence is recognized as a complex interplay between biology and environment. Indeed, the 1960s, the era that Mr. Murray blames for the moral failings that have driven poor and middle-class White America apart, was the very same era that stemmed the human rights abuse of involuntary sterilization. (Not coincidentally, it was the same era that began addressing the discrimination that entrenched Black poverty as well.)

The stigmatization of poor White families a century ago should provide a warning: behaviors that seem to have begun in the 1960s belong to a much longer and more complex history than ideologically driven writers like Mr. Murray would have us believe.

March 2012

What Is White America?

THE IDENTITY POLITICS OF THE MAJORITY

THE US PRESIDENTIAL ELECTION of 2016 altered the prevailing American ideology of race. Donald Trump's coy, borderline White nationalism helped turn people who previously happened to be White into "White people"—coded as White in an essential way, just as, for instance, Black people are coded as Black in an essential way. Many observers were slow to grasp the political ramifications of citizens who happen to be White voting first and foremost as White people. In the immediate aftermath of the election, commentators rushed to ascribe Trump's victory to economic disarray in the heartland and to a subset of voters lamenting their loss of jobs and stability. The election was all about class, they said.

It took a couple of years for journalists, pollsters, and scholars to find a sounder explanation: by and large, most White Trump supporters were not voting out of economic self-interest; rather, they were resentful of social changes that threatened their taken-for-granted position atop a social hierarchy—despite the fact that the vast majority of those who held political power were White (and male), White families' wealth was still six and a half times as great as Black families' wealth, and Black families headed by college graduates had about 33 percent less wealth than White families headed by high school dropouts.

Three new books seek to answer a few crucial questions. What do these White people want? According to these authors, they want

Trump, Brexit, guns, tax cuts, Republicans, Social Security, and Medicare. More than anything else, they want to protect their place atop society.

And what don't these White people want? Immigrants, Obamacare, and money for public schools. And above all, they don't want to be called bigots by multiculturalists; that kind of talk threatens them and encourages them to embrace White nationalism. They cannot imagine a multiracial society in which White people—however defined—peaceably take their place among others who are not White.

And who are these White people? That's what these books are about, and that's what makes them both interesting and, ultimately, vexing. All three authors seem to believe that it is possible to understand Whiteness ontologically, as a thing. But race is better understood as an ongoing discourse, not as a physical reality. Although racism and the discrimination that accompanies it clearly have measurable social and economic effects, race is a concept that should be described with verbs such as "to seem," as opposed to "to be." The belief in the reality of race as a biologically or otherwise fixed characteristic, however, is like the belief in witchcraft, as the sociologist Karen Fields said years ago: there's nothing one can say to disprove it. And, I would add, that belief produces clear material outcomes.

If there is no such thing as a stable, freestanding category of Whites, how can one make convincing claims about Whiteness and White identity politics? The solution to this problem, for these authors and many others, is to turn to data, measurements, charts, and graphs. Eric Kaufmann and Ashley Jardina analyze data from opinion surveys to make arguments about the roots of White resentment. Jonathan Metzl examines medical statistics and conducts interviews with individuals to understand why White-identifying people support a conservative political agenda that has had a deleterious effect on their own health and well-being. Kaufmann and Jardina focus on White identifiers' conservative politics but minimize the Republican Party's strategy of exploiting the enormous emotional power of Whiteness to advance regressive taxation, limit the social safety net, and disempower workers. All three authors recognize that so long as White identity is disconnected from economic (and, in the case of Metzl, biological) self-interest, politicians will remain free to pursue policies that benefit corporations and the wealthy but that do ordinary White people little good. But political issues that matter beyond White identity—for instance, voting rights and equal treatment under the law—hardly appear in these books. And none of the three books offers a convincing path out of the dangerous territory into which White identity politics has thrust the United States.

Eric Kaufmann, professor of politics at Birkbeck, University of London, is an expert on the politics of Northern Ireland and thus brings a sense of history to the subject of White identity, which he terms "White ethnotraditionalism." His book deals mostly with the United States, but Canada and Europe also come into view. By his reckoning, race is a genetic fact, and in a manner reminiscent of nineteenth- and early twentieth-century scientists' belief in temperamental differences based on race, he perceives a "White arch-type" that has certain recognizable cultural manifestations. He calls multicultural and multiracial populations in Western countries "mixed-race" and uses the term "unmixed" with scare quotes but without irony.

Kaufmann explores the attitudes of White people who oppose immigrants and refugees and voted for Brexit or Trump and argues that most of them are not power hungry or anti-Black. They're just normal human beings who, feeling threatened, are engaging in cultural self-defense. To prove that his claims rest on sound science, Kaufmann displays data in dozens of charts and graphs. But too often, they reduce or distort the reality they are supposed to represent. One chart, for example, shows two lines relating to the probability of someone voting for right-wing populists in a given country, correlated with whether the voter says safety is very important. The caption asserts that other variables were controlled for, but the reader is left wondering how that control has affected the stated probabilities. The graph offers no evidence for the direction of causation among the highlighted variables: the percentage of Muslims in the population, a person's level of concern for safety, and that person's propensity to vote for right-wing populist parties or candidates. But Kaufmann nonetheless suggests a particular causal direction, implying that the presence of Muslims stokes concerns about safety, which then encourage support for right-wing populists.

Kaufmann's main argument is that the kind of White identity politics that has taken the form of right-wing populism results from two threats: diversification through immigration, which reduces the size of the White majority, and an "anti-majority adversary culture" of "left-modernism," whose "most zealous exponents" inhabit college campuses, where they pursue their "mission of replacing 'Whiteness' with diversity." Kaufmann claims that the "anti-White narrative" of "radical left-modernists" has pushed some White people beyond mere opposition to immigration into extremist theories of "White genocide." To help White-identified people pull back from such extremes, Kaufmann proposes remedies for the short and the long term. In essence, Kaufmann wants to save White people from themselves.

But some of his proposals seem less like antidotes to extremism and more like accommodations of it. Take, for example, his suggestion for how to deal with the problems posed by refugees: keep them away from the majority White population and house them "on a long-term basis" in "camps" offering refuge but no prospect of permanent settlement. Such camps could be set up in "a less prosperous non-EU country like Albania." Western countries that oppose refugees would be willing to fund such camps, he writes, because "they care more about the cultural impact of refugee settlement than the economic costs."

Kaufmann's long-term solution to prevent the spread of extremist White identity politics is to speed what he sees as an inevitable "White shift": the emergence of a new definition of "White" that would include light-skinned people with heterogeneous ancestry and, at the same time, would conserve the "core myths and boundary symbols" of Whiteness. Of course, this is a phenomenon that has appeared in US history many times and in many guises. Over the centuries, as Kaufmann notes, definitions of Whiteness have come to incorporate formerly denigrated groups, such as Irish Americans, Italian Americans, and Jewish Americans. Consider, too, the centuries-old practice of members of the many-hued African American population passing for White in a deeply racist society—a topic Kaufmann ignores. Kaufmann is surely correct that ideas about who counts as White are bound to change. In Kaufmann's view, this shift will help maintain White supremacy. However, as I've written elsewhere, such an enlargement is in fact already weakening White supremacy by benefiting wealthy and educated people who do not identify as White.

To Kaufmann, the worries of "ethnotraditional nationalists" about "losing the country they know" are legitimate and not automatically worthy of condemnation. Those who condemn such thinking, he suggests, are peddling the "anti-White narrative" of the White-hating "modernist-left" and driving new followers into the arms of right-wing White nationalists. If these critics would just shut up, White people would settle down and admit other people into their world—provided they are light-skinned and willing to identify as White. But Kaufmann doesn't explain how non-White people would fit into this new polity, with its newly entrenched and enlarged White majority. Nor, crucially, does he reflect on how such a polity would fare when it comes to protecting the fundamental values of liberal democracy.

Less polemic and more modest than Kaufmann's book, Jardina's study applies multiple regression, the most widely used of all statistical methods, to opinion polling data. Jardina, an assistant professor of political science at Duke University, controls for variables representing resentment of Blacks, partisanship, gender, region, and political ideology and proposes to measure the influence of the degree to which White Americans identify as White, stripped of all other characteristics. Her measure of White identity has five categories, ranging from "being White is not at all important to my identity" to "being White is extremely important to my identity." Then she checks whether this measure of White identity allows her to predict political attitudes. It does.

She writes that perceived threats to White supremacy—a non-White US president, a Latina justice of the US Supreme Court, affirmative action, college courses on race—have made White people feel "outnumbered, disadvantaged, and even oppressed." Political responses have followed, as White voters have supported strict immigration controls and voter identification laws that reduce minority turnout. According to Jardina's analysis, a strong sense of White identification predicts negative attitudes toward immigration and positive attitudes toward Social Security, Medicare, and the policies of the Trump administration. But, Jardina contends, White identification alone does not predict opposition to policies and programs often viewed through a racial lens, such as affirmative action, welfare, and Medicaid. Rather, opposition to those things correlates with a strong sense of racial resentment that is distinct from merely identifying as White.

Jardina's methodology of applying multiple regression to opinion polling data is widely used in political psychology and other social sciences. But its pitfalls are well known, the most obvious being the problem of determining causality when the effects of certain variables are very small and predictions are therefore hard to make with confidence. A second pitfall lies in this methodology's inability to characterize change over time—to capture changing behaviors as populations adjust to one another. There is, further, the temptation to search among possible control variables or among variables to predict in order to find positive results. These pitfalls suggest that one should be skeptical of, for example, Jardina's assertion that "desires to preserve Social Security and Medicare are rooted in White racial solidarity"—a claim that seems to ignore the role of class and age in support for such programs.

Perhaps Jardina's most important argument is that "White identity is not defined by racial animus, and Whites who identify with their racial group are not simply reducible to bigots." Without passing judgment, Jardina writes that many White identifiers resent the notion that "expressing their identity would be seen, unfairly, as problematic or even racist." She cites as an example of this dynamic an episode in 2015 when a deli owner in New Jersey posted a sign at his business reading, "Celebrate your White Heritage in March. White History Month." The deli owner was baffled when some of his neighbors excoriated his sign as racist. But it's difficult to accept that support for a hypothetical White History Month would indicate nothing more than a blameless expression of White racial solidarity, portending no ill will toward other groups. After all, what might be celebrated during White History Month? Would it highlight heroic White people such as the Founding Fathers, even though they are already broadly celebrated? Would it commemorate events in US history such as the American Revolution, which very much included people of color? Would it herald the ethnic cleansing of Native Americans justified by Manifest Destiny? Answering the question of what White History Month might look like in practice would reveal the antidemocratic dimension of White identity and demonstrate why it cannot be celebrated as though it were historically neutral.

It's not hard to see how ethnic and racial minorities—and the polity at large—might be harmed when White-identifying citizens decide to vote and organize specifically as White people. But to what extent does such political behavior actually benefit White people on an individual level? Jonathan Metzl explores that question and finds that, at least in Kansas, Missouri, and Tennessee, White identity politics has resulted in physical and intellectual harm to actual White people. Metzl, a medical doctor and a professor of sociology and psychiatry at Vanderbilt University, has produced a data-driven book that alternates between narrative and analysis. Metzl also relies on personal interviews to shed light on how public policy affects particular people and how they process the conflicts between their physical well-being and their political convictions. He wants to know why "lower- and middle-class White Americans vote against their own biological self-interest as well as their own economic priorities."

Metzl begins in Tennessee with a White man he refers to as "Trevor" (Metzl uses pseudonyms throughout), who is poor, lacks health insurance, and suffers from an inflamed liver, hepatitis C, and jaundice. Trevor staunchly supports his state's refusal to embrace Obamacare by expanding Medicaid coverage, even though that refusal deprives him of the care he needs to save his life. "Of what was Trevor dying?" Metzl asks. The answer, he says, is the "toxic effects of dogma" and "American notions of Whiteness." That dogma, according to Metzl, equates Obamacare with intrusive government and intrusive government with threats posed by Mexicans and "welfare queens." Metzl calculates that "Tennessee's refusal to expand Medicaid cost every single White resident of the state 14.1 days of life," presumably on average.

Metzl also examines the health consequences of Missouri's 2016 "constitutional carry" bill, a piece of legislation that dramatically widened an individual's right to bear arms. He reports on conversations he had with members of a support group for people who have lost a loved one to suicide. Kim's father committed suicide with a gun after "he got worried about protection, security, you know, and terrorism and intruders." For Metzl, "terrorism and intruders" translates into fears associated with immigrants and the country's first African American president. His non-White interviewees, less fearful of the unknown, are less attached to their rights to own and carry firearms. Kim joins all the others in her suicide support group in rejecting proposals to strengthen gun control, even given the near certainty that someone attempting suicide with a gun—statistically most likely to be a White man—will succeed. "It's not the gun's fault," says one of the group's members. "Guns are important to us and to our liberties." But Metzl cannot come up with concrete means of saving White people's lives within the logic of Whiteness. His main advice is that White people should be less fearful of social change; they should understand that it is not a zero-sum game.

Racial identity, these three authors realize, is a gut-level belief that's very hard to shake. US history has shown the difficulty of getting masses of White people to further their economic self-interest by banding together with non-Whites—which might explain why all three balk at advocating fundamental political change, at least in the short run.

All three of these books portray White identity politics as conservative and Republican, as if being White-identified leads in only one direction politically. Although they evince varying degrees of sympathy for such politics, all three concur that they are harming American society. Even though Kaufmann and Jardina see White identity politics as a normal response to perceived threats, they also see a need to pull back from a reactionary trend. Kaufmann says White people need "reassurance," which will open the way "for a return to more relaxed, harmonious and trusting societies," as when White people sat securely on top.

Jardina is more fearful, seeing aggrieved Whites as an "untapped well . . . ready to be stoked by politicians willing to go down a potentially very dark path." Although she believes that an enlargement of Whiteness (along the lines of Kaufmann's White shift) will most likely occur, she sees it as insufficient. Like Metzl, she wishes White identifiers would become less fearful of social change. But she doesn't suggest any particular means of encouraging that outcome. For his part, Metzl concludes with a plea for what he terms "White humility" and asks, "What might American politics look like if White humility was seen not as a sellout or a capitulation but as an honest effort to address seemingly intractable social issues?" If only White Americans would attempt cooperation rather than domination, American society might move away from "a biology of demise."

It is true that vast numbers of White-identified people are unhappy with their loss of privileges. But those privileges depended on distortions of Western democratic values that produced a hereditary aristocracy of Whiteness. The question before Americans at this time concerns the value they place on their democracy when one of the country's two main political parties has embraced antidemocratic leadership and policies. Democracy will suffer as long as the Republican Party continues to function as a White people's party, as it increasingly does. The presidential election of 2016 offered some hope for the future, as some three million more voters opposed Trump than supported him. Now, three years later, the choice between Trump's White nationalism and the multiculturalism of the Democrats appears even starker. One can only hope that increasing numbers of Americans will conclude that standing at the top of a racial hierarchy is not worth the loss of American democracy.

November 2019

Ralph Waldo Emerson's Saxons

R ALPH WALDO EMERSON (1803–1882) towers over the American
Renaissance but does not, though he should, reign as philosopher-
king of American White-race theory. Widely hailed for his enormous intellectual strength and prodigious output, Emerson wrote the
earliest full-length statement of the ideology later termed "Anglo-
Saxonist." His "Saxons" are not, most emphatically, the same as
White Americans or White people.[1]

We ordinarily locate both White masculine gender panic and
spread-eagle Anglo-Saxonism at the turn of the twentieth century,
but Emerson laid them out half a century earlier, in the 1850s. In an
influential treatise and oft-repeated lectures, he portrayed *the American* as *Saxon* and the Saxon as manly man and separated the genealogy
of the American Saxon from that of the Celt. Deftly and subtly, Emerson elevated the Saxons and disappeared the Celts from the identity of the American. Emerson makes it crystal clear that "Saxon" (or,
later, "Anglo-Saxon") is *not* a synonym for "White," even though the
historiographical literature often seems to equate them.

Let me state categorically that I do not underestimate or ignore the
overwhelming importance of Black race in United States history. A
truly gigantic literature exists to explain the meaning and importance
of race when it means Black, to prove that race-as-Blackness really
and truly does exist (and, more recently, to show that it is no more
than a cultural construction). By concentrating on the White races, I
do not overlook or downplay the fundamental nature of concepts of
Black race. After all, the United States as a nation was founded by and

Emerson's English Traits with $100 Reward, 2022, ink and collage on paper, 12″ × 9½″.
Emerson starchily proclaimed race as the prime explanation for human power dynamics,
hardly considering the fundamentals of hierarchy in his country at the time, which the
text insert in the piece, borrowed from the history of Harriet Jacobs, gestures toward.

largely for the owners of enslaved Africans. Over the course of some two hundred years, federal, state, and local governments labored to define Black race, a history we recognize all too well. We now also recognize that concepts of Black-race identity have changed over time, in terms of naming and of ostensible biological basis. So far this sophistication has only barely begun to extend across the color line.[2]

Statutory and biological definitions of White race remain notoriously vague—the detritus of not-Blackness. But that vagueness does not indicate disinterest. Quite the contrary. Another gigantic literature of race exists, much less known today, explaining the meaning, importance, and honest-to-God reality of the existence of White races—*White,* the now usually unraced race. We may be accustomed to alterations in the meaning of colored race; we hear the passage from "colored" to "Negro" to "Black" to "African American" as changing discourse. But with the field of critical White studies nearly a century younger than Black studies, we are much less able to comprehend the less salient but equally mutable discourse of Whiteness. I further say White "races" in the plural because for the better part of a century Americans believed in the existence of more than one European race.[3]

During the hundred years of heavy working-class European immigration (c. 1830–1924), experts and laypersons labored to racialize people who were already considered White in phenotypical and purely legal terms. This history of the meanings of White race can be harder to see now, for the concept prevailing today—of one capacious White race—can obscure a complex past. We need to keep in mind that wide-scale acceptance of the idea of one big White race dates back only to the middle of the twentieth century, becoming hegemonic during the New Deal and World War II. In the 1930s and 1940s Southern Democrats' determination to keep the Negroes down permeated federal law, circumscribing, even prohibiting Black people's access to public services, notably through New Deal policies affecting housing. The war against German National Socialists delegitimized racist ideologies, and after the war a rising Black civil rights movement defeated legal segregation and disfranchisement. It also elevated the salience of Black/White difference. The emphasis on Black and White transformed White races into White ethnicities, obscuring the earlier history of plural Whitenesses.[4]

Here I want to go backward, back before the New Deal and World War II consolidated Euro-Americans into one White race, back before the early twentieth-century immigration of people from southern and eastern Europe inspired scholarly examination of the races of Europe, back to the time when impoverished, hardworking Irish immigrants were racialized as Celts. Back to the 1850s, when Ralph Waldo Emerson lent his golden pen to the ideology we know as Anglo-Saxonism.

Although Emerson gave American Anglo-Saxonism its most eloquent presentation, he did not invent it. Thomas Jefferson, among other Americans and Britons, also believed in the Saxon myth, a story of American descent from Saxons by way of England. Jefferson's fascination with the Saxons and Old English began during his student days at William and Mary College, and he carried a belief in Americans' Saxon roots to his grave. I want very briefly to review Jefferson's engagement with the Saxon myth, which in stressing politics differs from Emerson's infatuation with masculine brutality and beauty.

Thomas Jefferson's Saxons

For Thomas Jefferson, Saxon descent explained political differences between the patriots of the newly formed United States of America and the ruling class of Great Britain. He contrasted what he saw as the Saxon origins of positive English institutions to the Norman origin of the Tories. Laying out American claims in July 1774, Jefferson called English people "our ancestors" and the creators of the Magna Carta "our Saxon ancestors." Though the Norman Conquest dates from 1066 and the Magna Carta from 1215, Jefferson maintained that "our ancestors'" system of rights was already in place when "Norman lawyers" connived to saddle the Saxons with unfair burdens. In later writings Jefferson continued to associate Saxons with Whigs and Normans with Tories, as though liberal and reactionary parties had existed from time immemorial, perpetuating themselves immutably, one generation after the other, as though coursing through the blood.[5]

For Jefferson, "Saxon" stood for *English* liberty, not any trait particular to Germans. In ways that continually reappeared in American Anglo-Saxonism, Jefferson's Saxon genealogy of laws and blood skips over the inconvenient existence of actual German Saxons—in western Lower Saxony (Niedersachsen, around Hanover) and in eastern Saxony (Sachsen, around the prosperous cities of Dresden and Leipzig). That the oppressive English king was, in fact, a Saxon seems not to have troubled Jefferson's reasoning (or Emerson's, for that matter). George III, king of England, was also elector and later king of Hanover.[6]

In the great Philadelphia Continental Congress of 1776, Jefferson proposed embedding his heroic Saxon ancestors "Hengist and Horsa, the Saxon chiefs from whom we claim the honor of being descended," in the great seal of the United States. This proposition did not win approval, but Jefferson's pursuit of Saxons continued. In 1798 he wrote "Essay on the Anglo-Saxon Language," which equated the transmission of language with biological descent, a confusion then quite common. With its stress on the concept of purity, Jefferson's linguistic thinking sounds like race talk. He claimed not only that the Saxons stayed racially pure during the Roman occupation but also, amazingly, that their language remained pristine two centuries after the Norman Conquest.[7] One of Jefferson's last great achievements, the founding of the University of Virginia in 1819, institutionalized his interest in the Anglo-Saxon language. The University of Virginia was the only college in the United States offering instruction in Anglo-Saxon, and Anglo-Saxon was the only course it offered on the English language. By the mid-nineteenth century, Americans routinely spoke of "we Saxons." Those using such phrases included the bestselling novelist Harriet Beecher Stowe; Sarah Josepha Hale, author of "Mary Had a Little Lamb" and editor of the women's magazine *Godey's Lady's Book*; and the feminist Elizabeth Cady Stanton. And, of course, Ralph Waldo Emerson.[8]

As for Emerson, the mid-nineteenth century's foremost Anglo-Saxonist, it hardly seems necessary to underline his importance in

American cultural life. One of his well-read contemporaries described him as "the most American of our writers," the embodiment of "the Idea of America, which lies at the bottom of our original institutions." Those views still resonate today.[9]

By the mid-1850s Emerson had already been reviewed an astounding 644 times.[10] Today the Princeton University library holds 703 imprints with "Ralph Waldo Emerson" in their titles, including twelve volumes of Houghton Mifflin's 1903–4 *Complete Works of Ralph Waldo Emerson*, Harvard University Press's seven volumes (as of 2022) of the *Collected Works of Ralph Waldo Emerson*, sixteen volumes of Emerson's *Journals and Miscellaneous Notebooks*, and innumerable volumes of Emerson poems, sermons, essays, and correspondence. Considering his prodigious output, Emerson seems to have sprung from Harvard College in 1821 fully formed, lecturing and writing. In fact, much of his thought—Transcendentalist as well as Anglo-Saxonist—traces its roots to an education at the hands of his lifelong friend Thomas Carlyle.

Emerson and Thomas Carlyle

Thomas Carlyle (1795–1881), a reedy, six-foot-tall, stooped lifelong hypochondriac, was usually half sick with a cold. The twenty-four-year-old Emerson, also a tall, thin, narrow-shouldered hypochondriac, discovered Carlyle's unsigned reviews in the *Edinburgh Review* and the *Foreign Review* in 1827 and hailed the British author as "my Germanick new-light writer." It soon became clear that Carlyle's take on German mysticism would lay the foundation for American Transcendentalism. Carlyle served as Emerson's teacher of Transcendentalism, deepening the introduction Emerson's aunt Mary Moody Emerson had earlier furnished.[11]

One notion guiding both Carlyle and Emerson was their heroic figuration of what they termed the Saxon race and its transatlantic realm of Saxondom. In Carlyle's first letter to Emerson after the American had visited him in 1833, Carlyle proclaimed sentiments he attached to "all Englishmen, Cisoceanic and Transoceanic, that we and you are not two countries, and cannot for the life of us be; but only two *parishes* of one country, with such wholesome parish hospitalities, and dirty temporary parish feuds, as we see; both of which brave parishes *Vivant! vivant!*"[12]

Carlyle recognized the antithesis of the Saxon in the lower orders, who for him included Black people off in the Western Hemisphere, for whom he considered slavery the natural condition. And right in his own London, the local antithesis of Saxon was none other than the Celt. Carlyle termed the Irish "Human swinery." The epithet played, of course, on the commonplace analogy between Irish people and pigs. Not only were the Irish believed to live with their pigs, but pigs were also considered quintessentially Irish, as in the saying "as Irish as Paddy's pig." Over in Concord, Massachusetts, where Irishmen labored in mud and slept in shanties, Emerson saw no reason to dispute this libel. One of his rare comments on the districts of the poor, where he spent very little time, reveals his prejudice: "In Irish districts, men deteriorated in size and shape, the nose sunk, the gums were exposed, with diminished brain and brutal form." Like Carlyle in *Chartism* (1839), Emerson sidestepped the issue of whether Celtic race in and of itself made the Irish ugly. By and large, both men managed to skirt the unpleasant topic of the Irish poor, concentrating instead on elevating the exemplary qualities of the Saxon.[13]

Emerson saw himself as a New Englander and therefore as virtually an Englishman and therefore, as he constantly repeated, a "Saxon." From early in his career, he regularly inserted "we Saxons" language into his lectures, essays, and journals. An 1835 lecture, "Permanent Traits of the English National Genius," begins by connecting Americans to the English: "The inhabitants of the United States, especially of the Northern portion, are descended from the people of England and have inherited the traits of their national character." As for the French, whom Emerson saw as Celts, the unmanly vices of frivolity, corruption, and lack of practical know-how afflicted them. How else to view a people who invented the ruffle, while it took the English to invent the shirt? For manly practicality, look to the "English race." For the childish "singing and dancing nations," look south. That North/South dichotomy, often word for word in Emerson's lively formulation, would prove a durable theory, one Emerson repeated indefatigably and one followers such as the sociologist Edward A. Ross echoed in 1901.[14]

Another example appears in Emerson's classic 1841 essay "Self-Reliance," containing a typical throwaway line identifying him and his readers as Saxons: Emerson exhorts his readers to wake up the "courage and constancy, in our Saxon breasts." By 1853 Emerson was repeating a lecture entitled "The Anglo-American." He might well have been preening autobiographically in the lecture's reference to the "godly & grand British race . . . it is right to esteem without regard to geography this industrious liberty-loving Saxon wherever he works,—the Saxon, the colossus who bestrides the narrow Atlantic."[15]

While such people as Thomas Jefferson and Elizabeth Cady Stanton might look back to their putative Saxon ancestors and then move on, Emerson dedicated an entire book, *English Traits* (1856), to the subject. Cobbled together as race history, it drew on the eighth-century English historian Bede, on Norse mythology, and on prevailing versions of English history, notably the historian-bookseller Sharon Turner's wildly popular *The History of the Anglo-Saxons, from Their First Appearance above the Elbe, to the Death of Egbert.* Digging deep into Old Norse literature, Turner lumped Saxons and Norse together to come up with a list of permanent "traits," more temperamental than physiological, of the English race. Turner proclaimed liberty the first and foremost of these traits, which he believed persisted from the fifth-century Saxon/Norse conquest of England and endured in perpetuity. In *English Traits* New Englanders are the final product of a distillation that had earlier turned Norsemen into Englishmen over the course of a millennium. Even more English than the English, New Englanders were, in Emerson's terms, "double distilled English."[16]

English Traits

Like all of Emerson's books, *English Traits* collects various lectures delivered to various audiences. Part travelogue, part autobiography, and part historical ethnography, *English Traits* heightened Emerson's fame as his wittiest book. Within three months of publication, twenty-four thousand copies were in print in the United States and Great Britain, and the book was widely and positively reviewed. Its popularity endured well into the twentieth century, until its racial theories began to fall into disrepute.[17]

Saxon violence and manly beauty, two qualities Emerson lacked, fascinated him. A housebound intellectual when not lecturing before appreciative audiences, Emerson was infatuated with the primeval virility of outdoorsmen of physical strength. Many others shared similar anxieties and infatuations, enough to make scenes of frontier violence staples of popular entertainment in Britain and the United States.

The core chapter of *English Traits,* called "Race," begins in measured tones. Emerson enumerates the three components of the English population: first, the Celt, to whom he gives less than a paragraph; second, the German, also briefly noted; and third, the "Northmen," to whom Emerson devotes page after page. The balance of the chapter revels in ancient Viking history. The "Scandinavian" traits of personal beauty and bloodthirstiness explain the physical attractiveness and energy of Emerson's splendid English contemporaries.[18]

The "Race" chapter of *English Traits* expresses two thoughts rooted in anxieties over lack of virility and sex appeal Emerson shared with masses of Americans who relished his themes—two thoughts expressed as content and form. Brutality emerges as the chapter's prized quality, with manly beauty its outward sign. As natural outgrowths of early Saxon qualities, bodily strength, vigor, manliness, and energy emerge as admirable traits. Nature made Saxons/Norsemen as savages so they might endow their English descendants, in turn, with an "excess of virility."[19]

Homicidal history, synonymous for Emerson with gorgeous male energy, is embodied in his two quintessential "Norsemen," the brothers Horsa and Hengist, legendary founders of Saxon England, the same two whom Thomas Jefferson had sought to enshrine as American forebears. According to Anglo-Saxonist legend, the mid-fifth-century British warlord Vortigern invited Horsa and Hengist into what is now Kent in the southeastern tip of England to wrest the island from its

Celtic population and their Roman overlords.[20] Today Horsa and Hengist are considered Jutes from what is now Denmark, but tradition claims them as founders of the Anglo-Saxon nation that King Alfred raised to greatness in the late ninth century. Emerson cared little for the geographical particulars and lumped together Norsemen, Jutes, and Saxons as marvelous Scandinavian pirates, "a rude race, all masculine, with brutish strength . . . Let buffalo gore buffalo, and the pasture to the strongest!"[21]

Actual German Saxons hardly appear in *English Traits*. Making an exception for Johann Wolfgang von Goethe (born in Frankfurt in Hessen, though permanently associated with Weimar in Thuringia), for whom he named the family cat, Emerson questioned Germans' fitness to serve as models of any sort. Along with "the Asiatic races," he had said back in 1835, Germans lacked the racial constitution for political greatness, sharing as they did Asians' political impotence out of "a defect of will." Norsemen rather than Germans contributed the bonny figure of the Saxon-Englishman-American's ancestor.[22]

Scandinavia was another matter. It worked as the home of ultimate American Whiteness, but the Scandinavia of the 1850s presented Emerson a dilemma: it was backward and poor—a little nothing beside the British behemoth. How could Emerson reconcile that fact with his need for Scandinavian racial, hence inherent and permanent, brilliance? If the Norsemen endowed Britain with all its "Saxon" greatness, how could one explain the relative obscurity of contemporary Scandinavia? Why had Norwegians and Danes not invented the Industrial Revolution, grown rich on worldwide commerce, and colonized the globe? To explain Scandinavian deficiency, Emerson resorted to a favorite metaphor, that of the fruit tree. Scandinavia, he surmised, lost its best men during the Dark Ages—lost them to England and never recovered: "The continued draught of the best men in Norway, Sweden and Denmark to their piratical expeditions exhausted those countries, like a tree which bears much fruit when young, and these have been second-rate powers ever since. The power of the race migrated and left Norway permanently exhausted."[23]

Emerson did not lean on this lame theory heavily. For his purposes, the subsequent history of his Norsemen *in Scandinavia* need not loom large. His early Norsemen function as a handsome set of ancestors oversupplied with manliness and bloodthirstiness: perfect traits for Englishmen, the world's imperial rulers, and perfect traits for Emerson's Americans, aspiring rulers of the Western Hemisphere.

Emerson and Carlyle said "Saxons," but we know the ideology as Anglo-Saxonism and tend to locate it in the late nineteenth and early twentieth centuries. But it is worth remembering that Ralph Waldo Emerson fleshed out that notion in the 1850s. For Emerson and many nineteenth-century Americans, the stress on Saxon roots served to racialize both the Americans and the impoverished Irish and to seal the Irish in a spoiled Celtic racial destiny that for Emerson remained mostly, but not entirely, beneath notice. Ordinarily taking the racial high road, Emerson preferred to elevate his beautiful, virile, bloodthirsty Saxons rather than detail the deficiencies of the Celts.

For Emerson and his educated followers, to be American was to be Saxon. We recognize several exclusions from that identity: excluded were Native American Indians, Blacks, and Asian Americans. Also excluded in the nineteenth century were the Irish. After Emerson died in 1882, however, successive waves of European immigrants at the turn of the twentieth century pushed Irish Americans into the American fold as northwestern Europeans, as *Nordics*. But for Emerson in the 1850s, Saxon not only meant American; it meant *not* Celt. With Emerson as the embodiment of *the* American Renaissance, his fascination with Saxons—at the expense of all the others, including Celts—remains embedded almost unnoticed in fundamental notions of what it means to be an American, to belong within the notion of *the* American. For Emerson, among the White races, Saxons were the best. Emerson placed distinctions of race and genealogy at the foundation of Saxon-English-American racial temperament, leaving out many others we today consider White.

March 2009

VISUAL CULTURE

Malcolm X across the Genres

THE HISTORIAN IN ME distrusted a dramatic early scene in Spike Lee's *Malcolm X* set in Omaha, where the Ku Klux Klan comes pounding up to the Little family's house on horseback. Initially, the scene seems menacingly authentic—hooded White supremacy in its most recognizable guise bent on terrorizing a helpless Black family—but as soon as one recalls that this is supposed to be Omaha, Nebraska, in the 1920s, the sense of realism breaks down.

I assumed this to be yet another employment of the iconography of Southern White supremacy, which Americans still think of as the *real* White supremacy, to advance a narrative of Black life anywhere in the United States. Like the 1972 documentary of the same name and countless other evocations of Black life, Spike Lee's *Malcolm X* uses photos and footage from Southern history to hammer home the plight of Black people in American life everywhere. Considering that in Lee's film a still photograph from 1936 of a Florida lynch victim appears between cuts of the violence that met civil rights activists in Birmingham in 1963, it is hardly surprising that the need to show the Klan as always coming on horseback and riding off into the full moon triumphs again over regional and chronological verisimilitude. Once more in film, or so it appeared, D. W. Griffith's images cancel out the unlikelihood of twentieth-century, urban midwestern Klansmen making their rounds on horseback.

But I was wrong to think that Spike Lee had followed the dictates of film school; the image was not originally Lee's at all. *The Autobiography of Malcolm X* opens with this very scene. Lee and his screenwriters were following Malcolm X as though what he had said was history, which it was not. According to Bruce Perry's *Malcolm: The Life of a Man Who Changed Black America*, the story was Malcolm's own invention.[1] This vignette encapsulates the confusion about historical truth that surrounds the figure of Malcolm X in the two genres through which he is best known: his autobiography and Spike Lee's film.

Both *The Autobiography of Malcolm X* and the film *Malcolm X* simulate history by purveying autobiographical rather than biographical truths, for the source for each representation is Malcolm's own recomposition of his life from the vantage point of 1964. Alex Haley shaped the autobiography and took it from conversation to publication. A screenplay by James Baldwin, Arnold Perl, and Spike Lee recasts the published autobiography for the 1992 film. While each of these retellings—each step in crafting a work of art—invents a new narrative, neither the book nor the film is congruent with the life that Malcolm Little/Malcolm X lived, day by day, between 1925 and 1965.

The transubstantiations work on several different levels. First of all, autobiography, even when it is not "told to" another but is written by the person who lived the life, reworks existential fragments into a meaningful new whole, as seen from a particular vantage point. Even when autobiographies are not collaborations, narrators pass over much in silence and highlight certain themes that become salient in light of what narrators conclude they have become. When the subject is racialized, the narrative nearly always aspires to (or acquires in the marketplace) metonymic stylization, as captured in the dust-jacket blurb of *The Autobiography of Malcolm X* from 1965, which still served to promote the *Autobiography* in the mid-1990s: "In the agony of [his] self-creation [is] the agony of an entire people in their search for identity. No man has better expressed his people's trapped anguish." If Malcolm X is to work as a racial symbol, it's best not to look at him too closely.

The process of transforming an individual into a racial symbol alters the subject's life (with its false starts and, above all, with its intra-racial conflicts) into a narrative whose plot is coded in Black and White. Usually, the Black protagonist faces "White society" or the "White power structure." Such stark dichotomies are hardly the sign of history that is written sensitively. History grows out of evidence, the more the better, we say—or at least so we said until the late twentieth century, when evidence in absurd abundance threatened to paralyze historians by swamping the research phase of the work. History needs source documents, the more the better, we still think.

The best drama, the best art, in contrast, is spun out of the fewest number of documents, the least amount of detail and nuance. For the sake of theater, the less we know of thoroughly racialized figures like Malcolm X—the better. When we know enough about a man to analyze his childhood family dynamics, we know enough to realize that what happened between self, parents, and siblings counts as much as—more than?—the oppressiveness of segregation in the public sphere. It is hardly surprising that Spike Lee's movie has reached millions, while Bruce Perry's debunking biography, a 1991 imprint by a small publishing house called Station Hill, is hardly known at all. Even though the makers of Spike Lee's film conducted many interviews, for the purpose of the drama they chose to use a univocal source: *The Autobiography of Malcolm X.* The movie should have borne the same title, for it is autobiography rather than history.

As a means of buttressing the historical claims of his film, Spike Lee takes the process of stylization a step further and plays havoc with the distinction between feature and documentary. The results are mind-bogglingly effective as drama. At crucial junctures, the narrative, shot in color, is punctuated with scenes in which Denzel Washington, the actor who plays Malcolm X, appears in black and white—in the press conference in which Malcolm announces his departure from the Nation of Islam, as well as on the stretcher that bears his bullet-ridden body away from the Audubon ballroom. This faux footage replicates documentary technique like that in the 1972 documentary of Malcolm X by Marvin Worth and Arnold Perl, whose authority was also *The Autobiography of Malcolm X.* Spike Lee is so skilled at fabricating documentation that when Nelson Mandela appeared at the end of *Malcolm X,* I questioned *his* authenticity! The movie's credits reveal more faux footage, as in the black-and-white scene of the Kennedy assassination that is crosscut post-structurally with Denzel Washington's/Malcolm's reaction to the assassination.

This movie is not a documentary, but it wraps itself in manufactured images of documentary truth. When the images are real—as in footage of Martin Luther King Jr.'s remarks after the assassination of Malcolm X—the effect can be chilling, for viewers know that King would be the victim of assassination three years later. The verisimilitude of Spike Lee's faux footage is intensified by the cameo appearances of the Reverend Al Sharpton and former Black Panther Bobby Seale. Their roles as street-corner speakers establish a continuity of Black nationalist leadership from Malcolm X in the 1960s to the Panthers in the 1970s to Sharpton in the 1980s and 1990s. Given the tragic permanence of Black political grievances, notably police brutality and official harassment, this film may well reopen questions about the role of police and government in Malcolm X's assassination. If so, such an inquiry would underscore the political role of film in African American life and further blur the line between art and life, between symbolism and history.

Viewed as an artifact of this time rather than of the 1960s, the movie *Malcolm X* subordinates certain aspects of the problem of realism and accentuates others. Spike Lee's film heightens Malcolm's confrontation with police over the beating of Brother Johnson as though it were a major turning point rather than one of many steps (sideways and backward as well as forward) in the emergence of the Nation of Islam. For a 1993 audience, Denzel Washington is a good-enough Malcolm X: he looks and talks like Malcolm did in the 1960s; and, from this vantage point, it only matters slightly that Washington is significantly darker-skinned than Little/X and much older than Malcolm during much of the action. Although Washington is in his mid-thirties, Malcolm was a teenager during his years as a hustler. He went to prison before turning twenty and was only twenty-seven when he emerged from incarceration in Massachusetts and went to work as an organizer for the Nation of Islam. These are trivialities in racialized drama, where the conflict is posed mainly in terms of Black and White, and other questions are less intelligible. When what happens outside the Black-White nexus is not of much interest, the Black protagonist needs only enough family influence and youthful experience to foreshadow the anguish that will come of being Black.

In the movie, Malcolm X's siblings lose the roles they played in his personal and intellectual trajectory, roles the *Autobiography* clearly acknowledged. In life, four of his siblings joined the Nation of Islam before Malcolm did, and his family, particularly his brothers Philbert and Reginald, brought him into the fold while he was still in prison. Later on, when Malcolm was acting as Elijah Muhammad's national representative and building the Nation of Islam from 400 to 40,000 adherents, part of the hostility he encountered derived from the fear that by promoting the interests of his brothers, who were also ministers in the Nation, he was building a family dynasty intended to rival that of Elijah Muhammad. After Malcolm left the Nation of Islam in early 1964, his half sister Ella, a businesswoman in Boston, underwrote his pilgrimage to Mecca. While he spent months on end abroad in 1964–1965, Ella Little took over the leadership of his new organizations, the Muslim Mosque, Inc., and the Organization of Afro-American Unity, continuing to head them after his assassination. Given the kind of roles allotted to women in the Nation of Islam and in this and Spike Lee's other films, the effacement of the strong and complicated figure of Ella Little is hardly surprising.

Even though their roles are circumscribed, the female characters in Spike Lee's film have bigger parts than they did in *The Autobiography of Malcolm X*. His girlfriend Laura's place in the autobiography is small, although Alex Haley notes in his epilogue that Malcolm blamed his own shoddy treatment of Laura for her eventual ruin (which seems unlikely unless his role in her life was far larger than the autobiography indicates). In the feature film, the figure of Laura reappears at several junctures, first as the proper young Black woman whom the teenaged Malcolm deserts for a White woman named Sophia. Laura sharpens the point that the *Autobiography* makes obliquely by telling Malcolm, "I'm not White and I don't put out, so why would you want to call me, Malcolm?" Young Laura's purity contrasts with the figure she presents as the film progresses. When Malcolm arouses her sexually, she becomes willing to jettison her grandmother's prohibitions.

Later, she is naively vulnerable to the manipulation of a freeloading junkie boyfriend. Finally, as a prostitute at the bottom of the pit of degradation, Laura is seen giving a White john a blow job in a Harlem doorway. (Spike Lee does not explain how she gets from Boston to New York.)

At other points, Lee captures the patriarchal gender values of the Nation of Islam. Malcolm admonishes his wife, Betty, not to raise her voice in *his* home. A scene at a Saviours' Day rally hammers home the message, as the audience sees a banner stretched across the balcony in which the sisters are sequestered. It reads: "We must protect our women, our most valuable possession." Is Spike Lee using this prop ironically? I'm not sure, for popular Black nationalism, in the 1990s as in the 1960s, often espoused precisely this sort of gender ideal. Lee may be using the Nation of Islam to preach a gospel that he might also have found appealing.

Spike Lee's *Malcolm X* captures the strengths of the Nation of Islam in redeeming poor Black incarcerated men for useful lives. Elijah Muhammad wrote to Black inmates, many of whom lacked Malcolm's supportive family, and the Nation played a unique role in educating and empowering the most vulnerable men in American society. The content of the Nation's beliefs is not well explained, however, and Lee's film (like the autobiography and documentary film) glosses over the weirder themes in Elijah Muhammad's doctrine, learned from Master W. D. Fard in Detroit in 1931. (Fard's portrait appears on the walls of Elijah Muhammad's house in the feature film. Fard was even more light-skinned than Muhammad.) Fard taught that when Blacks separated from Whites, they would enter heaven on earth, after four hundred years of hell on earth under the control of White devils. Fard and Muhammad said that the Black man was the original man, and that Whites had been purposefully bred out of the original man six thousand years earlier in order to put Black people through hell. The end of time was near, and on a day of judgment Allah would defeat Whites and vindicate Blacks through racial separation.

Both the feature and the documentary films mention the Nation of Islam's apocalyptic vision of racial redemption, but neither fleshes it out. The Nation's solution to American racism, the creation of a Black state out of Georgia and Alabama, remains suitably vague. Spike Lee's film reveals why so many Black Americans were drawn to the Nation of Islam through Malcolm X's preaching of Black beauty and power; but, by deleting the inane portions of the creed, it eliminates the mystery of why so intelligent a person as Malcolm X would stay twelve years in such a narrow-minded movement. Answering that question means stepping outside the framework of Spike Lee's film.

The Nation of Islam combines two intellectual traditions: first, holiness religion of a sort common in working-class Black neighborhoods and that appeals primarily to women, and second, the masculinist tradition of Black nationalism continued by the Black Panthers in the late 1960s and early 1970s. Within urban African American life, the first tradition is strongly class-based, the second is highly gendered.

Holiness religion is perfectionist and apocalyptic, maintaining that the end is near and the faithful must prepare for judgment by purifying their thoughts, behavior, and bodies. Black Muslims, like acolytes of holiness churches, must take baths frequently, dress modestly, and eat healthfully (little or no meat, no pork, lots of fresh fruits and vegetables); they must not smoke, drink alcohol, use drugs, curse, gamble, steal, or fornicate. Men wear white shirts and suits; women wear long dresses, head coverings, and no makeup. Both holiness Christianity and the Nation of Islam have saved thousands of poor Blacks from the snares of vice-ridden neighborhoods.

Critics of the Nation of Islam have sometimes remarked on the paradox of Black nationalists' adopting the trappings of "the White middle class," but that designation is flawed. Muslims, like many other people of color in similar clothing, are dressing for respectability, not for racial transmogrification. Respectability, like the putative characteristics of economic class, are for many Americans color coded: the stereotypical vices of the poor (intemperance, laziness, fecklessness, immorality) are in the United States the stereotypical vices of Blacks; the supposed virtues of the middle class (thrift, hard work, sobriety, moral rectitude) are racialized as White.

Racial stereotype, which has long tended to lump all Blacks together, regardless of their class, gender, or region, deeded Black nationalism an intellectual inheritance with many of White supremacy's serious flaws. Malcolm X, in autobiography, documentary film, and feature film, exhibits one such weakness, a preoccupation with Whiteness, in three different guises. On the most obvious level, Whiteness provides the measure of beauty and desirability for young Malcolm Little, who undergoes excruciating pain in order to conk (straighten) his hair. In the film and in *The Autobiography of Malcolm X,* Malcolm and his composite sidekick, Shorty, display White girlfriends like trophies. In Malcolm's case, Whiteness alone does not quite suffice. In the *Autobiography,* he emphasizes Sophia's elegant clothing. Her relatively elevated class standing is also indicated in the feature film, as Sophia presents herself as a classy dame who is better than the trashy poor White women, "harps" (Irish Americans), with whom Black men were believed more likely to associate.

In the Nation of Islam, Malcolm X outgrows the aesthetic of Whiteness, but the gaze of the superego figure he terms "the White man" remains steady. While "the White man" is the devil and "the White man" has done only evil in this world, Malcolm X seems to agree with the judgment of "the White man" with regard to the self-destructive behavior of poor Blacks. Minister Malcolm X hectors his audience for ingesting the White man's poisons: pork, cigarettes, White women. "The White man sees you and laughs," says Malcolm, calling on the scorn of strange White people to induce dietary and sexual reform.

At the very end of the Spike Lee film, "the White man" goes from stern parent to Islamic brother. After his pilgrimage to Mecca in 1964, El-Hajj Malik El-Shabazz/Malcolm X wrote an open letter to the Muslim Mosque, Inc., in New York that is quoted in both films and reproduced in the *Autobiography.*[2] In the letter, Malcolm marvels at the color blindness he encounters in Mecca and reports that he has prayed and eaten and slept with brother Muslims whose skin was the whitest white and whose eyes were the bluest blue and whose hair was the blondest blonde. (Those White Muslims may have been Bosnians, the very people whom Serbs slaughtered and raped in the 1990s in quest of "ethnic cleansing.") The geography of the Muslim world is such that fair-skinned pilgrims in Saudi Arabia would have formed a small minority, who were remarkable to Malcolm X because the figure of "the White man" had acquired such salience in his own ideology. The great majority in Mecca would have been more or less brownish people from Asia and Africa.

In 1964 and early 1965, as Malcolm traveled widely and came into contact with Pan-Africanism and anti-imperialism, he grew intellectually and began to situate American racial issues within a broader context. Had he lived, he might well have outgrown the intellectually constricting aspects of Black nationalism. But in 1964, he knew he would not live much longer. The Nation of Islam (with official support?) assassinated him, in a spectacular and tragic example of Black nationalism's inability to tolerate intra-racial diversity. During most of his public life, Malcolm X, too, subscribed to the unifying tenets of the Nation, which lacked language with which to manage dissent or conceive of difference within the race.

The rhetoric of the Nation as preached so effectively by Malcolm X dwelled endlessly on "the White devil" and "the Black man." In Malcolm's own life, interracial conflict was not nearly so dramatic, for he was the victim of poverty as well as of racism. Spike Lee emphasizes the dramatic parallel between the burning of the Little family's home in Lansing, Michigan, and the firebombing of Malcolm's family home in New York, but the parallel, no matter how spectacular, is flawed: Malcolm called the Lansing fire a White-on-Black crime, while he blamed the conflagration in New York on the Nation of Islam.

A leading theme in Malcolm's life was actually intra-racial conflict, which, in the last analysis, took his life. Like Americans who lack a conceptual category for Black respectability, Malcolm X (and Black nationalists generally) found it difficult to envision a Negro race made up of people of different classes and clashing convictions. Malcolm much preferred to speak in the singular, as though all twenty-two million African Americans had identical interests and needs. The Nation of Islam offered solutions to "the Black man," no matter what "his" education or income. Women in the Nation were to accept the interests of Muslim men as their own.

Racial unity is the great ideal of the various strains of Black nationalism, and it is usually considered an attainable goal. If only Black people were united, so the reasoning goes, they could challenge racial oppression effectively; if only Black people were united, they could advance economically; if only Black people were united, they would represent a potent political influence. In this ideology, the impediment to unity is not the implausibility of tens of millions of people without their own governmental institutions or police power acting together in unison. Instead, racial unity is seen as being prevented by the actions of traitors who are in cahoots with Whites. Malcolm X identified race traitors as educated Blacks and house Negroes, and he usually treated these two kinds of people as one.

While he was proud of his own autodidacticism and wanted young Black people to educate themselves, Malcolm X doubted that formal education was good for Black Americans. He labeled Black PhDs "Uncle Thomases" and called them fakes and traitors, asking his audiences what a Black man with a PhD was called. Answer: "A n—er!" As if to say that for a Black person, formal education serves for naught.

For Malcolm X before 1964, formal education served for less than naught, because he saw a close connection between Blacks with education and what he called "the house Negro," the slave who loved his master better than himself or other Black people, that is, the traitor to his race. These lines always got a laugh when Malcolm appeared on television or on college campuses, and they still do in the movies that have appeared since his assassination. Even those who were skewered managed to laugh at their own expense, for, despite his harsh rhetoric, Malcolm X remained a good-humored man whose razor wit never became personal. This, at least, is my memory of seeing him in the early 1960s.

When he spoke at the University of California at Berkeley in the early 1960s, I was one of a handful of Black students in his audience, and I recall my realization that he was not talking to us. Malcolm X spoke around us to White people, even though educated Blacks like us were his rhetorical *bête blanche*. Like "the White man," we were a stereotype, but we were not nearly so interesting. As stereotype, we had a part to play in the drama of foiled race unity, but his real engagement was with the vast majority of his audience, whom he could bait and smile at with devastating effectiveness. As sidelined players in his American drama, we nevertheless relished Malcolm's appearance, for he was able to discomfort White people with an enviable skill that we did not possess. He was smart, assertive, funny, and, all in all, very entertaining. After he left the Nation of Islam, he realized what we had hoped, that he could do better than tailor his analysis to fit the demands of the Honorable Elijah Muhammad's creed.

The second and last time I saw Malcolm X was in West Africa in the fall of 1964. Perhaps because ideologically he was becoming more like us—the well-educated Afro-American community sheltering in Kwame Nkrumah's Ghana—our existence seemed to annoy him no longer. He was at home intellectually, but he was also utterly exhausted physically. When he returned to New York, Malcolm tried to implement what he had learned by founding new organizations that were still Black nationalist. He also moved to the left politically, which, had he lived, would have ultimately strained his racial ideals.

Given the Nation of Islam's willingness to shed blood, I doubt it would have been possible for Malcolm X to survive much longer. He certainly felt, when he finished his work with Alex Haley, that he would not live to see the publication of *The Autobiography of Malcolm X,* and he did not. Had he somehow managed to preserve his life, his intellectual trajectory would probably have continued leftward and away from Black nationalism. Would he still have inspired Huey Newton and Bobby Seale to found the Black Panther Party, which repeated much of the Nation of Islam's tragic history? Probably not, for by 1966–67, Malcolm X would have seen the danger inherent in a fascination with guns and come to resemble the Nelson Mandela of the late 1980s. Nelson Mandela, another symbol of race and manhood, is the figure with whom Spike Lee closes his film. The vision—still Pan-African—raises hopes for another round of consciousness-raising among Black nationalists.

April 1993

"...whatever she saw go on in that barn"

AFTER MANY YEARS as an academic historian, I undertook formal art study, earning a BFA from the Mason Gross School of the Arts of Rutgers University in 2009 and an MFA from the Rhode Island

Beloveds Gray, 2013, ink, graphite, and digital collage on paper, 6″ × 6″. One of four small prints in honor of Toni Morrison's *Beloved,* commissioned by *Women's Studies Quarterly,* a feminist journal that could not reproduce color within the body of the book. Two *Beloveds* appear in *Women's Studies Quarterly* 42, nos. 1 and 2 (Spring/Summer 2014).

School of Design in 2011, both in painting. More recently I've been combining my old and new lives into artwork with significant subject matter as well as visual meaning.

I just now reread Toni Morrison's tough, magnificent novel *Beloved* for the first time in about a quarter century. It left me devastated by the sheer cruelty of enslavement and the way it distorted humanity, even though as a historian, I was well acquainted with the institution's awfulness. I also saw in new ways Morrison's visual imagination, notably her insistence on the importance of color. Because the *Women's Studies Quarterly* cannot reproduce my pieces in color, grisaille will have to represent the meaning of Morrison's investment in color, though I have reproduced some of the work's haunting lines of text.

In addition to the grisaille print, three others exist in this series: one dominated by red; one dominated by orange; and one more graphic than the other three that appeared within the schema of the issue's cover.

Spring 2014

Alma W. Thomas (1891–1978)

OLD/NOT OLD ARTIST

FROM THE MOMENT SHE ARRIVED in New York City in 1972 and hit the big time, Alma Woodsey Thomas's age was a source of wonder—never disregarded, always worthy of remark. Harold Rosenberg (1906–1978), art critic for *The New Yorker*, singled her out by name in a long review. He decreed her work praiseworthy, after a mention of her age: "Alma Thomas, the eighty-one-year-old Black woman artist from Washington, D.C., has brought new life to abstract painting in the nineteen-seventies."[1] Even the art historian Judith Wilson (b. 1952), one of Thomas's most thorough and thoughtful critics, embedded the artist's age in the lede of her groundbreaking 1979 essay for *Ms. Magazine*: "In 1960, the late Alma W. Thomas retired from teaching and began to take herself seriously as a painter. She was 68 years old."[2]

Alma Thomas's age defines the figure of the painter Alma Thomas and is almost as central to her image as her unique and colorful abstraction. I'm hardly in her league as a painter, but as an old artist, I recognize this fascination with a woman's age, a phenomenon that she and I share. Her age, the geographies and chronologies of race, and successive eras in art history have all influenced how she pursued her art and how her art has been received. Her persona carries the mark of her age, even when she has been characterized as youthful as well as old. As an old woman, I also recognize the freedom that age brings women: freedom to spend your money as you please,

Fig. 1. *Evening Star,* April 27, 1972, page C-10 (detail). Alma W. Thomas Papers, The Columbus Museum.

because you're more likely when old than when you were young to have money; to do what you want to do, even if other people don't see your point in wanting to keep on doing it your own way.

In the 1970s, when mainstream critics in New York and Washington discovered Thomas and were fascinated by her advanced age, they were also marveling at the youthfulness of her paintings. "Somehow, Miss Thomas managed to retain a decisive spark of youth," said Benjamin Forgey (b. 1938) in the Washington *Evening Star,* whose review proclaimed her "A Charming 'Young' Painter" (fig. 1).[3] In *The New York Times,* James R. Mellow (1926–1997) wondered how such an "elderly woman . . . embraced total abstraction."[4]

Thomas herself announced that she wouldn't let age stop her: "There's aches and pains all over, but I have to keep going! . . . The older I become, the younger I feel. Most people grow old and feel old, but as I'm growing old, I'm feeling younger."[5] Even though she called herself "an elderly woman—born in the 'horse and buggy days,'" Thomas and her gorgeous paintings have inhabited successive art historical generations as she traversed segregated Washington, experienced art in Europe, and broke into the racially and geographically exclusionary art terrain of New York City.

Alma Thomas was, in fact, older—often very much older—than the people who shaped her education and advancement. Only in her 1920s studies as a Howard University student was she younger than her teachers, notably James V. Herring (1887–1969), who brought her into Howard's newly established art department as its first student and continued to mentor her until leaving as chair in 1953. That was about the end of her term as a relative youth. Everyone else in her life as an artist was younger than she, beginning with Herring's partner, Alonzo Aden (1906–1961), head of the Howard University Art Gallery, who, with Herring, operated the Barnett Aden Gallery out of their home from 1943. Showing her work very early on and welcoming her into the gallery's leadership, Herring and Aden encouraged Thomas in her beginnings as a professional, exhibiting artist. Howard University people, some older but mostly younger, were the first to lay down the stepping stones, offer helping hands, and praise her work to people who could get it shown where showing made all the difference in the art world.

Early in her career she collaborated with Howard people, not just Herring and Aden, but also the major painter and professor Loïs Mailou Jones (1905–1998). Jones included Thomas in an artists' club for schoolteachers, most likely with gestures of condescension. In the early 1950s Thomas broke away from Howard University's traditions of conventional fine art, of art-making intended to demonstrate Negro artists' mastery of prevailing standards. The leaders of this academic art of impeccable technique were Jones and James A. Porter (1905–1970), both born a decade and a half after Thomas. From 1953 until his death, Porter chaired Howard's art department, where Jones reigned as the artist of acclaim.

Jones and Porter were skilled twentieth-century modernists whose refined work, despite its technical mastery, has not been widely exhibited in decades. It's as though their expertise has damned their work as passé, especially in contrast with what was carelessly termed Thomas's spontaneity and naivete. Jones's and Porter's art belongs to the era before the Second World War, when Paris was the center of the international art world. After the war, the center shifted to New York City, where tastemakers seldom looked beyond Manhattan's confines or anywhere across the color line. When Thomas gained notice in New York City as an artist worthy of attention, it was because of a show at the Museum of the National Center of Afro-American Artists in Boston. There her work was exhibited with artists from that city and New York—as though art from Washington was so beneath notice it had to be presented as though from elsewhere.

Thomas's first steps out of obscurity took her five miles northwest of mostly Black Howard University to mostly White American University, a shift prompted by Aden at Howard and Ben "Joe" Summerford (1924–2015) at American in the early 1950s. The trip took her from Porter's and Jones's prewar styles to the postwar Washington Color School of the White painters Morris Louis (1912–1962), who taught at Howard; Kenneth Noland (1924–2010); and Gene Davis (1920–1985). Thomas knew Jacob Kainen (1909–2001) not only as her American University teacher but also as a paid, personal hands-on critic. Washington was still very much segregated in the 1950s, so her migration took her into a racial art world that had not previously welcomed Black artists. Even Jones, for all her skill, had had to submit her work incognito to the annual exhibitions at the Corcoran Gallery of Art during the 1930s and 1940s, before its desegregation in the late 1950s. Over the course of the decade of the 1950s, Thomas remade herself into the painter we recognize today, nowadays more likely to be categorized among color field painters than alongside African American figurative painters like Porter and Jones.

In addition to moving her from Black to White spaces in Washington, Thomas's purposeful later education reset her artist's clock, placing her in time with artists born in the 1920s and 1930s. A further geographical displacement took Thomas to Europe in summer 1958 with the Tyler School of Art of (mostly) White Temple University. Her passport puts her date of birth as 1894, rather than the actual date of 1891, and her height as 5'1" (fig. 2).[6] I don't know how European art inspired Thomas, but shortly after her return, she began working in the abstraction that has become her signature style.

Younger artists and curators advanced the career of the artist Thomas became in the 1960s and 1970s. Howard alumnus David Driskell (1931–2020), teaching at Fisk University, played a leading role by curating exhibitions of her work in the 1970s, which paved her way into the Whitney. The New York gallery director Harold Hart (1926–1997), Thomas's former junior high school student, neighbor, and protégé, helped her bridge the divide between Washington and New York City. Other art world leaders whom she did not know personally improved her fortunes by touting the excellence of her art, notably Edmund Barry Gaither (b. 1944) of the National Center of

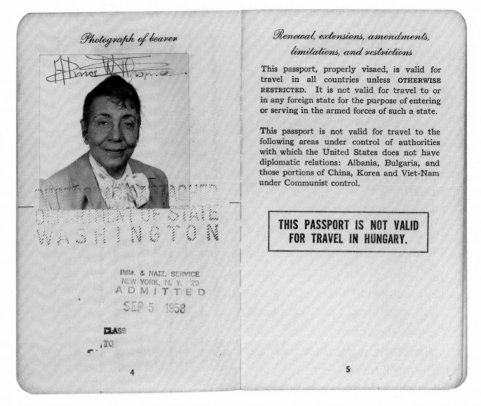

Fig. 2. Alma W. Thomas's passport, c. 1958. Alma Thomas Papers, c. 1894–2001, box 1, folder 19, Archives of American Art at the Smithsonian Institution.

Afro-American Artists in Boston and, in New York, the critic Hilton Kramer (1928–2012) in *The New York Times* and the painter Benny Andrews (1930–2006), who led the protests that prompted the desegregation of the exhibitions at the Whitney Museum of American Art.

Thomas was able to recast herself as a painter in the 1960s, thanks to the life she had already led as a teacher, reader, returning student, and pensioner. Teaching provided not only a constant immersion in the arts as practiced on the junior high school level but also a steady income that, as an unmarried woman, she expended entirely as she pleased. She didn't have to explain or share what she brought in or spent. She never married, shrugging off inquiries by saying marriage would just "create a lot of problems," plus, she was "liberated a long time ago."[7] Thomas's own money paved her way in the world, allow-ing her to attend summer school at Columbia University Teachers College in the 1930s and financially sustain the Barnett Aden Gallery, where she first showed her work in a professional setting in the 1940s. She had the money for her European trip in 1958.

The art world doesn't like to talk about money, preferring the pretense that good art always makes its way by and of itself. But Thomas's money enabled her to make and show her art over the course of four decades. From the 1940s Thomas's money paid for the art books she bought from Franz Bader (1903–1994), whose gallery represented her from the late 1960s until her death. She had the money to furnish the home inherited from her parents, keep up its garden, and purchase the supplies—stretchers, canvas, paint, brushes—plus the costs of shipping and storing the paintings she made on a heroic modernist scale.

Money sustained Thomas's independence, but money alone was not enough. Age gave her perspective. Age protected her from the peer pressure weighing on younger fellow students. She set her mind on succeeding as a painter and did what she knew needed to be done: attend art openings and galas, even as the only Black person, and pay attention to what artists beyond the confines of her city were making and saying in international art magazines. Age reinforced her firmness, her ability to stick to her own ways of making art, her steadfast determination to pursue art education even when she was the oldest one in class. And she probably always was the oldest one, starting at Howard University in her early thirties and graduating at thirty-four with the university's first fine art degree. She was forty-four when she received her master of arts from Teachers College, Columbia University. She was still teaching at Shaw Junior High School when she began taking classes at American University in her sixties. She painted steadily as art world politics changed around her.

Thomas was old enough to stay her own course in the 1960s, when Black Consciousness reshaped the work of artists like her esteemed Washington neighbor, associate, and sometime rival Loïs Mailou Jones. Younger artists, such as Jeff Donaldson (1932–2004), made the Black Arts Movement in the 1960s and brought Black Consciousness to Howard in 1970, when he became chair of the art department. Donaldson said Thomas, with her embrace of "beauty," didn't understand Blackness. While Black Consciousness art announced the importance of Black history, Thomas spoke of history as an impediment that the artist must be released from: "I have always enjoyed the progressive creativeness of the artist as he releases himself from the past."[8] In terms of the Blackness of the 1960s, for her this most certainly was true. In the era of Black Consciousness and the art of proud Black identity, she was definitely an old artist. She remained a turn-of-the-twentieth-century "Negro" rooted unwaveringly in the personal and visual aesthetics of her generation. Socially and politically, she emphatically did not adjust to the 1960s.

The formal freshness of Thomas's art stands in sharp contrast with her long-standing assumptions about race, which have not at all stood the tests of time. In the 1960s Howard University moved away from its famously entrenched intra-racial color lines and unrepentant colorism, but Thomas never shed her early twentieth-century preferences for light skin and straight hair. She always prized art for art's sake and continued to speak of the artist using the universal masculine "he." When it came to the color bar against Black artists, she would not go there. She never acknowledged racial discrimination (or sexism, for that matter), as the art historian Judith Wilson noted in 1978 (fig. 3).

Thomas ignored Black Consciousness all the while benefiting from it, riding the wave of protest that younger artists stirred up. She never, ever denounced discrimination (at least discrimination beyond her hometown of Columbus, Georgia, at the turn of the twentieth century) and, except for the 1963 March on Washington, never joined a protest. Fortunately for her art, others responded differently. Quiet protest arose from within the art world, notably on the part of Driskell and Gaither, who showcased her work by curating exhibitions that introduced Black artists to the big White art world, a world unrepentantly White. Outside existing institutions, protest organizations like the Black Emergency Cultural Coalition, led by Andrews in New York, negotiated Black artists into the Whitney. While protest shoved Thomas forward, her own aesthetic conservatism made her race and

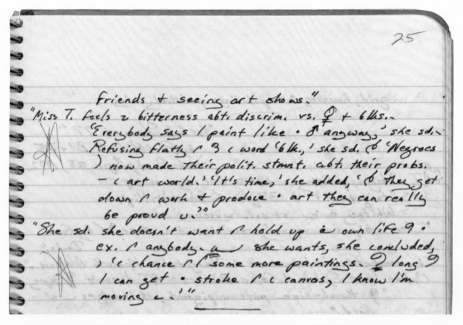

Fig. 3. Judith Wilson (b. 1952), "Alma Thomas: A One-Woman Art Movement," *Ms. Magazine,* Notebook, c. 1978, Judith Wilson Papers, 1966–2010, box 4, folder 2, page 32, Archives of American Art at the Smithsonian Institution.

her sex acceptable in the early 1970s and kept her buoyed long enough for people to focus on the originality and strength of her painting.

Pushed into desegregating its collections and exhibitions, the Whitney selected such abstract artists as Alvin Loving (1935–2005), Melvin Edwards (b. 1937), Frederick Eversley (b. 1941), and Frank Bowling (b. 1934), whose work eschewed angry figurative images against American White supremacy that would rile up the board: better to show work that would fit comfortably within established aesthetic norms that trustees were accustomed to, at least in the early 1970s.[9] With time, art world tastes continued to change. Between 1972 and now, two more art historical eras have intervened: the first welcoming Black Consciousness art into the mainstream and then deeming it the very definition of Black art, and the second discussing Black art as though it were sociology, its worth found in its analysis of American racism. The latter came as the art world continued to desegregate at the end of the twentieth century, realizing that not all Black artists made Black identity art and beginning to make room for more than one type of Black art and a range of Black artists, old as well as young. During the generation when identity art buried Black abstraction, Thomas's work was exhibited locally, as it had been before the watershed Whitney exhibition of 1972.

As Black abstraction is being widely rediscovered and appreciated, Thomas is now being hailed as a major artist, and her art is being discussed in the formal terms once reserved for the work of White men. Yet her generational autobiography follows her, making her an artist still noteworthy for her age. Once again, as in a *New York Times* review from 2019, she is a young artist remarkable for being old: "Ms. Thomas, an art teacher, . . . took up painting full time after retiring in 1960—and was the first Black woman to have a solo show at the Whitney Museum, when she was 80."[10] In the sixty years since Alma Thomas began painting full time, aesthetic tastes have changed, barriers in the art world have lowered, and yet one thing has not budged. Thomas, an old woman artist, is still remarkable for being old and for being singular because of being old. In an art world oriented around youth, an old artist's success seems unusual.

August 2021

Mary Quinn Sullivan, the Mysterious Founder of the Museum of Modern Art

Mary Quinn Sullivan (1877–1939)

THE IMAGE of the Museum of Modern Art founder Mary Quinn Sullivan published here isn't the only distinctive thing about her. Her name evokes Irishness three times in the early twentieth century and carries along with its Irishness powerful connotations of Catholicism, poverty, discrimination, the Democratic Party, and public (as opposed to wealthy, private) institutions. These connotations cannot be overlooked at a time when the rich Americans collecting art were more likely to be privately educated, Protestant, and, in politics, prominent Republicans. The heads of the families of both Lillie P. Bliss and Abby Aldrich Rockefeller—the museum's other two founders—were Republicans of national standing with roots in New England, where anti-Irish prejudice flourished.

But first, look at Sullivan's poised photograph, undated and lacking a credit line. Rich-lady photos of Bliss and Rockefeller, in contrast, manifest their self-assured affluence through clothing (Bliss) and domestic setting (Rockefeller): Bliss, in her ultrafashionable hat and fur coat, and Rockefeller in a home filled with books and fine furnishings.[1]

Sullivan's image, like much else about her, visualizes her difference—her distance—from the other two founders. I would guess Sullivan's photo to have been taken around 1930, in her middle age after the founding of MoMA but before the death of her husband in 1932 and the

Mary Quinn Sullivan. *Photo © The Museum of Modern Art / Licensed by SCALA / Art Resource, NY*

start of her financially straitened, hardworking life as an independent businesswoman. Her photograph reflects the manner of photographers like Berenice Abbott, who opened her New York City photographic portrait studio in 1929 and exhibited at the museum in 1932, and cosmopolitan Carl Van Vechten, who began portrait photography in 1930 but who needed a few years to develop his distinctive style of posing contemporary subjects such as the Harlem Renaissance writers Nella Larsen and Zora Neale Hurston—who in New York lived in a world apart from Bliss, Rockefeller, and Sullivan—before imaginative backgrounds in dialogue with their subjects' creativity.[2]

Mary Quinn Sullivan is artfully posed in a Parisian beret and asymmetrical scarf in just such a portrait, hands clasped meaningfully on the back of a chair of noteworthy handicraft. She sits in front of a memorable piece of modern art that looks like chicken wire in front of a bedsheet.[3] The photo portrays Sullivan as a shrewd denizen of the world of modern art. Knowledge was her forte. But getting to know her was not easy.

· · ·

All three founders of the Museum of Modern Art, being women, have been relatively little known in comparison with their achievements and the men around them. But Sullivan, originally Midwestern, working-class, and Irish American, is doubly obscure in the history of modern art in New York City. Finding Sullivan reminded me of doing research on a New York woman of the previous century, Sojourner Truth. Coming to understand both women meant quilting together tidbits of information. Truth did not read or write; Mary Quinn Sullivan obviously did. But given the paucity of her personal testimony, she also hides from the biographer.

My outline of Sullivan's career draws heavily upon the work of Howardena Pindell, a distinguished artist who was also a curator at MoMA early in her career. Pindell, whose basic research on Sullivan was published in the 1971 and 1999 editions of *Notable American Women,* wrote under word-limit constraints that prevented her from delving into themes that particularly interest me, such as the cultural significance of Sullivan's education, her employment in institutions of public education, her Irish Americanness, and her relationships with her contemporaries in modern art, especially with her friend Katherine S. Dreier.[4]

Sullivan was born Mary Josephine Quinn on a farm in west Indianapolis and kept close ties throughout her life with her seven younger siblings. Her paternal grandfather had immigrated to the United States in 1857 in the midst of the Irish famine and worked in manufacturing before following a familiar Irish American path through political patronage to become a fireman. I don't know why his son preferred farming, only that Mary was born on a farm. But the Quinn farm was close enough to town for her to attend Shortridge High School (public, not Catholic, likely for financial reasons). Her energy and artistic promise attracted Roda Selleck, a high school mentor who facilitated her move to New York City in 1899 to study art education and prepare for a teaching career, a common path for second-generation Irish American women in the early twentieth century.[5] Mary was not initially fated to work with Brahmins like Bliss and Rockefeller, the initial financial benefactors of the Museum of Modern Art.

In 1899 Mary Quinn went to Pratt Institute, a forward-looking private institution unusual for the times in welcoming students of all racial and ethnic backgrounds, women included. At Pratt she was a scholarship student, and according to the school's archives, her grades were mostly Bs, her teachers recording her as "bright" (many times), "intelligent," "enthusiastic," "energetic," "spirited," but also "uneven," despite her artistic talent, and in need of "more control of [her] work."[6] She graduated from the Department of Fine Arts' two-year Normal Course, which through classes in studio practices and art history prepared students to teach art education, in 1901.

At Pratt Mary met Katherine S. Dreier, born in the same year, an artist daughter of a wealthy, bohemian, public-spirited German American family in Brooklyn Heights. Dreier would become a close friend, traveling companion, and housemate. She will reappear in this essay as a kindred pioneer of modern art whose trajectory diverged from Mary Quinn's as personal character, tastes, and, especially, money came to play increasingly prominent roles in cultural-institution building in the late 1920s. But this is to run ahead of my story, where Quinn has graduated and begun to stand out as a leader, a leadership the New York Board of Education took cognizance of by sending her to Europe to survey art education as an investment in New York's public schools. This initial tour, underwritten by a public institution, was the first of her many art-centered European trips over the years and laid the foundation of her just reputation for deep knowledge of modern art. Her 1902–1903 traveling companions were Dreier and Dreier's eldest sister, Dorothea. Together they took an intense art and architectural historical grand tour from Paris to Florence, Venice, Ravenna, Rome, Pompeii, and several intervening cities.[7]

On her return to New York from Europe, Mary Quinn began a decade-long career teaching art at DeWitt Clinton High School in Lower Manhattan, then exclusively for boys. She was enough of a public education activist to serve as secretary of the New York High School Teachers' Association. During her years as a teacher, Quinn continued her own art education at the Art Students League and back at Pratt. In 1907, building on her existing friendship with Dreier, Quinn moved into the Dreier household, already well known for welcoming interesting people regardless of background. A friend later recalled

the Dreier home at 6 Montague Terrace as the "scene of many a con-
genial gathering, in which there was never the least hint of snobbism
or class consciousness. All were on the basis of wholesome equality."[8]
At the Dreiers', Quinn most likely did not experience the prevailing
prejudice against Americans of Irish descent.

In 1909 Quinn left DeWitt Clinton High School and returned to
Pratt as an instructor and department head in Household Design and
Household Arts and Sciences. While her courses were focused on
interior design, her next European trip, to London in 1909, focused
on fine art. She studied at the Slade School of Fine Art (which admitted women on an equal basis with men), where she absorbed the ideas
of the influential modernist art critics Roger Fry and Clive Bell. In
previous years Fry had come to admire French painting, especially the
work of Paul Cézanne and Édouard Manet. Fry's orientation toward
French painting and his theorizing on the importance of formalism in
connoisseurship deeply influenced Quinn. His understanding of the
role of the marketplace in art appreciation also likely shaped her as a
dealer and art adviser of impeccable taste with an oft-remarked-upon
talent for discovering and buying the work of young artists before
prices soared for their work.

The year 1913 was pivotal in American art history on account of
the International Exhibition of Modern Art, or Armory Show, which
introduced European avant-garde art to the American public. It also
signaled Mary Quinn's visibility beyond Pratt Institute. Three figures
who would become significant in her life were deeply involved with
the Armory Show: Arthur B. Davies, John Quinn (no relation to Mary
Quinn), and Lillie Bliss, all of them collectors and social movers who,
like Mary Quinn, helped to underwrite the monumental exhibition.
By then Quinn was evidently accompanying Bliss to galleries. It is
likely that Bliss brought Quinn into contact with Davies.

Around the time of the Armory Show, Quinn took another significant step beyond Pratt's classrooms through membership in the
Cosmopolitan Club, which offered lectures and other events on art,
literature, and current affairs to forward-looking (White) women.
Although the Cosmopolitan Club's founders "came from or were
allied to leading families of the city," its membership encompassed

artists and educated women with lively minds who were not social lions.[9] Abby Rockefeller helped to found it in 1911; Bliss joined the following year. Quinn belonged to the class admitted in 1913–14, as she was becoming a published author.

Shortly before the Great War, Mary Quinn established herself as an expert adviser in household design and in art, publishing the article "The Basic Work in Art in Preparing Teachers of Home Economics" and the book *Planning and Furnishing the Home: Practical and Economical Suggestions for the Homemaker,* both in 1914.[10] *Planning and Furnishing the Home*, which became a standard college textbook in home economics, imparts Quinn's general approach to design, which was one of simplicity, practicality, and a minimum of distracting detail. Though promising to serve the woman of modest means, the book begins by advising the homemaker to choose her architect as well as her neighborhood carefully. Quinn instructed her readers that "artistic expression and discrimination has a twofold value. The fine pleasure it brings to the individual is a reward in itself, but the beauty it creates in the home is an invaluable contribution to the happiness and joy of the family."[11] In 1915 she pivoted into art with "Modern Murals," an article reviewing an exhibition at the Carroll Galleries, published in *International Studio Magazine.* The 1915 rage for murals in New York also touched Davies and Dreier, who had founded the Cooperative Mural Workshop in 1914, a collective that painted murals and organized exhibitions of work by its members.[12] By then Quinn was not only an instructor at Pratt, but also an author with ambitions in modern art.

During this period Mary Quinn was less in contact with Dreier, who left the United States for Argentina during the war, and, possibly, in increasing contact with the wealthy women with whom she would found the Museum of Modern Art. In 1915, even before the United States became a belligerent in the war, Quinn and Rockefeller may have worked jointly to provide art therapy to servicemen, a cooperation sometimes cited as the initial source of their acquaintanceship. It's possible that this collaboration led Rockefeller to promote Quinn's commission to redecorate the Cosmopolitan Club at an unspecified date.[13] If Rockefeller truly were only aware of Quinn in 1915, after Quinn had joined the Cosmopolitan Club, Bliss would appear to be the person carrying Quinn over the distance separating the world of teachers from the realm of art collectors, from a world dominated by Irish American women workers into that of moneyed Anglo-Saxons.

Mary Quinn's life changed at forty, in 1917, when she married Cornelius J. Sullivan and left her teaching position at Pratt. Cornelius Sullivan was a successful lawyer from Holyoke, Massachusetts, whose clients included the New York Board of Education and the New York Giants baseball team. The son of an Irish immigrant, he was born into a more prosperous family than hers and was educated privately, first at Amherst College, then at Harvard Law School. Her late marriage would seem unusual among the wealthy Anglo-Saxons with whom she was now associating, but it was not unusual for the daughters of Irish immigrants, daughters who prioritized financial stability over early marriage.[14]

Her marriage put Mary Quinn Sullivan at a physical remove from the center of the New York art world, for she and her husband set up home not in Midtown Manhattan or Central Park West, but in Astoria, Queens, on the East River on Long Island. They lived in what they called the Hell's Gate Farm at 1801 Wolcott Avenue in a country house with handsome gardens. I don't know why the Sullivans moved to Astoria. Was it a question of money, Astoria being cheaper than Manhattan? Did they prefer a country estate to a city apartment? Did they have allergies? Was it a question of informal residential discrimination against Irish Americans in Midtown Manhattan? I don't know. I do know from the sparse remains of Sullivan's correspondence that she drew a map accompanied by a full page of written directions to guide—persuade?—colleagues to make the trip across the East River. Sullivan lived in Astoria until her death in 1939.[15]

Marriage also brought Sullivan into closer contact with John Quinn, the collector she likely first met around the Armory Show. John Quinn and Cornelius Sullivan's decades-long friendship had begun years earlier at Harvard Law School, and the two remained close in New York City. A fellow Irish American, Quinn came from a modest Ohio background and a scrappy education that included one year at the University of Michigan, law study at Georgetown, and one year at Harvard. Despite attaining wealth as a lawyer in New York, he remained touchy about his background and his relation to Irish-dominated city politics. Insulted by ethnic stereotypes of corrupt Irish politicians in New York City's powerful Tammany Hall intended to diminish him, he insisted, "I have never been a Tammany lawyer nor have I ever been a member of Tammany Hall."[16] During the First World War, Quinn intensified his connection with writers and activists associated with the Irish nationalist movement. He also ceased collecting the work of German artists.

With a taste for Irish objets d'art, Quinn began his collecting with manuscripts and rare books, moving on to American and European modernist painting and becoming, by the Armory Show, the foremost collector of French vanguard art in the United States. The painting Mary Quinn most admired in John Quinn's collection was Cézanne's *Madame Cézanne* (1872–77), which had been in the Armory Show. In May 1921, after one of many visits to John Quinn's gigantic collection of some twenty-five hundred objects in his apartment on Central Park West, Cornelius Sullivan admitted to his friend: "My wife, who knows pictures, says she would rather have your Cézanne than any other picture in the room."[17] Quinn's art collecting culminated in a furious pursuit of Henri Rousseau's *The Sleeping Gypsy* (1897), his last great purchase. The Sullivans were among Quinn's few close friends able to observe the continual growth of his collection, surely visiting his apartment in 1924 when he proudly showed off *The Sleeping Gypsy*, four months before his death.[18]

The Sullivans paid close attention to Quinn's collecting, which further oriented them toward French art. Marriage to a prosperous lawyer provided her—now as Mrs. Cornelius J. Sullivan—the means to put her art expertise to personal ends, and she and her husband built on his collection of rare books and paintings. After John Quinn's death in 1924, the Sullivans acquired their first major works, including *Madame Cézanne*, Henri de Toulouse-Lautrec's *Woman in the Garden of Mr. Forest,* and Georges Rouault's *Crucifixion.* By the late 1920s their large, eclectic collection included a wide range of Flemish, French, and American two- and three-dimensional works.[19]

Sullivan's newfound wealth and social standing, which enabled her to own works of art by the artists she had championed for over a decade, did not change the way she presented herself to the world. The most detailed description of her from this period—and also of her husband (containing a misidentification)—comes from the 1962–63 oral history of Edith Gregor Halpert, the legendary dealer and founder of the Downtown Gallery; it merits extended quotation here.

> There was a funny thing about Mrs. Cornelius Sullivan . . . Mrs. Sullivan came in. I didn't know who she was. She was wearing black cotton stockings—you know . . . this was before nylons, but silk stockings. She was wearing a seedy, sort of a rusty black wool suit, and I thought she was an old schoolteacher, a retired schoolteacher. She said, "I'd like to see some of the paintings."
>
> I thought, "Well, I'll be a nice person, and I'll show her something," and I kept showing her pictures. This [went] on and on and finally I thought, "This is enough already!"
>
> You know, I can be accommodating and kind to an old lady, but not that kind, but I went on being very pleasant, showing her things and finally she said, "I think that will do for today. Would you set those two pictures aside and I'll have my husband come in and look at them tomorrow."
>
> I said, "I'll be delighted to," and I put them right back where they were. I thought, "Good, Lord, such illusions of grandeur! Who would marry her with cotton stockings!"
>
> The next day up came a Rolls Royce, and all the kids in the neighborhood ran like hell—you know. They used to come running down for Mrs. Rockefeller's Rolls Royce too. This was [big] stuff. They'd never seen it before. A man came out, and he said, "There are two pictures being held for me. My wife selected them yesterday."
>
> I looked at this very elegant looking guy. He was Cornelius

Sullivan of Sullivan and Cromwell [*sic*]. Even I knew that name, and I almost fainted—you know, I had these awful shocks all the time. Then he told me, "I'm Mr. Sullivan."[20]

Marriage did not initially strain the Mary Quinn Sullivan–Katherine Dreier friendship, for Dreier—"Katrina dear"—was one of a very few friends Sullivan told of her engagement.[21] Dreier's wedding present, an Arthur Davies painting, delighted Sullivan, who was "glad it is from you—for all the years we had together—and the feelings of affection that I hope we will continue to have always."[22] While Sullivan was in her early years of marriage, Dreier toured Europe, returning to New York in 1920. That same year, with Marcel Duchamp and Man Ray, she founded the Société Anonyme as an experimental art organization whose subtitle was "Museum of Modern Art." But as Sullivan became more immersed in the social world of her husband in the 1920s, her friendship with Dreier weakened: in 1920 Sullivan joined the Société Anonyme as an "associate" at ten dollars per year; by 1923 she was an "acquaintance" at five dollars.[23] In early 1924 Dreier wrote to "My dear Mary": "I am so glad that our paths are crossing each other again."[24] By 1925 Dreier was asking "dear Mary" for twenty-five dollars to support the Société Anonyme, which had only ninety-two dollars on hand.[25] A year later Dreier was begging Cornelius Sullivan to make good on the twenty-five dollars he had promised to contribute, which he did, adding a bit more as well.[26]

The Société Anonyme was never able to afford a permanent home. Its penultimate act was the grand *International Exhibition of Modern Art*, an encyclopedic survey of postwar art that opened at the Brooklyn Museum in late 1926. The show reflected Dreier's eastern European tilt through its foregrounding of German and Russian artists such as Kurt Schwitters and Wassily Kandinsky, to whom she gave his first solo show in New York.[27] Ever since her 1912 discovery of European abstraction in the Cologne *Internationale Kunstausstellung des Sonderbundes Westdeutscher Kunstfreunde und Künstler*, Dreier had been drawn increasingly to abstraction. Sullivan remained faithful to more representational works, especially to figuration, as exemplified in an 1890 painting by Vincent van Gogh, known at the time as both *Adoles-*

cence and *Mädchen Brustbild Blau*, which Dreier had bought at the 1912 Cologne Sonderbund exhibition and the Sullivans purchased from her in 1929 for $20,000. (Today the painting is known by the title *Adeline Ravoux*.) Cornelius told Katherine that Mary had "always loved it."[28]

Dreier needed the money, for the Société Anonyme's big exhibition at the Brooklyn Museum was expensive and attracted less attention than it deserved, largely on account of being held in Brooklyn rather than Manhattan. Nonetheless, it counted some fifty-two thousand visitors and was reviewed widely. Was Mary Quinn Sullivan one of its visitors? Was she in the audience when Dreier gave a lecture on the exhibition at the Cosmopolitan Club in 1927? How far was Brooklyn from Queens in art miles? I don't know.

In the late 1920s Dreier and Sullivan were thus both deeply immersed in modern art in New York but active in different circles. One way this manifested was in their orientation toward art. Dreier's mystical philosophy saw modern art, especially abstract art, as a spiritual force benefiting society or as a means of improving the world. Sullivan seems to have emphasized formalist connoisseurship and buying art cheap and letting it appreciate over time.

In the second half of the 1920s, Sullivan also began turning her attention to the art needs of her hometown of Indianapolis, where she had kept close contacts over the years. In 1927 she encouraged Indianapolis's women "civic leaders" to form the Gamboliers, each paying twenty-five dollars annually toward enriching the collection of the John Herron Art Institute (now Herron School of Art and Design), a private art school and museum.[29] Until she opened her own business as a dealer after her husband's death in 1932, Sullivan purchased art—primarily works on paper by Maurice Prendergast, Modigliani, Matisse, and Toulouse-Lautrec—for the Herron Museum on behalf of the Gamboliers, 167 works in total. The collection of the Indianapolis Museum of Art still holds works given by the Gamboliers, which had inaugurated the museum's collection of modern art.[30]

After John Quinn's death in 1924, it was revealed that his will stipulated that the bulk of his collection be auctioned off to the public. The dispersal of this extraordinary collection prompted much wringing of hands among the friends of modern art in New York, who were likely expecting, or at least hoping, that the collection would remain intact. The auction finally took place three years later, in 1927. The Sullivans had meanwhile purchased André Derain's *Window at Vers* from the estate, which would eventually enter MoMA's collection.[31] The hand-wringing intensified with the dispersal of another famous collection, that of the painter and art promoter Arthur Davies, who died suddenly in 1928. After two storied collections of modern art were sold off and scattered through sale, the stage was practically set for the foundation of the Museum of Modern Art by Rockefeller, Bliss, and Sullivan, for obviously there needed to be a museum devoted to modern art with a permanent collection that would be safely housed.

A charming founding myth set on ships in exotic Near Eastern sites—Egypt or Jerusalem—has Bliss and Rockefeller meeting while traveling and Sullivan joining Rockefeller on board a ship somewhere before landing in New York City. According to this legend, the three women hatched the plan for the museum while traveling. We do have evidence from John D. Rockefeller Jr.'s datebook for March 20, 1929, that the Sullivans were shipboard guests that day.[32] Much more concrete is the additional history of a lunchtime meeting of the three women chez Abby, at which they invited A. Conger Goodyear, who had previously been president of Buffalo's Albright Gallery, to head the museum they already envisioned.

The name "Museum of Modern Art" already existed as the subtitle of Dreier's Société Anonyme, prompting her to protest the new museum's appropriation of her name. Alfred H. Barr Jr., the new museum director, and Nelson Rockefeller insisted the use of the name was really quite innocent, that it was truly "unwitting."[33] By 1929, obviously, Sullivan and Dreier had drifted far enough apart for Sullivan and her wealthy friends to appropriate the Société Anonyme's subtitle. No matter. Dreier's talk of cosmic vibrations and inner spiritual essences and the Société Anonyme's financial weakness made her Museum of Modern Art no match for the institution that became the Museum of Modern Art. As Dwight MacDonald observed in 1953, the museum's founders brought to it the "role and conspicuousness of names redolent of solid wealth [and] few Americans care to argue with a hundred million dollars."[34] The Société Anonyme, in contrast, wasted away. In 1941 Dreier gave to Yale University the organization's more than one thousand works and its archive, which were featured in the Yale University Art Gallery's 2012 exhibition *The Société Anonyme: Modernism for America*.[35]

On November 8, 1929, the Museum of Modern Art opened to the public. From the beginning the three founders divided their responsibilities. Rockefeller, with money and organizing savvy, was described by MoMA's architecture curator Philip Johnson as the "Queen Mother."[36] Thoughtful and more reticent, Bliss had the art collection that, rooted in acquisitions from the Armory Show, would soon become the foundation of the Museum of Modern Art's collection. Alfred H. Barr Jr. said "Abby and Lillie were a team" who approved expenditures.[37] Sullivan could not approve expenditures, but she knew not only modern art but also architecture, interior design, furnishings, and art education. At the founding, Rockefeller became treasurer; Bliss, vice president; and Sullivan, member trustee and chair of the Extension and Furnishing committees. Cornelius Sullivan served as the museum's counsel, drawing up the papers of incorporation. As Rockefeller and Bliss formed a tight team assuring institutional stability in terms of funding and the permanent collection, Quinn Sullivan, working with Associate Director Jere Abbott, performed the essential work of scouting and arranging exhibition space. Building on her long expertise in interior design and her preference for uncluttered display, she set up the first show's utterly indispensable visual infrastructure. Sullivan's gift was, in the words of an art historian, a "practical form of cultural capita."[38]

Mary Quinn Sullivan emerges from descriptions of the museum's very early days as a crucial figure whose essential expertise and hard work situated her between staff, whose regular presence was required, and the powerful team of Rockefeller and Bliss, who sat at an elevated remove. According to her biographer, Rockefeller appreciated Sullivan's "gaiety and charm and her luminous beauty," while friends described her "as [a] pure Irish mystic" who believed in elves—phrases that carry an element of stereotypical Irishness.[39] She was praised for her "pink cheeks over a brown skin" and admired as a "whizbang," but also patronized as a "church mouse."[40] Sullivan lacked children or other family members of wealth to continue her legacy at the museum. In contrast, after Bliss's death in 1931, her niece, Elizabeth Bliss Parkinson Cobb, succeeded to her trusteeship and continued the Bliss family's active leadership at MoMA. Cobb denigrated Sullivan, perhaps through ethnic bias, certainly through class prejudice: "Mrs. Sullivan did not have a collection because she wasn't rich. She didn't have money of that sort . . . She had a husband who was a lawyer and her contribution—she was a great friend of both Mrs. Rockefeller and Lillie Bliss—was that her husband gave them free legal advice."[41] In another interview, Cobb agreed to expand her brief remarks on Sullivan only while the oral historian's tape recorder was turned off.[42]

While in the museum's first few years, Sullivan was valued for her knowledge and enthusiasm, the centrality of her role did not endure. The combination of the Great Depression and her husband's death diminished Sullivan's finances as well as her standing.[43] In a heart-rending letter to Barr, in 1932, she expressed uncertainty over her role, voicing confidence in his leadership, respect for Rockefeller, and an offer to resign from her trusteeship: "I want to offer to drop out—to supplement, to do whatever work that may seem to you to be of help."[44] I don't know how wealthy the Sullivans actually had been before the crash—their holdings, their debts—but Cornelius's finances most certainly suffered in the downturn. In addition, his will, crafted during prosperous times, had left specific amounts to his family that decreased his widow's inheritance. In 1933 Quinn Sullivan left her active trusteeship. Two years later the trustees elected her an honorary trustee for life.

The Great Depression saw Sullivan working hard as a dealer. David Rockefeller, Abby's son, recalled: "Mrs. Sullivan perhaps I saw more of than [Miss] Bliss, because in addition to being a friend of Mother's, she was a dealer . . . So Mother saw her in other connections than in starting the museum."[45] Sullivan's correspondence reveals her pursuit of likely sales through personal contacts—to "Dear Mr. Swee-ney," to whom she offers an African sculpture she found in Ireland (Sweeney had recently curated a show of African art at MoMA), and to Paul J. Sachs at Harvard's Fogg Museum, whom she offers to meet in Cambridge or at her New York gallery.[46] Her galleries were called sim-ply "Mrs. Cornelius J. Sullivan," first on her own at 57 East Fifty-Sixth Street and later in two rooms within Lois Shaw's 460 Park Avenue gallery. As Sullivan concentrated on her own business, she withdrew from the Indianapolis Gamboliers due to conflict of interest.

An extended depiction of Sullivan as a businesswoman comes from Betty Parsons, who would later become an influential art dealer. Par-sons established her own elite bona fides rooted in an ancestral New York farm, education at Miss Chapin's, and a finishing school, such that "nobody could be more American."[47] As a broke painter, Parsons worked for Sullivan in her Park Avenue gallery for about a year and a half on a commission basis. Sullivan's flourishing business offered a variety of modern art and Irish silver, antiques, and paintings that Parsons thought had come from an estate sale that was most likely John Quinn's. Parsons's biographer, Lee Hall, described Sullivan as a "stern taskmaster," a judgment a friend echoed in 1939, deploring "Mrs. Sullivan's tyranny."[48] Nonetheless, Parsons met "a lot of artists through Mrs. Sullivan" and felt she had "great taste."[49] According to Hall, Parsons saw Sullivan as "clever in the management of her gal-lery. As an art dealer, she cannily combined her social life with her business, using parties and visits with friends to identify and court cli-ents."[50] These recollections paint her as a practical, persistent dealer who used her social standing and contacts to succeed in the art busi-ness, a pursuit in which she had an extraordinary depth of knowledge going back to the turn of the century.

Mary Quinn Sullivan's reckoning with reduced wealth meant not only dealing but also deaccessioning, beginning with an auction of proper-ties from her husband's estate and her own collection in 1937. When that sale did not suffice to support her in New York, she scheduled another auction for December 1939 with the intention of moving back to Indianapolis. In November of that year she made her sole gift of a work of art to MoMA, Aristide Maillol's *Portrait of Auguste Renoir,* in memory of her husband.[51] Tragically, on the night of December 5, the eve of her auction, she died of pleurisy and diabetes, at age sixty.[52]

The New York Times announced the December 6–7 auction at Parke-Bernet Galleries as "Noted Collection of Art to Be Sold."[53] A review afterward called the sale "one of the most important auction sales of modern art in recent years . . . dispersed before a packed house" and bringing in a total of $148,750.[54] Walter P. Chrysler paid the top prize of $27,500 for *Madame Cézanne,* the very Cézanne that had come from John Quinn's collection and that the Sullivans had coveted in Quinn's home. The *Times* article praised "this famous collection" for its "high level of taste . . . We can hardly fail at once to recognize the imprint of a rare collector's intelligence [and] discriminating taste."[55] Quinn Sullivan's several obituaries echoed this recognition of her art historical expertise and knowing connoisseurship.[56] The 1939 sale brought two more items from Sullivan's personal collection into the Museum of Modern Art, thanks to Abby Rockefeller's purchase of a Modigliani bust and the Derain painting that was Sullivan's signature piece.[57]

These two works, still in the Museum of Modern Art's collection, are the clearest trace of Mary Quinn Sullivan's crucial role in the museum's founding. For unlike Rockefeller and Bliss, whose families continued to exercise leadership into the twenty-first century, Sullivan lacked heirs in New York to extend her influence. For most intents and purposes, her memory faded with her death.

Mary Quinn Sullivan, the youngest and least known of the Museum of Modern Art's women founders, brought together young Mary J. Quinn's expertise in interior architecture, furnishings, and modern art and Mrs. Cornelius J. Sullivan's prestige as the wife of a wealthy lawyer and businesswoman's savvy. A long-standing, keen sense of value undergirded her impeccable taste, whose reputation survives in historical source materials rather than common wisdom. As one of the museum's three founders, she contributed a deep knowl-

Window at Vers, 1912, oil on canvas, 51½" × 35¼". By André Derain. © 2023 *Artists Rights Society (ARS), New York / ADAGP, Paris*

edge of modern art and interior design and sophisticated, formalist connoisseurship.

Much less appreciated but also of enormous importance is the energy she embodied as the granddaughter of immigrants. Unlike her wealthy and socially prominent Anglo-Saxon counterparts in the museum's founding, she had to cross enormous class and cultural distances and make her own way, intellectually, socially, and financially. She deserves to be well known as a remarkable pioneer in the American history of modern art. She should also be recognized within the history of twentieth-century New York, when being Irish American carried connotations she had to overcome to acquire her finely honed understanding of art. She embeds within the history of the Museum of Modern Art the energy, aspirations, and determination of America's rising immigrant classes.

March 2021

Whose Nation? The Art of Black Power

SOUL OF A NATION answers the complaint that Black visual artists have been making since the Harlem Renaissance of the 1920s, that their art suffers from a lack of serious engagement.

A few years ago, when I was a Fulbright Scholar in Britain, students gushed to me about their all-time favorite period in United States history: the heroic civil rights and Black Power era of the 1960s and 1970s. That's when America was really fascinating, they told me, when issues were clear, and the right Americans made their voices heard. Many Americans feel this way, too. It is true that the civil rights revolution enkindled the concept of Black Power, which galvanized Black artists—playwrights, choreographers, filmmakers, musicians, as well as visual artists—to make work that reflected the ideologies and energies of the era. It really did seem in the 1960s and 1970s that artists could make a difference in the struggle against racial discrimination by joining political activists as a force against White supremacy. Those young people in the UK were right to imagine a time when valiant Americans were outspoken and relatively united. And here I stress "imagine," because in fact, ideological disagreements had hardly disappeared at that time. Last year, an ambitious art exhibition captured these hopes and this variety of concepts in visual form.

I come to *Soul of a Nation: Art in the Age of Black Power* with two identities: as a historian and as a visual artist. I am interested in art history: in the machinations of history and memory as they apply to art, and in changes in taste and how they relate to power, money, and cultural visibility. As an artist, I'm attentive to how art is presented and actually looks in physical space. This essay, the first of a two-part review, focuses on the bound catalogue and how the works and ideas of the exhibition are represented in a book, an object that I hold in my hand in Newark, New Jersey (and an object of great beauty it is—a museum artifact in its own right). In a second piece, I will review the *Soul of a Nation* show at the Crystal Bridges Museum of American Art in Bentonville, Arkansas.

Black art is all too often characterized as solely a statement of identity, as commentary on Blackness in world history, or as a critique of racism. Work by Black artists is likely to get lumped together as *Black,* regardless of period, medium, and style. This kind of grouping occurred in the 1960s and 1970s, when protests against exclusion prompted White-run museums to attempt to desegregate their collections. Some, like the Newark Museum of Art in New Jersey, had already made intermittent efforts to show Black work. Others, like the Brooklyn Museum, had a steadier history. Still others had little idea even of where to start. Early museum outreach was prone to grasping at whatever works were easily obtained, then burying them in storage after protests calmed down. What little art criticism there was tended to neglect the visual meanings and value of the art.

Soul of a Nation, which originated at the Tate Modern in London, features some 170 works made by Black artists between 1963 and 1983. Co-curators Mark Godfrey and Zoé Whitley—who both curate the collection of international art at the Tate Modern—chose sixty-seven artists, living and dead, all but two of African descent: some of sustained prominence (for example, Romare Bearden, David Hammons, and Melvin Edwards); others who surged initially, then fell out of fashion (such as Charles White, Sam Gilliam, Dana C. Chandler Jr., and Kay Brown); and others, again, who produced steadily but have only recently achieved widespread acclaim. In this third group are two artists who experienced late but notable prominence, the sculptor Betye Saar, known for a wide range of styles starting with assemblages, and the vividly figurative painter Barkley L. Hendricks. The cover of the *Soul of a Nation* catalogue features *What's Going On*

(1974), a Hendricks painting of emphatically dark-skinned figures, one a nude woman, the others wearing luminous white suits and hats.

Black visual artists have hardly received extended commentary, especially when compared with writing on Black music. To this day, Black visual artists are rarely the subjects of lavish catalogues and lengthy personal essays. *Soul of a Nation* is certainly lavish, and while the catalogue spends time on individual artists, its strength lies elsewhere in its acknowledgment of the important part institutions play in art's creation and reception. Within the racist and sexist history of the American art world, Black curators, collectors, and galleries have exerted a crucial countervailing influence.

Organized in three parts intended as introductory surveys of the art, artists, and movements of the civil rights and Black Power period, *Soul of a Nation* is rigorous and encyclopedic. The first section, "Spiral to FESTAC," presents a history of institutions (voluntary organizations, galleries, art festivals) that showcased Black art in the 1960s and 1970s. It begins with Spiral, the 1963–1965 New York Black artists' cooperative (made up of all men except for the youngest member, the late Emma Amos) whose founding statement announced that they wanted to discuss "the commitment of the Negro artist in the present struggle for civil liberties," as well as the art historical project of documenting African American artists. Spiral dissolved in three years, as the artists did not agree with Romare Bearden, one of its founders, that members should embrace a uniform aesthetic. Older members, such as Hale Woodruff and Charles Alston, hesitated before making art they considered propaganda.

In addition, the question of how tightly to embrace the idea and the imagery of Africa also generated controversy in Spiral, as it did among other Black people, including artists across the United States. Spiral continued to inspire the artists involved and those who followed. Other collectives and organizations, like the Black Panther Party newspaper, the Studio Museum in Harlem, AfriCOBRA, and *The Black Photographers Annual,* are addressed as part of this survey. The section closes with the 1977 FESTAC festival in Nigeria, at the time the largest Pan-African cultural gathering, an event that exemplified Black American artists' embrace of a diasporic identity and identification with a "'trans-African' ethos: a prevailing African sensibility that remained identifiable despite geographic distance and diasporic dispersal."

The second section's two essays address abstraction and figuration. "American Skin: Artists on Black Figuration," by Zoé Whitley, begins with Hendricks and moves through a thoughtful survey of figurative artists like Faith Ringgold, best known for her narrative quilts, and the sculptor and graphic artist Elizabeth Catlett, both of whom created works that were explicitly political. Ringgold's *American People Series #20: Die* (1967) shows bloodied Black and White people fighting with one another, arms and legs splayed, as terrified children look on. Catlett's *Black Unity* (1968), a mahogany carved fist with two faces on the back, illustrates her interest in making art, as she said, "to service Black people—to reflect us, to relate to us, to stimulate us, to make us aware of our potential."

"Notes on Black Abstraction," by Mark Godfrey, covers ground that will likely be unfamiliar to many, as abstract Black art has long been ignored by museums and critics in favor of figurative representations of Black life. Godfrey's essay begins with the shaped canvases of Al Loving, who in 1969 became the first Black artist with a solo show in the Whitney Museum of American Art. The work of the Abstract Expressionist painter Norman Lewis, long ignored but recently selling well, and of the photographer Roy DeCarava—known for his pictures of Harlem in the mid-twentieth century, but who also experimented with light, shadow, and abstraction in the 1960s—is considered and luxuriously illustrated.

The third section, entitled "Recollections," focuses on figures integral to the fostering and reception of Black art during the Black Power era. While Black art history goes back to the Howard University philosopher Alain Locke's 1925 concept of African "ancestral arts" and the Howard artist James A. Porter's *Modern Negro Art* (1943), the 1960s and 1970s produced an outpouring of new commentary by art critics, historians, and curators such as David Driskell, Richard J. Powell, Deborah Willis, Lowery Stokes Sims, Cheryl Finley, and Camille Billops. In *Now Dig This! Art and Black Los Angeles, 1960–1980* and *South of Pico: African American Artists in Los Angeles in the 1960s and 1970s*, the art historian Kellie Jones (thanked, but not quoted) laid the groundwork for art of the Black Power era and for *Soul of a Nation*.

"Recollections" offers invaluable original, first-person reminiscences by many relevant artists, curators, gallerists, and publishers. The painter Samella Lewis founded *The International Review of African American Art* in 1976 to publish serious art criticism about Black artists who were otherwise ignored by mainstream journals. David Driskell, also a painter, curated the pioneering 1976 exhibition *Two Centuries of Black American Art: 1750–1950*, a cornerstone of Black art history. In 1976 Linda Goode Bryant founded the Fifty-Seventh Street gallery Just Above Midtown, which showed Black artists such as the painter Palmer Hayden, the photographer Dawoud Bey, and the performance artist Senga Nengudi. Even today, with the exception of the small minority of internationally prominent artists with major gallery representation, most artists, especially Black artists, lack means to widely share their work.

The British students I met on Fulbright imagined Black voices speaking as one against American racism. In a sense, *Soul of a Nation* represents a composite voice, made up of a wide range of artists, curators, and writers: the diverse soul of Black America at the time of Black Power. The title also seems to reference the fact that Black nationalism regarded Black America as a nation on its own. But "nation" in *Soul of a Nation* also implies that the art of this period confronts and concerns all Americans.

Near the beginning of the catalogue, Darren Walker, president of the Ford Foundation (a major funder of the project), writes that the "exhibition not only reflects on a particular period in American history, but reaffirms the integral role of art in the fight for social change." Walker hopes that *Soul of a Nation* will provide insight into our past and inspire "empathy and action in the days to come." The exhibition is explicitly intended to serve as a guide to art institutions seeking to desegregate their collections by race and gender, an issue that remains relevant today. Expanding what is seen and accepted as "American art," then, is a fundamental target of the show. *Soul of a Nation* itself is an effort, supported by major institutions, to break down habits of exclusion, to reshape American art history by increasing the visibility of Black artists then and now. But no single definition of Black art can usefully embrace the work of contemporary artists as disparate as Kara Walker, Adam Pendleton, Njideka Akunyili Crosby, Charles Gaines, Martin Puryear, and Joyce Scott. Although race alone can no longer serve as a useful category in visual art, *Soul of a Nation* takes a snapshot of a different time, a moment when the work of Black artists was most easily defined by race, and when Black work was most frequently and emphatically *Black*. It omits some work from the period that doesn't fit this criterion, such as the landscapes of Barkley L. Hendricks and Hale Woodruff. Nonetheless, the exhibition surpasses the limitations of twentieth-century museums by including a great deal of work that does not shout its racial identity.

For all its capaciousness, the catalogue suggests that the exhibition should more properly be titled "Soul of the US-American Nation," or even "Soul of the US-American Nation as Seen from Chicago and the Coasts." The art of Black Power in its British, West Indian, and South American manifestations is all but absent here, even though, as Cheryl Finley has noted, British curators have taken on the Black Arts Movement in exhibitions like Nottingham Contemporary's *The Place Is Here* last year. Within the US, provincial artists of the civil rights era, like Herman Kofi Bailey in Atlanta, remain invisible, despite his service to the Student Nonviolent Coordinating Committee as a graphic artist.

In our own Black Lives Matter times, when police brutality, racial discrimination, and voter suppression still disfigure American democracy, the issues that artists featured in *Soul of a Nation* sought to confront are very much still relevant. In trying to understand our current moment, we might look back to the American artists who worked to make sense of their nation in turmoil through creation, mutual support, and collective action.

February 2018

On the Gallery Walls

BLACK POWER ART IN ARKANSAS

L OOKING AT REPRODUCTIONS OF ART isn't really seeing art. If you want to experience art in the fullness of its materiality, you have to see it in person. You have to see it as it appears in exhibitions—at particular times on particular walls in particular buildings in particular cities or towns.

Given the usual tendency to talk about Black art in political and historical terms rather than as objects of art, I felt it was important to see *Soul of a Nation: Art in the Age of Black Power* in person. I didn't make it to the Tate Modern in London, where the exhibition originated, and I could have waited until this fall, when *Soul of a Nation* will come to the Brooklyn Museum. But Brooklyn is home to artists by the thousands and a museum with a distinguished collection of Black art. To me, it lacks the mystery of Bentonville, Arkansas, where *Soul of a Nation* went after London.

How would *Soul of a Nation*—this very Black art made in the 1960s to the 1980s—look in a museum situated in one of the Whiter areas of Arkansas? The Crystal Bridges Museum of American Art, founded by the Walmart billionaire Alice Walton, consists of several attractive buildings, thoughtfully and expensively designed by Moshe Safdie and nestled among hilly woods on the northern outskirts of Bentonville.

While the Crystal Bridges Museum feels East Asian in aesthetic style, downtown Bentonville speaks in another design register. Downtown is compact, with neat storefronts surrounding a grassy central square. Fitting in nicely among the storefronts is the Walmart Museum, a 1950s-themed general store and soda fountain where clean-cut young White people serve you with a smile. No hint of the anti-segregation 1960s civil rights sit-ins obstructs this historical reenactment. The Confederate monument (erected in 1908) towering over the town square has caused some well-mannered chagrin among the locals. Everybody is very, very nice, though little children in the soda fountain couldn't stop staring at me.

Bentonville is the home of Walmart, the world's second-biggest company (after Amazon), with 11,703 stores and clubs in twenty-eight countries, grossing $480 billion in sales. The company has been known for low wages, few benefits, insufficient health coverage, and hostility to unions. The founder's family is worth some $150 billion, and daughter Alice Walton is one of the wealthiest women in the world, with a net worth of nearly $44 billion. In a state where 17 percent of the overall population and a third of the African American population lives in poverty, there could hardly be a more glaring contrast to the values and material objectives of civil rights and Black Power. The juxtaposition of Walton riches and Black Power's art of "solidarity with the oppressed peoples of the world"—the words of one of Emory Douglas's posters in the exhibition—was something I had to see for myself.

As it turned out, all was tranquil. Crystal Bridges Museum attracted no "institutional critique," such as the 1971 controversy when the Guggenheim canceled the show of the artist Hans Haacke because of his exposé of the relationship between exploitative wealth and art sponsorship. *Soul of a Nation* opens with videos of activists—Malcolm X, Angela Davis, Martin Luther King Jr., and Stokely Carmichael—but no lines were drawn between their activism and the Walton wealth. Everyone, artists and audience, seemed pleased.

I thought I was well acquainted with the exhibition after my review of the Tate's catalogue, but at Crystal Bridges, the sheer variety of works stunned me. The limitations of the 10½″ × 8½″ pages of the catalogue had reduced the scale of the works and homogenized them. In true scale, some were huge (by Barkley Hendricks, for instance), others modest (Betye Saar), some flat (Alvin Loving); others projected from walls (Dana Chandler) or sat on the floor (Martin Puryear). Some were clearly didactic (Faith Ringgold), painted flatly in saturated reds and oranges (for instance, the Kool-Aid colors favored by Carolyn Lawrence that exhorted children to "Keep your spirits free"); other pieces conveyed their meanings through materials—leather, cloth, found articles, and metallic collage—that were not evident in the catalogue reproductions. Surface textures that had appeared muted in the printed image surged here into detail, only visible up close.

A daylong symposium accompanying the exhibition opening featured talks by Faith Ringgold and Lorraine O'Grady, as well as panels of artists now in their eighties discussing the activism of the 1960s and 1970s, networks of friendship and support, and losses suffered since the Black Power era. The abstract painters Melvin Edwards and William T. Williams lamented the absence of their friend Jack Whitten (1939–2018), a member of the cohort of Black artists working steadily from the 1960s right into the present but who only received commensurate professional recognition in the twenty-first century. Whitten symbolizes the real achievement of *Soul of a Nation*, which has reoriented the exhibition of Black art away from "sociology," as the photographer, critic, and exhibiting artist Dawoud Bey put it, and "towards the object"—that is, toward art as art.

One work that is strikingly different when seen in person is Whitten's *Homage to Malcolm* (1970). For decades prior to *Soul of a Nation*, *Homage to Malcolm* had been stored in Whitten's studio, unsold. In the catalogue, *Homage to Malcolm* appears as a triangular shape consisting of three dark triangles, each one inside the next. In reproduction you can hardly make out what is clear here—a sharp contrast between the nearly bare canvas's cloudy wash in the center and, around it, the thick, deeply scored acrylic paint. These textured lines, inflected with green in the middle and red at the bottom, were made with an Afro comb.

. . .

I was able to get close to Whitten's *Asa's Place* (1973), which is displayed next to *Homage to Malcolm* and demonstrates Whitten's pioneering use of acrylic paint with collage. He used acrylic practically as a sculptural medium, with techniques that foregrounded the materiality of painting.

Jae Jarrell's *Revolutionary Suit* (1969; remade 2010) is composed of wool, suede, silk, wood, and pigment. Produced in Chicago in the Afri-COBRA artist collective, *Revolutionary Suit* evokes a generalized Black struggle for freedom, and the bandolier, a favored symbol of the time, shows the struggle as an armed one. In place of bullets, however, Jarrell inserts brightly colored tubes of pigment from the artist's tool kit.

One of the most widely reproduced works of the Black Power era, Jeff Donaldson's *Wives of Sango* (1971), also came out of AfriCOBRA. In addition to displaying the high-keyed color and intense patterning characteristic of the collective, Donaldson's work also signals armed struggle through the motif of the bandolier. Once again, I found something I'd missed in the reproduction: Donaldson's use of gold and silver foil, in addition to acrylic paint on cardboard, to emphasize the metallic nature of armament and costume.

Donaldson's metallic armaments are representative of the exhibition's selection of works that demonstrate militancy as armored against racial violence rather than as armored with, say, a critique of economic exploitation. Even the figure in Emory Douglas's *What Is a Pig?*, a favorite theme and image of the Black Panther Party, is more policeman than plutocrat. The lack of clear engagement with issues of economic exploitation may explain the ease with which *Soul of a Nation* fits—as a celebration of racial empowerment—in a gorgeous art institution built with Walmart wealth. An amalgamation of art and money as old as the history of fine art.

April 2018

Seeing Police Brutality Then and Now

*We still haven't fully recognized
the art made by twentieth-century Black artists.*

WE CAN SEE BY NOW that the anti-police-brutality protests of 2020 differ profoundly from those of the 1960s. And I do mean *see*. We're seeing many protesters who are not Black and marches

Images, like Emory Douglas's depictions of cops as pigs, were central to the Black Panther Party's self-fashioning and mark its place in history. *Artwork by Emory Douglas / ARS / Art Resource*

in more places: large, small, urban, rural. These are protests ignited by *seeing,* seeing horrific videos of criminal acts again and again and again.

The very fact of the sameness of police brutality then and police brutality now intensifies an anger that remains totally justified. In the 1960s the Black Panther Party arose to confront police brutality, and the Panthers created a visual archive of justified outrage. Today's protesters know that their actions and the images they create will enter the political history of contesting injustice. This had not been the case for anti-police-brutality imagery created a half century ago, and even now, we still don't fully see the art made by those angry Black twentieth-century artists.

Back then, in California's Bay Area, where I grew up, police violence, including the killing of an unarmed Black teenager in San Francisco, prompted the organization, in October 1966, of the Black Panther Party for Self-Defense. The late Huey P. Newton and Bobby Seale, students at Merritt College in Oakland, bonded in reaction to an exclusionary version of California history that was being taught at the school. Then, as now, lily-White history was a part of the ideology supporting White supremacist policing.

I belong to Newton and Seale's generation, and I supported the BPP's denunciation of brutal police. But I never joined up, for reasons of neighborhood (I lived in Temescal, in North Oakland, next to Berkeley, where Kamala Harris grew up) and gendered (the BPP's gun-toting, masculinist self-fashioning). When the Panthers moved into community service and focused on programs such as free breakfasts for children and public health, women like Ericka Huggins came to the fore. Today's anti-racist activism, led by women, is beautifully feminist and eschews macho posturing.

The BPP announced a Ten-Point Program of goals for social and economic justice, which surely inspired Black Lives Matter's six-point platform of demands half a century later, and, as it matured, adopted an anti-colonial, internationalist stance. Nonetheless, armed opposition to police brutality remained the Panthers' heart and soul, the mission that attracted thousands into their ranks. Social and economic justice and the Panthers' (legally carried) guns sounded like communism to J. Edgar Hoover's FBI, which soon designated the BPP a threat to national security. FBI surveillance and infiltration, together with killings at the hands of the local police, helped destroy the organization by the early 1980s.

Images were central to the Black Panther Party's self-fashioning and mark its place in history. One of the best known is a photograph of Seale and Newton in their trademark black berets, leather jackets, and guns, standing outside the Black Panther Party storefront head-

"THE RACIST DOG POLICEMEN MUST WITHDRAW IMMEDIATELY FROM OUR COMMUNITIES, CEASE THEIR WANTON MURDER AND BRUTALITY AND TORTURE OF BLACK PEOPLE, OR FACE THE WRATH OF THE ARMED PEOPLE."

HUEY P. NEWTON, Minister of Defense

BLACK PANTHER PARTY
P.O. Box 8641, Emeryville, Calif.

Bobby Seale and Huey P. Newton at the Black Panther Party headquarters in Oakland.
Photograph from Alamy

quarters in Oakland. A group of Panthers had been photographed carrying guns into the California State capitol building in Sacramento to protest gun-control measures attempting to curb their then existing right to carry arms openly. It is likely that Howard L. Bingham took this photo, which served as a recruiting poster, because he took many other photographs of the Black Panthers. (In 2009 he published a collection of these photos titled *Howard L. Bingham's Black Panthers 1968*. Bingham died in 2016.) The image of Black men enacting armed self-defense now resonates as a counterweight to heavily armed White nationalists around the US demanding an end to public-health regulations meant to contain the coronavirus pandemic.

A drawing by Emory Douglas, the Black Panthers' minister of culture, shows children demanding an end to police brutality. *Artwork by Emory Douglas*

Bingham's photographs capture Panther activities in a documentary spirit. More intriguing to me now is the agitprop artwork of Emory Douglas, the BPP's minister of culture. Douglas's drawings were published in the *Black Panther* newspaper and plastered around the Bay Area as posters. Week after week, Douglas's searing wit visualized the urgency for action, such as this image of children carrying photographs showing police harassing children.

Armed women as mothers appeared frequently in Douglas's work, protecting their children and wearing natural hair. In this drawing, the police are shown as agents of an unjust system of property owning:

An Emory Douglas poster shows a mother holding her child and a gun. *Artwork by Emory Douglas*

Inspired by graphic design, woodcuts in particular, Douglas used bold black lines and often just one color. He combined patterns like Ben-Day dots and parallel lines, and added shading and layers to flattened images.

Douglas also popularized "pigs" as the epithet for policemen, and he would show "pigs" singularly or in twos or threes to represent not only local police but also the economic and political forces of war, Nixon, capitalism, and colonialism. The big-bellied "pig" character was often drunken and banged up, an emblem of the abuse of power; one image defined him as "a low natured beast that has no regard for law, justice, or the rights of people . . . a foul, depraved traducer, usually found masquerading as the victim of an unprovoked attack."

Right now, we are angry because police brutality and racism are so old, and they keep on happening. Art history needs to help us remember that our anger is not new, that half a century ago an organization and its artist confronted racial injustice resolutely.

Douglas's work belongs to American political history, but it should also figure in the history of twentieth-century American art. His body of work is one of several oeuvres needlessly missing from the art history canon. Among the missing, Charles White comes to mind immediately. My own narrative history, *Creating Black Americans: African-American History and Its Meanings, 1619 to the Present,* is not an art history but contains a great deal of Black art. Looking there, I find other vital works by Elizabeth Catlett, Jeff Donaldson, and Pat Ward Williams. The work of Betye Saar, Faith Ringgold, and Howardena Pindell, artists now in their deep maturity, who are also in *Creating Black Americans,* is only now becoming widely visible.

Here is art history for the moment that we are in, work that addresses themes of anti-Black violence and armed self-defense. Once this moment passes, we will need an accessible art history of righteous anger, as opposed to one that exiles these images to the margins. Why aren't these works part of the art history canon? Some of the answer lies in the definitions of fine art that prevailed during the twentieth century, when this art was made. A pertinent example is the cranky, conservative, influential *Times* art critic Hilton Kramer, who called Black art merely "social history" lacking "stringent esthetic criteria." When I was a student in art school in the early 2000s, I still encountered such judgments. Art was supposed to be "autonomous," speaking only to itself; engaged, activist art was dismissed as mere illustration.

Right now, the art history canon presents the 1960s as Abstract Expressionism and Pop Art, in images that depict an America without racial conflict and that celebrate consumer capitalism. Angry art inhabits a peculiar category of the art of protest, one peripheral to the history of American art. Let us recuperate the art that testifies to a long-standing, uncompromising opposition to police brutality. This furious art belongs not only to anti-racist heritage but also in the center of American art.

The 1960s art world, like American society at large, was so segregated that the absence of Black artists from galleries and museums was business as usual. Protesting against that color bar gave rise to anti-racist art organizations like Spiral, the Black Emergency Cultural Coalition, and the Studio Museum in Harlem, in New York, and the National Center of Afro-American Artists in Boston, all intended to lower racial barriers. The hard work of these institutions has weakened art world exclusion and discredited the outmoded distinction between art and social criticism. Today, the work of younger Black and engaged artists has been widely appreciated as art history. But the twentieth-century anti-racist art by Emory Douglas and others inspired by the Black Panther Party and Black Power has barely been rediscovered, has not made its way into the art historical canon that conveys both monetary and cultural value. Douglas's work is more easily found on tote bags being sold on behalf of Black Lives Matter than in the high-priced galleries and auctions that still decree which art matters.

In the half century between these two eras of rebellion, between the 1960s and 2020, the color bar and sexism in American society weakened, as we see in the diverse nature of the present uprisings. Today, women are at the forefront, and many non-Black people are in the streets. But more work remains to be done, specifically in the realm of images. If today's anti-racist awakening is to resonate culturally and art historically, the art world still has a big job left to do: to dismantle the color bar against twentieth-century Black artists. Let us recuperate the art that testifies to a long-standing, uncompromising opposition to police brutality. This furious art belongs not only to the anti-racist heritage but also in the center of American art.

Why, you may ask, am I talking about cultural history in a moment of soaring passion? Isn't art history a matter for later on, for museums and universities, when what we need now is action? True, art history is a cultural matter, but it is a keeper of popular memory, a version of how we see our past. American art history needs to acknowledge the art made by angry Black artists—as art. As American art.

June 2020

Archive to Brush

ARCHIVE TO BRUSH" discusses my use of a photographic archive in my painting practice and contrasts the ways archives function in the two facets of my work: as a historian bound by professional standards and as a painter relishing the freedom to follow visual impulse that comes with late style. For me as a historian, the archive—no matter how untrustworthy—held its own truths, in the senses that Michel Foucault theorizes. For me as an artist, however, the archive holds little inherent truth value, serving, rather, as source material and point of departure. As artist, I may copy, distort, and paint the contents of the archive in ways that bear little relation to the original creator's intent, because in painting, truth value resides in the visual appearance of the new work, not in its fidelity to the spirit of the source.

The archive inspiring my MFA thesis project consists of documentary photographs of Brooklyn in the 1970s and 1980s by Lucille Fornasieri-Gold, a collection now housed in the Brooklyn Historical Society. Executed under the sign of my patron saint, Robert Colescott, my paintings manifest the freedom of late style. My affinities lie with artists who use photographs, digital manipulation, collage, printmaking techniques, text, and historical narrative, notably Maira Kalman, Gerhard Richter, Romare Bearden, Fabian Marcaccio, Joyce Kozloff, and Huma Bhabha.

. . .

Self-Portrait Quilt, 2008, graphite, acrylic, and conte crayon on paper, 19¼″ × 24½″. This drawing is related to *Self-Portrait Skeleton,* revealing both my interest in the body and my attraction to fabric arts.

"Archive to Brush" begins with my transit from historical scholarship to visual art. As a historian, I found my scholarly raw material in archives, and they still play a role in my life as an artist. As a public figure whose status grows out of my scholarship, I donated my personal and professional papers to the archives of Duke University Library. Let that stand for the archive as historians understand it. And let Romare Bearden's musée imaginaire and Gerhard Richter's *Atlas* stand for the archive as artists understand it. As an artist I draw on this second kind of archive almost literally, for at this point in my thesis work a collection of photographs by Lucille Fornasieri-Gold offers a starting point for my ongoing series of paintings entitled simply *Brooklyn.*

The archives at the two ends of my work function in sharply contrasting ways. Professional ethics govern historians' use of archives: historians must respect the archive, whose authors must be cited with

346

care, for every document has an author. Not to cite an author is to plagiarize; to plagiarize is to call down professional censure. Historians need not agree with the archive's truth in order to respect it, and it is not up to historians to decide what in the archive merits respect. It *all* merits respect. This is the kind of archive—powerful in the shaping of discourse—that Michel Foucault describes in *The Archaeology of Knowledge and the Discourse on Language,* that Jacques Derrida dissects in *Archive Fever: A Freudian Impression,* and that Okwui Enwezor, as curator and art critic, contests in his essay "Archive Fever: Photography Between History and the Monument."[1]

In visual art, the archive cannot, of itself, lay claim to such power, for no such rules apply. The archive would seem to exist quite separate from any author, for here the author is dead. Truth is to be found more in appearance than in meaning. As a historian, I was careful to respect the coherence of the archive, citing authors and quoting with restraint. But now, as a painter, I throw verbal coherence to the wind. Heedless of the original appearance of my photographic archive, I copy, fracture, combine, and distort its images, disregarding the photographer's original intent according to my own eyes' impulse.

The Autobiography Behind My Art

I grew up in a left-leaning household in Oakland, California, surrounded by the counter–art historical tradition of Black American modernism, as in the work of Aaron Douglas, Charles White, Jacob Lawrence, and Elizabeth Catlett, my father's favorite artist. (In the mid-1980s my father visited Catlett in her studio in Mexico and brought back a print, inscribed by the artist to him, which I now own.) This was an unapologetically engaged art, produced at a time when images of Black people hardly appeared in American visual culture, and Black history was largely ignored outside Black institutions. During the civil rights and Black Power movements, Black artists continued to make art that carried strong positive messages. For these artists, as for my family, the discursive meaning of the work carried nearly as much importance as its formal qualities.

Many Black artists have stated clearly that they want to show the beauty of ordinary working people, a beauty that remains largely ignored. This goal continues to inspire Black artists today, including Whitfield Lovell, Faith Ringgold, Glenn Ligon, and Alison Saar, among international artists. Depicting Black history is not my goal, however, for I have had my say in print. Now I strive, as I once blurted out in a RISD class on contemporary art criticism, for meaninglessness. This is a gross overstatement on my part, for engaged art continues to inspire me now.

One of my important non-Black influences, Ben Shahn, was also on the Left and also made political art along social-realist lines. Growing up in Northern California and studying drawing at the California College of Arts and Crafts (now California College of the Arts), I absorbed the work of Richard Diebenkorn, who continues to influence my eye.

In the 1990s and early 2000s I began reengaging with visual culture through scholarship focusing on African American iconography rather than as an artist. I started by looking at how images function culturally. A chapter in *Sojourner Truth: A Life, A Symbol* (1996)—my biography of a feminist abolitionist, the best-known nineteenth-century African American woman—discusses Truth's use of photography in self-fashioning within the context of the history of photography. An essay, "*Ut Pictura Poesis*" (2004), directly addresses my own situation as I began to straddle the text and image divide. The bibliography of this thesis cites these essays and my 2006 book, *Creating Black Americans,* whose illustrations are Black fine art. Writing *Creating Black Americans* offered me a crash course in Black art history that has served me well at Mason Gross School of the Arts at Rutgers (2006–2009, BFA) and at RISD, where Black art history is largely ignored. These essays and books brought me back to a concentration on images for the first time in years.

As a BFA student in painting at Mason Gross, I mostly worked figuratively, closely studying the portraits of Max Beckmann and Alice Neel. The social commentary of early twentieth-century German expressionists (Otto Dix, Ernst Ludwig Kirchner, George Grosz) and their use of color (Karl Schmidt-Rottluff, Wassily Kandinsky, Gabriele

Münter, Franz Marc) also appealed to me. The work of contemporary painters who tackle social issues remains important to me, particularly if they play with art history as well as social convention with humor and fearless use of color. My prime inspiration in this regard is the late Robert Colescott, postmodernist avant la lettre.

Colescott (1925–2009) was from my hometown of Oakland. After serving in Europe during the Second World War, he earned a BFA in painting at the University of California, Berkeley, my undergraduate alma mater. He studied in France (as did I), earned an MFA from Berkeley, and taught in the Northwest US and Cairo. During the late 1960s he worked in the Bay Area beside West Coast artists like Roy De Forest, Mildred Howard, William T. Wiley, Joan Brown, Robert Arneson, and Peter Saul. Colescott's riotous, irreverent style dates from this tumultuous period and this rambunctious crowd. In the mid-1970s Colescott began receiving international acclaim, and in 1997 he became the first African American (and the second painter, after Jasper Johns in 1988) to represent the United States in the Venice Biennale.

Colescott's work is unabashedly multicultural and multiracial, to the point that figures in his paintings can be of several different hues and patterns within the self-same body, and he uses patterns unflinchingly. His crowded compositions depict space, but with a collage sensibility that throws figures upon one another along converging perspectives. Many of his paintings, especially those taking on art history, include self-portraits whose expressions often betray a look of puzzlement.

Colescott's work is clearly anti-racist, but his animation makes his paintings funny as hell. In his obituary, Roberta Smith said he pitted "the painterly against the political" in "giddily joyful, destabilized compositions that satirized, and offended, without regard to race, creed, gender or political leaning."[2] Like most twentieth-century Black painters, Colescott rejected the notion of making art purely for art's sake. Yet the originality and audacity of his work separate it sharply from the uplifting figurative art of Black modernists and the conservative, positive imagery of work that the Studio Museum in Harlem termed in 2002 the "Black Romantic."[3] Colescott did not feel the need to paint positive imagery, and, with a sound record of historical scholarship, nor do I.

My Paintings and Drawings

My work ranges from the more abstract to the more figurative, across four ongoing bodies of work since 2009: beauty, in historical paintings and Sylvia Boone drawings; self-portraits; nonrepresentational drawings and collages; digital + manual paintings (*Plantain* and *Brooklyn* paintings).

Personal beauty, a quintessentially visual characteristic, has fascinated me for years. My late mother, Dona Irvin, a beautiful, dark-skinned woman born in 1917, had a fraught relationship with her appearance that I inherited both intellectually and psychologically. My scholarship followed the intellectual dimension, most prominently in the theme of beauty threading through the book I published in 2010, *The History of White People*. This book shows how the theme of personal beauty influenced theories of race, beginning with the notion that people called Circassians, Caucasians, and Georgians were the most beautiful in the world. In a chapter entitled "White Slavery as Beauty Ideal," I show how this idea produced the figure of the odalisque, the beautiful young naked slave girl in nineteenth-century French academic paintings by Jean-Auguste-Dominique Ingres and Jean-Léon Gérôme. The following chapter, "The White Beauty Ideal as Science," opens with the pioneering art historian Johann Joachim Winckelmann.

These notions of beauty figure in three large (60″ × 60″ acrylic on unstretched canvas) figurative paintings I made in 2009–2010. The first depicts famous odalisques from Ingres, Gérôme, and Matisse against a map of the Black Sea region odalisques were supposed to come from. The second shows repeated images of Apollo Belvedere, the embodiment of ancient Greek male beauty, along with a sublime seascape composition appropriated from Caspar David Friedrich. The lower third of the painting quotes words from the eighteenth-century physiognomist Johann Kaspar Lavater on the sublimity of the Belvedere. The third painting repeats images of Michael Jackson at three different stages of his transformation from an African American into a White person, presumably a transit from ugliness into beauty.

The second part of my beauty works consists of nine small *Sylvia Boone Drawings* (2009, ink and collage on paper) that quote a photograph of two young women undergoing coming-of-age ceremonies in Sierra Leone in the 1970s in Sylvia Ardyn Boone's *Radiance from the Waters: Ideals of Feminine Beauty in Mende Art* (1986).[4] My drawings edit the photograph, changing its scale and repeating the figures and adding color and collage of African beads taken from other photographs. In some drawings the figures are clearly African; in others their setting obscures their identity so that the compositions emerge as only vaguely figurative.

My second body of work consists of self-portraits, most made in 2010 of acrylic, colored ink, and collage on paper or chipboard, paintings, drawings, and monotypes, 12″ × 12″. In my self-portraits, as in my paintings on canvas, I do not strive for clarity or coherence, nor is mimesis my aim. The self-portraits began as a means of addressing an issue of particular salience to artists of color who work figuratively: how to portray the colors of human skin. While some viewers read depictions of light skin as unraced and depictions of dark skin as raced, I am aware of the social connotations of everybody's skin color (not just Black people's). For me there is no such thing as neutral skin color. White people painted realistically are as colored as Black people painted realistically.

Herein lies a very big problem: a figure cannot *not* be situated racially, a challenge that pushes some artists toward abstraction. From my seat in a RISD audience, I once asked Julie Mehretu if abstraction offered her a means of avoiding the dilemma of skin colors' connotations. She said it did. I have faced up to skin color by painting myself in many colors, depending on line and shape to describe myself. I am not bound by a notion that people are defined by color, so I paint people of any race or ethnicity in all the colors I please. My self-portrait triptych from 2011 digitally manipulates a 2010 self-portrait collage, producing one in black, one in white, and one in the original bright colors. The first is *Self-Portrait Black;* the second is *Self-Portrait White;* the third is *Self-Portrait Normal.*

With affinities to the work of Richard Diebenkorn and the *Abstrakte Bilder* of Gerhard Richter, my *Bedside* and *Lake Clear Drawings* (both 2010) are abstract pieces in colored ink, gouache, and collage on paper between 8″ × 10″ and 11″ × 14″. Collaged material comes from pages torn from art magazines and *The History of White People.* Edited figurative imagery repeats in some of the drawings, while others combine line work and abstract colored shapes worked with a gestural touch. They belong to the tradition of abstract-representational painters like Amy Sillman and Huma Bhabha.

The Brooklyn Paintings of My MFA Project

In the summer of 2010 I developed a new way of working that carries over into the body of Brooklyn paintings of my 2011 MFA thesis project. Partly inspired by photography, partly inspired by printmaking methods, partly inspired by collage, this method is both digital and manual. In the *Plantain* paintings on canvas, I paint by hand on images that have been edited out of found photographs, recombined through Photoshop, and printed on canvas. The source photographs of the *Plantain* paintings come from Tibor and Maira Kalman's *Unfashion.*[5] My paintings are clearly figurative, but in imagery that is colored, composed, fractured, layered, and repeated in ways that testify to their digital manipulation. On top of images produced with Photoshop, I paint colors and patterns whose textures can only be produced by a painter's hand. I have carried this method over into my Brooklyn paintings, whose motifs came originally from an archive of photographs of Brooklyn in the 1970s and 1980s by Lucille Fornasieri-Gold (1930–2016) housed in the Brooklyn Historical Society.

Working in the spirit of Helen Levitt, Morris Engel, and Walter Rosenblum, Fornasieri-Gold conceived of her photographs as documents of a certain time and place. In retrospect we see her personal vision, her individual aesthetic at work. In no way do her photographs produce the banality that Gerhard Richter prefers in the source pho-

Back Man 1, 2011, acrylic, oil stick, and collage on canvas, 40″ × 40″. This was my last painting in art graduate school at the Rhode Island School of Design. I continued to paint like this for a few more years before text made its way into my drawings.

tographs in his *Atlas*. The very strength of her narrative encourages me to obscure her original compositions as I pick out facets of her photographs to reinterpret in paint.

The paintings proceed chapter by chapter, with each series consisting of three or four paintings and with each series taking a somewhat different approach to process, palette, and touch. The first series, consisting of four paintings with shared motifs (a dog fight, graffiti, and a woman's head), is very digital. In the second series, in which black helicopters supply unifying imagery, my touch is more gestural. The third series is far more graphic than the other two, with flatter space and use of color and the figure pulled up close to the viewer. The fourth series is not digitally printed, but composed through a combination of projection and collaged digitally printed photographs. Most of the paintings are 40″ × 40″ square, a format I chose for its neutrality. Squares convey a sense of timelessness, without pushing the viewer toward either the figurative or landscape expectations of vertical or horizontal orientations.[6]

Fornasieri-Gold's photographs are not nostalgic, and I also do not regard the past as a kinder or simpler time. Yet I found myself situating her figures from the 1970s and 1980s against backdrops of peril and disaster. Wild dogs fight to the finish. An older woman engages in conversation while the dreaded black helicopters swoop overhead. A man stands in his doorway, turning toward the viewer, unaware of the black helicopters heralding the onset of destruction. A fellow in a stingy-brimmed little hat doesn't realize that bombed-out Baghdad is burning behind him.

These paintings embody the fundamental personal quality of my work: freedom. Freedom from archival truth, freedom from clear meaning. The freedom of late style to play with composition, figures, color, and space. Freedom to find new narratives or make images with little narrative coherence. After a lifetime of expressing complicated notions clearly, I revel in the freedom to follow my visual impulses into spaces whose meaning I need not be able to express verbally.

As for the Future

I will continue to work on the Brooklyn series as a resident in the Gallery Aferro in Newark, New Jersey, into early 2012. I plan to apply to Yaddo in Saratoga Springs, New York, for a residence in 2012 to begin a new project, *Odalisque Atlas,* of drawings on paper. With inspiration from Andy Warhol, my new project follows the practice of Maira Kalman, whose books (online in *The New York Times* and bound)[7] combine painting, photographs, and text. I expect *Odalisque Atlas* to be a free-spirited take on history. This book will depart from my earlier books by emphasizing imagery rather than text and offering a coherent set of images on the perennially intriguing subject of personal beauty. It will bring readers unaccustomed to close looking to images at the basis of a topic that never fails to fascinate.

Acknowledgments

I owe many thanks to teachers and thesis advisers at RISD, notably Jennifer Liese, Roger White, and Jessica Dickinson. I also appreciate my Newark and New Jersey art world, the Gallery Aferro, the Aljira, a Center for Contemporary Art, and the Institute for Women and Art. My thesis project originates in the work of the photographer Lucille Fornasieri-Gold archived in the Brooklyn Historical Society (BHS). I thank the BHS and its director, Deborah Schwartz, for inviting me to use its collection.

Bibliography

Bey, Dawoud. "The Ironies of Diversity, or the Disappearing Black Artist." *Artnet Magazine Online*, April 8, 2004.

Copeland, Huey. "Truth to Power: Huey Copeland on Robert Colescott (1925–2009)." *Artforum International Magazine* 48, no. 2 (October 1, 2009): 59–60.

Elger, Dietmar, and Hans Ulrich Obrist, eds. *Gerhard Richter—Writings, 1961–2007.* New York: D.A.P./Distributed Art Publishers, 2009.

Huma Bhabha. Essay by Thomas McEvilley and interview by Julie Mehretu. New York: Salon 94 and Peter Blum, 2010.

L'Ambigu: Zeitgenössische Malerei zwischen Abstraktion und Narration [Contemporary painting between abstraction and narration]. St. Gallen, Switzerland: Kunstmuseum St. Gallen, 2010.

Marcaccio, Fabian. *Paintant Stories.* Zürich: Daros-LatinAmerica, 2005.

Memory and Metaphor: The Art of Romare Bearden 1940–1987. New York: Studio Museum in Harlem, 1991.

Merewether, Charles, ed. *The Archive.* London: Whitechapel Press, 2006.

Photography and Painting in the Work of Gerhard Richter: Four Essays on Atlas. Barcelona: Museu d'Art Contemporani de Barcelona, 1999.

Sims, Lowery Stokes, and Mitchell D. Kahan. *Robert Colescott, a Retrospective, 1975–1986.* San Jose, Calif.: The Museum, 1987.

Stillman, Steel. "In the Studio with Huma Bhabha." *Art in America,* November 2010, 85–93.

May 2011

I Knit Socks for Adrienne

L AST YEAR OF 2020 was a once in a lifetime for me—probably for you, too, though you'll probably be around in this world longer than I. Such upheaval! So much death and suffering, and in the nationwide, worldwide demonstrations against racist violence and White supremacy, for me, hope. All of this piled up together over the course of the year changed my art. Some of it became more political

I Knit Socks for Adrienne, page 1, 2020, graphite, ink, and digital collage. This triptych from coronavirus time in 2020, when we were exiled from home in Newark, voiced my loneliness as well as a novel willingness for me to come out of the closet as a knitter.

and talky, as in *American Whiteness Since Trump* made in Italy in February and March, and *From Slavery to Freedom* made in the Adirondacks in June. Even with the hopefulness, I was so exhausted that by the end of 2020, my art came out in a new way. Still with drawings, still with text. But newly confessional.

I Knit Socks for Adrienne is the most personally declarative piece of art I have ever made, more personal, even, than self-portraits, precisely because it is personally declarative in words that wrench the artist Nell Painter out of the closet as a knitter. For a long time I stayed closeted as a knitter. I previously thought, Let you see me as an artist, as a historian, as an artist who uses history, not let you see me as a knitter: a craftswoman, an old lady sitting around with her needles and yarn. That mental image wasn't one I had been able to expose.

But 2020 opened my closet door to reveal me knitting to hold myself together. There was all the death, searing painful deaths by the hundreds of thousands, especially of Black people. There was economic

I Knit Socks for Adrienne, page 2, 2020, graphite, ink, and digital collage. Adrienne is Adrienne Wheeler, distinguished Newark artist.

I Knit Socks for Adrienne, page 3, 2020, graphite, ink, and digital collage. The McCarter Highway mural shown here is by Adrienne Wheeler, using her favorite motif of her mother's white dress.

want. There was hunger. There was hope, in the hundreds of thousands of Americans in the streets calling down racism, denouncing White supremacy, declaring Black Lives Matter, roughing up, tearing down monuments to the Confederacy. The dead scared me. The demonstrators made me feel safer in the USA than ever before.

Even so, by Thanksgiving I had been away from home, away from Newark, for more than eight months, a coronavirus refugee in the far North Country of New York State, and missing my Newark people as I knitted—yes, to hold myself together. I knit socks for my husband; I knit socks for myself, and reaching across the miles to touch my friend in Newark, I knit socks for my Newark friend Adrienne. This piece in three panels shows self-portraits and, in the third, Adrienne's mural on McCarter Highway in Newark.

March 2021

Coda

Readers are amused by this book's title, for its forthrightness and, also, as though the terms of my persistence—*just keep*—were a sort of *non-dit*, as though they gestured toward an unspoken and perhaps inadmissible predicate, *Whether or not you're listening,* or, *Even if you're not paying attention.* To be confessional, I have to admit that for a long time, for decades, the predicate was *just.* I did *just keep talking,* even when it felt as though I were *just talking* to myself.

A drawing I repeat in these pages with "Regrets" (2000) and "The Truth of the Matter" (2022) captures that vexation:

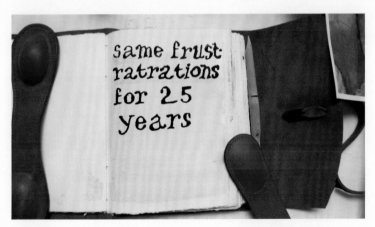

Same Frustrations, 2022, ink on paper, 5″ × 7¼″. This no longer feels so true.

That drawing expressed academic frustrations in 2000, and in 2022, my enduring struggle against the displacement of history and biography by art. Not that I'm against the power of art. In order to tap art's power, I have placed my art beside my text in these very pages. Their juxtaposition projects two different kinds of meaning, the one through discourse as text, the other visual through art. My frustration, however, springs from art's displacement of history, in this case, from the use of the literary art of the journalist Frances Dana Gage to evoke the historic Sojourner Truth. Gage's art, her journalism, invented the famous phrase "Ar'n't I a woman?" And now, all too often, merely quoting Gage functions as synecdoche for the person Sojourner Truth and testifies to art's power over history.

Sojourner Truth recognized the difference between history and art on the back and on the front of her cartes de visite photographs. My drawing quotes the text on the back that documents her power of copyright, a legal, historical power.

Sojourner Truth Entered According: Ink with Hands, Gray, 2022, an alternate version of the Sojourner Truth drawings from 2022.

On the front of her photographs, however, Truth famously contrasted art and historical person—herself—through the printed words "I sell the shadow to support the substance," the "shadow" being the photograph, the art, and the "substance" being her own physical being. Truth's use of both "shadow" and "substance" nods to the existence of two different kinds of power that coexist.

Interestingly, Truth did not quote Gage on her cartes de visite. I note this absence as the historian who has been insisting that *she did not say that* for a quarter of a century without making much of a dent in the power and reach of Gage's art. So, yes, I feel like I've been talking to myself.

I stress the emotional word, *feel,* rather than the facts of publication, reviews, promotions, and honors. While it *felt* to me as though few were reading what I wrote, scholarly recognition actually did come my way. I'm grateful for that recognition, even though I, like other women scholars, especially Black women scholars, continue to bemoan the scarcity of those citations that prove the existence of our work.

I should add that feelings have changed for me in this third decade of the twenty-first century, beginning in 2010 with the publication and bestsellerdom of *The History of White People,* a book that people admit out loud to reading, to *Old in Art School,* a sentimental favorite of artists and people old enough to sense themselves starting over. (In art school, old means you're over thirty-two.) I no longer feel as though I'm talking to just myself. A tragedy, a crime, that resonated globally in the spring of 2020 made all the difference in the world.

George Floyd's murder and the uprising of millions it inspired changed everything, is still changing everything, from the visibility of how race works in society to White Americans' understandings of themselves in history. In 2020 my work was read and heeded far more widely than ever before. I could even publish articles saying that in order to expose White as a meaningful racial category the term "White" should be capitalized. I could not have published such utterances before 2020—at least not without facing backlash and a lack of understanding—and certainly could not expect such sentiments to be widely read. Yes, the 2020 sacrifice of life made one difference in how widely my work was seen. None other than social media made another crucial difference; social media brought me lots of people to talk to who talked back.

Okay, social media didn't make *all* the difference between feeling I was talking to myself and now feeling that I am talking to some others who are paying attention. But social media—Facebook, then Instagram—gave me communities who not only "liked" my posts on Facebook or showered me with little red hearts on Instagram. Indeed, it was my Instagram community that commiserated with me when a *New Yorker* columnist quoted "ar'n't/ain't I a woman?" as Sojourner Truth.

Facebook (until it overflowed with self-hating Democrats and turned me off from the politics on its timeline) brought me an abundance of contacts, of "friends." At first it was people I already knew personally, many academics and some artists. Then people who knew people I knew. Then people who shared my interests but not my physical territory. People I came to know on Facebook, then met in person later on, and people I'll never know in the flesh. We talked. I talked to them about my books, including this one.

Back in the twentieth century I wrote books with the "informed layman" as my imagined audience. Though truth be told, I had a very particular audience in mind early on: my first graduate student advisee, Francille Rusan Wilson, from the University of Pennsylvania. Francille went on to her own academic career in Los Angeles, exceeding her role as my imagined reader, but she remains within reach as a Facebook "friend."

Here's another example of the difference Facebook could make: organizing the essays in this book, I asked my Facebook people if Southern history should have its own section or be folded into history. I had begun my scholarly career as a historian of the South and appreciated the original character of the society and histories of Southern people. At the same time, Southern history oughtn't be separated off as though not a part of American history. My Facebook people answered, some for distinction, others for incorporation. My organization here reflects this ambiguity. Most of all, enough of my "friends" paid attention to what I was thinking, attention not to be expected from history colleagues at my home institution.

As my work has leaned further into images, Instagram has become my preferred means of address. Here, too, my people responded. I

nellpainter Speaks for itself.

May 19

nellpainter ...

THE TRUTH OF THE MATTER

I admired Amy Davidson Sorkin's fine piece on the Republicans' shameful, bigoted manhandling of Judge Ketanji Brown Jackson's nomination to the Supreme Court (Comment, April 18th). Sorkin quotes a phrase—"Ain't I a woman?"—that was long held to have been spoken by Sojourner Truth, in an 1851 speech in Akron, Ohio. Yet, as I revealed in my 1996 biography, "Sojourner Truth: A Life, a Symbol," Truth never uttered those words. The phrase originated with Frances Dana Gage, a white abolitionist, women's-rights advocate, and journalist, who, in an article written twelve years after the speech, put "Ar'n't I a woman?" in Truth's mouth. (Gage was rebutting a careless essay by Harriet Beecher Stowe, in the April, 1863, issue of *The Atlantic Monthly*, which depicted Truth as quaint and, erroneously, as dead.) Elizabeth Cady Stanton and Susan B. Anthony reprinted Gage's piece in their book "History of Woman Suffrage," from 1881, which second-wave feminists would draw on as they forged the field of women's history in the twentieth century. By that time, the line had been reworked into a supposedly more authentic Southern Negro dialect, as "Ain't I a woman?" But a contemporaneous report of what Truth said, published by Marius Robinson, a white abolitionist minister, in the *Anti-Slavery Bugle*, does not include the line in any form. Although both Gage and Robinson were present at Truth's speech, Robinson was the designated amanuensis; it is hard to imagine that he would have omitted such a refrain. (Gage claimed that Truth repeated it four times.)

As a scholar, I find Robinson's account of Truth's speech more reliable than Gage's. "Ain't I a woman?" has nonetheless taken on a life of its own as a synecdoche for what we now term "intersectionality." The false quote flattens Truth into little more than a magical Negro savior of white women, and obscures her identity as a New Yorker who spoke standard English (as well as

Dutch). Unfortunately, it looms large in our country's historical imagination, my academic research as a Black woman frequently loses out to a slogan that my sister citizens *want* Truth to have said, and to the national hunger for simplifying history.
Nell Irvin Painter
Edwards Professor of American
History Emerita
Princeton University
Newark, N.J.

THE GLOBAL BBC

Sam Knight, in his article about the history of the BBC, discusses the organization's breadth and reach ("London Calling," April 18th). He could have also mentioned another important contribution in this vein—the BBC's services in international languages. Living in Quito, Ecuador, during the nineteen-forties and fifties, I grew up with the corporation's Spanish-language short-wave broadcasts. The content was outstanding: news, commentary, music, and literary presentations, among which I can recall masterly serial readings of "Don Quixote." The Spanish-language department of the BBC was then at its apogee, populated by luminaries from the expatriate community of Iberian writers and poets. Later, the service attempted to provide an objective perspective on the Falklands War between the U.K. and Argentina, in the face of governmental pressure to do otherwise. The BBC instituted similarly diverse and effective programming in a variety of languages, directed at other regions of the globe, through its World Service. I miss the Spanish-language radio transmissions to Latin America, which ceased in 2011, following budget cuts.
Pedro Lilienfeld
Lexington, Mass.

Letters should be sent with the writer's name, address, and daytime phone number via e-mail to themail@newyorker.com. Letters may be edited for length and clarity, and may be published in any medium. We regret that owing to the volume of correspondence we cannot reply to every letter.

SPECTACUL
AWAIT
AUG 29 – SEPT

us open

2022 MULTI-SES
TICKET PLAN
ARE AVAILABLE

USOPEN.O

ticketmaster

♡ ☐ ◁   ⊓

Liked by **philiphimberg** and **126 others**

Instagram "The Truth of the Matter" screenshot, 2022. Some viewers were already aware of what I was saying; those who weren't took the news in stride, a more mellow response than a quarter century ago.

Instagram Sojourner Truth screenshot. My Instagram community recognized Truth but was curious about the text.

could post an image, ask a question, and get answers. An example from my Sojourner Truth drawing assured me of engagement.

Among scores of others responding to this post were my dear personal friend Adrienne, of *I Knit Socks for Adrienne* (now on her second pair of socks), and Honorée, whom I don't know personally but whose work I admire. We'll meet face-to-face someday.

A historical document whose conventional mean-spiritedness galvanized my pen and engaged my Instagram community was Harriet Jacobs's owner's runaway-slave advertisement from 1835. All the while treating a person like property, it employs sexist language to denigrate Jacobs and to reveal its author as a prick. The advertise-

$100 Reward Triptych, 2022, ink on paper, 7″ × 15¾″. All three parts of the runaway-slave advertisement tell a story about the author—Harriet Jacobs's reputed owner—as well as about the legally enslaved young woman.

ment begins in capital letters with the phrase "$100 REWARD," capturing the insulting relationship between a young woman and the man claiming her ownership.

I made three text drawings to pause three times at the owner's self-revelatory language. But would others grasp what awfulness had caught my eye? My Instagram community read Jacobs's advertisement as I had, in all three of its atrocious claims. My piece remains a triptych, asking you to pause three times in its viewings.

"$100 REWARD" was too resonant a phrase to waste, so I used it again and again. In images, as in the middle of Ralph Waldo Emer-

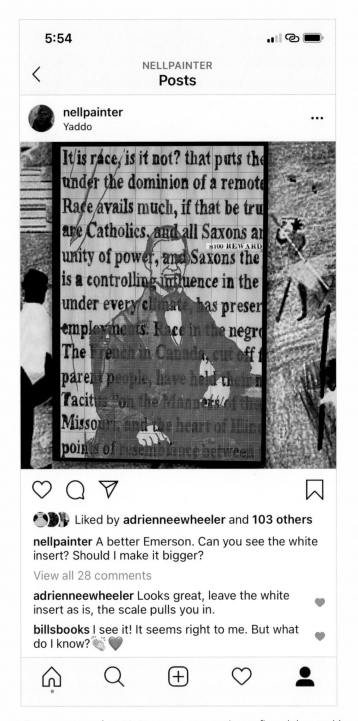

nellpainter
Yaddo

It is race, is it not? that puts the
under the dominion of a remote
Race avails much, if that be tru
are Catholics, and all Saxons ar
unity of power, and Saxons the
is a controlling influence in the
under every climate, has preser
employments. Race in the negro
The French in Canada, cut off f
parent people, have held them i
Tacitus "on the Manners of the
Missouri, and the heart of Illin
points of resemblance between

$100 REWARD

Liked by **adrienneewheeler** and **103 others**

nellpainter A better Emerson. Can you see the white insert? Should I make it bigger?

View all 28 comments

adrienneewheeler Looks great, leave the white insert as is, the scale pulls you in.

billsbooks I see it! It seems right to me. But what do I know? 👏🏻🖤

Instagram Emerson screenshot. My Instagram community confirmed they could see "$100 REWARD." They said they could.

son's White supremacist proclamation in *English Traits*. But could the crucial "$100 REWARD" be seen amidst his barrage of words in the image I had made? My Instagram community said yes, and so my image appears in these pages.

So thank you, my Instagram and Facebook communities, the twenty-first-century "informed layman" I write for with the confidence that you are really there. And thank you for the readers who have only recently discovered my work, due to any number of reasons.

Now I know you're there and that you are paying attention, and I am no longer just talking to myself.

Thank you very much.

August 2022

Acknowledgments

I am still talking. I am still writing. But this book passes an already full writing life before my eyes. I am exceedingly grateful to a world of good people over the passage of a great deal of time for my continuing life of reading, listening, learning, drawing, and writing.

The people to whom I owe thanks across my writing decades are literally innumerable. In too many cases, their names, the lessons they taught me, and the support they gave me lie buried under my memory's sands of time. But I want to acknowledge the entire community of scholars and readers who have accompanied me across the years, though I have dedicated this book to my friends of longest standing, and I do mean *long*-est standing: Jackie Bryant Smith, Jill Sheppard, Nellie Y. McKay in memoriam, Thadious M. Davis, and Glenn Shafer. All through the final decades of one century and the first decades of another, they have made sure I need not brave this world alone.

I Just Keep Talking began as a notion of Sarah Chalfant and Thomas Gebremedhin, its indispensable godparents. Working with them has always been an immense pleasure—truly gratifying. Thank you.

Further along, the completion of the book required the help of other institutions and individuals. I organized its chapters at Mac-Dowell and made new images at Yaddo, both residencies sustaining concentration on this work. Sarah Lewis and Courtney Baker read a draft of the introduction early on, when draft reading especially counted. My Facebook and Instagram communities weighed in with support and opinions to remind me I belong to a good-size virtual community. As a physical artifact this book needed the dedication and multiple and deeply appreciated talents of Jackie Ko and Johanna Zwirner, whose generous support and engagement have buoyed me over distance and time. Designers John Fontana and Maggie Hinders have combined text and images creatively, which I deeply value as a writer and visual artist. For shepherding my manuscript into a book, I am grateful to my production editor, Kathleen Cook, and copy editor, Carol Rutan, and the essential team that takes the book to the outside world: Michael Goldsmith, Milena Brown, and Roméo Enriquez. Thank you.

Notes

DIFFERENCE, SLAVERY, AND MEMORY: SOJOURNER TRUTH
IN FEMINIST ABOLITIONISM

1. For more information on Frances Dana Gage (1808–1884), see Edward T. James, Janet Wilson James, and Paul S. Boyer, eds., *Notable American Women* (Cambridge, Mass., 1971), 1:2–4.

2. [Olive Gilbert and Frances W. Titus], *Narrative of Sojourner Truth; A Bondswoman of Olden Time Emancipated by the New York Legislature in the Early Part of the Present Century; with a History of Her Labors and Correspondence Drawn from Her "Book of Life"* (Battle Creek, Mich., 1878; rpt. New York, 1968, and Salem, N.H., 1990), pp. 131–35. This narrative went through several reprintings and three main editions: the first, in 1850; the second, which added material from Truth's scrapbook, in 1875/1878; and the third, which added a memorial section in 1884, after her death.

3. Jean Fagan Yellin, *Women and Sisters: The Antislavery Feminists in American Culture* (New Haven, Conn., 1989), p. 81.

4. Ellen Carol DuBois, *Feminism and Suffrage: The Emergence of an Independent Women's Movement in America, 1848–1869* (Ithaca, N.Y., 1978), p. 24.

5. William L. Andrews, ed., *Sisters of the Spirit: Three Black Women's Autobiographies of the Nineteenth Century* (Bloomington, Ind., 1986), pp. 2–3; Elizabeth Cady Stanton, Susan B. Anthony, and Matilda Joslyn Gage, *History of Woman Suffrage*, 6 vols. (Rochester, N.Y., 1889–1922; rpt. New York, 1970), 1:384; Nellie McKay, "Nineteenth-Century Black Women's Spiritual Autobiographies: Religious Faith and Self-Empowerment," in Joy Webster Barbre et al., eds., *Interpreting Women's Lives: Feminist Theory and Personal Narratives* (Bloomington, Ind., 1989), pp. 137–54.

6. Blanche Glassman Hersh, *The Slavery of Sex: Feminist-Abolitionism in America* (Chicago, 1978), pp. 17, 121–36.

7. DuBois, *Feminism and Suffrage*, pp. 24–25.

8. Stanton et al., *History of Woman Suffrage*, 1:380.

9. Gerda Lerner, *The Grimké Sisters from South Carolina: Pioneers for Women's Rights and Abolition* (New York, 1967), pp. 306–8.

10. Feminist scholarship refigures the categorization of women's reform. Nancy Hewitt's *Women's Activism and Social Change: Rochester, New York, 1822–1872* (Ithaca, N.Y., 1984), a study of women's activism in Rochester (a city in which Sojourner Truth had very good friends and spent a great deal of time), outlines three communities of women's reform, all of which were tinged more or less with Protestant Christianity. Mary P. Ryan, *Cradle of the Middle Class: The Family in Oneida County, New York, 1790–*

1865 (New York, 1981), testifies to the unrestricted reach of antislavery societies in Oneida and Utica, New York, in the 1830s. Ann Braude, *Radical Spirits: Spiritualism and Women's Rights in Nineteenth-Century America* (Boston, 1989), illustrates the tight relationship between spiritualism and other social reforms like women's rights at midcentury. Yellin's *Women and Sisters*, focusing on the iconography of women's abolitionism, traces the racial heterogeneity in feminists' cultural productions.

11. Salem, Ohio, *Anti-Slavery Bugle*, March 29, April 2 and 5, 1851. In the spring of 1851, Oliver Johnson was editing the *Bugle*. Marius Robinson succeeded him at midyear.

12. Ibid., June 7, 14, and 21, 1851.

13. For example, the New York *National Anti-Slavery Standard*, June 26, 1851, and the *Rochester Daily American*, June 4, 1851.

14. Harriet Beecher Stowe, "Sojourner Truth, The Libyan Sibyl," *The Atlantic Monthly* 11, no. 66 (April 1863): 480. My analysis of Stowe's essay differs from Yellin's excellent discussion in *Women and Sisters*, pp. 81–87, in that Yellin stresses the transcendent passivity and mystery of Stowe's "Libyan Sibyl."

15. Frederick Douglass, "What I Found at the Northampton Association," in Charles A. Sheffield, ed., *History of Florence, Massachusetts. Including a Complete Account of the Northampton Association of Education and Industry* (Florence, Mass., 1895), pp. 131–32.

16. *Narrative of Sojourner Truth*, pp. 201, 221, 227.

17. Douglass, "What I Found at the Northampton Association," p. 132; Carleton Mabee, "Sojourner Truth, Bold Prophet: Why Did She Never Learn to Read?" *New York History* 86 (January 1988): 55–77.

18. For Harper, see Dorothy Sterling, ed., *We Are Your Sisters: Black Women in the Nineteenth Century* (New York, 1984), pp. 159–64. See also Hazel Carby, *Reconstructing Womanhood: The Emergence of the Afro-American Woman Novelist* (New York, 1987); Frances Smith Foster, ed., *A Brighter Coming Day: A Frances Ellen Watkins Harper Reader* (New York, 1990); and Bettye Collier-Thomas, "Frances Ellen Watkins Harper: Abolitionist and Feminist Reformer, 1825–1911," in Ann D. Gordon and Bettye Collier-Thomas, eds., *African-American Women and the Vote, 1837–1965* (Amherst, Mass., 1997).

19. Gerda Lerner, ed., *Black Women in White America: A Documentary History* (New York, 1972); Sterling, *We Are Your Sisters*, pp. 126–33, 175–80; Marilyn Richardson, ed., *Maria W. Stewart, America's First Black Woman Political Writer: Essays and Speeches* (Bloomington, Ind., 1987), p. 68. See also Dorothy B. Porter, "Sarah Parker Remond, Abolitionist and Physician," *Journal of Negro History* 20 (July 1935): 287–93; Ruth Bogin, "Sarah Parker Remond: Black Abolitionist from Salem," *Essex Institute Historical Collections* 110 (April 1974): 120–50; R. J. M. Blackett, *Building an Anti-Slavery Wall: Black Americans in the Atlantic Abolitionist Movement, 1830–1860* (Baton Rouge, La., 1983); R. J. M. Blackett, *Beating against the Barriers: Biographical Essays in Nineteenth-Century Afro-American History* (Baton Rouge, La., 1986); and Dorothy Sterling, *Black Foremothers: Three Lives*, 2nd ed. (New York, 1988).

20. Anthony quoted in Dorothy Sterling, *Ahead of Her Time: Abby Kelley and the Politics of Antislavery* (New York, 1991), p. 338, emphasis in original; *Pittsburgh Saturday Visiter*, November 23, 1850.

21. Nancy Leys Stepan, "Race and Gender: The Role of Analogy in Science," in David Theo Goldberg, ed., *Anatomy of Racism* (Minneapolis, Minn., 1990), p. 47; Gloria T. Hull, Patricia Bell Scott, and Barbara Smith, eds., *All the Women Are White, All the Blacks Are*

Men, But Some of Us Are Brave: Black Women's Studies (Old Westbury, N.Y., 1982); Patricia J. Williams, *The Alchemy of Race and Rights: Diary of a Law Professor* (Cambridge, Mass., 1991), pp. 55–56, 222.

"INTRODUCTION" IN *INCIDENTS IN THE LIFE OF A SLAVE GIRL, WRITTEN BY HERSELF*

1. Frances Smith Foster notes that the title page of the first edition of Jacobs's book bears only the subtitle, leading later reprinters and critics to call the book simply *Incidents in the Life of a Slave Girl*. The spine of the first edition bore the name "Linda," and thus, in the nineteenth century the author was known by her pseudonym, "Linda Brent." See Francis Smith Foster, "Resisting *Incidents*," in *Harriet Jacobs and Incidents in the Life of a Slave Girl*, ed. Deborah M. Garfield and Rafia Zafar (New York: Cambridge University Press, 1996), 69.

2. For example, Louisa Picquet's autobiography, *Louisa Picquet, the Octoroon; or, Inside Views of Southern Domestic Life*, as told to the Reverend Hiram Mattison, also appeared in 1861. It reflected above all Mattison's prurient interest in Picquet's sexuality. See William L. Andrews, *To Tell a Free Story: The First Century of Afro-American Autobiography, 1760–1865* (Urbana: University of Illinois Press, 1986), 243–46.

3. This last point is Hazel Carby's in *Reconstructing Womanhood: The Emergence of the Afro-American Woman Novelist* (New York: Oxford University Press, 1987), 39, 45–61.

4. The "happy darky" genre outlived Harriet Jacobs, notably in continual restagings of *Uncle Tom's Cabin* as a proslavery play and movie well into the twentieth century.

5. Jacobs calls the crawl space in which she hid for nearly seven years a "loophole of retreat."

6. Wilma King and Nellie McKay both compare to wartime the conditions under which slave children developed. See Wilma King, *Stolen Childhood: Slave Youth in Nineteenth-Century America* (Bloomington: Indiana University Press, 1995); and Nellie Y. McKay, "The Girls Who Became the Women: Childhood Memories in the Autobiographies of Harriet Jacobs, Mary Church Terrell, and Anne Moody," in *Tradition and the Talents of Women*, ed. Florence Howe (Urbana: University of Illinois Press, 1991).

7. According to Jean Fagan Yellin, the definitive authority, Jacobs was born "around 1813." See Jean Fagan Yellin, introduction to Harriet A. Jacobs, *Incidents in the Life of a Slave Girl, Written by Herself*, ed. Jean Fagan Yellin (Cambridge, Mass.: Harvard University Press, 1987), xv. However, Rohanna Sumrell Knott, in "Harriet Jacobs: The Edenton Biography" (unpublished PhD dissertation, University of North Carolina at Chapel Hill, 1994), uses Jacobs's Mount Auburn Cemetery gravestone to calculate her dates. Edith Grinnell Willis, daughter of Cornelia Grinnell and Nathaniel Parker Willis, erected the stone in 1917, after the death of Harriet's daughter, Louisa Jacobs, presumably using Louisa's dates. By this reckoning, Harriet Jacobs would have been born in 1815; her brother, John S. Jacobs, born in 1819; and her daughter, Louisa, in 1837. Harriet's son, Joseph, who died in Australia, presumably in 1863, is not buried in Mount Auburn Cemetery. Yellin gives Joseph's birthdate as 1829 (Knott, p. 33, fn. 1; p. 75, fn. 15). This essay uses Yellin's dates unless otherwise indicated.

8. In her introduction to the 1987 edition of *Incidents in the Life of a Slave Girl*, Jean Fagan Yellin calls Harriet Jacobs's father Daniel. She corrected the name in "Harriet

Jacobs's Family History," *American Literature* 66, no. 4 (December 1994): 765–67. Yellin also explains that after the death of Harriet's mother, Elijah married a free woman, with whom he had a second family, including a son born in about 1824, also named Elijah. The younger Elijah, surnamed Knox, eventually settled in New Bedford, Massachusetts, the widowed father of two children. He subsequently remarried and had a son, whom he also named Elijah. Louisa Jacobs, Harriet's daughter, recognized Elijah Knox and his family in her will.

9. Harriet Jacobs, *Incidents in the Life of a Slave Girl* (Boston: Published for the Author [self-published], 1861), 9. All page numbers refer to this edition.

10. John S. Jacobs, "A True Tale of Slavery," *The Leisure Hour,* February 1861, and Stevens and Co., London, 1861, 233. All page numbers refer to the London edition.

11. John S. Jacobs, "A True Tale of Slavery," 235.

12. Rohanna Sumrell Knott, "Harriet Jacobs," 56, 78. All the enslaved would have been considered to be Negroes, but their number would also include people of European and American Indian descent.

13. John S. Jacobs, "A True Tale of Slavery," 256.

14. Rohanna Sumrell Knott, "Harriet Jacobs," 128.

15. According to Jean Fagan Yellin (*Incidents,* 268), Samuel Tredwell Sawyer died in 1865; in this instance, I have followed Rohanna Sumrell Knott ("Harriet Jacobs," 114), who adds that Sawyer is buried on Long Island.

16. Rohanna Sumrell Knott, "Harriet Jacobs," 130–34.

17. Harriet Jacobs, *Incidents,* 9.

18. P. Gabrielle Foreman speculates enticingly on the possible familial entanglements motivating Horniblow's sale and emancipation, her possession of her son, and her purchase of a grand house in the center of town for $1. See Foreman's "Manifest in Signs: The Politics of Sex and Representation," in *Harriet Jacobs and Incidents in the Life of a Slave Girl,* ed. Deborah M. Garfield and Rafia Zafar, 92.

19. John S. Jacobs, "A True Tale of Slavery," 243.

20. The quotes are on pages 58 and 39 of Harriet Jacobs, *Incidents.* See also pages 4 and 57.

21. Hannah Decker points to the phenomenon of the sexual abuse of the sweet young thing (*das süsse Mädel*) in Freud's Vienna. See Nell Irvin Painter, "Three Southern Women and Freud: A Non-Exceptionalist Approach to Race, Class, and Gender in the Slave South," in *Feminists Revision History,* ed. Ann-Louise Shapiro (New Brunswick, N.J.: Rutgers University Press, 1994), 205–6.

22. Harriet Jacobs, *Incidents,* 61–62.

23. Harriet Jacobs, *Incidents,* 59.

24. Harriet Jacobs, *Incidents,* 61–62.

25. Harriet Jacobs, *Incidents,* 18, 60–61.

26. Deborah M. Garfield, "Earwitness: Female Abolitionism, Sexuality, and *Incidents in the Life of a Slave Girl,*" in *Harriet Jacobs and Incidents in the Life of a Slave Girl,* ed. Deborah M. Garfield and Rafia Zafar, 121–22; and Harriet Jacobs, *Incidents,* 86.

27. Rohanna Sumrell Knott, "Harriet Jacobs," 83, 115.

28. Rohanna Sumrell Knott, "Harriet Jacobs," 227.

29. Nell Irvin Painter, "Soul Murder and Slavery: Toward a Full Loaded Cost Accounting," in *US History as Women's History: New Feminist Essays,* ed. Linda K. Kerber, Alice Kessler-Harris, and Kathryn Kish Sklar (Chapel Hill: University of North Carolina Press, 1995), 137–38.

30. Frederick Douglass (1818–1885), the leading African American antebellum feminist abolitionist and postwar statesman, wrote three autobiographies and edited several newspapers over the course of an illustrious public career.

31. Willis's father-in-law supplied half their annual income. See P. Gabrielle Foreman, "Manifest in Signs," 91.

32. The exact quote is Carolyn Karcher's, rather than Child's. See Carolyn L. Karcher, ed., *A Lydia Maria Child Reader* (Durham, N.C.: Duke University Press, 1997), 330.

33. Jean Fagan Yellin, "Written by Herself: Harriet Jacobs' Slave Narrative," *American Literature* 53, no. 3 (November 1981): 481.

34. Nathaniel Parker Willis's sister, the popular novelist Fanny Fern, suspected he married Cornelia Grinnell for her money; Cornelia Willis's inheritance paid for their Hudson River mansion, Idlewild, where Harriet Jacobs was the senior housekeeper and surreptitiously wrote *Incidents*. See P. Gabrielle Foreman, "Manifest in Signs," 97.

35. Jean Fagan Yellin, "Through Her Brother's Eyes: *Incidents* and 'A True Tale,'" in *Harriet Jacobs and Incidents in the Life of a Slave Girl*, ed. Deborah M. Garfield and Rafia Zafar, 46, 45.

36. Jean Fagan Yellin, "Through Her Brother's Eyes," 47.

37. This material comes from Jean Fagan Yellin's "Chronology," in Yellin, ed., *Incidents*, 224–25.

38. P. Gabrielle Foreman, "Manifest in Signs," 80. Sojourner Truth's *Narrative* was meant to raise money to support her in her old age. She was in her midfifties when it appeared.

39. See "Introduction," in *Narrative of Sojourner Truth*, ed. Nell Irvin Painter (New York: Penguin Books, 1998).

40. See Jean Fagan Yellin, "Harriet Ann Jacobs, c. 1813–1897," *Legacy: A Journal of Nineteenth-Century American Women Writers* 5, no. 2 (Fall 1988): 56, 60–61. This article includes the text of Jacobs's first letter to the editor, written in 1853.

41. New York *National Anti-Slavery Standard*, February 23, 1861.

42. Milton Meltzer and Patricia G. Holland, eds., *Lydia Maria Child: Selected Letters, 1817–1880* (Amherst: University of Massachusetts Press, 1982), 357–59, 378–79. See also Carolyn L. Karcher, *The First Woman in the Republic: A Cultural Biography of Lydia Maria Child* (Durham, N.C.: Duke University Press, 1994), 435–37.

43. Frances Smith Foster, "Resisting *Incidents*," 69.

44. Jean Fagan Yellin, "Through Her Brother's Eyes," 56.

45. William C. Nell, letter to the editor, *Liberator*, January 25, 1861.

46. New York *National Anti-Slavery Standard*, February 23, 1861. By this time, Lydia Maria Child had been out of the editorship nearly twenty years.

47. New York *National Anti-Slavery Standard*, August 17, 1861, quoted in Jacqueline Goldsby, "I Disguised My Hand," in *Harriet Jacobs and Incidents in the Life of a Slave Girl*, ed. Deborah M. Garfield and Rafia Zafar, 23.

48. New York *Weekly Anglo-African*, April 13, 1861.

49. Child to Henrietta Sargent, February 9, 1861, in *Lydia Maria Child: Selected Letters*, ed. Milton Meltzer and Patricia G. Holland, 374–75.

WHO DECIDES WHAT IS HISTORY?

1. Mary Beth Norton, David M. Katzman, Paul D. Escott, Howard P. Chudacoff, Thomas G. Paterson, and William M. Tuttle Jr., eds., *A People and a Nation* (Houghton Mifflin, 1982).

FRENCH THEORIES IN AMERICAN SETTINGS: SOME THOUGHTS ON TRANSFERABILITY

1. Readers seeking a deeper understanding of the assumptions embedded in this *Annales* essay would do well to consult Karen Offen's informed explanation, "Defining Feminism: A Comparative Historical Approach," *Signs* 14 (Autumn 1988).

2. Scott read her paper at the December 1985 meeting of the American Historical Association. It was published as "Gender: A Useful Category of Historical Analysis," *American Historical Review* 91 (December 1986) and is included in her book of essays *Gender and the Politics of History* (New York, 1988).

3. It is as though the low wages paid Southern workers in, say, the textile industry did not affect the jobs of Northern textile workers, as though Southern White workers' wages were unaffected by the reserve of Black workers, who were ordinarily paid much lower wages.

4. For an example of such controversies in labor history, see Herbert Hill, "Myth-Making as Labor History: Herbert Gutman and the United Mine Workers of America," *International Journal of Politics, Culture and Society* 2 (Winter 1988), and Nell Irvin Painter, "The New Labor History and the Historical Moment," *International Journal of Politics, Culture and Society* 2 (Spring 1989).

WHAT EIGHTEENTH- AND NINETEENTH-CENTURY INTELLECTUALS SAW IN THE TIME OF TRUMP: AMERICAN UNIVERSITIES, MONUMENTS, AND THE LEGACIES OF SLAVERY

1. Harriet Ann Jacobs (February 11, 1813–March 7, 1897) was an African American writer who escaped from slavery and was later freed. She became an abolitionist speaker and reformer. Jacobs wrote an autobiographical novel, *Incidents in the Life of a Slave Girl,* first serialized in a newspaper and published as a book in 1861 under the pseudonym "Linda Brent." It was a reworking of the genres of slave narrative and sentimental novel, and was one of the first books to address the struggle for freedom by female slaves and explore their struggles with sexual harassment abuse and their effort to protect their roles as women and mothers.

2. After studying in Jesuit schools and spending four years as an officer and mapmaker in Canada, Crèvecoeur chose in 1759 to remain in the New World. He wandered the Great Lakes region, took out citizenship papers in New York in 1765, became a farmer in Orange County, and was married in 1769. Torn between the two factions in the American Revolution, Crèvecoeur languished for months in an English army prison in New York City before sailing for Europe in 1780, accompanied by one son. In London he arranged for the publication of twelve essays called *Letters from an American Farmer* (1782).

Within two years this book—charmingly written, optimistic, and timely—went through many editions. He was appointed French consul to three of the new American states. Before assuming his consular duties in 1784, Crèvecoeur translated and added to the original twelve essays in *Lettres d'un cultivateur américain,* 2 vols. (1784). When he returned to America, Crèvecoeur found his home burned, his wife dead, and his daughter and second son with strangers in Boston. Reunited with his children, he set about organizing a packet service between the United States and France. During a two-year furlough in Europe, he brought out a larger second edition of the French *Lettres,* 3 vols. (1790). Recalled from his consulship in 1790, Crèvecoeur wrote one other book on America, *Voyage dans la haute Pensylvanie et dans l'état de New-York* [Travels in Upper Pennsylvania and New York], 3 vols. (1801). He lived quietly in France and Germany until his death.

3. His comic novel *The Pickwick Papers* (1837) made him the most popular author of his time in England. His novels *Oliver Twist* (1838) and *Nicholas Nickleby* (1839) were followed in 1841 by *The Old Curiosity Shop* and *Barnaby Rudge.* Exhausted, Dickens took a five-month vacation in the United States, where he was lionized. His reactions to America—many negative—found expression in *American Notes* (1842) and *Martin Chuzzlewit* (1844). *A Christmas Carol* (1843), written in a few weeks, entered immediately into modern mythology. It was the first and the best of his annual Christmas novels and stories, which also included *The Cricket on the Hearth* (1846).

SOUL MURDER AND SLAVERY: TOWARD A FULLY LOADED COST ACCOUNTING

1. Fox Butterfield, "Why America's Murder Rate Is So High," *New York Times,* July 26, 1998, sec. 4, 1.

2. Philip Greven is exceptional among historians in investigating child abuse carefully. However he does not focus upon child abuse associated with enslavement. See Philip Greven, *The Protestant Temperament: Patterns of Child-Rearing, Religious Experience, and the Self in Early America* (New York: Knopf, 1977) and *Spare the Child: The Religious Roots of Punishment and the Psychological Impact of Physical Abuse* (New York: Knopf, 1991).

3. Daniel Paul Schreber, *Memoirs of My Nervous Illness,* translated and edited by Ida Macalpine and Richard A. Hunter, with a new introduction by Samuel M. Weber (Cambridge, Mass.: Harvard University Press, 1988), xii–xiii. See also Sigmund Freud, "Psycho-Analytic Notes on an Autobiographical Account of a Case of Paranoia (Dementia Paranoides)" [1911], in *The Standard Edition of the Complete Psychological Works of Sigmund Freud,* edited and translated by James Strachey (London: Hogarth Press, 1958), 9–82; Jacques Lacan, "On a Question Preliminary to any Possible Treatment of Psychosis" [1955–56], in *Ecrits,* translated by Alan Sheridan (New York: W. W. Norton, 1977); and Leonard Shengold, *Halo in the Sky* (New York: Guilford, 1988). The great legal reformer Anselm von Feuerbach was the father of the philosopher Ludwig Feuerbach. My thanks to Ulrich Struve for help in sorting out the story of Kaspar Hauser.

4. Leonard Shengold, *Soul Murder: The Effects of Childhood Abuse and Deprivation* (New Haven, Conn.: Yale University Press, 1989), 1–5; James A. Chu, "The Repetition Compulsion Revisited: Reliving Dissociated Trauma" (paper presented at the International Conference on Multiple Personality and Dissociative States, November 6, 1987), 1. I am grateful to Becky Thompson for bringing this paper to my attention.

See also Leonard Shengold, *Soul Murder Revisited: Thoughts about Therapy, Hate, Love, and Memory* (New Haven, Conn.: Yale University Press, 1999).

5. Ian Hacking, "Memoro-politics: Trauma and the Soul" (Davis Center Seminar Paper, Princeton University, September 25, 1992; used with the permission of the author), and "The Making and Molding of Child Abuse," *Critical Inquiry* 17 (Winter 1991): 253–88; Carol Tavris, "Beware the Incest-Survivor Machine," *New York Times Book Review*, January 3, 1993.

6. See Louis Althusser, "A Letter on Art," in *Lenin and Philosophy and Other Essays*, translated by Ben Brewster (New York: Monthly Review Press, 1971), 221–27, and Pierre Macherey, *A Theory of Literary Production* (1966), translated by Geoffrey Wall (London: Routledge and Kegan Paul, 1978), esp. 82–97; Judith Lewis Herman, *Trauma and Recovery: The Aftermath of Violence—From Domestic Abuse to Political Terror* (New York: Basic Books, 1992) and *Father-Daughter Incest* (Cambridge, Mass.: Harvard University Press, 1981).

7. Stanley Elkins, *Slavery: A Problem in American Institutional and Intellectual Life* (Chicago: University of Chicago Press, 1959), 122–23 (Elkins's emphasis). See also Ann J. Lane, ed., *The Debate over Slavery: Stanley Elkins and His Critics* (Urbana: University of Illinois Press, 1971); Peter Kolchin, *American Slavery: 1619–1877* (New York: Hill and Wang, 1993), 135–39; Peter J. Parish, *Slavery: History and Historians* (New York: Harper and Row, 1989), 7, 67–70; and Herbert Aptheker, *American Negro Slave Revolts* (New York: International Publishers, 1943).

8. Herbert Gutman, *The Black Family in Slavery and Freedom, 1750–1925* (New York: Oxford University Press, 1976).

9. Karl Marx and Friedrich Engels, "Feuerbach: Opposition of the Materialist and Idealist Outlook," in *The German Ideology, Part One* [written 1845–46], edited by C. J. Arthur (New York: International Publishers, 1947, 1970), 47–49 (emphasis in the original).

10. Alexis de Tocqueville, *Democracy in America*, edited by J. P. Mayer (Garden City, N.Y.: Doubleday, 1969), 345, 375–76, 585–88.

11. Althusser sees the family as one of the potent "ideological state apparatuses" that silently inculcate ideology alongside whatever coercion the state may employ. Lacan speaks of the "paternal metaphor" and "the name of the father" as means by which children are initiated into the conventions and power relations of social life. Althusser, *Lenin and Philosophy*, 143–45, 150–58, 189–220; Lacan, *Ecrits*, 65–73, 142–43, 196–97, 201–20, 252.

12. Quoted in Brenda Stevenson, "Distress and Discord in Virginia Slave Families, 1830–1860," in *In Joy and in Sorrow: Women, Family, and Marriage in the Victorian South, 1830–1900*, edited by Carol Bleser (New York: Oxford University Press, 1991), 111.

13. Kenneth Stampp, *The Peculiar Institution: Slavery in the Ante-Bellum South* (New York: Knopf, 1959, Vintage ed.), 141.

14. William Wells Brown, *Narrative*, quoted in John Blassingame, *The Slave Community: Plantation Life in the Antebellum South*, rev. ed. (New York: Oxford University Press, 1979), 186; Nell Irvin Painter, ed., *Narrative of Sojourner Truth* (1850; reprint, New York: Penguin Books, 1998), 26.

15. Theodore Rosengarten, *All God's Dangers: The Life of Nate Shaw* (New York: Knopf, 1974), 6–11.

16. Stampp, *Peculiar Institution*, 144 (irregular capitalization in original); Alice Miller,

For Your Own Good: Hidden Cruelty in Child-Rearing and the Roots of Violence (New York: Farrar, Straus and Giroux, 1983, 1990), 58, 65, 88.

17. Concerning attachment, the three-volume work of John Bowlby is crucial: *Attachment* (London: Tavistock Institute of Human Relations, 1969; reprint, New York: Basic Books, 1982), *Separation: Anxiety and Anger* (New York: Basic Books, 1973), and *Loss: Sadness and Depression* (New York: Basic Books, 1980).

18. Michael Tadman, *Speculators and Slaves: Owners, Traders, and Slaves in the Old South* (Madison: University of Wisconsin Press, 1996), 12, 26. See also Parish, *Slavery*, 86; Kolchin, *American Slavery*, 96–98, 125–39. The dust jacket of Kolchin's book shows a slave auction in which a Black mother on her knees reaches vainly for her baby, whom the auctioneer holds up for sale by one arm and on whom a gentleman bids. In the lower right corner, a soon to be sundered slave family huddles in tears.

19. Harriet A. Jacobs, *Incidents in the Life of a Slave Girl, Written by Herself*, edited by Jean Fagan Yellin (Cambridge, Mass.: Harvard University Press, 1987), 27–28, 33. See also Nell Irvin Painter, ed., *Incidents in the Life of a Slave Girl* (New York: Penguin, 2000), xv–xvii.

20. Mary Chesnut quoted in Lee Ann Whites, "The Civil War as a Crisis in Gender," in *Divided Houses: Gender and the Civil War,* edited by Catherine Clinton and Nina Silber (New York: Oxford University Press, 1992), 6.

21. Gayle Rubin, "The Traffic in Women: Notes on the 'Political Economy' of Sex," in *Toward an Anthropology of Women,* edited by Rayna R. Reiter (New York: Monthly Review Press, 1975), 157–210.

22. Andrew Jackson, *Narrative and Writings of Andrew Jackson of Kentucky* (Syracuse, N.Y.: Daily and Weekly Star, 1847), 24. I thank Walter Johnson for bringing this anecdote to my attention.

23. Herman, *Father-Daughter Incest*, 81–83, and *Trauma and Recovery*, 106.

24. Catharine A. MacKinnon, *Sexual Harassment of Working Women: A Case of Sex Discrimination* (New Haven, Conn.: Yale University Press, 1979), 29, 40, 45. MacKinnon also notes that "racism is deeply involved in sexual harassment" (31).

25. David Finkelhor with Sharon Araji, Larry Baron, Angela Browne, Stefanie Doyle Peters, and Gail Elizabeth Wyatt, *A Sourcebook on Child Sexual Abuse* (Newbury Park, Calif.: Sage Publications, 1986), 152–64.

26. Benjamin Mays, *The Negro's God as Reflected in His Literature* (Boston: Chapman and Grimes, 1938), 22, 87.

27. John Hope Franklin, "Slavery and Personality: A Fresh Look," *Massachusetts Review* 2 (Autumn 1960), and Earl E. Thorpe, "Chattel Slavery and Concentration Camps," *Negro History Bulletin* 25 (May 1962), both quoted in August Meier and Elliott Rudwick, *Black History and the Historical Profession, 1915–1980* (Urbana: University of Illinois Press, 1990), 140, 248.

28. Unfortunately, due to the state of the historiography, I cannot elaborate on the cultural and psychological situation of the millions of enslaved people who lived outside Black communities, for this, like much in studies of the psychology of households that included Whites and Blacks, remains to be investigated. Historical scholarship on non-plantation Southern Blacks is virtually nonexistent. Historians writing on Northern slavery have tended to examine those people's conditions of life rather than their actual experiences. One exception to this rule is Shane White, *Somewhat More Independent: The End of Slavery in New York City, 1770–1810* (Athens: University of Geor-

gia Press, 1991). The first two chapters of my biography of Sojourner Truth, *Sojourner Truth: A Life, A Symbol* (New York: W. W. Norton, 1996), deal with the personal experience of enslaved people in New York State.

29. Blassingame, *Slave Community*, 191; Deborah Gray White, *Ar'n't I a Woman? Female Slaves in the Plantation South* (New York: W. W. Norton, 1985), 119–41.

30. Gail Elizabeth Wyatt and M. Ray Mickey, "The Support by Parents and Others as It Mediates the Effects of Child Sexual Abuse: An Exploratory Study," in *Lasting Effects of Child Sexual Abuse*, edited by Gail Elizabeth Wyatt and Gloria Johnson Powell (Newbury Park, Calif.: Sage Publications, 1988), 211–25.

31. Albert Raboteau, *Slave Religion: The "Invisible Institution" in the Antebellum South* (New York: Oxford University Press, 1978); Gayraud S. Wilmore, *Last Things First* (Philadelphia: Westminster Press, 1982), 42, 77; James H. Cone, *God of the Oppressed* (San Francisco: Harper San Francisco, 1975), 32, 57, 175.

32. Arthur A. Stone, Lynn Helder, and Mark S. Schneider, "Coping with Stressful Events: Coping Dimensions and Issues," in *Life Events and Psychological Functioning: Theoretical and Methodological Issues*, edited by Lawrence H. Cohen (Newbury Park, Calif.: Sage Publications, 1988), 187–88.

33. Catherine Clinton, *The Plantation Mistress: Woman's World in the Old South* (New York: Pantheon, 1982), 165.

34. Caroline [Howard] Gilman, *Recollections of a New England Bride and of a Southern Matron*, rev. ed. (New York: Putnam & Co., 1852 [*Southern Matron* originally published 1837; *New England Bride*, 1834]), 297, 384.

35. Elizabeth Fox-Genovese notes that the family "figured as a central metaphor for southern society as a whole." "Family and Female Identity in the Antebellum South: Sarah Gayle and Her Family," in Bleser, ed., *In Joy and in Sorrow*, 19.

36. On White women in the fields, see Stephanie McCurry, "The Politics of Yeoman Households in South Carolina," in Clinton and Silber, eds., *Divided Houses*, 28–31.

37. Painter, ed., *Narrative of Sojourner Truth*, 36–39.

38. [Theodore Dwight Weld], *American Slavery as It Is: Testimony of a Thousand Witnesses* (New York: American Anti-Slavery Society, 1839), 51–52.

39. Elizabeth Fox-Genovese, *Within the Plantation Household: Black and White Women in the Antebellum South* (Chapel Hill: University of North Carolina Press, 1988), 24, 97, 308–14.

40. Quoted in [Weld], *American Slavery*, 54–55 (emphasis in the original).

41. Thomas Jefferson, *Notes on the State of Virginia* (1787; New York: W. W. Norton, 1972), 162. Similarly, an advice manual for slave-owning mothers published in 1830, *Letters on Female Character*, noted that slave owning encouraged "all the most malignant vices of his nature" in the child. Quoted in Clinton, *Plantation Mistress*, 91.

42. Philip G. Ney, "Triangles of Abuse: A Model of Maltreatment," *Child Abuse & Neglect* 12 (1988): 363–73.

43. See Virginia Walcott Beauchamp, ed., *A Private War: Letters and Diaries of Madge Preston, 1862–1867* (New Brunswick, N.J.: Rutgers University Press, 1987).

44. Stephanie McCurry, *Owners of Small Worlds: Yeoman Households, Gender Relations, and the Political Culture of the Antebellum South Carolina Low Country* (New York: Oxford University Press, 1995), 86–91.

45. A. Leon Higginbotham Jr., *In the Matter of Color: Race and the American Legal Process: The Colonial Period* (New York: Oxford University Press, 1978), 40–47; Peter W.

Bardaglio, *Reconstructing the Household: Families, Sex, and the Law in the Nineteenth-Century South* (Chapel Hill: University of North Carolina Press, 1995), 37–78.

46. Daniel Blake Smith, *Inside the Great House: Planter Family Life in Eighteenth-Century Chesapeake Society* (Ithaca, N.Y.: Cornell University Press, 1980).

47. Carol Lawson, "Violence at Home: 'They Don't Want Anyone to Know,'" *New York Times*, August 6, 1992.

48. Ronald C. Summit, "Hidden Victims, Hidden Pain: Societal Avoidance of Child Sexual Abuse," in Wyatt and Powell, eds., *Lasting Effects of Child Sexual Abuse*, 40.

49. Jeffrey Moussaieff Masson, *The Assault on Truth: Freud's Suppression of the Seduction Theory* (New York: HarperCollins, 1984, 1992).

50. Richard L. Bushman, *The Refinement of America: Persons, Houses, Cities* (New York: Knopf, 1992), xiv, 55, 288; Jay Fliegelman, *Declaring Independence: Jefferson, Natural Language, and the Culture of Performance* (Stanford, Calif.: Stanford University Press, 1993), 79–129, 189–200.

51. Lillian Smith, *Killers of the Dream*, rev. ed. (New York: W. W. Norton, 1961), 83–89, 121–24.

OF *LILY*, LINDA BRENT, AND FREUD: A NON-EXCEPTIONALIST APPROACH TO RACE, CLASS, AND GENDER IN THE SLAVE SOUTH

1. I am coming to Freud's writing from a different direction from that of literary critics and most Lacanians. Although Freud's work is the starting place for object relations theory, it, too, would be more useful to me than certain Lacanians (notably Jane Gallop, whose insights are valuable here) if object relations analysts were not so relentlessly mid-twentieth-century middle class. The family structure that object relations scholars—such as Nancy Chodorow—envision is strictly nuclear, whereas many nineteenth-century Southern families included parental figures who were not related to children by birth.

2. Abram Kardiner and L. Ovesey, *The Mark of Oppression: Explorations in the Personality of the American Negro* (New York, 1951).

3. I should add that family relations also affect more than women and girls; men and boys deserve—and will ultimately receive—a far larger place in this piece of work in progress than they currently occupy.

4. See, for example, Lenore Davidoff, "Class and Gender in Victorian England: The Diaries of Arthur J. Munby and Hannah Cullwick," *Feminist Studies* 5 (Spring 1979): 87–141; and Maria Ramas, "Freud's Dora, Dora's Hysteria," in Judith L. Newton, Mary P. Ryan, and Judith R. Walkowitz, eds., *Sex and Class in Women's History* (London, 1983), 72–113.

5. Sue Petigru King Bowen, *Lily* (New York, 1855), and Jean Fagan Yellin, ed., *Incidents in the Life of a Slave Girl, Written by Herself*, by Harriet A. Jacobs (Cambridge, Mass., 1987). Although I am aware of the controversy surrounding the designation of genre of *Incidents*, I am treating it here as autobiography.

6. Orlando Patterson, *Slavery and Social Death: A Comparative Study* (Cambridge, Mass., 1982), 50, 229–30, 261.

7. Hortense Spillers makes some tantalizing observations in this regard in "Mama's Baby, Papa's Maybe: An American Grammar Book," *Diacritics* 17 (Summer 1987): 76–77.

8. Virginia Ingraham Burr, ed., *The Secret Eye: The Journal of Ella Gertrude Clanton Thomas, 1848–1880* (Chapel Hill, 1990).

9. Psychologists call cues that something is being withheld "deception clues" and the inadvertent disclosure of such material "leakage." Both deception clues and leakage are associated with the phenomenon of self-deception, which Gertrude Thomas practiced in regard to unpleasant personal truths that she did not want to confront.

10. Harriet Martineau, *Society in America*, 3 vols. (New York, 1837), 2:112, 118; Fredrika Bremer, *Homes of the New World: Impressions of America*, 2 vols. (London, 1853), 1:382; C. Vann Woodward and Elisabeth Muhlenfeld, *The Private Mary Chesnut: The Unpublished Civil War Diaries* (New York, 1984), 42 (March 18, 1861).

11. Bowen, *Lily*, 206, 227–28. W. J. Cash also utilizes Spanish-ness to hint at the Blackness within White Southerners. See Cash, *The Mind of the South* (New York, 1941), 25.

12. Bowen, *Lily*, 278. *Sigmund Freud: Collected Papers,* trans. Joan Riviere (New York, 1959), 4, 207. According to Freud, well-brought-up women who have been taught that sex is distasteful and who reject their sexuality tend to be inexperienced, inhibited, and frigid in marriage. This means that their husbands, who also regard the sex act as polluting, relate to their wives more as judges than as joyous physical partners. Hence only love objects who seem to these men to be debased—prostitutes, women of the lower class—can inspire in them full sensual feelings and a high degree of pleasure. This explains why these men keep lower-class mistresses (207, 210–11).

13. Yellin, *Incidents in the Life of a Slave Girl,* 27, 28.

14. Ibid., 27–28, 33.

15. Moses Roper, *A Narrative of the Adventures and Escape of Moses Roper from American Slavery,* 5th ed. (London, 1843), 9–10, quoted in Frances Smith Foster, *Witnessing Slavery: The Development of Antebellum Slave Narratives* (Westport, Conn., 1979), 78; and Frederick Douglass, *Narrative of the Life of Frederick Douglass, an American Slave* (Boston, 1845), 4.

16. See Jane Gallop, "Keys to Dora," in *The Daughter's Seduction: Feminism and Psychoanalysis* (Ithaca, N.Y., 1982), 137, 141–45, 147. Other commentators on the case include Elisabeth Young-Bruehl, ed., *Freud on Women: A Reader* (New York, 1990); Jim Swan, "Mater and Nannie: Freud's Two Mothers and the Discovery of the Oedipus Complex," *America Image* 31 (Spring 1974); Hannah S. Decker, *Freud, Dora, and Vienna 1900* (New York, 1991); Maria Ramas, "Freud's Dora, Dora's Hysteria," in Newton, Ryan, and Walkowitz, *Sex and Class in Women's History;* and to a certain extent, Mary Poovey, "The Anathematized Race: The Governess and *Jane Eyre,*" in Poovey, ed., *Uneven Developments: The Ideological Work of Gender in Mid-Victorian England* (Chicago, 1988).

17. Jeffrey Moussaieff Masson, *The Complete Letters of Sigmund Freud to Wilhelm Fliess, 1887–1904* (Cambridge, Mass., 1985), 241.

18. Ibid.

19. Decker, *Freud, Dora, and Vienna 1900,* 109.

20. See also Freud's "'Civilized' Sexual Morality and Modern Nervous Illness" (1908) and *Civilization and Its Discontents* (1930), in which he surveyed what he saw as the psycho-sexual dysfunctions associated with civilization. In "'Civilized' Sexual Morality" Freud makes some observations that might be useful in Southern history: "In her [the girl's] mental feelings [as she marries] she is still attached to her parents, whose authority has brought about the suppression of her sexuality; and in her physical behaviour she shows herself frigid, which deprives the man of any high degree of sexual enjoyment. I do not know whether the anaesthetic type of woman exists apart from

civilized education, though I consider it probable. But in any case, such education actually breeds it . . . In this way, the preparation for marriage frustrates the aims of marriage itself." Young-Bruehl, ed., *Freud on Women*, 176.

21. Drew Gilpin Faust, *James Henry Hammond and the Old South: A Design for Ownery* (Baton Rouge, La., 1982); and Carol Bleser, ed., *Secret and Sacred: The Diaries of James Henry Hammond, a Southern Slaveholder* (New York, 1988).

ERIC FONER'S *RECONSTRUCTION:* AMERICA'S UNFINISHED REVOLUTION

1. Published as *Nothing But Freedom: Emancipation and Its Legacy* (Baton Rouge, La., 1983).

2. E.g., Suzanne Lebsock, *The Free Women of Petersburg: Status and Culture in a Southern Town, 1784–1860* (New York, 1984); Barbara Jeanne Fields, *Slavery and Freedom on the Middle Ground: Maryland during the Nineteenth Century* (New Haven, Conn., 1985); Dolores E. Janiewski, *Sisterhood Denied: Race, Gender, and Class in a New South Community* (Philadelphia, 1985); Orville Vernon Burton, *In My Father's House Are Many Mansions: Family and Community in Edgefield, South Carolina* (Chapel Hill, N.C., 1985); Paul D. Escott, *Many Excellent People: Power and Privilege in North Carolina, 1850–1900* (Chapel Hill, N.C., 1985); Allan Kulikoff, *Tobacco and Slaves: The Development of Southern Cultures in the Chesapeake, 1680–1800* (Chapel Hill, N.C., 1986); Elizabeth Fox-Genovese, *Within the Plantation Household: Black and White Women of the Old South* (Chapel Hill, N.C., 1988).

3. Elisabeth Muhlenfeld, *Mary Boykin Chesnut: A Biography* (Baton Rouge, La., 1981), 128.

4. Jacqueline Jones, *Labor of Love, Labor of Sorrow: Black Women, Work, and the Family from Slavery to the Present* (New York, 1985), 51–58.

5. John W. Blassingame, *The Slave Community: Plantation Life in the Antebellum South*, particularly the first edition, New York, 1972, although the androcentric vision persists in the revised 1979 edition; Herbert G. Gutman, *The Black Family in Slavery and Freedom, 1750–1925* (New York, 1976).

6. Jones, *Labor of Love*, 69–72.

7. Linda Gordon, *Heroes of Their Own Lives: The Politics and History of Family Violence* (New York, 1988). Gordon says that "family violence has been historically and politically constructed . . . violence among family members arises from family conflicts which are not only historically influenced but political in themselves, in the sense of that word as having to do with power relations" (3).

8. In 1866 Andrew Johnson called intermarriage a logical consequence of Congress's policies (250), and in 1868 "Conservatives" raised potentially embarrassing questions of interracial marriage and mixed schools (which also came right back to interracial marriage) "at every turn" (321). Feminist historians have been pointing to the gendered nature of politics since the early 1980s, as in Joan Scott's important essays, including "Politics and the Profession: Women Historians in the 1980's," *Women's Studies Quarterly* 9 (Fall 1981), "Women in History: The Modern Period," *Past and Present: A Journal of Historical Studies* 101 (1983), and "Gender: A Useful Category of Historical Analysis," *American Historical Review* 91, no. 5 (December 1986).

9. Foner does mention that after emancipation Black families wanted to withdraw daughters and wives from work situations in which they were sexually vulnerable (86).

10. Martha Hodes, "Sex Across the Color Line: White Women and Black Men in America, 1680–1880" (PhD dissertation, Princeton University, 1990), and Nell Irvin Painter, "'Social Equality,' Miscegenation, Labor, and Power," in Numan V. Bartley, ed., *The Evolution of Southern Culture* (Athens, Ga., 1988).

THE SHOAH AND SOUTHERN HISTORY

1. Daniel J. Goldhagen, *Hitler's Willing Executioners: Ordinary Germans and the Holocaust* (New York: Alfred A. Knopf, 1996).

2. Stanley Elkins, *Slavery: A Problem in American Institutional and Intellectual Life* (Chicago: University of Chicago Press, 1959).

3. Wilma King, *Stolen Childhood: Slave Youth in Nineteenth-Century America* (Bloomington: Indiana University Press, 1995).

RALPH WALDO EMERSON'S SAXONS

1. Ralph Waldo Emerson, *The Collected Works of Ralph Waldo Emerson*, vol. V: *English Traits*, ed. Robert E. Burkholder, Douglas Emory Wilson, and Philip Nicoloff (Cambridge, Mass., 1994). Ralph Waldo Emerson's Anglo-Saxonist lectures include "Permanent Traits of the English National Genius" (1835), "The Genius and National Character of the Anglo-Saxon Race" (1843), and "Traits and Genius of the Anglo-Saxon Race" and "The Anglo-American" (both 1852–53).

2. The vast literature on Black race goes back to David Walker, *David Walker's Appeal to the Coloured Citizens of the World*, ed. Peter P. Hinks (1835; University Park, Pa., 2000). For useful, though now dated, introductions to racial theory, see Kimberle Crenshaw et al., eds., *Critical Race Theory: The Key Writings That Formed the Movement* (New York, 1995); and Richard Delgado, ed., *Critical Race Theory: The Cutting Edge* (Philadelphia, 1995). The professionalization of the field of Black history began with Carter G. Woodson's founding of the Association for the Study of Negro Life and History (now the Association for the Study of African American Life and History) in 1915 and the founding of *The Journal of Negro History* (now *The Journal of African American History*) in 1916.

3. The literature of critical White studies reaches back to the mid-twentieth century, to Lillian Smith, *Killers of the Dream* (1949; New York, 1961). But the recognized founding texts of the field are David R. Roediger, *Wages of Whiteness: Race and the Making of the American Working Class* (London, 1991); and Noel Ignatiev, *How the Irish Became White* (New York, 1995). Other important books in the field include Theodore W. Allen, *The Invention of the White Race: The Origin of Racial Oppression in Anglo-America* (London, 1994); Grace Elizabeth Hale, *Making Whiteness: The Culture of Segregation in the South, 1890–1940* (New York, 1998); George Lipsitz, *The Possessive Investment in Whiteness: How White People Profit from Identity Politics* (Philadelphia, 1998); Matthew Frye Jacobson, *Whiteness of a Different Color: European Immigrants and the Alchemy of Race* (Cambridge, Mass., 1998); and Thomas A. Guglielmo, *White on Arrival: Italians, Race, Color, and Power in Chicago, 1890–1945* (New York, 2003). Useful anthologies include Ian Haney López, *White by Law: The Legal Construction of Race* (New York, 1996); and Richard Delgado and Jean Stefancic, eds., *Critical White Studies: Looking behind the Mirror* (Philadelphia, 1997).

4. On the emergence of White race in the New Deal era and World War II, see Gary

Gerstle, *American Crucible: Race and Nation in the Twentieth Century* (Princeton, N.J., 2001), 128–37; and Lizabeth Cohen, *Making a New Deal: Industrial Workers in Chicago, 1919–1939* (Cambridge, Eng., 1990), 251–89.

5. Thomas Jefferson, "A Summary View of the Rights of British America," in *The Papers of Thomas Jefferson*, ed. Julian P. Boyd et al. (Princeton, N.J., 1950), 1:121–35.

6. On George III and his grandfather and predecessor, George II, also elector of Hanover, see *Encyclopaedia Britannica Online*, s.v. "George II" and "George III."

7. For Thomas Jefferson's remarks on Hengist and Horsa, see John Adams to Abigail Adams, Aug. 14, 1776, in *Familiar Letters of John Adams and His Wife Abigail Adams, during the Revolution, with a Memoir of Mrs. Adams*, ed. Charles Francis Adams (Boston, 1875), 210–11. For the other side of the seal, Jefferson suggested the children of Israel in the wilderness; see ibid. See also Dumas Malone, *Jefferson and His Time*, vol. VI: *The Sage of Monticello* (Boston, 1981), 202. Thomas Jefferson, "Essay on the Anglo-Saxon Language," in *The Writings of Thomas Jefferson*, ed. Andrew A. Lipscomb, 20 vols. (Washington, 1904), 18:365–66. This 5,400-word essay was not published until 1851, a quarter century after Jefferson's death. It appeared with a postscript Jefferson had written in 1825.

8. Stanley R. Hauer, "Thomas Jefferson and the Anglo-Saxon Language," *PMLA* 98 (Oct. 1983), 883–86, 891; Harriet Beecher Stowe, *Uncle Tom's Cabin: Or, Life Among the Lowly* (Boston, 1852), 43, 75, 76, 302, 803; Nina Baym, "Onward Christian Women: Sarah J. Hale's History of the World," *New England Quarterly* 63 (June 1990), 260–65; Susan M. Ryan, "Errand into Africa: Colonization and Nation Building in Sarah J. Hale's *Liberia*," *New England Quarterly* 68 (Dec. 1995), 565. On Elizabeth Cady Stanton, see her woman suffrage speeches from 1867 and 1869 in *History of Woman Suffrage*, ed. Elizabeth Cady Stanton, Susan B. Anthony, and Matilda Joslyn Gage, vol. II (New York, 1882), 193, 353–55; and Nell Irvin Painter, *Sojourner Truth: A Life, A Symbol* (New York, 1996), 228–31.

9. Theodore Parker in 1850, quoted in Neil Baldwin, *The American Revelation: Ten Ideals That Shaped Our Country from the Puritans to the Cold War* (New York, 2005), 61.

10. Robert D. Richardson Jr., *Emerson: The Mind on Fire* (Berkeley, Calif., 1995), 522–23.

11. Emerson, quoted in Kenneth Marc Harris, *Carlyle and Emerson: Their Long Debate* (Cambridge, Mass., 1978), 10. For unsigned reviews written by Thomas Carlyle, see "Jean Paul Friedrich Richter," *Edinburgh Review* 46 (June 1827); "State of German Literature," ibid. (Oct. 1827); "Signs of the Times," ibid., 49 (June 1829); "Taylor's Historic Survey of German Poetry," ibid., 53 (March 1831); "Characteristics," ibid., 54 (Dec. 1831); "Goethe's Helena," *Foreign Review*, 1 (April 1828); "Goethe," ibid., 2 (July 1828); "Life of Heyne," ibid., 2 (Oct. 1828); "Novalis," ibid., 4 (July 1829); and "Jean Paul Friedrich Richter Again," ibid., 5 (Jan. 1830). These essays and reviews indicate Carlyle's immersion in German literature and preceded Thomas Carlyle, *Sartor Resartus* (London, 1836). See the work of his research assistant and factotum, Henry Larkin, *Carlyle and the Open Secret of His Life* (1886; New York, 1970), 13. Phyllis Cole, *Mary Moody Emerson and the Origins of Transcendentalism: A Family History* (New York, 1998), 5, 164, 170, 180, 242, 307.

12. Thomas Carlyle to Ralph Waldo Emerson, Aug. 12, 1834, in *The Correspondence of Thomas Carlyle and Ralph Waldo Emerson, 1834–1872*, ed. Charles Eliot Norton, vol. I (http://www.gutenberg.org/dirs/1/3/5/8/13583/13583.txt); Harris, *Carlyle and Emerson*, 138.

13. For the use of "human swinery" to describe the Irish, see Thomas Carlyle, "Car-

lyle in Ireland," *Century* 24 (June 1882), 251; and Thomas Carlyle, "Carlyle in Ireland," *Century* (July 1882), 430. Emerson, *Collected Works of Ralph Waldo Emerson*, vol. V: *English Traits*, ed. Burkholder, Wilson, and Nicoloff, 170; Thomas Carlyle, *Critical and Miscellaneous Essays* (London, 1839); Thomas Carlyle, *The French Revolution: A History* (London, 1837); Carlyle, *Sartor Resartus*; Thomas Carlyle, *Chartism* (London, 1840), 28–31.

14. Ralph Waldo Emerson, "Permanent Traits of the English National Genius," in *The Early Lectures of Ralph Waldo Emerson*, ed. Stephen E. Whicher and Robert E. Spiller, vol. I: *1833–1836* (Cambridge, Mass., 1959), 233, 234–35; Emerson, *Collected Works of Ralph Waldo Emerson*, vol. V: *English Traits*, ed. Burkholder, Wilson, and Nicoloff, 54; Edward A. Ross, "The Causes of Racial Superiority," *Annals of the American Academy of Political and Social Science* 18 (1901), 67–89, esp. 79.

15. Ralph Waldo Emerson, "Self-Reliance," in *Anthology of American Literature*, ed. George McMichael et al. (New York, 1989), 1100; "The Anglo-American" is quoted in Harris, *Carlyle and Emerson*, 147–48. See also Phyllis Cole, "Emerson, England, and Fate," in *Emerson: Prophecy, Metamorphosis, and Influence; Selected Papers from the English Institute*, ed. David Levin (New York, 1975), 83–105.

16. Sharon Turner, *The History of the Anglo-Saxons, from Their First Appearance above the Elbe, to the Death of Egbert* (London, 1799). On Sharon Turner's book, see Hugh A. MacDougall, *Racial Myth in English History: Trojans, Teutons, and Anglo-Saxons* (Hanover, N.H., 1982), 26–37, 56–62, 81–86, 91–92; and Ralph Waldo Emerson, "The Genius and National Character of the Anglo-Saxon Race," in *The Selected Lectures of Ralph Waldo Emerson*, ed. Ronald A. Basco and Joel Myerson (Athens, Ga., 2005), 7–18.

17. On the printing, circulation, reception, and wit of Emerson's *English Traits*, see Philip Nicoloff, "Historical Introduction," in *Collected Works of Ralph Waldo Emerson*, vol. V: *English Traits*, ed. Burkholder, Wilson, and Nicoloff, xiii–xiv. For a description of *English Traits* as Emerson's "wittiest book," see Wallace E. Williams, "Historical Introduction," in *The Collected Works of Ralph Waldo Emerson*, vol. IV: *Representative Men*, ed. Wallace E. Williams and Douglas Emory Wilson (Cambridge, Mass., 1987), xlix.

18. Emerson, *Collected Works of Ralph Waldo Emerson*, vol. V: *English Traits*, ed. Burkholder, Wilson, and Nicoloff, 24–40. On the book's "almost countless" instances of racial thought, see Philip L. Nicoloff, *Emerson on Race and History: An Examination of* English Traits (New York, 1961), 120. For a twenty-first-century genetically based appraisal of the demographic role of Vikings in the British Isles, see Bryan Sykes, *Saxons, Vikings, and Celts: The Genetic Roots of Britain and Ireland* (New York, 2006), 173–75, 255–66, 277–88.

19. Emerson, *Collected Works of Ralph Waldo Emerson*, vol. V: *English Traits*, ed. Burkholder, Wilson, and Nicoloff, 155.

20. Vortigern was said to have invited Hengist (stallion) and Horsa (horse) to come from Jutland, the southern part of Denmark, to England in 449 to help repulse attacks by the Picts and Scots. Vortigern gave them the southeastern Isle of Thanet in gratitude. Bede, *Ecclesiastical History of the English People*, 1:15. The *Anglo-Saxon Chronicle* makes Hengist and Horsa joint kings of Kent.

21. Emerson, *Collected Works of Ralph Waldo Emerson*, vol. V: *English Traits*, ed. Burkholder, Wilson, and Nicoloff, 23.

22. Emerson, "Permanent Traits of the English National Genius," 242.

23. Emerson, *Collected Works of Ralph Waldo Emerson*, vol. V: *English Traits*, ed. Burkholder, Wilson, and Nicoloff, 33.

MALCOLM X ACROSS THE GENRES

1. Bruce Perry, *Malcolm: The Life of a Man Who Changed Black America* (Barrytown, N.Y., 1991), 3.

2. Malcolm X, *The Autobiography of Malcolm X*, with the assistance of Alex Haley (New York, 1965), 339–42.

ALMA W. THOMAS (1891–1978): OLD/NOT OLD ARTIST

1. Harold Rosenberg, "The Art World: Being Outside," *New Yorker* (August 22, 1977), 84.

2. Judith Wilson, "Teacher, Painter, Patron, Pioneer. Alma Thomas: A One-Woman Art Movement," *Ms. Magazine* (February 1979), 59.

3. Benjamin Forgey, *Evening Star* (Washington, D.C.), April 27, 1972, Alma Thomas Papers, c. 1894–2001, box 2, folder 52, Archives of American Art, Smithsonian Institution (hereafter Alma Thomas Papers).

4. James R. Mellow, *New York Times*, April 29, 1972, Alma Thomas Papers, box 2, folder 52.

5. Alma Thomas to Harold Hart, and Hart to Judith Wilson, in 1978. Judith Wilson Papers, 1966–2010, box 4, folder 3, page 11, Archives of American Art, Smithsonian Institution (hereafter Judith Wilson Papers).

6. Alma Thomas passport, Study Abroad Trip, 1958, Alma Thomas Papers, box 1, folder 19.

7. Harold Hart quoted in Judith Wilson Papers, box 4, folder 3, page 7.

8. Alma Thomas in *Alma Thomas* (New York: Whitney Museum of American Art, 1972), 3, in Judith Wilson Papers, box 4, folder 1.

9. See Jonathan P. Binstock, "Apolitical Art in a Political World: Alma Thomas in the Late 1960s and Early 1970s," in *Alma W. Thomas: A Retrospective of the Paintings*, ed. Sachi A. Yanari (San Francisco: Pomegranate, 1998), 54–70.

10. Jillian Steinhauer, "Alma Thomas," *New York Times*, October 11, 2019, C15.

MARY QUINN SULLIVAN, THE MYSTERIOUS FOUNDER
OF THE MUSEUM OF MODERN ART

Acknowledgments: I could not have found all this information on Mary Quinn Sullivan without the assistance of friends and colleagues in art history and history history. They include Hasia Diner, Julia Van Haaften, Laurette McCarthy, Robert Storr, Mike Wallace, Deborah Willis, and Jerilea Zempel. Thanks also to Romy Silver-Kohn for tireless research and to Sarah Resnick for editing the earlier version. I owe very special thanks to Avis Berman for a generous and knowingly detailed reading of my 2021 draft.

1. Rona Roob calls Bliss "a woman of privilege who never married . . . dressed conservatively, wore little make-up and was unpretentious." In Roob, "A Noble Legacy," *Art in America*, November 2003, 73. Bliss had her correspondence destroyed after her death.

2. Julia Van Haaften, *Berenice Abbott* (New York: Aperture Foundation, 1988) and *Berenice Abbott: A Life in Photography* (New York: W. W. Norton, 2018).

3. In her notes on this essay, Avis Berman suggested that the backdrop is netting in the (unidentified) photographer's studio, an avant-garde backdrop perhaps taken from the theater world, such as what Florine Stettheimer might have used in *Four Saints in Three Acts,* a 1928 opera composed by Virgil Thomson with a libretto by Gertrude Stein.

4. Howardena D. Pindell, "Sullivan, Mary Josephine Quinn (1877–1939)," in *Notable American Women, 1607–1950,* ed. Edward T. James, Janet Wilson James, and Paul S. Boyer (Cambridge, Mass.: Harvard University Press, 1971), 3:408–10. See also Roob's research file on Sullivan in the Roob Papers, folder 2.D.55, Museum of Modern Art Archives, New York.

5. Hasia Diner notes that "in the first decade of the twentieth century, daughters of Irish parents made up the largest group of schoolteachers in New York City." In Diner, *Erin's Daughters in America: Irish Immigrant Women in the Nineteenth Century* (Baltimore: Johns Hopkins University Press, 1983), 97.

6. Quinn's performance evaluation card, Sullivan file, Vertical Files Collection, PI-VF, Pratt Institute Archives, New York.

7. Katherine Dreier, journal documenting trip to Europe, 1902–1903, box 149, and Dorothea Dreier, journal documenting trip to Europe, 1902–1903, box 127, folder 2871, Katherine S. Dreier Papers/Société Anonyme Archive, Yale Collection of American Literature, Beinecke Rare Book and Manuscript Library, Yale University, New Haven, Connecticut.

8. Dorothy M. Browne, "New York City Museums and Cultural Leadership, 1917–1940" (PhD diss., CUNY, 2008), 68.

9. Lucienne S. Bloch, "In the Company of Women," in *In the Company of Women: 100 Years at the Cosmopolitan Club,* ed. Sophia Duckworth Schachter, Caroline Zinsser, and Cynthia V. A. Schaffner (New York: Cosmopolitan Club, 2009), 71.

10. Quinn's article was published in *Journal of Home Economics* 7 (February 1914): 35–40.

11. Mary Josephine Quinn, *Planning and Furnishing the Home: Practical and Economical Suggestions for the Homemaker* (New York: Harper & Brothers, 1914), 38.

12. Eleanor S. Apter, "Regimes of Coincidence: Katherine S. Dreier, Marcel Duchamp, and Dada," in *Women in Dada: Essays on Sex, Gender, and Identity,* ed. Naomi Sawelson-Gorse (Cambridge, Mass.: MIT Press, 1998), 367.

13. Bernice Kert, *Abby Aldrich Rockefeller: The Woman in the Family* (New York: Random House, 1993), 269.

14. Diner, *Erin's Daughters in America,* 18–25, 66–67, 73, 116–18, 161.

15. "Map of 1801 Wolcott Avenue, Astoria, Long Island," c. mid-1930s, folder 4.38.a, Early Museum History: Administrative Records, MoMA Archives.

16. Benjamin Lawrence Reid, *The Man from New York: John Quinn and His Friends* (New York: Oxford University Press, 1968), 573–74, and Judith Zilczer, *The Noble Buyer: John Quinn, Patron of the Avant-Garde* (Washington, D.C.: Hirschhorn Museum and Sculpture Garden, 1978), 62. A large collection of John Quinn's art and literature correspondence resides at the New York Public Library.

17. Cornelius Sullivan addressed John Quinn as "My Dear Quinn" and wrote about "a delightful two hours" at his home. Sullivan to Quinn, May 23, 1921, reel 37, box 43, folder 5, John Quinn Papers, Manuscripts and Archives Division, New York Public Library, and Zilczer, *The Noble Buyer,* 55–56.

18. Judith Zilczer, "John Quinn and Modern Art Collectors in America, 1913–1924," *American Art Journal* 14, no. 1 (Winter 1982): 65.

19. This list of the Sullivans' collection comes from Howardena D. Pindell, "Sullivan, Mary Quinn (24 November 1877–05 December 1939)," in *American National Biography* (Oxford: Oxford University, 1999), https://doi.org/10.1093/anb/9780198606697.article.1701216. See also Dianne Sachko Macleod, *Enchanted Lives, Enchanted Objects: American Women Collectors and the Making of Culture, 1800–1940* (Berkeley: University of California Press, 2008), 158.

20. Halpert, interviewed by Harlan Phillips, 1962–63, transcript, Archives of American Art, Smithsonian Institution. Halpert has confused Cornelius J. Sullivan with Algernon Sydney Sullivan of Sullivan and Cromwell, which makes Cornelius into a fancier lawyer than he might have been. In a separate anecdote, Halpert notes Sullivan's refined taste in clothes, recalling how Sullivan recognized a dress worn by Halpert as a design by the Ukrainian-French artist Sonia Delaunay, whose works were so high-end that even Bliss claimed that she could not afford them.

21. Mary Sullivan to Dreier, n.d., Holyoke, Massachusetts, box 34, folder 981, Dreier Papers/Société Anonyme Archive.

22. Mary Sullivan to Dreier, n.d., Holyoke, Massachusetts, Dreier Papers/Société Anonyme Archive.

23. "an 'associate' at ten dollars per year": Letters from a custodian of Société Anonyme to Sullivan, May 28 and December 11, 1920, box 34, folder 981, Dreier Papers/Société Anonyme Archive; "an 'acquaintance' at five dollars": Société Anonyme membership card belonging to Sullivan, 1923, box 92, folder 2354, Dreier Papers/Société Anonyme Archive.

24. Dreier to Mary Sullivan, January 12, 1924, box 34, folder 981, Dreier Papers/Société Anonyme Archive.

25. Dreier to Sullivan, April 1, 1925, box 34, folder 981, Dreier Papers/Société Anonyme Archive.

26. Dreier to Cornelius Sullivan, December 1, 1926, and Cornelius Sullivan to Dreier, December 2 and 3, 1926, box 34, folder 980, Dreier Papers/Société Anonyme Archive.

27. "Katherine S. Dreier," Solomon R. Guggenheim Foundation, accessed November 15, 2022, https://www.guggenheim.org/history/katherine-s-dreier.

28. Cornelius Sullivan to Dreier, December 18, 1928, box 34, folder 980, Dreier Papers/Société Anonyme Archive.

29. The art school and museum separated in 1967, with the art school joining Indiana University–Indianapolis and, in 1969, the Art Association becoming the Indianapolis Museum of Art. Since 2017 the museum has been part of the Newfields art and nature campus.

30. Harriet G. Warner, Martin F. Krause, and S. L. Berry, *The Herron Chronicle* (Bloomington: Indiana University Press, 2003), 50.

31. Rona Roob, "Cos Club," folder 3.5, Roob Papers. See also the entry for *Window at Vers* in the Provenance Research Project, Museum of Modern Art, accessed November 15, 2022, https://www.moma.org/collection/works/80136.

32. John Rockefeller Jr.'s Egypt and Palestine notebook, 1929, box 42, folder 376, Series 2: Personal Papers, Rockefeller Jr. Papers, Rockefeller Archive Center, Sleepy Hollow, New York. The calendar also notes that on March 7, 1929, "Cornelius Bliss and his sister [Lillie] and daughter lunched with us." They were in Bethlehem.

33. Nelson Rockefeller to Dreier, April 30, 1950, box 26, folder 738, Dreier Papers/

Société Anonyme Archive. Jennifer R. Gross writes that Barr drafted the letter on behalf of Rockefeller. See "Believe Me, Faithfully Yours," in *The Société Anonyme: Modernism for America,* ed. Jennifer R. Gross (New Haven, Conn.: Yale University Press, 2006), 5.

34. Dwight MacDonald, "Action on West Fifty-Third Street," *New Yorker,* December 12, 1953, 50.

35. Martha Schwendener, "A Vast Collection That Predates MoMA," *New York Times,* December 21, 2012.

36. Rona Roob, "Women of the Modern: The Women Who Helped to Fulfill the Mission of the Museum of Modern Art," folder 3.5, Roob Papers, MoMA Archives.

37. Roob, "A Noble Legacy," 81.

38. Sachko Macleod, *Enchanted Lives, Enchanted Objects,* 161–62.

39. Kert, *Abby Aldrich Rockefeller,* 268; and Russell Lynes, *Good Old Modern: An Intimate Portrait of the Museum of Modern Art* (New York: Atheneum, 1973), 7.

40. Lynes, *Good Old Modern,* 7–8.

41. Elizabeth Bliss Parkinson Cobb, interviewed by Sharon Zane, July 6, 1988, transcript, Oral History Program, MoMA Archives.

42. Cobb, interviewed by Paul Cummings, November 30–December 17, 1970, Archives of American Art, Smithsonian Institution. Tamara L. Follini asks, "Why had the interviewer not seen fit to include this dialogue, especially as documentation about Mary Sullivan is practically non-existent? Had the comments been unflattering? Were there aspects of the lives of Bliss or Sullivan which friends or executors had thought better left to silence?" In "Discretion, Devotion, and the Founders of the Museum of Modern Art," in *Before Peggy Guggenheim: American Women Art Collectors,* ed. Rosella Mamoli Zorzi (Venice: Marsilio, 2001), 152–53.

43. Lynes, *Good Old Modern,* 149. Cornelius Sullivan's collection was sold in three sessions at the Anderson Galleries.

44. Mary Sullivan to Barr, n.d., folder 1.A.6, Alfred H. Barr Jr. Papers, MoMA Archives.

45. David Rockefeller, interviewed by Sharon Zane, January 17, 1991, transcript, Oral History Program. Like Eliza Cobb, Rockefeller is skeptical of the shipboard version of the Museum of Modern Art's founding. Cobb goes so far as to say of the myth: "I'm sure that's not true. [Abby Aldrich Rockefeller and Lillie P. Bliss] must have been already talking about it for a long time." Cobb, interviewed by Zane.

46. Mary Sullivan to Sweeney, October 30, 1935, folder 4.38.a, Early Museum History: Administrative Records, MoMA Archives; Mary Sullivan to Sachs, November 8, 1937, Papers of Paul J. Sachs, folder 1806, Harvard Art Museums Archives, Harvard University, Cambridge, Mass.

47. Parsons, interviewed by Paul Cummings, June 4–9, 1969, transcript, Archives of American Art, Smithsonian Institution.

48. Lee Hall, *Betty Parsons: Artist. Dealer. Collector* (New York: Harry N. Abrams, 1991), 68, 70.

49. Parsons, interview; Hall, *Betty Parsons,* 68.

50. Hall, *Betty Parsons,* 68.

51. Maillol's *Portrait of Auguste Renoir* is now in the collection of the Metropolitan Museum of Art. It was sold as part of a 1947 inter-museum agreement between the institutions under which the Metropolitan purchased a number of older works from MoMA to enable the younger institution's acquisition of newer ones. The agreement was terminated five years later.

52. There would be another auction in February 1940 of Sullivan's furnishings, decorative arts, and silver.

53. Edward Alden Jewell, "Noted Collection of Art to Be Sold," *New York Times,* December 5, 1939.

54. "Sullivan Prices," *Art Digest,* December 15, 1939, 23.

55. Jewell, "Noted Collection of Art to Be Sold."

56. "Mrs. Sullivan, Art Patron and Collector, Dies," *New York Herald Tribune,* December 6, 1939, and "Mrs. C. J. Sullivan; Aided Modern Art," *New York Times,* December 6, 1939.

57. Abby Rockefeller's accountant made sure her purchase was conducted in such a way to assure her tax benefits. Mr. Keebler to Rockefeller, December 18, 1939, FA 314, Series E: Cultural Interests, Office of the Messrs. Rockefeller Records, Rockefeller Archive Center. In addition to the Modigliani head and Derain painting that Rockefeller purchased from Sullivan's estate sale in 1939 and gave to the Museum of Modern Art, there are eleven works in the collection labeled "Mrs. Cornelius J. Sullivan Fund" and accessioned between 1948 and 1949 that have no further identification.

ARCHIVE TO BRUSH

1. Jacques Derrida, *Archive Fever: A Freudian Impression* (1996), and Michel Foucault, *The Archaeology of Knowledge and the Discourse on Language* (1972), both quoted in Okwui Enwezor, "Archive Fever: Photography between History and the Monument," in *Archive Fever: Uses of the Document in Contemporary Art* (New York: International Center of Photography, 2008), 11–12, 37–42.

2. *New York Times,* June 9, 2009.

3. *Black Romantic: The Figurative Impulse in Contemporary African American Art* (New York: Studio Museum in Harlem, 2002).

4. Sylvia Ardyn Boone, *Radiance from the Waters: Ideals of Feminine Beauty in Mende Art* (New Haven, Conn.: Yale University Press, 1986).

5. Tibor Kalman and Maira Kalman, *Unfashion* (New York: Abrams Books, 2000).

6. See Rudolf Arnheim, *The Power of the Center: A Study of Composition in the Visual Arts, The New Version* (Berkeley: University of California Press, 1988), 96–97, and Arnheim, *Art and Visual Perception: A Psychology of the Creative Eye, The New Version* (1954; Berkeley: University of California Press, 1974), 10–16.

7. E.g., Maira Kalman, *And the Pursuit of Happiness* (New York: Penguin Press, 2010); William Strunk Jr. and E. B. White, *The Elements of Style,* illustrated by Maira Kalman (New York: Penguin Books, 2007).

Index

Page numbers in *italics* refer to illustration captions.

Permissions Acknowledgments

Grateful acknowledgment is made to the following for permission to reprint previously published material:

The American Historical Review: "Malcolm X across the Genres" in *The American Historical Review* (April 1993). Reprinted by permission of *The American Historical Review*.

Condé Nast: "Seeing Police Brutality Then and Now" in *The New Yorker* (newyorker .com) on June 18, 2020. Copyright © 2020 by Condé Nast. Reprinted by permission of Condé Nast. "The Truth of the Matter: Letter to the Editor" in *The New Yorker* (new yorker.com) on May 23, 2022. Copyright © 2022 by Condé Nast.

Cornell University Press: "Difference, Slavery, and Memory: Sojourner Truth in Feminist Abolitionism," from *The Abolitionist Sisterhood: Women's Political Culture in Antebellum America,* edited by Jean Fagan Yellin and John C. Van Horne. Copyright © 1994 by the Library Company of Philadelphia. Reprinted by permission of Cornell University Press.

Foreign Affairs: "What Is White America? The Identity Politics of the Majority" in *Foreign Affairs* (November/December 2019). Reprinted by permission of *Foreign Affairs*.

Georgia Historical Society: "Of *Lily,* Linda Brent, and Freud: A Non-Exceptionalist Approach to Race, Class, and Gender in the Slave South" in *The Georgia Historical Quarterly* (Summer 1992). Reprinted by permission of the Georgia Historical Society.

Guardian News & Media Ltd: "How We Think about the Term 'Enslaved' Matters" in *The Guardian* (theguardian.com) on August 14, 2019. Copyright © 2019 by Guardian News & Media Ltd. Reprinted by permission of Guardian News & Media Ltd 2022.

Johns Hopkins University Press: "French Theories in American Settings: Some Thoughts on Transferability" from *Journal of Women's History* (Spring 1989). Copyright © 1989 by Journal of Women's History, Inc. Reprinted with permission by Johns Hopkins University Press.

Oxford University Press: "Ralph Waldo Emerson's Saxons" in *The Journal of American History* (March 2009). Copyright © 2009 by Oxford University Press. Reprinted by permission of Oxford University Press.

Pantheon Books: "Hill, Thomas, and the Use of Racial Stereotype" by Nell Irvin Painter, copyright © 1992 by Nell Irvin Painter. Originally appeared in *Race-ing Justice, Engendering Power: Essays on Anita Hill, Clarence Thomas, and the Construction of Social Reality,* edited by Toni Morrison. Reprinted by permission of Pantheon Books, an imprint of the Knopf Doubleday Publishing Group, a division of Penguin Random House LLC. All rights reserved.

Princeton University Press: "The Shoah and Southern History" originally published in *Jumpin' Jim Crow: Southern Politics from Civil War to Civil Rights* (Princeton University Press, 2000), edited by Jane Dailey, Glenda Elizabeth Gilmore, and Bryant Simon. Reprinted by permission of Princeton University Press.

The University of Illinois: "Martin R. Delany: Elitism and Black Nationalism" by Nell Irvin Painter, from *Black Leaders of the Nineteenth Century*, edited by Leon Litwack and August Meier. Copyright © 1988 by the Board of Trustees of the University of Illinois. Reprinted by permission of the University of Illinois.

The University of North Carolina Press: "Soul Murder and Slavery: Toward a Fully Loaded Cost Accounting" in *U.S. History as Women's History: New Feminist Essays,* edited by Linda K. Kerber, Alice Kessler-Harris, and Kathryn Kish Sklar. Copyright © 1995 by the University of North Carolina Press. Reprinted by permission of the University of North Carolina Press.

Several pieces originally appeared in the following publications:

"I Knit Socks for Adrienne" (March 2021) and "From 1872 to 1876 in the Space of One Year" (January 2022) in *Hoosac Journal;* "I Knit Socks for Adrienne" also appeared in *Womb of Violet, Volume II: Blackness, Resistance, and Being* by fayemi shakur (2021); "Introduction" in *Incidents in the Life of a Slave Girl* (Penguin Classics, 2000); "Regrets" in *Signs* (Summer 2000); "Who Decides What Is History?" (March 6, 1982) and "Reparations: Be Black Like Me" (May 22, 2000) in *The Nation;* "Long Divisions" (October 11, 2017) and "Improving American Democracy Means Working Locally for the Common Good" (December 2, 2022) in *The New Republic;* "'. . . whatever she saw go on in that barn'" in *Women's Studies Quarterly* (Spring/Summer 2014); "On Horseback" in *The Paris Review* (www.theparisreview.org) on June 19, 2020; "Humanity, Scholarship, and Proud Race Citizenship: The Gifts of John Hope Franklin" in *The Journal of African American History* (Summer 2009); "Whose Nation? The Art of Black Power" (February 4, 2018) and "On the Gallery Walls: Black Power Art in Arkansas" (April 1, 2018) in *The New York Review of Books;* a shorter version of "Capitalize White" as "Why 'White' Should be Capitalized, Too" in *The Washington Post* (July 22, 2020); "Mary Quinn Sullivan, the Mysterious Founder of the Museum of Modern Art" in *Women of MoMA: The First Generation* (Spring 2023); "Hers: Whites Say I Must Be on Easy Street" (December 10, 1981), "Hers: A Sense of Place" (December 17, 1981), "It Shouldn't Be This Close. But There's Good News, Too." (November 5, 2020), "What Whiteness Means in the Trump Era" (November 12, 2016), and "When Poverty Was White" (March 24, 2012) in *The New York Times.*

Illustration Credits

About the Author

Nell Irvin Painter, Edwards Professor of American History, Emerita, Princeton University, is the author of *Old in Art School*, a finalist for the National Book Critics Circle Award; *The New York Times* bestseller *The History of White People*; and *Sojourner Truth: A Life, A Symbol*. A fellow of the American Academy of Arts and Sciences since 2007, she has received several honorary degrees from institutions such as Yale, Wesleyan, the University of North Carolina at Chapel Hill, and Dartmouth, and has also served as president of the Organization of American Historians and the Southern Historical Association. Painter earned degrees in painting from Mason Gross School of the Arts at Rutgers and the Rhode Island School of Design after a PhD in history from Harvard. She lives and works in East Orange, New Jersey, and when not writing essays and drawing self-portraits, she makes artist's books that visualize people and history. She has served on the nonfiction jury of the National Book Awards three times and is currently Madam Chairman of MacDowell.